# Women of Japan and Korea

C O N T I N U I T Y   A N D   C H A N G E

*Edited by*

*Joyce Gelb*

*and*

*Marian Lief Palley*

*Temple University Press*

*Philadelphia*

Temple University Press, Philadelphia 19122
Copyright © 1994 by Temple University. All rights reserved
Published 1994
Printed in the United States of America

Library of Congress Cataloging-in-Publication Data
Women of Japan and Korea : continuity and change / edited by Joyce Gelb and
Marian Lief Palley.
p.   cm. — (Women in the political economy)
Includes bibliographical references and index.
ISBN 1-56639-223-3 (alk. paper). — ISBN 1-56639-224-1 (pbk. : alk. paper)
1. Women—Japan—Social conditions.   2. Women—Korea (South)—Social conditions.
3. Japan—Social conditions—1945–    4. Korea (South)—Social conditions.   I. Gelb,
Joyce, 1940–     II. Palley, Marian Lief, 1939–     III. Series.
HQ1762.W67   1995
305.42'09519—dc20                                                    93-46966

# Contents

## II ❖ KOREAN WOMEN

# Preface

DURING the last half of the 1980s and the early years of the 1990s we directed much of our research to the study of women's rights movements in Asia, Gelb in Japan and Palley in the Republic of Korea (ROK). When we discussed our respective experiences we concluded that a comparison of the role of women in two strikingly similar but clearly distinct Asian industrial nations could provide new insights into the clashes that have arisen between tradition and change. Moreover, it seemed that the observations and analyses garnered from our studies of these two nations might provide new perspectives applicable to women's lives and experiences in other nations as well. The focus of this coauthored and coedited volume is the political, economic, and social participation of women, and their changing roles and status in Japan and the ROK.

The actual "voices" of the women—social scientists and practitioners—who are living in these two countries and are, therefore, experiencing societal changes first-hand are incorporated into this collection. Their articles consider patterns of family life, educational systems, health care—encompassing issues of sexuality and reproductive health—work-force participation and employment patterns, and changes in patterns of political participation. The introductory chapter discusses the similarities and differences in the two cultures and considers the relationship between cultural constraints and behavioral change.

We assume that there is no one "correct" way to implement change and that there is no one "right" behavioral adaptation to economic modernization.[1] The perspectives provided by the voices in this volume will underscore this perspective.

Many people and organizations provided us with support and assistance during the years we were involved in developing this volume. The Murray Center at Radcliffe College furnished Gelb with the opportunity to spend a semester at the center working on this volume. Also, the Japan Society for the

Promotion of Science, the Social Science Research Council, the Asia Foundation, and the Fusae Ichikawa Memorial Association provided Gelb with opportunities to complete her research in Japan. Special thanks are due to Professor James Shields and the City College Japan Initiatives Program (sponsored by the U.S.–Japan Friendship Commission) and to Professor Nozomu Kawamura, her host professor at Tokyo Metropolitan University. These two institutions provided Gelb with her initial opportunity in 1987 to visit Japan and introduced her to Japanese society. Most recently, a research visit to the Research School of Social Sciences at the Australian National University in Canberra provided an opportunity for reflection on the materials included in this volume.

Palley was a Fulbright Scholar at the Women's Research Center at the Ewha Woman's University in 1988 and she returned to Ewha in 1990 as a visiting scholar. In 1993 she received a grant from the Korea Research Foundation to return to Korea and Ewha Woman's University to complete her research. Also, the University of Delaware provided her with a General University Research Grant, an International Studies Grant, and a College of Arts and Science Research Grant to help support the completion of this work.

We would like to thank several people in particular for their assistance during the years we were working on this project. Gelb would like to thank Junko Shiota, Naoko Ota, and Momoe Tomono for their invaluable assistance as interpreters and translators. Dawn Lawson did an outstanding job of translating the essays by Ueno and Shinotsuka into English. Palley would especially like to thank Fred Carriere, former director of the Korea Fulbright Foundation; Professor Ahn Byong Man, president of Hankuk University for Foreign Studies; and Professor William W. Boyer, University of Delaware, for their initial encouragement and support for this project. Also, Professor Cho Hyong and Professor Chang Pil Wha, both of the Ewha Woman's University, provided Palley with contacts at each stage of her work and assumed the responsibility to locate very competent and helpful student assistants. We are both grateful to the numerous participants at professional meetings who responded to some of our initial thoughts and observations. Finally, Michael Ames, editor-in-chief at Temple University Press, encouraged us at all stages of this project. We would like to thank him for his ongoing enthusiasm for this project and for his unwavering support.

*Joyce Gelb*
*Marian Lief Palley*

# NOTE

1. Marian Lief Palley, "Women's Rights as Human Rights: An International Perspective," *Annals of the American Academy of Political and Social Science* 515 (May 1991): 164.

*Women of Japan and Korea*

# 1

## Introduction

JOYCE GELB and MARIAN LIEF PALLEY

THE focus of this volume is the changing role of women in Japan and Korea. In order to understand both the pressures for change and the constraints that limit change, it is necessary to examine political culture and the political opportunity structure in which social movements and individuals seek modifications in their status and conditions.

Lucian Pye defined political culture as "the set of attitudes, beliefs and sentiments which give order and meaning to a political process and which provides the underlying assumptions and rules that govern behavior in the political system. It encompasses both the political ideas and operating norms of a polity."[1] In *The Civic Culture*, Gabriel Almond and Sidney Verba discussed political culture and emphasized "political knowledge and skill, and feelings and value orientations toward political objects and processes—toward the political system as a whole, toward the self as participant, toward political parties and elections, bureaucracy, and the like. Little or no stress was placed on attitudes toward public policy."[2]

Political culture can be a useful analytical framework because it is multidimensional and descriptive of the numerous factors that influence how we behave as political beings. However, some of the major discussions of political culture provide an incomplete prism through which comparative analysis of women's roles in non-Western nations can be successfully undertaken. It is necessary to move beyond this concept and provide a more complete framework in which to consider issues related to women and efforts to seek social changes. Five sets of factors must be understood before any meaningful discussion of Japanese and Korean women and their changing roles can begin:

values and value manipulation, economic growth and development, political structures and processes, social and demographic forces, and international dynamics such as trade and communications. All of these factors influence the constraints and opportunities that influence the environment in which social movements advocate system change. Moreover, a consideration of these factors underscores the idea that political culture is a dynamic process and not a static construct.

In Japan and Korea, as in most other societies, the constraints imposed on political behavior have been established by men and historically have advantaged men and excluded women from being significant participants in the political process. Put in somewhat different terms, "politics always sets limits on universalisms as it defines 'we's' and 'they's,' citizens and foreigners."[3] Women may be citizens but nonetheless they are often regarded as the "they's." Thus, without an understanding that politics extends beyond the public sphere and an acceptance of the position that "what is significant in our time is the diffusion of the political . . . [and] the absorption of the political into non-political institutions and activities,"[4] it is not possible to understand the traditions and changes in the past several decades that have affected women's roles and relationships.

## CONTEXT FOR CHANGE

The post–World War II era brought dramatic changes in political rhetoric and structures to Japan and Korea. Each nation adopted an American-style constitution. In addition, rapid industrial development transformed Japan into a leading postindustrial society and Korea, after the Korean War, into an emerging industrial giant. (Korea was occupied by Japan from 1910 to 1945, leaving an imprint on Korean society.) These nations experienced growth of their middle classes and a concurrent increase in educational opportunities for both men and women.

Second-wave women's rights movements began to emerge in most nations from the mid 1970s into the 1980s. In part, universal calls for improved conditions for women gained currency in both Japan and Korea due to enhanced contact between women activists, fostered in large measure by the United Nations Decade for Women (1975–1985). Also, media communications, expanded educational opportunities for women, and an increase in international travel and training reinforced these calls for women's rights. As in Western nations, each of these women's movements originated with educated middle-class and upper-class women. Such women tend to share many concerns and aspirations that transcend national differences despite their respective cultural traditions.[5]

Much of the rhetoric of Western, and especially American, democratic thought has been integrated into the discourse of women's movements as their leaders call for improved conditions and more equitable conditions for women. However, the preconditions and expectations of American liberal democratic thought, rooted as it is in notions of the centrality of the individual, individual freedom, and pluralism, are confronted by the realities of political systems based on other traditions.

In Japan and Korea great stress is placed on the individual's conformity to group norms. "Consciousness of hierarchy and loyalty to the family, work place and nation may take precedence over equality and independence."[6] Thus, in both nations traditional values based on the centrality of relationships, hierarchy, the distinctive roles and duties of women, and the importance of conformity to group values often confront the alien Western traditions with a resultant gap between expectations and reality for those women seeking Western-style equity in their lives.

## VALUES AND CULTURE

In traditional Confucian societies women were in a disadvantaged position. A hierarchical social structure consisting of a royal monarchy, strong class consciousness, and a patriarchal, large family system in which maintaining the family line is important tended to maintain separate and unequal roles for women and men. One of the tenets of Confucianism requires three obediences of women: to the father when young, to the husband when married, and to the son in old age. Also, the three-generation Confucian family was the model for many centuries. The father, and after his death the first-born male, served as the legal family head, and he exercised authority and control over joint property and family members.

### The Korean experience

Confucianism has a stronger hold in Korea than in any other nation in the world. In fact, a discussion of Korean society would be incomplete without some understanding of the moral code that is associated with Confucianism, and more specifically, an understanding of the changing roles and status of women in Korea requires some sense of the centrality of this moral code in the evolution of that society. Though most Koreans adhere to a Confucian moral code, they also maintain religious affiliations that most often are Buddhist or Christian.

During the Yi dynasty (1392–1910) a Confucian moral code was accepted in Korea. This led to a deteriorating position for women. From 1486 to 1636, Confucianism became firmly established and entrenched in Korea and Confucian precepts were used to justify a secondary and unequal position for women.

Systematic "control and subjugation of women" evolved when the government launched a series of legal measures to ensure conservative Confucian views of "womanly virtues."[7] As in Japan, most of the restrictions that were established during these years were imposed on royal women and other upper-class women. Not until later did the strict Confucian moral code and the legal mandates that controlled it begin to influence the lives of the less affluent population.[8]

In the late nineteenth century, when Korea opened its doors to the West, female Christian missionaries became active in trying to improve the position of women in Korean society. Education became an issue in the late 1800s, and in 1886 the first women's schools were opened. Though upper-class women were sometimes educated in their homes prior to this time, this was the first opportunity for them to have formal schooling.[9]

However, women's education was separate and different from men's. Until 1892 at the Ewha Woman's University, the oldest and most prestigious women's higher educational institution in Korea, men lectured to women from behind a screen so that the presence of women would not distract them.

Despite the centuries of inequality between the sexes and the inferior position of women in traditional Korean society, industrialization and modernization have brought changes in female lives. Thus, to the casual observer, women do not appear to be disadvantaged or oppressed. Today, women can be found working in offices, businesses, and commercial enterprises. They move freely and unescorted in public places, and they have access to educational opportunities. However, the system tends to remain gender stratified.

Traditional values have been tested by economic and demographic changes since the 1950s. The Confucian value base has been modified, and Koreans often talk about the "new Confucianism." But the centrality of relationships over the individual is still used to justify the distinct sex roles that tend to handicap women in economic and political competition. Moreover, as recently as the late 1980s, a Seoul newspaper quoted a survey in which 60 percent of Korean teenage girls said they would rather be boys if they could be born again.[10] Kim Chong Ui wrote in *Korean Women Today*, a publication of the Korean Women's Development Institute, a government agency, that "because of the wrong socialization process in our society which has continued for too long, not only men but also women themselves tend to recognize the inferiority of women at least unconsciously. This is what remains as the major obstacle to achieving equality between men and women." [11]

## The Japanese experience

Japanese values can best be understood in the context of the assimilative tendency in Japanese culture. Historically, Japan has adopted various religious and moral traditions. (Today, while most Japanese claim no religious allegiance, they turn to Shintoism for life crises and Buddhism for funerals.) Though different traditions were absorbed, the addition of new ideas was not used to uproot the existing value systems. Rather, they were incorporated into an amalgam that itself might be termed the "Japanese religion." Notable in this process is continuity and harmony rather than value conflict or discord. In some measure, cultural homogeneity has been enhanced by Japan's isolated geographic situation and dense population concentration. [12]

Shintoism and Buddhism, as they fused during the seventh and eighth centuries in Japan, provided a religious base for the nation. However, it was during the Edo or Tokugawa period (1603–1868) that Samurai Confucianism and feudalism altered the face of Japanese society. Samurai Confucians assigned loyalty to one's lord prior to one's family. When a choice had to be made, loyalty to one's lord was assumed to override the filial relation. [13] This structure, with its hierarchical relationships, may have served as a precursor of today's corporate structure.

In the earlier Kamakura period (1192–1333), neo-Confucianism—the revival of Confucian teaching with its concern for learning and harmonious relationships among people—was adopted by Zen priests who were attracted by the blending of Buddhist and Confucian thought. Later, the Tokugawa government formally adopted neo-Confucian teaching as the ideological basis for its rule. Once this occurred, Confucian precepts began to influence the lives of the ordinary people. [14] In this belief system the role of women became primarily "heir providers." The view that women were important largely as vessels to insure paternity and that the husband was the absolute lord and master of his family was not unlike the view that prevailed in Korea. [15] The imposition of feudal values reinforced Confucian morality and further constrained opportunities for women in Japan.

While the Meiji period experienced the end of feudalism, the rise of industrialization, and new employment opportunities for women, little improvement in women's status was actually evident. Tightly circumscribed roles and responsibilities for women were upheld by the Meiji Code, though some women did gain limited rights to own property, with their husbands as managers, and the right to divorce was established, with husbands maintaining custody of the children. Men were awarded rights and privileges while women were given duties and obligations. In 1872 education for women was introduced in order to produce *ryosai kembo* (good wives and mothers).[16]

Significantly, the Peace Preservation Law, which was enacted in 1887, prohibited women and minors from joining political organizations, attending political meetings, or initiating such meetings. This was justified by the need for women to "concentrate on domestic responsibilities." While in 1922 women were able to press for a change in the law that permitted them to attend meetings, the ban on political organization and joining political parties remained in effect until the post–World War II period.[17]

*The similarities in national experiences*

In Japan and especially Korea, Confucian belief systems have been used to justify the persistence of loyalty to authority (the state, the company) and to hierarchy. A highly ordered chain of relationships has meant that women were subservient to men, and men to the rulers. Individual rights and equality were secondary to values emphasizing the primacy of the family and the group.[18]

Traditional role relationships and status expectations are often used to define and justify strict and limited roles for women in Japan and Korea. Moreover, it is difficult to alter role relationships in either country since many women, as well as men, accept the legitimacy of the traditional relationships.[19]

Buddhism, which still has many adherents in both Japan and Korea, also maintains a secondary status for women. A woman's only hope for salvation is to be reborn as a man.[20] The continued prevalence of these attitudes could be seen in Japan as recently as 1989 when 71 percent of surveyed Japanese women agreed with the statement "Women take care of the household; husbands work outside of the home."[21]

## CHANGING PATTERNS OF ECONOMIC PARTICIPATION

Major industrial growth and development in Korea commenced in the 1960s under the regime of Park Chung Hee. Park's economics have been characterized as "guided economic development." With strong and guided encouragement from the state, some of Korea's most successful enterprises grew into *chaebol* (huge conglomerates). The *chaebol* began to dominate Korea's economic development as they benefited from government contracts and patronage. They were given government protection that enabled them to monopolize spheres of activity and accumulate capital to finance diversification of production.

The two Chinese characters that form the word *chaebol* also form the Japanese word for industrial conglomerates, *zaibatsu*. The *chaebol* and the *zaibatsu* began as small enterprises that, because of government protection, were able to expand and monopolize economic development in the two nations.[22]

*The Korean experience*

Despite profound changes in Korean society in the past three decades that have had some impact upon women's expectations and roles, a secondary status for women has been retained. Some observers of industrial development in Korea have observed that Korea's "economic miracle" was possible because women worked at the repetitive, dead-end, and poorly paid jobs that are generated by industrialization. Thus, a segregated female labor force has provided the employees for electronics, textiles, and toy factories.[23] In other words, the industrial conglomerates have absorbed women into factory positions. They have not, however, welcomed women into the corporate offices, except as secretaries.

The public sector has also been unreceptive to women professionals. In part this is a function of nepotism reinforced by cultural norms and expectations. Nepotism in Korea exists in both the private and the public sectors. It is part of the behavioral culture that seems to work to exclude women from full participation in both the labor force and the political structure.

According to the February 1989 *Korea Statistics Monthly*, labor-force participation in January 1989 was 69.4 percent for men and 39.9 percent for women. Not all women want to work; most women leave the paid work force when they have their first child, and since women college graduates often have difficulty finding positions appropriate to their level of education and training, sometimes they choose not to seek paid positions. Further, men were more likely than women to hold the higher paying and more prestigious positions. Thus, 68.3 percent of professional, technical, and administrative positions were held by men, and only 31.7 percent by women.

It is important to note too that "all professional, technical and administrative positions are not created equal" and that women tend to be in positions that have less authority and lower pay than men—a condition that appears to be nearly universal. For example, in central government service, women hold 13 percent of lower-ranked positions but fewer than 1 percent of higher civil-service positions. In the private, nongovernmental sector there are token female appointments but few women who enter career-path employment in the *chaebol*. Female college graduates seen in corporate offices are generally hired as secretaries.[24] In contrast, in the service sector, women hold 60.6 percent of all of the jobs, while men fill 39.4 percent of these positions.

As women have achieved higher educational levels, one of the few sectors of the economy that has been receptive to them has been teaching. The proportion of women who have entered teaching has increased substantially. In particular, there have been notable increases in the number of women elementary and secondary school instructors. Women constitute almost 44 percent of elementary school, 39 percent of middle school, and 21 percent of secondary school teachers.[25]

The above discussion does not take into account two groups of women who should be considered when employment opportunities and income prospects are considered. Farm women and lower-class women have worked outside of their homes even when the norm was for women not to be so employed. In poor families all able-bodied people must work in order to provide income necessary for survival. In agricultural households, though the work that women perform may be different from men, female participation in the farm chores is always assumed. Women work in the rice paddies and they care for vegetable gardens. They do these jobs in addition to the traditional household chores usually designated as "women's work."

There continues to be significant employment discrimination in Korea that is rooted in perceptions of appropriate role divisions between men and women. There is unequal access to jobs and inequality in earnings. In 1989, the average annual pay for women was 52.4 percent of the average male's. Often the inequality in opportunity and earnings is justified on the basis of Confucianism and what is believed to be the necessary role relationships rooted in the multigenerational family. However, it is worth noting that according to a 1985 housing census, 80.5 percent of Korean households are composed of five or fewer people. This reflects the preference for fewer children as well as the movement away from the multigenerational family. This trend seems to have accelerated in the years since 1985 as the birthrate has continued to decline. Both of these tendencies may free women from some of the traditional, time-consuming household and family responsibilities assumed to be part of a "women's role."[26]

### The Japanese experience

In 1989, 77 percent of Japanese men and 49 percent of all Japanese women were members of the work force. This level of participation is comparable to other industrial societies. Japanese women workers comprise 54.9 percent of the service-sector workers. While women hold 42 percent of the professional and technical/managerial positions in Japan, they constitute only 7.9 percent of the higher-level managers and officials. This marks an increase from 5 percent in 1980.[27]

As in other nations, female participation in the labor force is circumscribed by domestic responsibilities. In Japan, as in Korea, women are expected to leave their paid positions when they have their first child. Thus, women's employment patterns in Japan (and Korea) look like M-shaped curves. In other words, female labor-force participation is not continuous. It peaks between the ages of 20 and 25, when 75 percent of women are employed, and then it again begins to rise at gradually increasing rates between the ages of 35 and 50, when women no longer have children at home for whom they must provide care.[28]

Care-giving responsibilities for women do not end with children. Japanese women are often called upon later in their lives to care for their elderly parents or in-laws. This pattern exists because there are few well-developed public programs to care for the elderly and life expectancy in Japan is the longest in the world. There is an expectation that children will care for their aged parents and in-laws. (The same tendencies exist in Korea.) The pattern of interrupted labor-force participation—in both the beginning and ending work years—disqualifies women from joining the ranks of the privileged employees "whose lengthy and continuous service is rewarded with promises of lifetime employment" and creates a system in which women have been viewed as transient members of the work force.[29]

The pattern of interrupted labor-force participation and the primacy of domestic roles has several consequences for women workers. In the main, women are limited to relatively low-status work that tends to be part-time and temporary in nature. These jobs may in fact involve full-time hours but they are poorly paid and they do not provide benefits. Benefits such as housing and dependent allowances are especially important in determining workers' actual incomes. However, such benefits are normally paid only to male heads of households (though in recent years this issue has been litigated with some success by women plaintiffs and attorneys).

Until recently, companies preferred to hire female graduates of high school and junior college rather than college, since the former were deemed "more expendable." This pattern has been buttressed by the disproportionate number of women who attend junior college in Japan. In 1989, 24 percent of women high school graduates attended junior college, while just 13.7 percent attended a university. The comparable figures for men were 1.7 percent and 34.1 percent.[30] Even among women who do attend a university, a large portion are enrolled in women's colleges and few attend the prestigious national universities that provide access to career mobility. Also, women are likely to major in such traditional fields as home economics, literature, or education, a pattern similar to that found in Korea. It is not surprising, given their distinctive educational background and the patterns of labor-force participation, that women workers experience a significant wage gap relative to their male colleagues. In the 1980s and early 1990s this gap has ranged from 50 percent to 60 percent, which is one of the highest in the industrialized world.[31]

*The similarities in experiences*

In Japan and Korea there is an unusually large gender-based wage gap. Japanese and Korean women have been denied access to the jobs, skill training, life-time employment, seniority, and job security that are characteristic of their male counterparts. Traditionally, women were forced to leave the paid work force upon marriage or childbearing. Though the 1985 Equal Employment Opportunity Act in Japan and the 1988 Equal Employment Opportunity Act in Korea specifically define these practices as illegal, old habits and culturally reinforced expectations are difficult to change. In addition, in both nations the equal employment legislation is weak and limited in its impact. (These laws do not affect farm women and poor women who work despite their family status or entrepreneurial women who have carved out their own niches as business owners.) If women return to the labor force after their children are grown, they tend to be limited to part-time, temporary positions. As a consequence of these patterns, in both nations there are very few women who hold high-status professional and managerial positions.[32]

To an extent unusual in the industrial world, women continue to comprise a segregated segment of the labor force that is low skilled, low paid, and of low status. Even among women who are university educated and trained, equal employment opportunity remains an elusive goal. Japan and Korea, which have produced dramatic gains in industry and technology, remain male-dominated societies.[33] Women's roles continue to be defined in terms of a "gendered duality," circumscribed by family, life-style, and social life.[34]

## WOMEN AND POLITICS

To understand the changes that are confronting the traditions in Japan and Korea, political representation, group and movement activism, and efforts to influence public policy development must be appraised. In particular, one must ask whether women's movements can gain recognition and have a lasting impact on policy formation given the cultural constraints discussed above.

### The Korean experience

Article 8 of the 1948 Korean Constitution provides that all citizens are equal before the law and bars discrimination in political, economic, social, and cultural life on account of sex, religion, or social status.[35] The reality is sometimes at variance with the American-influenced constitution.

Korea is not a liberal democracy. Concern with relationships, social order, and community takes precedence over regard for individual freedom. Moreover, in the post–World War II era politics has been dominated by a single party that, until 1993, was controlled by authoritarian "strong men" with military support. During the 1980s, political turmoil was a regular occurrence in South Korea. Demands for democratization, reunification with North Korea, and human-rights reforms were the three pillars of discontent that articulated and fueled the country's ongoing strikes, protests, and demonstrations.[36] Ultimately this led to the downfall of the government in 1987 and the promulgation of a new constitution and more open elections in 1988 and 1993.

Despite the fact that women participated in the protests that led to the downfall of the government and the writing of a new constitution, in 1993 there were only three women cabinet ministers and all of the female candidates for district seats in the National Assembly were defeated. There were five women members of the National Assembly but they were all appointed by their parties to these positions. It is worth noting, however, that all of the parties courted women's votes and the government has begun to pay lip service to women's concerns.

Prior to the April 1988 election there were elected women district representatives to the 299-member National Assembly. The electoral mechanism was altered for that election and the double-member districts that had been in place were replaced by single-member districts. It is possible that voters who had supported women representatives along with men when there were double-member districts found it more difficult to vote only for a woman.[37] Another possible explanation for the complete failure of women to be elected to positions in the National Assembly in 1988 and 1993 may be related to the manipulation of the male-dominated parties that allowed women to run only in peripheral districts where there were few hopes for the party's electoral success.[38]

Though the 1988 and 1993 electoral failures were disappointing to female activists who were hoping to establish themselves in the new electoral system, women are continuing to work to get into positions of influence and power in the recently organized autonomous local governments. In the 1991 basic-level local elections (i.e., districts), 122 women were candidates for local office. This figure represented 1.2 percent of the 10,120 candidates for the newly created local positions. The largest number of female candidates (54) were from Seoul, followed by the other large metropolitan cities, such as Kwangju, Inchon, Taejŏn, and Pusan. The nonurban areas had far fewer female candidates. The highest success was in Seoul, where twenty-two women were elected to local council positions.[39]

There has been a rapid expansion of women's issue-oriented groups, service organizations, consumer groups, and church-based groups.[40] Women's organizations have been focusing their attention on schools, parks, health facilities, and the like. Women's research centers have been organized at a number of universities, and there is an active Women's Studies Organization. In 1983, in response to pressure from women's organizations, the government established the Korean Women's Development Institute (KWDI). The KWDI has been working to improve conditions for women and end the formalized discrimination against women in Korea. It acts as a bridge between organized women's interests and the government.

All of these organizations have worked to foster changes in the status of women. In 1988 the Equal Employment Opportunity Act became law. Many of the women's organizations along with the KWDI were instrumental in influencing government officials to pass this legislation. The law calls for an end to employment discrimination, equal pay for equal work, equal working conditions, an expansion of child day-care centers and a child-care leave system, and a dispute mediation system.[41] Though the legislation itself does not have an enforcement mechanism, it does provide the basis for improving workplace conditions for women.

Also, in 1991 changes in the Family Law of Korea became operational. The Family Law maintains a system of patrilineal family headship, defines relationships for a woman's family differently than for a man's, and restricts marriage between people with the same name and place of origin, even if they are very distant relatives. The changes in the law did, however, eliminate some of the more offensive (to women's rights activists) elements of the law. In particular, the law ended the differential inheritance provisions that provided a greater portion of family inheritance to the elder son than to the other children or the widow.

Women's groups in Korea provide the building blocks for a developing women's movement. However, despite an American-style constitution, Korea is not a pluralist democracy, and apparent similarities to American interest groups are misleading. Nonetheless, the over forty national women's organizations that are associated with the two major umbrella organizations of women's groups represent an array of interests and concerns. They range from very traditional groups (housewives and mothers groups, mainstream service organizations such as the YWCA, church affiliated groups) to more radical organizations that have been concerned with democratization, reunification with North Korea, and the human-rights violations of the government. Some of the latter groups have been in the forefront of recent activities focused on violence against women. In particular, the Women's Hot Line and the Korea Sexual Violence Relief Center have been in the forefront of the campaign to limit gender violence. At times, the various groups work together to try to pressure for change, as was the case with the modifications in the Family Law and in the campaign to end sexual violence against women. There are also occasions when the groups fail to cooperate. Thus, the more radical groups did not support the Equal Employment Opportunity Act because it lacked an enforcement mechanism.

### The Japanese experience

Political conditions in Japan are somewhat different from those in Korea. Less authoritarian in structure than Korea, the Japanese system has rested on a triumvirate of power based on the Liberal Democratic party, business groups, and the bureaucracy. Prior to the late 1980s, when opposition parties were able to gain control of the less powerful Upper House of the Diet, electoral competition was limited and state legitimacy was assured by economic success. Then, in 1993 a seven-party reform coalition headed by Morihiro Hosokawa of the New Japan party took control of the government. The thirty-eight-year-long rule of the Liberal Democratic party came to at least a temporary halt, and the major opposition party, the Social Democrats, suffered a crushing defeat.

Like Korea, Japan too has an American-style constitution. The 1947 constitution, a legacy of the American occupation after World War II, appeared to set the stage for equal rights for women and men when it stipulated in article 14 that "all people are equal under the law" and "there shall be no discrimination in political, economic, or social relations because of sex." Article 24 states that "marriage shall be maintained with the equal rights of the husband and wife as a basis," specifying that property rights, inheritance, divorce, and other spousal relationships should reflect "the equality of the sexes." The attainment of women's rights, as articulated in the Japanese constitution, has not been fully realized. Unequal social status for women has been justified in terms of traditional cultural expectations that are shared by both men and women.

Japanese women have lacked a vigorous feminist movement with a mass grass-roots base or a strong national presence. The absence of such a movement is rooted in the entrenchment of gender-based distinctions at all levels of the society that have limited opportunities for the creation of a new type of consciousness among women.

Japan lacks a tradition of liberalism and individual rights that might be invoked to mobilize advocacy and group activity. Also, outspoken dissent, especially by women, is frowned upon in Japan. Nonetheless, feminism in Japan can be traced back to the late nineteenth century when socialist feminists and "Bluestockings" fought for suffrage and to raise women's consciousness about their status in society and the family.

In the post–World War II era women in Japan, as in Korea, have been active in consumer and environmental movements as well as in the peace movement, especially in opposition to the U.S.–Japan Security Treaty in the early 1970s. Community groups have been organized by local housewives, their primary focus being social welfare policies and the family. In the main, activities that do not challenge prevailing attitudes and are extensions of home and domestic activities have dominated the efforts of Japanese women activists.[42] In her study of urban housewives, Anne Imamura found among her respondents a general lack of interest in political activity, a limited concept of citizen participation, and a general absence of community in terms of solidarity-producing institutions outside the family.[43]

Nonetheless, there is women's movement in Japan, and like its counterparts elsewhere, it is characterized by diverse interests and is divided into moderate and more militant wings. A reformist oriented "liaison group" to the government is comprised of fifty-two organizations representing women's groups, labor unions, and representatives of the political parties. Among the participating groups is the Fusae Ichikawa Memorial Association, which resembles an amalgam of the League of Women Voters and the National Women's Political Caucus. The coalition pressed for passage of the Equal Employment Opportunity Act of 1985 and continues to pressure for changes in women's unequal status, including a "National Plan of Action—Toward the Year 2000," which emphasizes increased representation and equal rights for women. The groups have also fought government efforts to restrict abortion. On several occasions in the 1970s and 1980s feminist activists along with other groups have vigorously opposed proposed restrictions in the Eugenic Protection Law, which freely permits abortion for economic reasons. In 1990 similar efforts to oppose newly imposed bureaucratic restrictions on the period in which legal abortions could be performed were unsuccessful.

Local groups have organized around workplace discrimination issues in numerous urban areas and company settings. Though such organizations are numerous, they have been limited in their impact on society. These groups are localized and fragmented, and are unlikely to evolve into national organizations or coalitions to influence policy making.[44]

Other avowedly feminist organizations have evolved that address issues of women's consciousness. Agora was founded as a resource center for women to engage in consciousness raising, sensitivity training, and political activity. The (International) Women's Action Group, born during the International Decade of the Woman, has remained active with working groups on work, discrimination, and the media.[45] Finally, despite the fact that Japan is not a litigious society, since 1966 over thirty lawsuits have been brought into the courts by women and activist female attorneys questioning their unequal status, most recently focused on sexual harassment. They have met with varying degrees of success.

In addition to the involvement of Japanese women in groups that are working to improve their status, some women have become active in electoral politics. These women have tended to be members of the Upper House, the less powerful of the two houses in the Diet. The more powerful Lower House of the Diet had 512 members as of 1994, elected for four-year terms (the Upper House had 252 members). Election to the Lower House has been based on a system of multimember districts (usually three to five members per district). Voters have had one nontransferable vote. Candidates could thus be elected with a small portion of the vote, making it possible for small parties and even independent candidates to win electoral victories. In theory this system would seem to foster the election of numerous women candidates. However, in practice this has not occurred and in 1993 women held just 2.7 percent of the seats in the Lower House and 15 percent of the seats in the Upper House.

In 1989 a woman, Takako Doi, was designated as the leader of the opposition Socialist party in Japan. In 1993 she was chosen as speaker of the Upper House by the Hosokawa government. Though the latter is a position with limited power, it has symbolic importance. In the elections of 1993, the number of women candidates increased slightly, while the role of women voters seemed less central to the process than it had been in 1989. Two Liberal Democratic party women won seats in the Lower House for the first time since 1980, and three women were appointed to the twenty-one-member cabinet.

The political system is in flux, and patterns of alignment and electoral representation appear to be changing more at this writing than at any time during the postwar period. The impact on women voters and elected representatives is not entirely clear.

In the arena of local politics, including prefectures, cities, towns, and villages, the representation of women was just 3.1 percent of all elected officials in 1991 (up from 2.3 percent in 1987). Only the Communist party has tended to field a large number of successful female candidates.[46] Finally, in a system in which the bureaucracy plays a central role in the decision-making process, fewer than 1 percent of senior government posts are held by women, and at the most senior level the figure is even lower.

### The similarities in national experiences

In both Japan and Korea women are entering the political arena as both voters and candidates. Although their successes have been limited, Japanese women seem to be making more headway, albeit slowly and incrementally, into electoral politics than Korean women. In both countries politicians are seeking women's votes in response to political instability and an awareness that women may become decisive in determining electoral outcomes. This recognition has led to the appointment of more women to political office and perhaps an increased awareness and attention to some women's concerns.

Groups that articulate concerns for the improved social, economic, and political status of women have become the building blocks of women's movements in both societies. These organizations have helped to raise issues related to the unequal status of women. However, given constraints on their full involvement in the political system as well as the difficulty new groups have in gaining access to the decision-making process in both Korea and Japan, they have found it difficult to achieve their desired goals. In both countries equal employment opportunity laws were enacted in response to pressures from women's groups, but the scope of the laws are limited and enforcement mechanisms are lacking. Thus despite recognition of unequal employment opportunities for women, only a symbolic response has thus far been achieved.

## PROSPECTS FOR THE TWENTY-FIRST CENTURY

There are several factors that may induce women and men to accept substantial changes in sex-role relationships in both Korea and Japan. Increasingly the need for two incomes is becoming more acceptable in order to meet the demand for consumer and luxury goods, the need for retirement income, and the high cost of educating children. Also, the internationalization of both nations means increased exposure to alien cultures and interest in the life-styles of people elsewhere, potentially adding to the reinforcement of international feminist principles and networks.

Change appears to be predicated on transformations in women's consciousness and on the broader needs of the political and economic system. With regard to the former, both Japanese and Korean women apparently perceive of childbearing and rearing as an increasing burden. Birth rates in both nations have dropped to among the lowest in the world: fewer than 1.54 for women of childbearing age in Japan and 1.7 in Korea.

Both Japanese and Korean women have been made increasingly aware of discrimination in the workplace. Corporate norms that stress lifetime employment and seniority may break down due to the desire of employers to lower costs, although they will be counterbalanced by the desire to maintain a homogeneous work force. Also, when employment opportunities decrease, women are the first to be laid off.

Moreover, the continued reluctance of many women in both countries to enter the labor force on a permanent basis because of the long hours, limited opportunities, and domestic expectations could contribute to a continuation of gender-based distinctions in the workplace and at home. Women's attitudes are further complicated by the need to choose alternative life-styles. Very few women are able to balance professional careers and domestic expectations in societies in which Confucian role relationships and neotraditional values justify women's unequal status in society.

In addition to the cultural and economic barriers to equity and choice, political constraints operate in both societies to exclude women from full participation. The two political systems provide few opportunities for political advocacy and involvement, and women who wish to pursue social change find few avenues for attaining access and success.

The language of feminism has been adopted by a minority in both Japan and Korea and newly enacted legislation reflects the rhetoric, if not the reality, of pluralism and equal rights. However, the persistence and pervasiveness of culturally determined gender-based role distinctions for men and women suggests that equal opportunity for women is a goal yet to be achieved in both Japan and Korea.

## NOTES

1. Lucian Pye, "Political Culture," in *International Encyclopedia of the Social Sciences* (New York: Free Press, 1968), 218.

2. Gabriel A. Almond, "The Intellectual History of the Civic Culture Concept," in *The Civic Culture Revisited*, ed. Gabriel A. Almond and Sidney Verba (Newbury Park, Calif.: Sage Publications, 1989), 27.

3. Lucian Pye, *Asian Power and Politics* (Cambridge, Mass.: Belknap Press of Harvard University Press, 1985), 12.

4. Sheldon Wolin, *Politics and Vision* (Boston: Little, Brown, 1960), 353.

5. Marian Lief Palley, "Women's Rights as Human Rights: An International Perspective," *Annals of the American Academy of Political and Social Science* 515 (May 1991): 164.

6. Roger Buckley, *Japan Today* (New York: Cambridge University Press, 1990), 83.

7. Kim Yung Chung, *Women of Korea* (Seoul: Ewha Woman's University Press, 1976), 84.

8. *Ibid.*

9. *Ibid.*, 402–3.

10. Ben Kremenak, "Women's Progress in Korea: Promise, Progress, and Frustration," *Asia Foundation Quarterly* 2 (Summer 1988): 1.

11. Kim Chong Ui, "On Male Chauvinistic Cultural Attitudes," *Korean Women Today*, no. 19 (Seoul: KWDI, Spring 1988), 4.

12. Agency for Cultural Affairs, *Japanese Religion: A Survey* (Tokyo: Kodansha International, 1987), 12.

13. Agency for Cultural Affairs, *Japanese Religion*, 112.

14. *Ibid.*, 22.

15. Dorothy Robins-Mowry, *The Hidden Sun: Women of Modern Japan* (Boulder, Colo.: Westview Press, 1983), 24.

16. Joyce Lebra, Joy Paulson, and Elizabeth Powers, *Women in Changing Japan* (Boulder, Colo.: Westview Press, 1976), 13.

17. Robins-Mowry, *Hidden Sun*, 64.

18. Dorinne Kondo, *Crafting Selves: Power, Gender, and Discourses of Identity in a Japanese Workplace* (Chicago: University of Chicago Press, 1990).

19. Marian Lief Palley, "Women's Status in South Korea: Tradition and Change," *Asian Survey* 30 (December 1990): 1153.

20. Lebra *et al.*, *Women in Japan*, 9.

21. Sandra Buckley, "Altered States: The Body Politic and Gender in Contemporary Japan," in *Postwar Japan as History*, ed. Andrew Gordon (Berkeley: University of California Press, 1992), 347–372.

22. Lee Chong Sik, "South Korea: The Challenge of Democracy," in *Minidragons*, ed. Steven M. Goldstein (Boulder, Colo.: Westview Press, 1991), 121.

23. Vincent S. R. Brandt, "South Korean Society," in *Korea Briefing, 1991*, ed. Lee Chong Sik (Boulder, Colo.: Westview Press, 1991), 87.

24. Kremenak, "Women's Progress in Korea," 2.

25. *Ibid.*, 3.

26. *Ibid.*, 1.

27. Japanese Institute of Women's Employment, *Japan's Working Women Today*, (Tokyo: JIWE, 1991), 5, 8. As in Korea, not all technical/managerial positions are comparable in responsibility, status, and pay.

28. Mary Brinton, "The Social/Institutional Bases of Gender Stratification: Japan as an Illustrative Case," *American Journal of Sociology* 94 (September 1988): 309.

29. Bernard Eccleston, *State and Society in Post-War Japan* (Cambridge, England: Basil Blackwell, Polity Press, 1989), 182.

30. Japanese Institute of Women's Employment, *Japan's Working Women*, 10.

31. Brinton, "Gender Stratification," 308.

32. *Ibid.*; Cho Hyoung, "Labor Force Participation of Women in Korea," in *Challenges for Women*, ed. Chung Sei Wha (Seoul: Ewha Woman's University Press, 1986), 159–63.

33. Joyce Gelb, "Japanese Women: Continuity and Change," *Kaleidoscope* 5 (Spring 1992): 14–17; Palley, "Women's Status."

34. Takie Sugiyama Lebra, "Gender and Culture in Japanese Economy," presented at the Japanese Political Economy Research Group, Tokyo, 18 January 1988, 4.

35. Korean Women's Development Institute, *Status of Women in the Republic of Korea* (Seoul: KWDI, 1985), 7.

36. Palley, "Women's Status," 1138.

37. Ahn Byong Man, Professor of Political Science, Hankuk University of Foreign Studies, Seoul, Korea, interview with Marian Lief Palley, 25 June 1988.

38. Kremenak, "Women's Progress in Korea," 4.

39. "Women Candidates for Local Election," *Korean Women and Politics Newsletter* (Seoul: Korean Center for Women and Politics, May 1991), 4.

40. Palley, "Women's Status," 1144–1145.

41. Korean Women's Development Institute, *Korean Women Today* (Seoul: KWDI, Summer 1989), 4–5.

42. Margaret McKean, *Environmental Protest and Citizen Politics in Japan* (Berkeley, Calif.: University of California Press, 1981), 127.

43. Anne Imamura, *Urban Japanese Housewives* (Honolulu: University of Hawaii Press, 1987), 105–129.

44. See McKean, *Environmental Protest*, 162, for discussion of a similar point.

45. Vera Mackie, "Feminist Politics in Japan," *New Left Review*, no. 167 (January–February 1988): 72.

46. Kimiko Kubo, "Japanese Women's Participation in Politics," presented at International Seminar on Women and Elections, Seoul, 6–7 October 1989, 9–10.

# I ❖ JAPANESE WOMEN

# 2

# Women and the Family in Transition in Postindustrial Japan

CHIZUKO UENO

---

LIKE most other industrial societies, over the past two decades Japan has undergone a period of restructuring from an industrial to a postindustrial economy. This process has greatly affected the lives of both working women and nonworking housewives, and in turn, their families. If the changes that women have undergone since the period of high economic growth were to be summarized briefly, "the advance of women into the workplace" would express the situation pretty well. According to the *1982 Basic Survey of the Employment Structure*, more than half (50.8 percent) of married women work. The year 1982 is particularly noteworthy as the year in which the number of married women who work surpassed the number of full-time housewives, placing the latter in the minority for the first time.

How have Japanese women changed over the past twenty years? Emiko Shibayama, a women's labor economist, identifies the following eight changes in women workers since the 1973 oil crisis.

1. The percentage of middle-aged and older women who work has increased to more than 30 percent.
2. The percentage of women in the labor force has increased to over 40 percent.
3. The percentage of women workers who are employees (as opposed to workers in family businesses and self-employed workers) now exceeds 70 percent.
4. The percentage of all employees who are women has now climbed to 40 percent.

5. The average age of women employees has risen to the mid thirties, and the number of employees who have been married (i.e., who are married, widowed, or divorced) has increased to 70 percent.
6. About 70 percent of women employees work in tertiary industries.
7. The number of women employees who are part-time workers has climbed to 20 percent, and their patterns of employment have become both diverse and unstable (for example, they are sent from site to site or used as temporary or day workers).
8. More women are employed in the field of high technology.[1]

From these facts, we see that the reality of women's advance into the workplace has not been so much an increase in the number of "career women" who were so glamorized at one time, but rather an increase in the unstable and low-paying employment of middle-aged and older women—in other words, the phenomenon that can be referred to as the "marginalization of women's labor."

Described in terms of their personal histories, these middle-aged women who are entering the workplace fall into the category of "workers who return to work after a hiatus"—those who left the workplace to marry and have children and then returned to work. By contrast, "continuous workers"—those who never stopped working, even when having or raising children—are, contrary to predictions, increasing by a surprisingly small margin.

The National Life Bureau of the Economic Planning Agency commissioned a study by Kiyomi Morioka and others that was published in 1987 as *Searching for a New Way of Life for Women.*[2] This survey of women by life pattern carefully examined the relationship between women's work and family life, placing 655 women into six categories, according to their life patterns:

Pattern 1: unmarried, no children, continue to work
Pattern 2: married, no children, continue to work
Pattern 3: married, have children, continue to work
Pattern 4: married, have children, quit work
Pattern 5: quit work to marry or have children, return to work after raising children
Pattern 6: married, have children, never worked

The study showed that Pattern 3 women, those who have children and continue to work, accounted for only 21.7 percent of participants in the survey. In terms of age, 27.8 percent of Pattern 3 women were in their thirties, 25.2 percent in their forties, and 27.9 percent in their fifties. If only employees (as opposed to workers in family businesses and self-employed workers) are considered, there are no significant fluctuations: 14.3 percent were in their thirties, 14.4 percent in their forties, and 12.1 percent in their fifties. When you consider the fact that the percentage of self-employed women is decreasing, you can see a gradual increase in the number of employees who do not stop working when raising children, but because the total was only 27.8 percent the increase does not affect enough of a majority to be labeled "an increase in the number of career women who do not quit working even if they marry or have children." The majority of women in their thirties (57.2 percent) leave work to marry and have children. (This total is reached by adding together the number of women in the Pattern 4 category, that is, those who become full-time housewives when they get married and have children, and the number in the Pattern 5 category, that is, those who return to work after raising their children.) Thus the biggest change in women's lives since the period of high economic growth in the 1960s is that the "return to work after raising children" pattern, which was nearly nonexistent among employees at the beginning of the period, became the option selected by the majority of women.

As is well known, however, the working conditions awaiting the middle-aged and older women who returned to the workplace were terrible: unskilled positions at low wages with no job security. Shibayama says, "women's patterns of employment have become more diverse," but in this case "diverse" also means "not secure." We must also exercise caution when considering the data claiming that over 20 percent of women employees are part-time workers. If you consider women workers over age thirty-five, the number of part-timers increases to 1 in 3. Furthermore, the government's definition of part-time labor as "those who work fewer hours than regular employed workers" does not take into account the regulation of work hours.[3] So there are those treated as "part-timers" who work nearly the same number of hours as full-time workers and who even work overtime while being paid by the hour or by the day. Thus, the phenomenon of nonsecure employment can be seen to extend even farther than is ordinarily imagined. To summarize, the burden of women's advance into the workplace has been borne by middle-aged women who have undergone many changes, including a marginalization of women's labor.

## CHANGES IN THE INDUSTRIAL STRUCTURE

In order for the social phenomenon of women's advance into the workplace to take place, conditions on the demand side and the supply side of the labor market had to coincide. On the supply side, forces pushing women out of the home—the decrease in the birthrate and the automation of housework—emerged in the 1950s and have increased steadily ever since.[4] But it would be difficult to say that conditions on the demand side allowed for the assimilation of women into the workplace. In that sense, the changes in the demand side that created such a large increase in employment opportunities for middle-aged women were, Shibayama points out, the changes in the industrial structure that followed the 1973 oil crisis; in other words, the process of restructuring the economy.

The changes in the industrial structure greatly increased the proportion of tertiary industries in the Japanese economy. These changes made the economy softer and more information and service oriented. The heavy industries like iron, steel, and shipbuilding that had supported the economic growth of the 1960s had reached a dead end. Now, the information and service industries were supporting the growth. The Japanese economy had rushed from the industrial age to the postindustrial age.

As Veronica Beechey notes, citing the example of the OECD countries, since the 1973 oil crisis women's employment has grown dramatically in nations like Japan and the European countries, which are advanced industrialized economies.[5] Beechey emphasizes the structural depression and consequent "paradoxical increase in the employment of women when there is a high rate of unemployment." "A high rate of unemployment" means unemployment among adult male workers who normally have secure employment; "an increase in the employment of women" means an increase in nonsecure jobs for middle-aged women. This does not mean, as is often claimed, that women have "usurped" men's jobs. First, the jobs women are getting didn't exist before because they are new kinds of jobs in growing industries. Second, the jobs that women are being given have such poor conditions attached to them that there is no reason that any adult male worker would accept them.

The number of women workers increase during times of change in the industrial structure for the following reasons.

1.  Because of the softening of the economy, a worker's gender becomes less of an issue, relatively speaking.
2.  In the service sector, there is an increase in the number of irregular-shift jobs with hourly and seasonal variations.
3.  These latter jobs, considered "suitable for women," are made into "part-time jobs" because they are "women's work."[6] Thus, the new employment opportunities for women are jobs with low salaries and no job security that an adult male worker would not accept; in other words, "jobs for pin money."

There is a uniquely Japanese aspect of this trend that is not common to the other OECD countries: Japan has no immigrant laborers. Since the high economic growth period of the 1960s, the Japanese labor market has consistently suffered from a labor shortage. Having lost its overseas colonies and being bound to a policy of "peaceful growth," Japan has not opened its labor market to foreigners. Under the 1990 Immigration Control Act, the foreign workers permitted to enter Japan must be trained workers "who perform a job that cannot be performed by a Japanese." The labor shortage experienced during the high economic growth period, however, was one of unskilled workers. One way that companies addressed this labor shortage was by the introduction of factory automation and robotization. But for the jobs they still needed to fill they had no choice but to depend upon the ranks of the latent unemployed: married women. Consequently, married middle-aged women workers filled unskilled jobs that couldn't be done by machines; jobs that in other advanced industrialized nations might be filled by immigrant workers. National policy regarding the introduction of immigrant workers and trends in the employment of women are thus very closely connected. This is because the two groups would compete against each other directly for unskilled jobs.

Claudia von Werlhof calls this marginalization of women's labor, paradoxically, "the housewife-ization of labor."[7] The phrase "participation in the marginal labor market" connotes that the fence marking the boundary between the paid labor of the formal sector and the unpaid labor of the informal sector has been lowered so that women can easily go back and forth between the two. A "housewife," then, is someone who is always on call to respond to the demands of the informal sector, which normally means family responsibilities such as child rearing and taking care of the elderly, usually her parents-in-law.

## THE DIVERSIFICATION OF WOMEN'S LIFE-STYLES

When thinking about the increase in the number of women who return to work after an interruption, it becomes clear that the realities of women's advance into the workplace may have constituted changes not entirely welcomed by women. If we confine our discussion to married women with employment experience who have children, we find the following three groups of women.[8]

1. Full-time working wives (women who don't stop working when they marry)
2. Part-time working wives (women who stop working to marry and/or have children but later return to work)
3. Full-time housewives ("nonworking" women)

As mentioned above, Group 1 (full-time workers) constitutes about 14 percent of thirty-year-old employees and is not increasing significantly. Group 3 (full-time housewives) is on the decline. In the mid 1980s, the households in

Japan with two incomes exceeded 60 percent. The number of workers in their forties also exceeded 60 percent, which means that the proportion of wives over age thirty-five who do not work is now only in the 30 percent range.

The group that has gone from near invisibility to being an overwhelming majority over the past twenty years is Group 2, women who have returned to work after an interruption. These women, now in their forties and fifties, came of age during the period of high economic growth, and when they left work to marry and have children they had no idea that they would ever return to the workplace. At that time, women did not really have the concept of a life in which they would stop working for a time and then return. It wasn't until twenty years later that the restructured economy would so greatly increase the number of women workers. By this time they were completely unprepared for their return to the workplace, and, now middle-aged, they had no idea what the workplace they were returning to would be like. Women thus faced a new experience for which there was no historical precedent.

Today women's options have become more varied, and that raises the following question: When women choose from among the options available to them, what is the determinant variable? Women in the three groups above face two decisive times in life. The first is when they are about to have children and have the choice of leaving work or continuing. The second is when they are in the post–child-raising stage of life and have the choice of returning to work or remaining at home. Many variables, including her educational background, her sense of self as an independent being, and the structure of her family, will influence a woman's decision, but statistics show that ultimately it is a material reality—her husband's income—that matters most.

According to the 1989 *Basic Survey of the Employment Structure*, which divides household income into five levels, each comprising 20 percent of the population, nearly 50 percent of wives in the first four levels (i.e., from the lowest to the second highest) work. There is not much difference in the percentages of working wives among those levels, which together constitute 80 percent of the population. This 50 percent figure is close to the average rate of participation in the labor force by married women. By the fifth level, that is, among the top 20 percent of the population in terms of household income, the number of working wives suddenly drops about 10 percent to 38.1 percent. The dividing line between the fourth and fifth levels is an annual income of 7 million yen. In other words, it takes an annual income of that much or more for a wife to be able to be a full-time housewife. This is also clear from the fact that the first motivation women cite for going to work part-time is economic necessity, "to supplement household income."[9] Between 1986 and 1989, the percentage of working wives increased by approximately the same degree at all income levels, except Level 5, which had the highest increase. It is difficult to explain why the number of working wives in the fifth level has increased so steeply, but this may simply reflect the presence of two-career couples in which the wives earn as much as the husbands.

Incidentally, an advanced educational background does not always correlate with a high rate of employment. In Japan, which has a strong tendency toward hypergamy (marrying "up," particularly above one's educational background), women college graduates almost always marry men college graduates. Because men with a good educational background are often comfortably off financially, there is a tendency for women with a good educational background to end up in the privileged group of "nonworking wives."

Among full-time working wives, there is a high rate of concentration in the three "women's professions": kindergarten teacher, grade-school teacher (primarily at the lower end of the educational spectrum), and nurse. Although these three professions have some educational requirements, they have been "feminized" and are thus low-paying, low-status, semiprofessions. If you add civil servants to this list, you have a list of occupations women can easily engage in without interruption. It is unclear whether women in these professions work continuously simply because it is readily possible for them to do so or whether they initially chose these occupations with the intention of working continuously. Women in these professions have a tendency to meet and marry men in the same field. And so the reason that few women civil servants and teachers stop working when they get married and have children is not simply that their jobs have features like parental leave that make it easy for them to keep working, it is because they can't afford to suffer a reduction in their two-income family budget.[10]

According to the Hakuhodo Comprehensive Life Research Institute's 1988 survey of 1,485 households of employed workers in the Tokyo metropolitan area, another variable, in addition to their husband's income, that affects women's decisions about work is "parental assets."[11] In other words, it is not only household income but family background that determines a woman's choice of life-style. According to the survey, one of the conditions cited as necessary to enable a woman to be a full-time housewife was her husband's family's assets. Even if her husband's income doesn't reach 7 million yen (the boundary between Levels 4 and 5), if his parents have money the younger couple's own potential disposable household income increases. On the other hand, it is the wife's family's assets that support full-time working wives. First of all, in order to be able to give their daughter the education needed to qualify her to enter a specialized occupation, her family would either have to have a strong educational background itself (and thus take it as a given that a daughter should receive higher education) or be comfortable enough financially to be able to afford the expense of giving a daughter a higher education. Since more than 80 percent of Japanese parents still say that they would like to give their son four years of college and their daughter two years of junior college, there remains a gender bias regarding higher education. Most parents do not want to spend much money for their daughter's education because they do not anticipate a return on that investment since their daughter is likely to marry and thus become a member of another family. If a woman has a four-year college degree, therefore, she is likely to have come from a wealthy family. Her family will tend to support her, implicitly and explicitly, even after she gets married. The phrase "triple income" has been coined to refer to households such as this, which receive help from the wife's family in the form of goods or services, and in some cases even in the form of money. The matrilineal kinship tie is thus stronger among urban families with family property.

According to the Hakuhodo survey, women who return to work after an interruption belong to couples in which neither husband nor wife receives any family assistance, causing them to be at a disadvantage in terms of both cash flow, stock, and real property. The majority of these women return to work motivated by a desire to supplement household income, but because of the limit on the amount that a wife can earn and still be declared as a dependent for tax purposes (the so-called 1-million-yen wall), this supplementing amounts to less than 25 percent of total household income.

As a result, full-time housewives are women whose husbands have ample cash flow and come from wealthy families; women who continue working after marriage receive some help from their family but form a double-income couple with their husbands in order to increase household cash flow; and women who stop working for a time but then go back have neither stock, nor real property, nor cash flow. If you consider working by women simply in terms of economic factors, the sheer reality is that women who have to work have long been working, and those who don't have to, don't.

## GENDER NORMS AND THE VIEW OF MARRIAGE OF WOMEN WHO RETURN TO WORK

The problem is that both women who are continuous workers and women who return to work after a hiatus are counted as "working women." Women in these two categories differ markedly in terms of their working patterns, occupations, status at work, and earnings. In fact, it is not productive to lump Groups

1 and 2 together as "working women" in contrast to Group 3, "nonworking women." Group 2 includes both "women who didn't particularly want to but returned to work because they had to" and "women who wanted to continue working but had to stop due to a variety of factors," but in any event they are all women who made child rearing a priority over work during the child-rearing years. Looking at various data, it is clear that in terms of their view of gender roles in marriage and gender norms, Group 2 women are much closer to Group 3 women than they are to Group 1 women. A survey of gender norms conducted in 1990 by the city of Toyonaka in suburban Osaka shows that the working patterns of women in Group 2 do not affect their gender roles in marriage, nor do they change men's behavior in the household, thus leaving the power structure of the husband-wife relationship in its traditional form.[12] Thus, Group 2 women have a dual role or dual burden, that is, they continue to bear the burden of 100 percent of the housework along with the renewed burden of paid work.[13] The traditional sociological hypothesis that this dual burden of being a wage earner and a housekeeper occasions a role conflict is negated in the case of Group 2 women, however. First of all, these women usually return to work during the third stage of life, when their children have stopped needing constant care. Second, their income is used mainly to pay back home loans and for their children's extra (nonregular school) educational expenses. And third, since facilitating the process of children's second socialization is now left to professionals and thus has become something that can be bought, earning the money needed to give children a "better education" has emerged as one of the qualifications required of a "good mother." As Natalie Sokoloff points out in *Between Money and Love*, going out of the home to work thus does not occasion a conflict with the mother role.[14]

The group that conforms to Group 2's view of gender norms and the husband-wife relationship is Group 3, the full-time housewives. In that respect, Group 2 women might be referred to as "women who wanted to be full-time housewives but unfortunately failed to be." If it is the husband's economic status that differentiates Groups 2 and 3, the differentiation between the women who return to work and those who stay home can be attributed to the increase in the class gap over the past two decades.

## THE GROWING CLASS GAP AMONG WOMEN AND NEW TRENDS

The diversification of women's life patterns and the disintegration of social classes experienced over the past two decades were historically unprecedented and thus gave women historically unprecedented experiences. One might even call the changes that are taking place in the 1990s a type of historical judgment that is being rendered by these women's experiences. Let us consider the new trends manifested among young women separately in terms of working and nonworking women.

According to the results of a Ladies' Forum survey of 2,990 women workers at 114 private companies, including Nippon Telephone and Telegraph Corporation (NTT) and Fujitsu, 25 percent of all women wanted to continue working after marriage.[15] But that percentage grew smaller the younger the respondents were, with only 16 percent of women in their early twenties and 6 percent of women under twenty wanting to continue working. At all age levels, more than half of the respondents wanted to become a housewife eventually. Fifty-five percent of those under twenty wanted to become full-time housewives.

The results of this survey coincide with those of other surveys of women college students. Even according to the results of a survey I myself conducted each year of women in the classes at the junior college where I formerly taught, in 1988, 60 percent said they wanted to become full-time housewives, in contrast to the early 1980s when a majority voiced a preference for the return-to-work pattern, indicating that the return-to-work pattern has lost its appeal for young women and has been replaced by the desire to become a full-time housewife. The proportion of those wanting to continue working increased slightly, into the 20 percent range, but this is still very far from being a majority.

What does it mean when the number of women who want to become full-time housewives increases while the number of actual full-time housewives drops to a minority? There are several possible explanations for this. First, as the number of full-time housewives has decreased, the reality of the housewife who has returned to work has emerged for all to see, and in the course of this has lost its appeal. During the 1970s, when women began returning to work in great numbers, the model woman, who balanced working and taking care of her family, received the government's stamp of approval. The redundant term "full-time housewife" first appeared in the early 1970s. Among these women, whose identity was threatened by the increase in the number of working housewives, the phrase "just a housewife" began to be used.

When the number of women who returned to work began to constitute the majority, the realities of their lives became obvious. The burden of housework remained, working conditions were poor, and life itself was more onerous because of the dual burden. In exchange for a more stressful life they received mere pin money. As these realities became obvious there were more women on the borderline of this class who chose to risk not returning to work even when a job opportunity presented itself. The appeal of the option of both work and family that women had earlier demanded in order to fulfill all their desires had faded in the face of reality.

Second, as the disintegration of classes continued, it became inescapably clear that what separated the women who returned to work from the women who stayed at home was an economic factor. Being a full-time housewife had become proof of economic sufficiency. This becomes evident when you ask women students what images they associate with the phrase "full-time housewife." Whereas in the research I conducted among women college students in the 1970s full-time housewives were saddled with such labels as "overworked hausfrau," "hag," and "faceless," ten years later they began to be described as "attractive" and "well-off." The image of the full-time housewife evolved from a negative to a positive from the 1970s to the 1980s.

At the same time, the life of a full-time housewife was not necessarily confined to the home. Although these housewives didn't enter the workplace, they left their homes to engage in local activities and networking. Kanai Yoshiko, a scholar of women's studies, calls them "full-time activist housewives," meaning that they work full-time at activities leading to self-realization rather than housekeeping. Being a full-time housewife no longer requires a full-time dedication to a husband and children.

According to a survey I myself conducted of grassroots activists in suburban Osaka with the support of Dentsū, which included a statistical survey of 300 participants and 26 group interviews in 1987, in order to be active in self-realization activities women need both time and money.[16] There were more than the average number of full-time housewives among my interviewees, and they had a higher-than-average educational background and economic status.

Full-time housewives are no longer the prisoners that Hannah Gabron described them as being in *The Captive Wife*.[17] They are becoming a privileged class of people who choose not to go to work because they place priority on their own activities. Thus, young women who want to become full-time housewives are not unlike women who want to raise their social class through marriage. The only problem with them is the gap between desire and reality. In spite of the fact that nearly 60 percent of women would like to become full-time housewives, the number of men in the economic class who can actually help them fulfill that goal is only 30 percent (of men in their forties), and this number is predicted to fall to nearly 20 percent when the men presently in their twenties reach their forties. The majority of women who wish to become full-time housewives but are not able to will have to join the category of women who return to work to supplement household income after child rearing. The fate that awaits these women when they reach middle age, who will be cast into an inferior marginal labor market with no preparation, is the same as that being suffered today by the many women who have already returned to work. Thus, because the desires of these women conform to those of the full-time housewives, another generation of wives frustrated at not being able to get what they want is coming into existence.

## THE EFFECT OF THE EQUAL EMPLOYMENT OPPORTUNITY LAW

In the age of women's advance into the workplace, with the marginalization of women's labor having become a reality, the Equal Employment Opportunity Law was promulgated hastily in 1985 to meet the requirements for ratification of the United Nations treaty for women, which the Japanese government unwillingly signed in Copenhagen in 1980. With provisions for equality without protection and provisions specifying "good faith" compliance by employers without penalties, the law is like a sieve, but the impression of the workplace the law gives to women students who have not yet begun working is of a place where women can work and compete as the equals of men, even if tokenism exists. To address the requirements of the law, companies immediately introduced two-track personnel advancement systems consisting of a career track and a noncareer track, changing gender discrimination into "personal choice," but less than one percent of newly hired women graduates enter the career track. Moreover, "equal opportunity" applies only to individuals with identical academic credentials, so discrimination on the basis of educational background is practiced boldly against women graduates of junior college. In spite of the shoddy realities of the Equal Employment Opportunity Law, the commonly held image is an illusion of "equality of opportunity" in which "women can be professionals if they want to be," but this illusion is not that attractive to young women today. That is because for women this means that they will have equal opportunity to be engulfed in a competition with men. The only ones who welcome this competition are a small elite who do not mind working the long hours that men do and educational high achievers who have not yet known the reality of the workplace. Furthermore, women have caught on to the fact that success in this competition is gained only through extraordinary effort and by shouldering extraordinary burdens. Some of the reasons that may explain why the number of women who work continuously has not increased drastically over the past twenty years are (1) there has been absolutely no improvement in the conditions under which women must balance working and child raising and (2) young women, who have seen women succeed largely by shouldering the burdens individually and making personal sacrifices, do not find the life-style attractive. Akiko Chimoto, a specialist in the economics of women's labor, has noted that the heightened desire of young women to become full-time housewives exists, paradoxically, not "in spite of the Equal Employment Opportunity Law" but "because of the Equal Employment Opportunity Law."[18]

Although the Equal Employment Opportunity Law was, during the process of its establishment, reduced from being an "equal employment law" to being merely an "equal employment opportunity law," many are not aware of the strong reaction against it expressed at women's discussion groups and by feminist groups such as the Women's Group to Make Our Own Equal Employment Opportunity Law. These women opposed the law when it was proposed, anticipating that the modification of the protection provisions of the old Labor Standards Law coupled with the new law's "equality without protection" would strengthen competition among women workers and worsen working conditions for women. The government's attempt to force a choice of either equality or protection—a reference to the fact that American women work on equal terms with men without being accorded protection—is not acceptable if "equality" is not applied to unpaid work done at home as well. Moreover, for Japanese women to "catch up" to the more than two thousand hours per year worked by Japanese men would be destructive to family life. For women to give up the existing protections that prohibit them from working excessively long hours and irregular shifts would therefore be the least desirable alternative.

With the experience since the enactment of the Equal Employment Opportunity Law, it is possible to say that nearly everything predicted by those who opposed that law, along with the Dispatch Enterprise Law and the changes in the work-hours regulations in the Labor Standards Law inaugurated at the same time, has come to pass. The Equal Employment Opportunity Law promoted the differentiation of women workers into the elite and the nonelite. One sector of elite women workers gained the opportunity to work on a career track like men, but the vast majority of nonelite women workers face a marginal labor market based on the assumption that women cannot work like men. Since the Equal Employment Opportunity Law, women's employment patterns have diversified to include part-time work, work under contract, dispatch work, work at home, and rehiring. There are also places like Isetan, one of Japan's biggest department stores, which has introduced a "sometime" workers program under the slogan, "you can work at your convenience," and Jusco, a nationwide chain store, which initiated a reentry system that gives priority to previous employees. However, the steps to becoming a regular full-time employee with job security are divided up into many gradations, and it is difficult to return to one's previous position. So, although many people are talking about "women's potential," all it really means is that they are being received into marginal labor markets in a variety of forms.

In the midst of this process, a quiet change is taking place among the women who were hired as full-time company employees before the Equal Employment Opportunity Law. According to the Labor Ministry's *Basic Survey of the Wage Structure*, the average length of service by women employees (excluding part-timers) has increased 1.7 years over ten years, from 5.3 years in 1976 to 7.0 years in 1986. The proportion of women with over ten years of service has increased to 25 percent. Women with ten years of service as of 1986 were of course hired before the Equal Employment Opportunity Law. These women were not given the option to enter the career track and are given "supplementary work suitable for women," without the chance for reassignment or advancement, so they are now experienced office workers. One reason for the lengthening years of service by women is the growing tendency for women to marry later. In 1991 the average age of a woman at the time of her first marriage reached nearly twenty-seven. Another factor is that women have had the opportunity to observe the fate that awaits women who leave work and return later, and they have decided to protect themselves from the insecurity of rehiring by holding on to a stable job despite the boring tasks they are given. These women aren't necessarily making a significant contribution to their companies, nor do their companies expect a lot from them. They have remained in their jobs longer than was expected and are often referred to by their employers as "dead stocks," but they are motivated by the quest for job security rather than a desire to work or particular interest in the job. The Child Care Leave Law passed in 1991 was welcomed because it enhances job security, even though it does not guarantee that women will be paid while on leave.

The changes that working women have undergone have had some side effects at the workplace. At ongoing employee training sessions, seminars to "recharge" women employees with more than five years of service have become popular, but rather than being an indication of a change in company attitudes toward women employees because of the Equal Employment Opportunity Law this is proof that, finding themselves confronted with women who are staying with them longer than expected, companies are beginning to think seriously about how to utilize their potential. The differences in the treatment of women employees hired before the law and those hired since the law is a newly emerging concern for personnel managers.

Women employees on the noncareer track hired since the law are also showing a tendency to remain in their positions longer than before. But the gap in wages and promotion has widened between the career track and the noncareer track. Noncareer-track women have begun to regret the choice they made at the outset of their employment and the fact that their work has remained "supplementary" in nature. To improve the morale of such women, some companies introduced ways of switching from the noncareer track to the career track. There are many restrictions on such switches, however, and the chance of realizing such a switch is small.

Surprisingly, women on the career track have tended to leave their jobs earlier than expected, for a variety of reasons. One is that they are mistreated at their companies because the men are unaccustomed to treating women as their equals. But the main reason is the extremely hard work they must do in order to reach the male standard. Equality means having to be a male clone, and women are showing their refusal to do this by leaving their privileged positions. The sole survivors on the career track, the women middle managers who are promoted, have no family responsibilities. Some are single and some get help from their mothers or their mothers-in-law.

### CHANGES FOR FULL-TIME HOUSEWIVES

There is a new wave of activity among nonworking housewives. There are two classes of women over forty who are now full-time housewives: (1) women who chose not to return to work even after the expansion of employment opportunities for middle-aged women and (2) women who were too old to be hired when the labor market shifted. Gender discrimination in recruiting and hiring was prohibited by the Equal Employment Opportunity Law, but age discrimination is still rampant, and there are few employment opportunities for women over forty. Women's networking activities center on women in their late forties and fifties. For women to be engaged in grassroots activities, they must be in the "empty nest" stage of life, completely free of the burdens of child rearing and educational expenses. Even if they have their own income, in order for their earnings to constitute 100 percent disposable income, their children must be completely independent of them. Women of this generation have the most resources in terms of time and money (and in addition they are physically able) because their child-rearing responsibilities are completed and their husbands have not yet reached retirement age.

At the same time that other women have been making advances into the workplace, these women have accumulated experience in local activities and networking, and these accomplishments have fostered new, independent, women's enterprises. Paid volunteering, profit-making club activities, and co-operative workers' collectives are the new forms of urban self-employment in which the women can control the quality of labor and manage themselves.[19] They began as consumers of non–profit-making activities but later began to engage in creative and productive activities of their own. The cooperative workers' collectives are particularly interesting. The women involved in them are members of consumer cooperatives that created their own autonomous circulation of goods and services as producers outside the market economy. In contrast to traditional women's self-employment in family-based businesses, most of the husbands of these women are employed elsewhere. Because the women do not work out of economic necessity, they can afford to question the quality of work and self-management of these organizations.

This new self-employment by housewives is both a result of women's having been excluded from regular employment and a product of their having opted against it. According to labor economists, many self-employed people are members of a social minority that suffers systematic discrimination in the labor market, and because women are, in that respect, a social minority, they formed their own work pattern independent of regular employment. Paradoxi-cally, in the midst of the pervasive trend toward women becoming employees, some middle-aged and older women who missed being hired experimented with a way of working that questioned conventional work styles, and some have succeeded. However, this way of working, which pays less than the hourly rate of part-time work, must also be considered a product of economic sufficiency.

## THE BREAKDOWN OF THE FAMILY AND THE DIVERSIFICATION OF LIFE-STYLES

I have argued that the structural changes in Japanese society over the past twenty years have led to the further differentiation of classes of women. These changes will inevitably cause further differentiations in family types as well. Now that getting married and becoming a housewife have ceased to be a woman's sole option, the realities of family life will change drastically accord-ing to the choices women make.

Although it can be said that women's options have become more diverse, they will probably continue to fall into the three groups described above—working continuously, stopping work and then returning, and being a full-time housewife—and variations thereof. As noted earlier, the variable that will differentiate the three will largely be economic—the woman's class. However, whereas previously a woman's class was determined solely by her husband's income, now other elements have come into play, such as her own income and the wealth of the parents of both husband and wife. Although this statement may open me to charges of being an economic determinist, in reality the fact is that the economic strength of a husband and wife has the most influence on the balance of power and interdependence of that couple. When there is abundant cash flow, stock, and real property on the wife's side, the traditionally patrilineal Japanese family structure might have a tendency to become more matrilineal. This is already manifesting itself in the increased desire of parents to live with their daughters and in the increase in extended matrilineal families in urban areas. Furthermore, a wife's having independent income doesn't necessarily always lessen the interdependence of husband and wife. Hakuhodo's research shows that when the annual income of a wife surpasses 3 million yen, the husband becomes more dependent on her; he does not want to lose her income. It is also possible that the effort to maintain a household budget built on the assumption of a wife's income might make a family more cohesive. As the wealth of a husband's or wife's family increases in value, the couple's coherence may increase rather than decrease as it unites to preserve the property. The Hakuhodo report called this type of strongly coherent family the family bound together by profit ties rather than blood ties.

The life of a couple or family will vary greatly according to which of the three working groups the wife follows. The way of life and use of time of working and nonworking wives differ so drastically that it would not be an exaggeration to say that they belong to different modes of life. Not only do they exist in different time zones and spaces, there are even instances in which their needs and interests conflict regarding such things as PTA activities and the disposal of garbage. In terms of household expenditures, working women must take into account increased social, communications, and commuting expenses, so in terms of their consumption habits working and nonworking wives differ greatly as well. Their ideas about the rationalization of housework and the priority it should be given differ too.

More than anything else, these women differ greatly in terms of what they expect of a spouse and their criteria for choosing one. Group 3 women expect their husbands to have economic strength, while Group 1 women expect to have a partnership. The age difference between husband and wife also differs between Group 1 and Group 3 women; the former tend to choose a spouse close to their own age, while the latter tend to choose older men. Although the average age difference between husband and wife in first marriages has remained unchanged at two to three since the early 1970s, marriage between people of the same age has recently become the most frequent occurrence, followed by marriage between people with a greater-than-average age gap.

According to Anne Imamura's survey "The Japanese Housewife," housewives feel "happiness" when their expectations and their role coincide.[20] In that respect, "unhappiness" results in the case of mismatches, for example when a husband expects a wife with a strong desire to work to be a housewife or when a woman who desires to be a full-time housewife marries a man without financial resources. The problem is whether men will experience enough diversification of life-style to correspond to the diversification women have attained. According to 1990 census data, there are nearly 100,000 more single men than single women between ages twenty and twenty-four. Women are tending to stay single much longer than before: 30 percent of women between ages twenty-five and twenty-nine are single (as are 60 percent of men; 30 percent of men in their thirties remain single). Considering the fact that, until recently, the accumulated marriage rate at age forty was over 95 percent, it appears that men now have less chance of finding a spouse. This shortage of brides is in part being met by importing brides from other Asian countries, but this solution causes other problems.

The life of the modern family as defined in terms of the gender-differentiated roles of the full-time housewife and the working husband is on the brink of major changes. The life of a married couple—their interests, the way they spend their leisure time, whether their lives are centered on their children, their consumption habits—will vary greatly depending on the life-style chosen by the wife. We are at a point in history when family norms and realities are in transition, and this has much to do with changes undergone by women rather than by men.

NOTES

1. Emiko Shibayama, "Changing Structure of Employment and Conditions of Women's Employment," in Committee for Peaceful Economic Planning and Editorial Board for White Paper on Economy, eds., 1987 People's White Paper on Economy: Women's Labor and the Changing Japanese Society (Tokyo: Nihon Hyōronsha, 1987), 45.

2. National Life Bureau, Economic Planning Agency, ed., *Searching for a New Way of Life for Women* (Tokyo: Printing Bureau, Ministry of Finance, 1987).

3. Shibayama, *People's White Paper*.

4. Chizuko Ueno, "The History of Housewives in the Postwar Period," in Ueno, ed., *Reading the Domestic Labor Debate*, vol. 1 (Tokyo: Keiso Shobo, 1982).

5. Veronica Beechey, *Unequal Work* (London: Verso, 1987).

6. *Ibid.*, 163. In its *1990 Basic Survey of Part-Time Workers*, the Ministry of Labor defines "part-time workers" as "those who work less than regular workers." It does not mention how many fewer hours they work. It includes "those who work as long as regular workers" among part-time workers as well. As the labor economist Osawa Mari points out, these people are treated as part-time workers regardless of their working hours because, in the Japanese employment system, "part-time workers" are determined by their status rather than by the hours they work. See Mari Osawa, *Beyond the Corporation-Centered Society: Reading Japanese Society from the Gender Perspective* (Tokyo: Jiji Tsushinsha, 1993), 83–86.

7. Claudia von Werlhof, " 'Schattenarbeit' oder Hausarbeit? Zur Gegenwart und Zukunft von Arbeit. Eine feministische Kritik an Ivan Illich," in Thomas Olk and Hans-Uwe Otto, eds., *Soziale Dienste im gesellschaftlichen Wandel*, vol. 2 (Neuwied, 1984).

8. I do not include in this breakdown the nearly 20 percent of women who are self-employed because their work style does not render working and being at home incompatible. For a detailed discussion of this, see Ueno Chizuko, "Twenty Years of Japanese Women," in *Annual Report for Women's Studies*, no. 10 (Tokyo: Women's Studies Society of Japan, 1989).

9. This reason was given by 66.2 percent of women surveyed. Ministry of Labor, "Basic Survey of Employment in the Third Industry," in Takahashi Hisako, ed., *Changing Women's Labor* (Tokyo: Yuhikaku, 1983), 120.

10. In 1991 the Child-Care Leave Law was made applicable to all private corporations, but it remains difficult for women in such corporations who have to work long hours to continue working after they have children. The relative stability of work hours and the long holidays of lower-level civil servants and schoolteachers make it possible for them to continue working even after having children. This would not be true of women with a company position higher than that of middle manager, however.

11. Hakuhodo Comprehensive Life Research Institute, *The Family in the 1990s* (Hakuhodo, 1989). Hakuhodo is the second largest advertising agency in Japan, after Dentsu.

12. Center for the Promotion of Women's Issues, City of Toyonaka, "Report on a Survey of Citizens' Views of Gender Roles: Men's Independence in Their Daily Lives," March 1989.

13. Chizuko Ueno, *Patriarchy and Capitalism* (Tokyo: Iwanami Shoten, 1990).

14. Natalie Sokoloff, *Between Money and Love: The Dialectics of Women's Home and Market Work* (New York: Praeger Publishers, 1980).

15. "Young Women Want to Be at Home the Most: A Ladies' Forum Sur-

vey Finds That Many Women Want To Be Full-Time Housewives," *Asahi Shimbun* (morning edition), 23 May 1989.

16. Chizuko Ueno and Dentsu Network Research Institute, *Women's Networking Changes the World* (Tokyo: Nihon Keizai Shimbunsha, 1989).

17. Hannah Gavron, *The Captive Wife: Conflicts of Housebound Mothers* (Routledge and Kegan Paul, 1966).

18. Akiko Chimoto, Lecture series at St. Agnes Women's College, 1986.

19. Details on cooperative workers' collectives can be found in Masako Amano, "From Passive Work to Talent-Based Work: The Experiment of Workers' Collectives," in Yoshiyuki Sato, ed., *Women's Life Networks* (Tokyo: Bunkado, 1988).

20. Anne Imamura, "The Japanese Housewife," in International Women's Studies Association, ed., *Report on the International Women's Studies Association's 1978 Tokyo Meeting* (Tokyo: NHK Books, 1978).

# 3

## Women's Education and Gender Roles in Japan

KUMIKO FUJIMURA-FANSELOW

*and* ATSUKO KAMEDA

---

SINCE the 1960s numerous discussions have been undertaken and various proposals set forth by governmental bodies for the improvement and reform of the Japanese educational system. All of them, however, have failed seriously to address issues related specifically to the education of women. This neglect or indifference can be traced in part to the presumption widely prevalent in Japan that, since the reforms of the educational system following the end of World War II under the direction of the American occupation firmly established the principle of gender equality in education, there no longer exist any problems. The lack of attention may also be traced to the fact that most people have not really thought it important or desirable to have women participate in society in the same capacities as men, and therefore have not been concerned with the question of how girls and women are educated. As a result, there has been little effort to look carefully at manifestations of sexism and gender inequality at various levels of education, to investigate ways of dealing with them, or to try to redress sex imbalances in educational participation and achievement.

However, the women's movement that appeared in the 1970s, together with the birth of women's studies on college and university campuses from the latter part of the 1970s, and the example of American and British research in the field have given rise to a growing concern among feminist educators and researchers regarding gender issues in education. Moreover, in an attempt to understand why, despite the abolition of legal and structural barriers to educational access for women, gender differences persist, educators and scholars, as well as groups of concerned women, have begun to examine the issue of gender equality not only in terms of educational access but also in terms of actual outcomes. Their goal is to analyze how sexism and gender stereotyping at various levels of the educational system function to perpetuate inequality.

This essay explores both change and continuity in patterns of female participation and achievement in education at various levels. We will also explore the factors, within and outside of schools and the educational process that contribute to the perpetuation of sex-based disparities in educational outcomes. We will examine efforts underway to combat sexism and eradicate barriers to the realization of gender equality. The last section of the essay is devoted to an examination of some of the most recent trends and developments pertaining to women's education, including the growth of women's studies in institutions of higher education, the increasingly uncertain future of women's colleges and universities, and the growing presence of nontraditional students, particularly women, in higher education institutions.

## GENDER DIFFERENCES IN EDUCATIONAL PARTICIPATION

### Postwar growth in female educational participation

In the wake of the reorganization of the Japanese educational system that took place following World War II, women were granted the legal right to pursue their education as far as their abilities would permit, at whatever types of institutions and in whatever fields they might choose. The various sex-segregated streams or tracks that had existed beyond elementary school were consolidated at each level, resulting in a single-track structure with each level qualifying students for the next higher level. University status was granted to various existing institutions, including many of the women's colleges. Compulsory education was extended from six to nine years, and a 6-3-3-4 structure was adopted (six years of elementary school beginning at age six, three years of lower secondary school, three years of upper secondary school, and four years of university or two years of junior college). Coeducation, which had formerly been limited to the early years of elementary school, was extended to all levels, including the university, and a common curriculum was instituted in all schools. These reforms, embodied in the School Education Law and the Fundamental Law of Education of 1947, established the necessary legal and structural basis for gender equality in terms of access to educational opportunity.

Since that time, remarkable progress has been made in terms of attendance at various levels within the educational system. Nearly all girls and boys receive nine years of compulsory education, and the percentage of girls

TABLE 3-1  *Percentages of Graduates from Lower Secondary School Attending Upper Secondary School (Selected Years, 1950 to 1991)*

| Year | Females (%) | Males (%) |
|------|-------------|-----------|
| 1950 | 36.7 | 48.0 |
| 1960 | 55.9 | 59.6 |
| 1970 | 82.7 | 81.6 |
| 1980 | 95.4 | 93.1 |
| 1990 | 96.2 | 94.0 |
| 1991 | 95.8 | 93.5 |

SOURCE: Mombusho (Ministry of Education), *Gakko Kihon Chosa* (School Basic Survey) for various years.

graduating from lower secondary school and continuing on to upper secondary school has increased from just 37 percent in 1950 to 96 percent in 1991 (see Table 3-1).

The expansion in upper secondary school attendance has been reflected, in turn, in a dramatic growth in enrollment both among females and males at institutions of postsecondary education. The growth has been especially striking, however, in the case of females: There was a fourfold increase in the proportion of girls entering junior colleges and universities between the years 1960 and 1986. The proportion of females in the relevant age group entering college (that is, the number of college entrants as a proportion of the total number of females who graduated from lower secondary school three years prior to a given year) rose from just 5.5 percent in 1960 to 18 percent in 1970, 33.5 percent in 1986, and 39.2 percent in 1991. Since 1989 the figure has exceeded that of males. There are a variety of social and economic factors that have promoted this expansion in women's postsecondary enrollments, including (1) the growing prosperity of the Japanese people brought on by the dramatic economic growth experienced in the 1960s; (2) the general improvement in the Japanese living standard, coupled with a reduction in the number of children per family, which has meant that more family resources are available to educate daughters as well as sons; (3) the growing shift from an elite to a mass system of higher education, which has led people to view college attendance as a matter-of-course for those belonging to the middle-class and upper-class; and (4) a change in social attitudes toward acceptance of the desirability of providing higher education for women.

*Gender differences in patterns of college enrollment*

While these figures appear impressive, they conceal numerous persisting gender differences, which are most readily apparent at the postsecondary level.[1]
Of the roughly 366,000 women who entered college in 1990, just four out of
ten went into four-year universities. The remaining 60 percent entered junior
colleges. In contrast, nearly all (95 percent) of the 361,000 males entering
college went to four-year universities (see Table 3-2).

Female university enrollment has increased in recent years, especially
since the mid 1980s. Nevertheless, women continue to be a minority (see
Table 3-3), and their proportion lags behind that found in most of the industrialized societies. Female representation is especially small at the most
prestigious coeducational universities, such as Tokyo University (a national
university), where just 10 percent of the students are women, and Waseda
University (a private university), where they make up 20 percent of the undergraduates. About 25 percent of all female university students are enrolled in
women's universities, of which there are 91 (82 private, 2 national, 7 public)
out of a total of 514 universities.

The comparatively low rate of female enrollment at four-year universities means that women continue to be a small minority of graduate students,
although in terms of both absolute numbers and relative proportions women's
representation has increased in recent years. In 1990 women comprised about
20 percent of all students enrolled in master's degree programs and slightly
under 18 percent of those in doctoral programs.[2]

Gender differences are also evident in the programs of study women
and men pursue in college. In recent years university women have made
inroads into traditionally male-dominated faculties such as law, political science, economics, and industrial management, and in turn there has been a
decline in the relative proportion enrolled in education and home economics.
Nevertheless, 55 percent of all women enrolled in universities in 1991 were
concentrated in the traditionally female fields of humanities, education, and
home economics. By contrast, the largest proportion of men were majoring
in the social sciences, followed by engineering. Relatively few women receive training for business and professional careers except in fields such as
teaching or pharmacy. At the junior colleges there has been a considerable
increase in the proportion of women majoring in the social sciences and in
health-related fields and a decrease in those majoring in home economics,
although that, together with the humanities, is still the most popular major (see
Table 3-4).

TABLE 3-2  *Relative Proportions of Female College Entrants
Entering Universities versus Junior Colleges
(Selected Years, 1950 to 1990)*

| Year | University (%) | Junior College (%) |
|------|----------------|--------------------|
| 1950 | 63.2 | 36.8 |
| 1960 | 45.3 | 54.7 |
| 1970 | 36.7 | 63.3 |
| 1980 | 37.0 | 63.0 |
| 1990 | 40.6 | 59.4 |

SOURCE: Compiled from Mombusho (Ministry of Education) *Gakko Kihon
Chosa* (School Basic Survey) for various years.

TABLE 3-3  *Percentages of Females among All Students
Enrolled in Universities and Junior Colleges
(Selected Years, 1955 to 1991)*

| Year | University (%) | Junior College (%) |
|------|----------------|--------------------|
| 1955 | 12.4 | 54.0 |
| 1960 | 13.7 | 78.7 |
| 1965 | 16.2 | 74.8 |
| 1970 | 18.0 | 82.7 |
| 1975 | 21.2 | 86.2 |
| 1980 | 22.1 | 89.0 |
| 1985 | 23.5 | 89.8 |
| 1990 | 27.4 | 91.5 |
| 1991 | 28.3 | 91.6 |

SOURCE: Mombusho (Ministry of Education), *Gakko Kihon Chosa* (School
Basic Survey) for various years.

## Gender differences at the secondary level

Gender differences found at the postsecondary level represent the culmination
of a process that begins much earlier in the educational process. There appears
to be little gender differentiation at the compulsory elementary and lower secondary levels, where a common, uniform curriculum and program of study is
pursued by all students, mostly in coeducational classrooms. By the time students apply for upper secondary school, however, differences based on gender

TABLE 3-4 *Percentage of Students at Universities and Junior Colleges by Various Faculties and Departments (Selected Years, 1965 to 1991)*

| | Women | | | |
| --- | --- | --- | --- | --- |
| | 1965 | 1975 | 1991 | 1991, Men |
| **UNIVERSITIES** | | | | |
| Humanities | 45.2 | 36.2 | 35.3 | 7.3 |
| Social sciences | 5.2 | 15.0 | 22.1 | 47.0 |
| Natural sciences | 2.3 | 2.0 | 2.2 | 3.9 |
| Engineering | 0.5 | 0.8 | 3.2 | 26.3 |
| Agriculture | 0.8 | 1.5 | 2.7 | 3.5 |
| Medicine/Dentistry | 8.6 | 7.7 | 7.8 | 4.8 |
| Home economics | 9.4 | 8.1 | 6.2 | 0.0 |
| Education | 20.1 | 19.6 | 13.0 | 4.4 |
| Art | 6.6 | 6.3 | 5.5 | 1.2 |
| Other | 1.3 | 2.8 | 2.0 | 1.6 |
| **JUNIOR COLLEGES** | | | | |
| Humanities | 26.6 | 23.9 | 28.0 | 5.7 |
| Natural sciences | 4.3 | 6.9 | 11.5 | 31.4 |
| Engineering | 0.6 | 0.4 | 1.6 | 42.4 |
| Agriculture | 0.3 | 0.2 | 0.3 | 5.8 |
| Health | 0.5 | 3.0 | 5.5 | 7.7 |
| Home economics | 52.1 | 32.2 | 26.3 | 0.8 |
| Education | 11.9 | 25.8 | 17.3 | 1.9 |
| Art | 3.6 | 5.5 | 4.5 | 4.2 |
| General education | 0 | 2.1 | 5.0 | 0.1 |

SOURCE: Figures compiled from Mombusho (Ministry of Education), *Gakko Kihon Chosa* (School Basic Survey) for each year.

become apparent. Today, the percentage of girls graduating from lower secondary school and continuing their studies in upper secondary school exceeds that of boys. Significant differences are apparent, however, when we examine the types of high schools female and male students enter and the curricula they pursue, reflecting in turn differing aspirations and expectations regarding postsecondary education.

First, despite the fact that the postwar educational reforms called for the adoption of the principle of coeducation at all levels, many students are still found in single-sex high schools. Private high schools comprise about 24 percent of all high schools and enroll about 30 percent of female and 27 percent of male high school students.[3] More than 60 percent are single-sex schools, and the most competitive schools are exclusively male. Public high schools in major urban centers such as Tokyo and Kyoto these schools are coeducational, but in many other areas of the country (notably the northern Kanto and Tohoku regions) a significant number are single-sex institutions. High schools established after World War II are invariably coeducational, but many prewar boys' middle schools or girls' high schools have remained single-sex institutions.

Second, while more girls than boys are enrolled in the general academic program in high school, fewer are found in the most competitive and prestigious academic high schools. At the top public high schools in Tokyo that were formerly boys' middle schools, such as Hibiya, more than two-thirds of the students are male. Of those who choose a vocational program in high school, girls are apt to take home economics or enter commercial studies in preparation for taking clerical jobs after graduation, whereas boys tend to study technical subjects. The proportion of students going on to four-year universities is much higher among technical students than those in commercial or home economics programs.

Although high school attendance has become nearly universal in Japan, it is not compulsory, and admission to high school is determined on the basis of entrance examinations. High schools are informally ranked on the basis of their success rate in preparing students for admission to the nation's most prestigious (coeducational) universities. Youngsters aiming for admission into one of these schools begin preparing for the entrance examinations in lower secondary school, if not earlier, by attending special extra-study schools known as *juku* or by getting a private tutor. It appears that by the time girls reach the second or third year of lower secondary school many of them have lowered their ambitions and decided to attend a junior college rather than a four-year university. They are, therefore, less likely to seek admission to top-ranking high schools. A survey conducted in 1985 with third, fifth, and eighth graders and their mothers in Tokyo found that the percentage of students aspiring to four-year universities was about the same among boys and girls in the third grade (39 percent and 41 percent), somewhat higher among boys than girls in the fifth grade (45 percent and 33 percent), and more than twice as high among boys in the eighth grade (71 percent and 32 percent). On the other hand, the percentage of girls aspiring to junior college was much higher among eighth graders (29 percent) than among third- and fifth-graders (8 percent and 13 percent).[4]

Within academic programs in high school there is often sex-linked track-ing. In the second and third years students are given the choice of specializing either in literary or scientific studies. Those electing to pursue literary studies take more courses in English and in Japanese literature, while the science majors take more math and science courses. The majority of male students opt for the science course, while most females go into literature. There may be further differentiation based on whether a student plans to apply to a national university or a private one and whether he or she anticipates applying to a science-related faculty or a literary faculty. Students are then given inten-sive preparation for the entrance examinations in the subject areas required by the institutions and faculties to which they plan to apply.[5] For those planning to attend a junior college, the preparation is much less rigorous. Most of them do not require entrance exams, merely recommendations, and those that do require applicants to be tested in just two or three subjects.

What we find is that young women, on the whole, elect to pursue pro-grams in high school that prepare them to enter the humanities or social science faculties at universities rather than the scientific or technological fields, or they decide to forego the rigorous and competitive preparation for univer-sity admission altogether and instead aim for a junior college. Those that do apply to universities tend to be a much more select group than their male counterparts in terms of social class as well as academic ability.

## SOCIAL NORMS AND ATTITUDES REGARDING WOMEN'S EDUCATION AND GENDER ROLES

The differences in patterns of educational participation and attainment de-scribed above reflect in large part dominant cultural norms and attitudes regarding the role of women in society and the purposes of education, particu-larly higher education, for women within this culturally defined role. Such notions as "a man should be better educated than his wife," "a girl who's too brainy isn't endearing to a guy," "too much education will make a woman too proud and therefore unfit to be a good wife," "the goal of women's education should be to produce good wives and wise mothers," and "the woman's place is in the home," old-fashioned though they may sound, summarize many Japanese people's attitudes regarding women and women's education.

Nationwide public opinion surveys conducted in recent years reveal that while there has been a general rise in the levels of education that the Japanese desire for children of both sexes, parents continue to assign higher priority to the education of sons. Most parents want their daughters to receive at least a

TABLE 3-5   *Attitudes regarding Gender Roles, in Response to:*
*"How do you feel about the idea that men should*
*work and women should stay at home?"*

| | Women | | Men | |
|---|---|---|---|---|
| | 1987 (%) | 1990 (%) | 1987 (%) | 1990 (%) |
| Agree | 36.6 | 25.1 | 51.7 | 34.7 |
| Disagree | 31.9 | 43.2 | 20.2 | 34.0 |
| Neither | 29.3 | 29.1 | 26.4 | 29.7 |

SOURCE: Sorifu (Office of the Prime Minister), *Fujin ni kansuru yoron chosa* (Public Opinion Survey on Women, 1987 and 1990).

high school education, but beyond that they are likely to think in terms of a junior college for their daughters and a four-year university for their sons. In a 1988 national opinion poll by NHK (Japan Broadcasting Corporation), 33 percent of the respondents indicated they wanted daughters to receive a four-year university education (45 percent wanted them to go to a junior college), in contrast to 78 percent in the case of sons.[6] These results are similar to those derived from the survey of third, fifth, and eighth graders and their mothers in Tokyo referred to earlier, in which 68 percent of the mothers indicated they wanted a four-year university education for sons and just 37 percent in the case of daughters.[7] Those parents with more education and a higher socioeconomic level who reside in large urban centers are more likely to want a university education for their daughters. Yet at every level, Japanese parents exhibit higher aspirations for sons than for daughters and place a higher priority on getting sons into good universities. This tendency reflects in large part the assumption that women will marry and have children and not take up careers following completion of their education. Thus, the general cultural-enrichment type of education that junior colleges provide is considered sufficient. The view that "men should work and women should stay at home" has only recently come to be questioned by a substantial proportion of women themselves, while among men it continues to have considerable support (see Table 3-5).

Looking more closely at socialization, we find that from the time children are born many Japanese have very different expectations of boys and girls. Today, we are much less likely to hear the "Oh, too bad it's not a boy!" when a daughter is born, but comments such as "Daughters are much easier to bring up," "With sons you have to worry about getting them into good col-

TABLE 3-6 *Attitudes regarding Socialization for Daughters and Sons*

| Country | Favor sex-differentiated socialization (%) | Favor bringing up boys and girls the same (%) | Others/ don't know (%) |
|---|---|---|---|
| Japan | 63 | 34 | 3 |
| United States | 31 | 62 | 7 |
| Philippines | 28 | 67 | 5 |
| Great Britain | 20 | 76 | 4 |
| West Germany | 20 | 75 | 6 |
| Sweden | 6 | 92 | 2 |

SOURCE: Sorifu (Office of the Prime Minister), *Fujin mondai ni kansuru kokusai hikaku chosa* (Comparative International Survey on Women's Issues, 1982).

leges but with daughters you don't have such worries," and "You must have great expectations for your son's future" are still often heard. In addition there is considerable emphasis on the notions of "femininity" and "masculinity" and on instilling what are viewed as behaviors appropriate to each sex. In an international comparative study, Japanese women were the most likely to favor bringing up children differently according to sex (see Table 3-6).

Many of the women students we have taught have mentioned how the consciousness of being a female has been impressed upon them time and again by comments made by parents as well as teachers and peers, such as "You are a girl, so it's natural that you should help with housework" (said by a mother), "Be quiet, you must behave like a lady" (by a teacher), or "You act pretty smart-alecky for a girl" (said by a junior high school male classmate to a girl who asked the teacher a question in class). There seems to be some set standard of "femininity" and feminine-appropriate behavior that is widely accepted within society to which girls are expected to conform. The same can be said of many societies, of course, but our impression is that in Japan this standard is defined much more rigidly, is more universally accepted, and is more strictly imposed. This standard of feminine behavior is enforced, for example, by a distinctive "woman's language" that is characterized by, among other features, politeness and tentativeness and the use of special vocabulary (including verb forms and sentence structures, as well as by a distinctive tone of voice and carriage). Recent studies that have systematically looked at gender differences in speech point to a gradual convergence in the linguistic forms used by women and men, especially among youth.[8] At the same time, though, parents continue to teach children to use language appropriate to their sex, and parents as well as teachers persist in correcting children—girls in particular—who use forms of speech thought to be reserved for the other sex.

Messages about gender-appropriate behavior are conveyed through the mass media as well. To give just one example, recently we find cooking programs on television directed at children. While such programs are good in the sense that it is important for children to learn basic skills necessary for daily life, the children who appear on these programs are always girls, thereby reinforcing the notion that "females do the cooking, boys do the eating."

## SEXISM AND GENDER STEREOTYPING IN EDUCATION

We will now examine some practices within schools and the educational process that contribute to the perpetuation of sex differences in educational outcomes and the efforts that are being made to bring about changes.

### Gender stereotyping in textbooks

Roughly 400 million copies of textbooks are printed each year for use by elementary and lower secondary school students in Japan. Although the textbooks are put out by private publishers, they undergo rigorous inspection by the Ministry of Education prior to publication. Gender issues are not taken into account in this inspection procedure, however, and gender biases permeate school textbooks.

An analysis of textbooks used in elementary schools and lower secondary schools made by a women's group in 1975 revealed several significant facts.[9] The majority of figures and main characters who appeared in the Japanese language arts textbooks were male; in some sixth grade texts none of the main characters was a female. The overwhelming majority of the textbook authors were male. Scattered throughout the texts were illustrations that depicted traditional gender roles. In the social studies texts women were often portrayed as homemakers. The occupational roles in which they were shown were limited to nurses, teachers, waitresses, and other female-dominated jobs. Finally, in English textbooks, sentences that dealt with activities such as baking and washing dishes consistently used the pronoun "she" or a female proper name for the subject.

Subsequently, representatives from many women's groups got together with textbook publishers and sought their cooperation in eliminating gender stereotyping in textbooks by hiring as textbook writers and editors women and men who were sensitive to the need for promoting gender equality. Over the years we have seen some improvement. Textbooks today are more likely to include illustrations and pictures of fathers grocery shopping or preparing meals and women working in a variety of occupations. However, when the League of Japanese Lawyers conducted a study in 1989 to examine the extent to which gender discrimination had been eliminated in textbooks, it found that not a great deal had changed over the previous ten years.[10] For example, while more males were likely to be depicted in texts used in home economics classes, they were more likely to be pictured in the role of "overseer," examining or inspecting the work of others, in contrast to females, who were pictured actually doing the laundry or cooking. Thus, while the fact that males are appearing in such textbooks represents a step forward, the ways in which they are depicted only serves to further buttress existing ideas regarding gender roles.

Recently, many teachers have begun to question the sexism and gender-stereotyping found in textbooks and other teaching materials and to seek changes. Many other teachers, however, are not aware of these issues, due in part to the fact that no attention is paid to gender issues in the training of teachers.

*Sex differentiation in the formal curriculum*

We mentioned above that educational reforms instituted following World War II mandated that all students pursue a common, uniform curriculum and program of study. As part of this policy, home economics was made a mandatory subject for both girls and boys at the elementary level; in lower secondary school students were offered a choice between taking home economics or industrial arts. What happened over the years was that most girls took home economics while most boys went into industrial arts. In 1973 course requirements were altered, making the study of home economics in upper secondary school mandatory for girls only. Since then, various women's groups as well as organizations comprised of teachers, including the Women's Action Group (*Kodo suru onnatachi no kai*) and the Association for the Promotion of the Study of Homemaking by Both Sexes (*Kateika no danjo kyoshu o susumeru kai*) campaigned vigorously to bring about a change in this requirement. After Japan signed the United Nations Convention on the Elimination of All Forms of Discrimination against Women in 1980, the government was forced to take up this issue as part of the task of establishing a uniform curriculum for males and females, as called for in article 10 of the convention. Finally, under the new Course of Study for Upper Secondary Schools announced by the Ministry of Education in 1989, home economics was made a required subject for both girls and boys starting in the 1994 academic year. In addition, changes were made in the field of physical education enabling girls and boys to take either martial arts (judo and kendo, or Japanese-style fencing) or dance.

*Sexism and gender stereotyping in classroom practices*
*and school rituals*

A close look at various practices that go on in the daily life of the school or classroom also reveals a common and almost universal tendency to place priority on males. These practices are not something that are set by any institutional regulation but are rather done as a matter of custom. Repeated over and over again in the course of daily school life, however, these customary practices, which make up the hidden curriculum, often function to reinforce certain attitudes and assumptions about the sexes and their respective positions and roles in society.

DIFFERENTIATING THE SEXES: CALLING THE ROLL.    One of the pervasive features of Japanese schools, and of Japanese society as a whole, is the tendency to distinguish the two sexes in one way or another. The school bags carried by elementary school pupils are almost invariably black in the case of boys and red in the case of girls. Paint boxes, which are usually purchased through the school, are blue for boys and red for girls. Likewise, in some cases boys are given black or blue library cards while girls get a red or pink. Boys and girls are lined up separately, and boys are paired with boys and girls with girls, for a variety of activities. Also, girls and boys are often placed in separate teams for sports and other competitive activities.

One such practice that is almost universally followed by Japanese teachers in classrooms at all levels and one that has become a subject of controversy in recent years, is that of having separate registers for boys and girls and consistently calling the boys' roll first. The same order is often followed when returning test results, giving out report cards, or reading students' names at school entrance and graduation ceremonies. A survey of elementary schools in the Tokyo metropolitan area showed that a mere 0.5 percent of the schools followed the practice of mixing girls' and boys' names.[11] A group of Japanese women who attended the International Women's Conference in Nairobi in 1985 conducted an informal survey of representatives from nine countries to find out whether such a practice was followed elsewhere. What they found was that apart from Japan and India, the usual practice was to list girls and boys together according to alphabetical order. Upon their return to Japan, these women began to bring this matter to the attention of the mass media, and in recent years it has attracted growing attention. Various schools have started to experiment with alternatives that do not entail separating girls and boys, for example, mixing the sexes and calling the roll by alphabetical order or, in some elementary schools, according to the children's date of birth. The issue is currently under consideration by school boards and city councils throughout the country. In the city of Sakai, near Osaka, a decision was made by the city council in 1990 to institute mixed-sex listing of students' and teachers' names, from kindergarten through lower secondary school. Councilwoman Ayako Yamaguchi was instrumental in pushing through this reform.

PARTICIPATION IN STUDENT COUNCILS AND CLUB ACTIVITIES.　As in many countries, each Japanese school has a self-governing student council or association that makes decisions regarding such matters as rules of student conduct and budgets for club activities. The chair, vice-chair, treasurer, and secretary are elected from among those standing for office by the student body. Theoretically, any student can run for office, but there seems to be a common understanding that while it is all right for girls to run for vice-chair, treasurer, or secretary, the top office should be occupied by a boy. Some schools have a regulation stipulating that the student council chair must be a boy, and this has become an issue. Even in the absence of such formal regulations, a girl who seeks the top position is likely to be accused by boys of "trying to put on airs" or "lacking in feminine appeal."

The view that the leader or group representative ought to be a male is, of course, reflected in adult society, where men clearly dominate the top positions in politics and business. Even community volunteer groups and parent-teacher associations are often headed by men, in spite of the fact that most often women do the actual work within these organizations. Some teachers have proposed that student council offices be shared equally by girls and boys.

Sexual differentiation in school-sponsored club activities is another issue. To take one example, baseball clubs are very popular in Japanese high schools and are given considerable support by schools, both in terms of financial resources and time devoted to training. Nationwide competitions among high schools are held twice a year and these attract considerable media coverage. Membership in baseball clubs includes girls, but they participate not as players but as "managers," whose role is to put away the baseball equipment, wash the uniforms, and prepare meals and snacks for the players. In short, they perform a supporting role for the male players. Girls are, moreover, prohibited from entering the grounds at the national competitions.

Even if the formal setting of schools and classrooms is coeducational, as at the elementary and lower secondary school level, daily exposure to the kinds of customs and practices described above instills in many youngsters a consciousness of gender differences and male superiority. This is not to say that sex-role socialization is always or necessarily "successful." As has been shown in other societies, there are many girls (and boys) who resist the dominant messages regarding appropriate sex-role attitudes and behaviors, and there are also teachers at all levels who strive to convey very different kinds of messages to their students.[12] Thus, both authors have encountered women in our college classes who resisted efforts by their parents or high school teachers to discourage them from applying to college or who possessed the critical capacity to question such taken-for-granted practices and regulations as that which requires girls in lower and upper secondary school to wear skirts to school and girls, but not boys, in upper secondary school to study domestic science.[13]

*Gender-based tracking*

Earlier in this essay we noted that females are less likely than males to enter the most competitive high schools as well as four-year universities. One influencing factor we mentioned was the lower level of aspirations parents have for daughters' as opposed to sons' education. There is also evidence suggesting that teachers and guidance counselors in many instances tend to "cool down" the aspirations of female students and steer them to less competitive high schools and colleges while encouraging male students to aim for the leading institutions. Some of the college women we teach have reported being advised by the teachers in junior or senior high school to aim for a junior college rather than a four-year university. The usual argument given is that "it's a waste of both time and money for a girl to go to a university, since you're going to get married soon."

One of the reasons teachers tend to track female students into less competitive schools is that, as recent evidence have shown, some public high schools practice discrimination in their admission procedures. In Tokyo, for example, it has been revealed that the top public high schools, which were formerly boys' middle schools, require a higher score on the entrance examinations for girls and maintain admission quotas for girls. In addition, there have been reports from other parts of Japan of administrators at coeducational high schools urging their counterparts in lower secondary schools to discourage female students from applying to their schools and to send more boys. While the scope of such discriminatory practices has yet to be ascertained, such practices frequently reveal the notion that while girls may score high on high school entrance examinations, once they are admitted they don't work as hard as boys to get into the top universities, thereby reducing the number of successful applicants to such universities and causing the reputation of the high school to decline.

While many issues remain to be tackled, a promising development is that through the efforts mainly of various women's groups, we are at last witnessing a growing awareness and public discussions of the various practices that embody and perpetuate sexism and gender stereotyping in education. And as the above discussion has pointed out, this awareness has given rise to some efforts at change and reform.[14]

## GENDER INEQUALITIES IN THE TEACHING PROFESSION

Conspicuous gender differences characterize the teaching profession at all levels, and these have important implications for female education in terms of providing role models for students, reinforcing stereotypes regarding gender roles in the larger society, and limiting professional opportunities for women who pursue graduate training.

Teaching at the elementary or secondary school level was the most common profession among women in prewar Japanese society. There were very few women professors apart from those teaching at women's higher normal schools or at women's colleges. For a variety of reasons teaching is still a popular occupation among women, particularly those who aspire to lifelong careers. There is no overt sex discrimination, for example in pay or retirement age. In addition there is a system of maternity and child-care leave. Nevertheless, as in the past, the proportion of women declines as one moves up the educational ladder, and women are likely to be found teaching subjects traditionally considered feminine, such as home economics, literature, and art. Few women are found in administrative positions.

Kindergartens are staffed almost exclusively by women (94 percent), yet only 49 percent of kindergarten principals are women. In elementary schools, women account for 58 percent of the teachers—up from 45 percent in 1960—but just 4 percent of the principals. Women comprise about 36 percent of the teachers and a mere 0.7 percent of the principals in lower secondary schools, and the corresponding figures at the upper secondary school level are 20.5 percent and 2.4 percent.[15] Women's low representation in administrative posts at these levels attests in part to the difficulties women teachers, like other working women, face in trying to advance in their career while at the same time having to bear the major part of household responsibilities. Also, when both the wife and husband are teachers there is an unwritten regulation in some places that only one of them can be made a principal. There is still a widely held prejudice against women being placed in the position of principal or head teacher based on the preconception that women lack the necessary qualities of leadership and toughness. An acquaintance who recently took and passed the written examination qualifying her to become a head teacher at the elementary level was repeatedly questioned during the subsequent oral examination about her ability to fulfill all of the necessary responsibilities, including dealing with other teachers, especially men.

At the college level, more women teach in junior colleges than in universities. Women make up 38 percent of all faculty members in junior colleges, 9.2 percent of four-year university faculty, and just 4 percent of graduate-level faculty. The higher the professional rank, the smaller is the representation of females: Women comprise just 5 percent of full professors at universities and 25 percent of those at junior colleges, and 4 percent of university and 13 percent of junior college presidents.[16] Moreover, within universities, women's representation on faculties is higher at the private than at the national universities, at all-female than at coeducational universities, and at the more recently established ones than at the older, more prestigious institutions. As of 1982, women represented a mere 1.1 percent of the faculty at the former imperial universities, which include Tokyo and Kyoto universities, the most prestigious universities in the country.[17] To take another example, at Waseda University, which is one of the oldest and most prestigious private coeducational universities, in 1991 there were forty full-time female faculty members at the instructor/assistant professor level and above (compared to twenty-nine in 1980), representing just 4 percent of the total. Women employed as assistants and adjuncts accounted for 11 percent of the total, up from 7 percent in 1980.

Women's underrepresentation in college and university faculties is a manifestation of the highly rigid and closed organizational nature of Japanese universities, particularly the national universities. Positions are rarely announced publicly, so that women do not have an opportunity to compete openly for a university teaching or research position. Faculty members and research staff tend to be recruited from particular networks through a patronage system, and women are generally excluded from those networks. There are few networks, however, that function as a source of recruitment for women. Moreover, there are no affirmative action programs designed to promote the hiring of women and to redress gender imbalances. As a consequence, fewer women than men are able to obtain employment following completion of master's and doctor's degree programs. In 1990, 3,578 women completed the master's degree program (compared to 22, 226 males); 18 percent of these women (and 15 percent of the men) went on for further study, while less than 50 percent (compared to 77 percent of the men) obtained employment. Of the 696 women (compared to 5,116 men) who completed the doctor's degree program the same year, just 48 percent found employment, in contrast to 67 percent of the men.[18] Many women continue teaching as adjuncts on a yearly contract basis at two or three institutions without ever obtaining a full-time position. A factor that further aggravates this problem is that job transfers are very common within Japanese companies, so that an academic woman married to a businessman faces the prospect of having to give up a position in order to accompany her husband to another location. The various forms of discrimination that exist in academia are likely to prove much more difficult to attack than those found in business and industry.[19]

## RECENT TRENDS AND DEVELOPMENTS IN WOMEN'S EDUCATION

There are several recent trends and developments that have important implications for women's education. One has been the growth since the mid 1970s of women's studies within higher education. Another is the declining popularity of junior colleges and women's universities and the growing popularity of co-educational universities among young women, accompanied by a shift away from traditionally female fields of study to hitherto male-dominated fields. A third development has been the growing presence of nontraditional students, particularly older women, in universities.

### The emergence of women's studies

The growth of women's studies in the United States had an important influence on the development of such studies in Japan in the years just preceding International Women's Year (1975). A number of colleges and universities, particularly women's institutions, began to set up courses in women's studies. Between 1983, when the National Women's Education Centre began conducting its annual surveys, and 1990 the number of colleges and universities offering courses in women's studies at the undergraduate level more than tripled, to 251 or about 23 percent of all such institutions. Of the 251, 155 are women's junior colleges and universities. Many women's colleges have set up courses in women's studies as one way of trying to attract applicants in the face of a growing trend away from women's colleges. The number of course offerings has increased fivefold, to 463,[20] and while in the past courses with such titles as "Women's History" or "Women and Literature" were most common, today we find a much greater diversity of courses, such as "Theory of Motherhood," "Feminism," "Sociology of Women," "Women and the Law," "Women and Welfare," and "Women's Labor."

While these are encouraging signs, several things need to be pointed out. Although women's courses are offered at more than one out of five colleges and universities, in most cases only one or two courses are taught. Moreover, the number of students enrolled in such courses in 1990 amounted to roughly 39,000, or a mere 1.5 percent of all students enrolled in higher institutions. And of the 39,000 students, just 5,500 were male.[21] A major problem is that there is no institution that has a women's studies department or faculty and awards a degree in this field. Were an institution to set up such a program, it would have to be approved by the Ministry of Education. An underlying factor is that women's studies has yet to be fully recognized and accepted as a legitimate academic discipline within Japanese higher education. Time and again we hear colleagues raise such questions as "What is women's studies?" and "If we're going to have a course in 'Women and Psychology,' why not also have one in 'Men and Psychology?'"

## A trend away from women's colleges

"Women's Colleges Struggle to Adapt," "The Rise and Fall of Six Women's Universities," "Desperate for Survival—Women's Universities": Such headlines, which are frequently seen in newspapers and magazines, attest to a continuing decline in the popularity of women's junior colleges and universities since about the mid 1980s. Their struggle for survival is expected to become increasingly acute with the eighteen-year-old population expected to decrease by nearly one-half million from 1992 to 2000.

Financial problems and changes in the job market account for the decline in the popularity of junior colleges (of which about 60 percent enroll women exclusively) and women's universities (which numbered 91 in 1991, or around 18 percent of all four-year universities). In the past, many women preferred to go to junior colleges because employment opportunities for women graduating from junior colleges were much better than those available to university graduates. While companies welcomed junior college graduates as "OLs" or "office ladies," who performed routine clerical work, they were reluctant to take on university graduates for such positions because they were more expensive and also presumably had fewer years remaining until they left their jobs to get married. At the same time, university-educated women were usually denied access to jobs of similar status as those available to male graduates. Many companies have had a policy of not recruiting female university graduates at all.

Several recent developments have opened up employment opportunities for female university graduates. One is the passage of the Equal Employment Opportunity Act in 1985. Even more significant has been the acute labor shortage, which has forced companies to turn to a hitherto untapped source of talent and skills to fill positions formerly reserved for male graduates. Many major companies, most notably financial institutions and trading companies, now offer university-educated women a choice between traditional women's work (i.e., support-level clerical work) and the career path (sogoshoku), traditionally reserved for male university graduates. Employment rates among female university graduates went up from between 55 percent to 70 percent in the years prior to 1985 to more than 80 percent in the early 1990s, a figure comparable to that among male university graduates, though still lower than the figure for female junior college graduates. The downturn in the Japanese economy in the early 1990s has unquestionably hurt women university graduates in the marketplace. It is difficult to foresee what the future trend will be, but university-educated women have definitely made significant inroads into jobs and positions hitherto closed to them, and many employers have come to recognize their capabilities.

With the opening up of the job market, women have begun to choose more marketable fields of study, such as law, commerce, economics, political science, international relations, engineering, and psychology (see Table 3-4). While the number of females entering four-year universities has increased by 2.4 times over the past twenty years (from 62,000 in 1970 to 148,000 in 1990), those going into the social sciences has increased by four- and fivefold, while those going into engineering has increased by tenfold. Because such courses are generally not offered at women's universities, where the focus has been on such fields as English literature and home economics, many women have begun to turn toward coeducational universities. At the same time, many young women are attracted to coeducational universities simply because they want to study and participate in various extracurricular activities with men.

Consequently, the number of applicants to women's colleges and universities has steadily declined since the mid 1980s. Tsuda College, Japan's oldest and certainly one of the most prestigious colleges for women, experienced a 22 percent drop in applications between 1985 and 1990, while Japan Women's University, another well-established institution, saw a 26 percent decline between 1986 and 1989. Compounding the problem is the fact that in recent years it has become much more difficult for Japanese universities to obtain sufficient resources from either public or private sources. In Tsuda's case, whereas in 1982 it received aid from the government to cover 32 percent of its annual budget, in 1990 the figure was cut to 15 percent.[22] The figure for those enrolled in women's universities as a percentage of females enrolled in all four-year universities has declined from close to 30 percent in 1965 to 25 percent in 1991.

In response to this trend, women's universities have adopted various survival strategies. One strategy has been to redesign or add faculties and programs that are more professionally oriented. For example, in 1990, Japan Women's University added a major in Integrated Arts and Social Science—a combination of sociology, psychology, and education. Others have added programs in management and science. Women's universities have attempted to attract students by emphasizing their unique strengths as women's institutions, for example, by setting up courses in women's studies. Another strategy has been to go coed; those adopting this strategy have attempted to expand enrollment by adding faculties designed to attract male students, such as economics and international relations.

Junior colleges, which have tended to be regarded as "bride-training schools," are suffering even more than women's universities. Between 1980 and 1990, the proportion of female college entrants going into junior colleges as opposed to four-year universities decreased from 63 percent to 59 percent. A combination of factors contributed to this trend: the growing affluence of the Japanese people, a decline in the birthrate, and the fact that as college attendance has become more and more a common practice the prestige of a junior college education has declined. With fewer children and more money available, more parents can and want to send daughters, as well as sons, to college, and increasingly to a four-year university, thereby providing their daughters with an edge, both in terms of employment and marriage prospects.

As a consequence, a number of junior colleges have closed down in recent years. Others have adopted various strategies, some similar to those undertaken by women's universities, in order to survive, such as transforming themselves into four-year women's universities, becoming coed, and adding more specialized, professionally oriented programs to their curriculum, such as communications and business.

*The growing presence of nontraditional students*

Unlike the United States, Canada, Australia, and many European countries, where people aged twenty-five and older comprise a substantial proportion of students in institutions of higher education, in Japan 90 percent of college enrollments are drawn from the eighteen- to twenty-two-year-old population. Most Japanese tend to view higher education as something restricted to people within a certain age group, which is to be pursued on a full-time basis. It was not until 1978 that older students were first admitted to universities, and then only in the evening division and on the basis of special recommendations. In 1979 the law faculty of Rikkyo University in Tokyo became the first university to admit nontraditional students through a system of special entrance examinations. In 1989, nineteen national universities, eight public universities, and over sixty private universities were admitting such students. So far, however, the number of students admitted has been limited. For example, the number of "adult students" admitted to the law faculty at Rikkyo is restricted to roughly 5 percent of the total.

Given the anticipated decline in the college-age population, colleges will increasingly be forced to try to attract not only traditional full-time students but also nontraditional part-time students in order to survive. A substantial proportion of these nontraditional college students are likely to be women—housewives in their thirties and forties who want to return to school now that their children are older and employed women who wish to acquire or upgrade knowledge and skills required for their current jobs or to make a career change. One way for women's colleges and universities to try to survive the coming years is to begin to emphasize and strengthen their functions as institutions for women's lifelong or recurrent education. Similarly, junior colleges, which have until now functioned mainly as the "women's track" in higher education, might become more like American community colleges. As Kitamura emphasizes, the influx of large numbers of nontraditional students into Japanese colleges and universities will inevitably pose a serious challenge to traditional Japanese higher education, forcing them to reexamine many of their existing assumptions and practices, including curricula and teaching methods.[23] As this process unfolds, its impact on the education of Japanese women will be watched with interest by many.

CONCLUSION

In many respects, the way education has been and continues to be perceived with respect to women by educators, educational institutions, society in general, parents, and young women themselves is out of tune with the reality of women's lives today and in the years to come. There has not been a full recognition of the related ways in which women's lives have changed and are changing, nor a serious appraisal of the ways in which education ought to adapt to the changing needs of women. What is now required is for those involved in the educational process to take into account the entire life span of women, to look at education as serving women in the many roles they will perform and to prepare them for new realities and opportunities in their lives.

At the same time serious attention must be directed toward eradicating sexism and gender inequality throughout the entire educational system, from the bottom up. As Fujieda has noted, in a centralized system of education such as Japan's, the Ministry of Education exercises both direct and indirect power and authority over the conduct of education, from determining curricula to inspecting textbooks prior to publication.[24] Yet, it has not sought to exercise that authority toward realizing gender equality in education. Of all the various recommendations and proposals for educational reform that have been set forth by Ministry of Education appointed and cabinet-level advisory bodies, such as the Central Council for Education, the Ad Hoc Council on Education, and the University Council, none has dealt with any of the many serious gender issues we have discussed here.

Various grass-roots women's organizations as well as teacher and parent groups have led the way in this respect. The Women's Action Group, founded in 1975 and made up chiefly of female activists and teachers, has taken up several issues, including sexism in textbooks and classroom practices, and played a leading role in pressing the Ministry of Education to make the study of home economics in high school mandatory for both sexes. It has also appealed to the Ministry of Education to allocate more funds, which at the present are very limited, toward the promotion of gender equality in education. The League of Japanese Lawyers has sought to investigate and publicize sex discrimination in textbooks. In addition, several feminist educators and researchers have begun to work with local school boards to produce teaching materials and textbooks aimed at promoting nonsexist perspectives among youngsters. The Yokohama Board of Education is one such example.[25] The board of education, teachers, and parents of Kunitachi City in Tokyo have for many years endeavored to promote gender equality in their schools. Recently, recognizing that change must begin with the teachers, the board produced a guide designed to bring to the attention of elementary teachers various aspects of gender inequality and discrimination in schools.

Thus, here and there, mostly on the local level, we see important and promising initiatives and developments. What is clearly needed at this point, however, is for these and other efforts to be carried forth in a systematic manner at all levels and in all aspects of education, beginning with teacher training. A heightened consciousness and acceptance on the part of both women and men in Japanese society of gender equality as a social and educational goal, coupled with a commitment and resolve on the part of leaders in government and education to realize this goal, are imperative. Whether progress will be made in the near future is questionable, given the priorities that continue to dominate Japanese education. The emphasis on competition, efficiency, and control and the subordination of education to the demands of the marketplace are in many respects at odds with the goals genuine equality of educational opportunity and valuing and nurturing the potential of each individual, regardless of social class, ethnicity, regional background—or sex.

## NOTES

1. For a fuller treatment of this topic, see Kumiko Fujimura-Fanselow, "Women's Participation in Higher Education in Japan," in James J. Shields, Jr., ed., *Japanese Schooling: Patterns of Socialization, Equality, and Political Control* (University Park: Pennsylvania State University Press, 1989).

2. Mombusho (Ministry of Education), *Mombu tokei yoran* (Summary of educational statistics) (Tokyo: Ministry of Education, 1991).

3. *Ibid.*, 54–55.

4. Kiyoshi Takeuchi, "Joshi no seito bunka no tokushitsu" (Special characteristics of female student culture), *Kyoiku shakaigaku kenkyu* (Research in the Sociology of Education) 40 (1985).

5. In Japan, students apply to a particular faculty within a university, and entrance examinations are prepared by each faculty, although recently more institutions are taking advantage of the examinations prepared by the University Entrance Examination Center.

6. NHK (Japan Broadcasting Corporation), *Nihonjin no ishiki chosa* (Survey of the consciousness of the Japanese) (Tokyo: NHK, 1988).

7. Takeuchi, "Joshi no seito bunka no tokushitsu," 25.

8. See Yoko Kawaguchi, "Majiriau danjo no kotoba" (Mixing of men's and women's language), *Gengo seikatsu* (Linguistic life), no. 429 (July 1987), 34–39. See

also Orie Endo, *et al.*, "Dansei no hanashi kotoba" (The spoken language of men), *Kotoba* (Language) 11 (1990): 1–88, and "Josei no hanashi kotoba" (The spoken language of women), *Kotoba* (Language) 10 (1989): 1–84.

9. Fujin Mondai Konwa-kai, *Fujin mondai konwa-kai kaiho, 22—kyokasho no naka no danjo sabetsu* (Twenty-second report of the Fujin Mondai Konwa-kai Association: gender discrimination in textbooks) (Tokyo: 1975), and *Fujin mondai konwa-kai kaiho, 24—kyokasho wa danjo byodo o sodatenai* (Twenty-fourth report of the Fujin Mondai Konwa-kai Association: Textbooks do not promote sexual equality) (Tokyo: 1976).

10. Masako Owaki, *Kyokasho no naka no danjo sabetsu* (Sex discrimination in textbooks) (Tokyo: Meiseki Shoten, 1991).

11. "Yatta!! Danjo Kongo Meibo" (We did it!! Mixed-sex class rolls), *Asahi Shimbun* (Asahi newspaper), 23 February 1990.

12. See, for example, Stephen Walker and Len Barton, "Gender, Class, and Education: A Personal View," in Stephen Walker and Len Barton, eds., *Gender, Class and Education* (Barcombe, England: The Falmer Press, 1983), and Kathleen Weiler, *Women Teaching for Change* (Westport, Conn.: Bergin and Garvey, 1988).

13. As noted earlier, this latter regulation has been changed, so that from the 1994 academic year domestic science or home economics will be a required subject for both girls and boys.

14. For a description of these efforts, see Atsuko Kameda and Kaoru Tachi, "Gakko ni okeru sexism to danjo byodo kyoiku" (Sexism in schools and equal education), in *Joseigaku Koza 4—Onna no Me de Miru* (Lectures in women's studies, vol. 4: From a woman's perspective) (Tokyo: Keiso Shobo, 1987).

15. Mombusho, *Mombu tokei yoran*, 43–58.

16. *Ibid.*, 84–85.

17. Yoshimasa Kano, "Nihon no josei kenkyusha—sono genjo to rekishiteki hendo" (Women researchers in Japan: Their current status and historical changes), in Michiya Shimbori, ed., *Daigaku kyojushoku no sogoteki kenkyu—academic profession no shakaigaku* (A comprehensive study of the college academic profession: Sociology of the academic profession) (Tokyo: Oga Shuppan, 1984), 194, table 7.

18. Mombusho, *Mombu tokei yoran*, 96–97.

19. For additional discussion of women academics in Japan, see Katsuko Saruhashi and Shobei Shiota, eds., *Josei kenkyusha* (Women researchers) (Tokyo: Domesu Shuppan, 1985); Kano, "Nihon no josei kenkyusha"; Takako Michii, "The Chosen Few: Women Academics in Japan" (Ph.D. diss., State University of New York at Buffalo, 1982); and Masako Bando, Michiko Noguchi, and Yoko Shinyama, eds., *Josei to gakumon to seikatsu-fujin kenkyusha no raifu saikuru* (Women, study, and life: The life cycle of women researchers) (Tokyo: Keiso Shobo, 1981).

20. National Women's Education Centre, *Survey of Courses on Women's Studies and Related Subjects in Institutions of Higher Education in Japan (Fiscal 1990)* (Saitama, Japan: National Women's Education Centre, 1991), 8, table 2.

21. *Ibid.*, 9, table 3.

22. "Women's Colleges Struggle to Adapt," *Japan Times*, 8 August 1990.

23. Kazuyuki Kitamura, "The Future of Japanese Higher Education," in Edward R. Beauchamp, ed., *Windows on Japanese Education* (Westport, Conn.: Greenwood Press, 1992).

24. Mioko Fujieda, *"Women's Studies in Japan: Its Past, Present, and Future,"* paper delivered at the Asian Women's Conference, Tokyo, 2–5 April 1992.

25. An example is a twenty-four-page booklet titled *Doshite wakeruno?* (Why do we make distinctions?), which was issued in 1992 by the Yokohama City Board of Education under the leadership and guidance of Kaoru Tachi of the Institute for Women's Studies at Ochanomizu University. The booklet, directed at third- and fourth-graders, is aimed explicitly at promoting attitudes conducive to gender equality.

# 4

## Abortion and Women's Reproductive Rights: The State of Japanese Women, 1945–1991

### MIHO OGINO

---

In 1922, Margaret Sanger argued that a liberated woman "should have the right over her own body and say if she shall or shall not be a mother, as she sees fit."[1] From her time to our own, a woman's right to control her own body has been one of the major issues of the international feminist movement. Women in Western countries fought hard for access to birth control and abortion; in many places they are still fighting for that access. In Japan, however, women received the means of fertility control as "a gift from above" as early as 1948, when a new national population policy was introduced along with other post–World War II reforms. While the legalization of abortion and the subsequent popularization of contraception that it entailed brought about a significant drop in the birthrate within a short period of time and paved the way for the economic growth of the 1960s, the new policy also produced less happy consequences for the contraceptive behavior and consciousness of Japanese women. Herein I examine the postwar pattern of fertility control that this policy helped to create, showing why this pattern has persisted as well as the role it has played in the formation of concepts about women's reproductive rights in post–World War II Japan.

### THE PRE–WORLD WAR II PERIOD

A wealth of folkloric evidence suggest that in the period before the Meiji Restoration of 1868 abortion and infanticide were widely practiced throughout Japan. Expressions such as *kaesu* (return) and *modosu* (send back), which mean killing an unwanted child immediately after birth, and *nagasu* (let run out)

69

or *orosu* (pull down), denoting abortion, existed in every part of the country. *Mabiki*, which means thinning out too many plant shoots, was another word commonly used to express infanticide. Traditional methods of inducing abortion included inserting pointed objects like sticks or plant roots into the uterus, applying strong pressure to the lower abdomen, and orally or vaginally ingesting poisonous abortifacients.[2] According to historical demographers, widespread practices of abortion and infanticide helped to keep Japanese popuation growth at almost stagnation levels during the eighteenth and early nineteenth centuries.[3]

At the very beginning of the Meiji era (1868–1912), however, the new imperial government issued a proclamation forbidding abortion and the sale of abortifacients. In 1880 the first modern penal code, modeled after the French penal code, for the first time made abortion—both by a pregnant woman herself and by other persons—a crime. The 1907 penal code, revised under the influence of the German penal code, provided for even severer penalties for abortion, and this Law of Abortion (Chapter 29, Article 212 of the penal code) has persisted to the present time.

However, since criminalization of abortion was adopted more as a part of modernization efforts by a government anxious to catch up with Western nation-states than as a Japanese tradition, abortion practices did not die out easily at the popular level. After the victory in the Russo-Japanese War in 1906, nationalist proponents of *fukoku kyohei* (a wealthy country and a strong army) policies furiously denounced illegal abortion, fearing widespread toleration for abortion would impede the population increase that economic and military development seemed to require. For example, in 1907, Kure Ayatoshi, a statistician, angrily claimed that the number of abortions performed in Japan at that time was three times as many as were done in Europe and argued as follows: "There are about 150,000 stillbirths every year in Japan. What if we take better care of them prenatally so they can be born safely? If we could make some sort of society to look after these babies, I think more than 70,000 out of 150,000 would be saved at the least. After ten years, we can afford to fight a battle with them! Not only a military battle, 70,000 people will constitute materials to increase power in Manchuria in the peacetime war. . . . We cannot develop national strength without people."[4]

The number of abortion cases that resulted in guilty verdicts greatly increased from 293 in 1904 to 672 in 1910 and stayed at high levels during the 1910s.[5] Japanese women were encouraged by the government and its supporters to bear as many children as possible to reinforce national human resources, and the population of Japan rapidly increased. By the time the first national census was conducted in 1920, some people had begun to express concern and speculate on the ramifications of overpopulation. The previous population of about thirty-five million at the beginning of Meiji era was now approaching fifty-six million.[6]

The 1910s and 1920s saw the birth of a women's movement among the educated middle-class women. Some of early feminists in this movement encountered issues of abortion and birth control in their quest for the liberation of women and joined in the movement for propagation of contraceptive knowledge and liberalization of the abortion law. Margaret Sanger's visit to Japan in 1922 combined with the general economic distress fueled the movement, and Japan's first contraception clinics were founded in Osaka and Tokyo in 1930. But since the solution for overpopulation that the Japanese government chose was expansion and war overseas, blatant cries of "*umeyo fuyaseyo*" (bear children and strengthen the nation) increasingly assailed women in the 1930s. The scanty information on contraceptive methods that had appeared in women's magazines disappeared, retailing of contraceptive goods was banned, and birth control clinics were shut down.

In 1940 the National Eugenic Law (*Kokumin yusei-ho*) was promulgated. It was patterned after the 1933 Hereditary Disease Law of Nazi Germany, and it stipulated that induced abortion and sterilization for any reasons except for eugenic ones were strictly prohibited. Women were encouraged to fulfill "the national mission of motherhood" by marrying young and bearing more children than ever. As a part of this campaign, the Welfare Ministry gave awards to 10,336 families with ten or more children in November 1940.[7] During the war years, any attempt for birth control or abortion was stigmatized as the deed of a *hikokumin* (unpatriotic traitor), and some of the activists in the birth control movement were arrested and imprisoned.

FERTILITY CONTROL AFTER THE WAR

Following the defeat in World War II, Japan immediately faced a serious overpopulation problem. While the national territory was reduced by 40 percent due to the loss of overseas colonies, large numbers of Japanese returned home as demobilized soldiers or repatriated citizens. With the help of postwar baby boom, the population that was about seventy-two million in October 1945 had increased by 15 percent to more than ten million by the end of 1950.[8] Amid starvation and confusion due to a near-complete devastation of the social and economic infrastructure, people resorted to illegal abortion, child abandonment, and infanticide to deal with unwanted pregnancies. Since there was such a great demand, obstetrician gynecologists (ob-gyns) were joined by surgeons, otolaryngologists, dentists, and even ex–hospital corpsmen and veterinarians, who performed illegal abortions under filthy and dangerous conditions.[9] Among those who endured illegal abortions in the immediate postwar years were women repatriates who had been raped in Korea and Manchuria by foreign soldiers after the Japanese surrender. Upon their arrival at Japanese ports, many such repatriates were found to be pregnant and were sent to secret hospitals. Of 380 patients housed in a hospital in Hakata port from March to December 1946, 213 women are recorded as receiving illegal abortions. The operations were conducted without any anesthesia.[10]

The Japanese government and the occupation administration quickly responded to this "state of national emergency" by passing the Eugenic Protection Law (*Yusei hogo-ho*) in June 1948. This law, which is still in effect today, had many points in common with the National Eugenic Law, and the first part of Article 1 clearly states that the purpose of the law is to prevent the birth of "inferior descendants," as defined by a eugenic point of view. The law further states that another purpose for its enactment is the protection of the life and health of the mother. As the fact that eight out of ten Diet members who introduced the bill were physicians suggests, the law was designed to protect the professional interests of legitimate ob-gyns, and it permits only certified ob-gyns to perform induced abortions. Under this law, induced abortion was made legitimate not only for eugenic reasons, rape, or leprosy of the pregnant woman or her spouse, but also "when the continuation of the pregnancy or childbirth would be physically detrimental to the health of the mother" (Article 14, Sentence 4). In the next year, economic reasons were added as legitimate grounds for abortion. Another amendment in 1952 made the previously required investigation of each abortion application by a local screening committee unnecessary, and consent of the attending ob-gyn became the only prerequisite for the operation. Since there was no stipulation of specific economic criteria for the physician to apply in deciding whether or not the applicant was qualified for legal abortion, Japanese women were thus given abortion on request. Although the Law of Abortion itself was not abrogated, prosecution under it became extremely rare because the economic criteria for abortion were so broad.

Under the new law, the number of induced abortions reported by ob-gyns doubled between 1949 and 1950 and skyrocketed thereafter from 489,111 cases in 1950 to the peak of 1,170,143 cases in 1955.[11] It is said that the actual number of abortions was far greater, however, being somewhere from one and a half to four times the reported figure because ob-gyns in private practice tended to underreport the number of operations to escape taxation.[12] In concert with the rapid rise in the number of abortions, the crude birthrate dropped from 34.3 per thousand in 1947 to 28.1 in 1950 and 19.4 in 1955.[13] Undoubtedly, the great success in suppressing fertility and subsequent economic reconstruction would have been impossible, or at least much retarded, without this abortion liberalization.

Given the drive to increase national fertility ever since the Meiji Restoration, such a prompt and smooth realization of "popularization of abortion"[14] at first sight seems to be a puzzling phenomenon. Apart from the pressing need for population control in the postwar confusion and the unabashed realism of the government, an explanation may lie in the lack of strong opposition from Japanese religious groups and the persistence of a traditional ethos permissive to abortion. Even though the two major religions in Japan, Shinto and Buddhism, do not approve of the act of abortion, they almost never voice opposition openly, as does the Catholic Church.[15] As I will discuss below, some of the Buddhist temples capitalize on the practice of abortion for private profit.

In contrast with prompt legalization of abortion from above and ready acceptance of it at the popular level, changes in contraception and family planning were relatively slow to occur. In 1951 cabinet members agreed on the necessity of substituting contraception for abortion in order to reduce injuries and health hazards inflicted on the maternal body as a result of rampant abortions, and the training of nurses, public health nurses, and midwives as contraception counselors began the following year. This program did not prove very successful, however, because some midwives were indignant at the government's complete turnabout from its pronatalist policy during wartime, and additionally they feared diffusion of contraception would inevitably lead to a decrease in the number of delivery cases.[16]

In 1954 two private organizations, the Japan Family Planning Association and Japan Family Planning Federation, were founded for the purpose of spreading contraceptive knowledge, and the Fifth International Family Planning Conference was held in Tokyo the next year. The term "family planning" began to filter into popular minds, and contraception succeeded in transforming itself from an immoral deed to be repressed, as in prewar and wartime Japan, into a new national morality befitting new life in a new state. Popular magazines also contributed to the spread of knowledge on fertility control methods. According to the nationwide polls on family planning conducted since 1950 by the Population Problems Research Council, a private organization sponsored by the *Mainichi* newspaper, the number of couples that had no experience with contraception constantly decreased from 63.6 percent in 1950 to 41.5 percent in 1955, 28.5 percent in 1961, and 15.1 percent in 1992.[17]

## RECENT TRENDS

In inverse proportion to the diffusion of contraception, the reported number of induced abortions declined after 1955, and a rapid decline ensued from the 1960s into the 1990s (Table 4-1). The 1991 figure is 37 percent of the peak figure.[18]

In spite of such a sharp decline, Japan still ranks very high among the so-called "developed countries" in the number and rate of abortions. What is peculiar about Japanese abortion is that the majority of the women who request induced abortion are neither teenagers nor unmarried—as, for example, in the United States—but are married women. As shown in Table 4-1, up to the mid-1980s women in their late twenties and older were most apt to undergo abortion. Although the marital status is not recorded in the official data, we can safely presume that a large majority of them were married because of very low rates of unmarried women in these age groups. In 1985, while 81.4 percent of women between ages 20 and 24 were unmarried, the figures for those between 25 and 29, 30 and 34, and 35 and 39 were 30.6, 10.4, and 6.6 percent, respectively.[19] The changes in this pattern appearing in the 1990s might be related to the general rise in age at first marriage and the increase in the rate of unmarried women between ages 25 and 29 (40.2 percent in 1990).

It is true that the reported number of pregnancies and abortions among teenage girls has been increasing since the mid 1970s, while the overall abortion rate has been declining constantly. Marriage and childbearing by women in their teens were not rare in the pre–World War II period, but as a result of the extension of compulsory education to age fifteen after the war and of the popularization of higher education in the 1970s and 1980s (in 1989, 95.3 percent of girls entered senior high school, while the rate for boys was 93.0 percent, marriage of teenage girls is quite an exception in present-day Japan.[20] In 1985 the rate of teenage marriage in the total population of teenage girls was only 0.2 per thousand.[21] Accordingly, almost all of the recent teenage applicants for induced abortions have been unmarried girls, and much attention has been directed to the gradual increase in their number as constituting a grave social problem. Although the teenage pregnancy rate in Japan is still much lower in comparison with other countries (see Table 4-2), a particular problem is that many teenage girls apply for induced abortion only after

TABLE 4-1    *Number of Reported Abortions and Abortion Rates*

| Year | Reported Abortions | Rate per 1,000 Women by Age | | | | | | | |
|------|--------------------|-------|----------|-------|-------|-------|-------|-------|-------|
|      |                    | Total | under 20 | 20–24 | 25–29 | 30–34 | 35–39 | 40–44 | 45–49 |
| 1955 | 1,170,143 | 50.2 | 3.4 | 43.1 | 80.8 | 95.1 | 80.5 | 41.8 | 5.8 |
| 1960 | 1,063,256 | 42.0 | 3.2 | 40.2 | 73.9 | 74.0 | 62.7 | 29.4 | 3.8 |
| 1965 |   843,248 | 30.2 | 2.5 | 31.1 | 56.0 | 56.0 | 38.0 | 21.2 | 2.5 |
| 1970 |   732,033 | 24.8 | 3.2 | 26.4 | 42.2 | 44.7 | 32.9 | 14.7 | 2.1 |
| 1975 |   671,597 | 22.1 | 3.1 | 24.7 | 34.3 | 38.4 | 29.2 | 13.8 | 1.5 |
| 1980 |   598,084 | 19.5 | 4.7 | 23.3 | 29.3 | 33.2 | 26.8 | 12.0 | 1.3 |
| 1985 |   550,127 | 17.8 | 6.4 | 22.0 | 24.6 | 31.5 | 26.2 | 11.2 | 1.1 |
| 1990 |   456,797 | 14.5 | 6.6 | 19.8 | 19.7 | 25.4 | 22.7 | 10.3 | 0.8 |
| 1991 |   436,299 | 13.9 | 6.9 | 19.1 | 19.1 | 23.7 | 21.7 |  9.3 | 0.8 |

SOURCE: Kosei-sho, *Yūsei hogotōkei hōkoku* (1992): 42–43.

TABLE 4-2    *Comparison of Teenage Pregnancy Rate (1985)*

| Country | Population of Women 15–19 yrs. | Pregnancy Rate per 1,000 |
|---------|-------------------------------|--------------------------|
| Denmark | 190,000 | 22.0 |
| France | 2,070,000 | 23.9 |
| West Germany | 620,000 | 20.8 |
| East Germany | 2,430,000 | 73.0 |
| Italy | 2,250,000 | 34.3 |
| Sweden | 290,000 | 22.9 |
| England | 2,270,000 | 32.0 |
| USSR | 10,140,000 | 33.9 |
| Canada | 990,000 | 34.1 |
| United States | 8,780,000 | 63.0 |
| India | 41,360,000 | 40.8 |
| South Korea | 2,070,000 | 29.3 |
| Japan | 4,400,000 | 3.3 |

SOURCE: Ishihama, *Jūdai no ninshin to chūzetsu* (1989): 78–80.

they have entered the second trimester of pregnancy because of their sense of shame, hesitancy, fear, or lack of knowledge of sexual matters. In 1987, for instance, one out of five pregnant teenagers received a midterm abortion, which is more dangerous and causes much greater physical and mental stress than abortion during the first trimester.[22]

### FEATURES OF JAPANESE FERTILITY CONTROL

Married women account for the great majority of abortions in Japan. The results of past surveys indirectly substantiate this fact. In a sex survey conducted among 1,500 married women by Yasuda in 1965, 49.6 percent of them replied that they had had one or more induced abortions in the past.[23] In another large-scale research project sponsored by Kyodo News Service in 1982, 58.2 percent to 64.1 percent of respondents had experienced abortion.[24] In Mainichi family-planning surveys, the rates of respondents with abortion experience were 32.8 percent in 1965, 37.5 percent in 1975, 39.8 percent in 1984, and 28.9 percent in 1992.[25]

One explanation for these high marital abortion rates lies in the peculiarity of contraception patterns among Japanese couples. In all of the research conducted from 1947 to 1992 in which couples or married women were asked what kind of contraceptive methods they were or had been using, condoms invariably were first, with rhythm methods second. In the Yasuda report, for example, condoms were named by about half of the respondents, followed by the Ogino rhythm method by 17.9 percent, basal body temperature (BBT) by 10.4 percent, contraceptive jelly (6.4 percent), tablet-form spermicide (3.7 percent), male and female sterilization (3.6 percent), IUDs (2.6 percent), and diaphragms (2.0 percent).[26] The results of the longest-running and most exhaustive Mainichi family-planning surveys are summarized in Table 4-3.

It is also noteworthy that Japanese couples tend to use condoms in conjunction with other traditional methods, especially rhythm. Although some people prefer BBT, the most widely used rhythm method is Ogino. Couples make a guess relying on this method to project "dangerous" days of the female cycle, during which conception is most likely to occur, and use condoms on these days and do without them during the presumably "safe" period. In other words, condoms plus rhythm has been the most popular contraceptive method from post–World War II Japan to the present. This is a remarkable difference from contraceptive patterns in other developed countries, where there is more variation of methods and modern methods such as the IUD, pill, and sterilization are more widely used.

Why are condoms so popular in Japan? In the prewar period, the use

TABLE 4-3  *Changes in Percentage Distribution of Contraceptive Methods in Use, 1950–1992 (Multiple Answers Allowed)*

| Method | 1950 | 1955 | 1961 | 1967 | 1973 | 1979 | 1984 | 1990 | 1992 |
|---|---|---|---|---|---|---|---|---|---|
| | | | | | Year | | | | |
| Rhythm | 27.4 | 44.1 | 42.5 | 37.4 | 29.7 | 23.1 | 20.2 | 15.3 | 16.5 |
| Coitus interruptus | 12.7 | 8.1 | 11.5 | 7.4 | 6.2 | 5.2 | 4.2 | 6.5 | 7.6 |
| Condom | 35.6 | 56.8 | 60.5 | 65.2 | 75.0 | 81.1 | 80.4 | 73.9 | 75.3 |
| Douching | 4.9 | 3.4 | 1.6 | 1.2 | 1.3 | 1.6 | 0.8 | 1.2 | 0.9 |
| Spermicide | 14.2 | 8.7 | 6.9 | 5.9 | 4.2 | 2.3 | 0.6 | 1.0 | 1.2 |
| Jelly | 15.4 | 10.5 | 10.4 | 6.6 | 4.0 | 1.9 | 0.2 | | |
| Sponge | — | 2.7 | 1.4 | 0.4 | 0.0 | — | — | — | — |
| Diaphragm | 7.8 | 6.2 | 5.9 | 4.9 | 3.6 | 1.1 | 0.2 | 0.3 | 0.1 |
| IUD | — | — | — | 6.1 | 9.0 | 8.3 | 6.3 | 4.7 | 4.9 |
| Pill | — | — | — | — | 2.4 | 3.2 | 2.2 | 1.0 | 1.3 |
| Sterilization (female and male) | — | 3.6 | 8.0 | 3.6 | 3.6 | 4.0 | 10.5 | | |
| Sterilization (female) | | | | | | | | 7.4 | 5.0 |
| Sterilization (male) | | | | | | | | 2.4 | 1.2 |
| Others | 15.0 | 7.6 | 5.3 | 4.2 | 5.2 | 2.4 | 5.4 | 2.5 | 2.2 |

SOURCE: Mainichi, *Kiroku nihon no jinkō*, rev. ed. (1992): 59.

of condoms was linked to the shady image of prostitution and venereal diseases as it was in Western countries. In the national turnabout from prewar pronatalism to postwar population control, however, condoms were acknowledged both politically and socially as a simple and effective means for fertility control, and their image shifted from negative to positive. Family-planning organizations actively promoted the use of condoms because income from condom sales constituted the main source of their funds. The Japan Family Control Association, for example, purchased condoms from a major manufacturing company for a fourth of the retail price and supplied them at wholesale price to family-planning workers, who then sold them to their clients at or below the retail market price and kept the profit.[27] Technical innovations in manufacturing and quality improvements that produced very thin, strong, and colorful condoms accelerated further popularization of condom use, and Japan quickly became the largest condom-producing country in the world. In 1980, Japan produced 6,575,000 gross of condoms, of which 1,439,000 gross were exported to other countries.[28]

Condoms are simple to use, safe for health, and one can purchase them easily at supermarkets, drugstores, vending machines, through door-to-door saleswomen, or by mail order. They are very effective if they are used correctly and consistently. But they have their own shortcomings, namely, interruption of intimate mood and cumbersomeness. Also, their effectiveness can be largely reduced if they are used in a haphazard and inconsistent manner. Since a female menstrual cycle changes very easily according to physical, mental, and environmental conditions, it is too unreliable and dangerous as a contraceptive method to calculate ovulation by the Ogino method alone and refrain from using condoms during "safe" days. The unreliability and danger become even greater if knowledge of the Ogino method is incorrect, as in "one week before the period and one week after are safe."[29] The alternate use of condoms and rhythm that is adopted by so many Japanese couples can thus result in unwanted pregnancies rather frequently, and induced abortion is resorted to as a solution to this "miscalculation." In other words, high marital abortion rate in Japan is a byproduct of its characteristic contraceptive pattern that depends so heavily on the condom-plus-rhythm method.

Lack of firm resolution to avoid conception by any means might be cited as another factor. When people know that abortion is easily available, it is possible that men and even women worry less about effective contraception, thinking that "even if it fails, there is still another card." In such cases, abortion is regarded as just one more alternative in birth control.

## WOMEN'S ATTITUDES TOWARD CONTRACEPTION AND THEIR BODIES

Even though induced abortion is available on request, the procedure is an unpleasant and humiliating experience in most cases and may hurt the woman both physically and mentally. It is quite natural to presume that no woman would like to have an abortion, much less repeat the experience over and over again. Nevertheless, there do exist women who resort to abortion many times. Perhaps one of the most extreme cases is a woman who was reported to have experienced three childbirths and thirty-five abortions during eighteen years of marriage to the same husband.[30] Apart from such an extreme case, 28.9 percent of women in the Mainichi family-planning survey conducted in 1992 replied that they had experienced abortion. Most (59.2 percent) had had only one abortion; 28.4 percent, two; 9.7 percent, three; and 2.8 percent, four or more.[31] As would be expected, the number of abortions increases with the age of women and also as the number of pregnancies increases. The correlation between abortion and pregnancy suggests that too frequent pregnancies or

TABLE 4-4  *Number of Abortions by Number of Pregnancies*

| Number of Abortions | Number of Pregnancies | | | | |
|---|---|---|---|---|---|
| | One | Two | Three | Four | Five or more |
| One | 4.6 | 5.7 | 33.1 | 35.7 | 15.0 |
| Two | 0.0 | 0.5 | 3.8 | 27.7 | 33.2 |
| Three | 0.0 | 0.0 | 0.3 | 1.5 | 27.0 |
| Four or more | 0.0 | 0.0 | 0.0 | 0.0 | 8.8 |

SOURCE: Mainichi, *Kiroku nihon no jinkō*, rev. ed. (1992): 81.

those taking place after the intended number of children (two in many cases) have been born tend to end in abortions (Table 4-4).

Many women get pregnant even when they do not want to give birth in part due to the unequal relationship between men and women. Effective contraception by condoms or coitus interruptus (which is used more frequently than the pill or IUD in Japan) requires male cooperation and care. The high reliance on these methods, especially condoms, however, does not mean that Japanese men are eager to take on responsibility for birth control or are satisfied with the method. Condoms are chosen only because they are easiest to obtain and use, because "everybody uses them," and because many Japanese couples find it embarrassing or troublesome to visit and consult with ob-gyns or other health-care specialists about alternative contraceptive methods. Since many Japanese men dislike using condoms, as do men in other countries, they tend to neglect using them thoroughly and correctly and sometimes try to force intercourse without them in spite of objections from women. When Coleman interviewed twenty-two couples living in various areas of Japan in 1976, it was husbands' dislike of condoms that the interviewed wives cited most frequently as the disadvantage of this method, which the majority of them, like so many Japanese couples, were using.[32]

Generally speaking, women are supposed to be more keenly motivated to control fertility than men because it is their bodies and their health that are at stake. But many Japanese wives, especially those who are economically dependent on their husbands, find it difficult to reject sexual approaches from their husbands even when they do not want intercourse. In a 1983 survey conducted by *Waifu* (Wife), a women's magazine, 39.4 percent of economically dependent wives in their twenties and thirties and 69.0 percent of those in their forties or above replied that they always acquiesced to their husbands regardless of their own feelings. Some of the reasons they gave for such obei-sance were "My husband always carries it through anyhow once he decides to do it, so it's useless to protest" (a woman in her twenties); "I obey against my will because he gets very nasty if I reject him" (a woman in her thirties); "He gets angry and won't go to work for about a week if I don't comply with him" (another woman in her thirties); and "I was beaten two or three times in the past when I rejected him. It's easier and ends faster if I accept him" (a woman in her forties).[33]

One cannot expect that under such circumstances wives dare to demand husbands' cooperation in contraception very strongly. Furthermore, many Japanese women are socialized to believe that it is not "feminine" to be self-assertive against men. What is expected of them is *otto o tateru* (husband first), to treat a husband with due respect as the leader of the household. It is also a taboo for women to act knowledgeable about sexual matters and to give instructions to men, because this suggests that they have had many sexual experiences with other men in the past. Although changes are taking place gradually among the younger generations, many Japanese—male and female—still think that passivity, reliance on men, and innocence are syn-onyms for "ideal femininity." Thus, many women prefer maintaining a passive stance toward sex and leaving contraception in men's hands to discussing these matters thoroughly and openly with men or to assuming responsibility for themselves. The following are two such examples.

> Mrs. T (forty-nine years old): Has been using condoms for contraception. Although her husband has been rather cooperative, she sometimes becomes afraid of having sex. Despite several experiences with induced abortion, she has never thought of trying other methods, as she believes "It is a man's responsibility to think of contraception." She hopes her husband will have a vasectomy, but this has not been realized as yet.

> Mrs. I (thirty-two years old): Uses condoms for contraception but has never seen them with her own eyes because she leaves everything to her husband. When she received an induced abortion, the husband came to the hospital with her and, weeping openly, said "It's my fault. It's because I was not steady enough. I am sorry for giving you a hard time." But now he seems to have forgotten this, because "Once on shore, we pray no more."[34]

As implied here, vasectomies in men, which are often called (in English) "pipe cuts," are not very popular in Japan. The reporter of the above cases describes a typical reaction of men to this issue:

I asked a thirty-four-year-old man with two children about contraception. He lives in an apartment with two bedrooms, a living-dining room, and a kitchen, and he told me he wanted no more children because his housing condition would not permit it. His wife had an induced abortion after she gave birth to their second child and is now wearing an IUD. I asked him why he would not choose a "pipe-cut" if he really intends to have no more children. At first he replied that it is "troublesome" and that "it looks painful," but when I further questioned him, asking "Isn't abortion more troublesome and painful?" he finally confessed his real feeling, saying "Rationally I know that there will be no harm to my sexual potential even if I undergo a vasectomy. But somewhere in my heart it makes me feel emasculated and I cannot accept it psychologically." [35]

Nor do some Japanese wives welcome the idea. In addition to the vague feeling of "unnaturalness" accompanying surgical operation, they fear that the operation will increase the possibility of their husbands' having extramarital affairs. As a result, it is more often wives than husbands that have the operation when sterilization is chosen as their method of fertility control. According to the Eugenic Protection Statistics, the reported number of sterilizing operations from 1969 to 1988 is 198,959 (98.3 percent) for women and 3,428 (1.7 percent) for men. These figures are supposed to be far below the actual number, however, and one of the researchers of the Mainichi family-planning survey estimates it to be approximately 789,000 and 317,000 respectively. [36]

Women's ignorance or fear of their own bodies is another important factor that makes effective contraception difficult. Many women (and sometimes even men) display embarrassment in talking about matters relating to sex due to strong sexual repression, one of the deep-rooted effects of Confucian tradition. For these women, the idea of seeing or touching their own genitals, or furthermore inserting their fingers into the vagina, is repulsive and fearful because they regard these parts of their bodies as filthy and disgusting. For this reason, most women prefer sanitary napkins to tampons during menstruation, and mothers sometimes forbid their daughters to try tampons. The remarkably low and ever-decreasing rates of diaphragm and spermicide use among Japanese couples can be largely explained by such widespread resistance to handling women's genitals (see Table 4-3). Although these methods were tried in the early days of family-planning campaigning, they were quickly abandoned for condoms and IUDs during the 1960s and 1970s.

Fear or indifference to their own bodies also hinders women from using BBT or other ovulation observation methods, such as mucus observation, correctly and effectively to control their fertility. Since these methods require of women far greater motivation and commitment than the Ogino method, many women don't want to bear such burdens.

One tragic example that illustrates how ignorant and repressed Japanese women have been about their own bodies is the Fujimi Obstetrico-Gynecological Hospital case that was exposed in 1980 in Tokorozawa City, Saitma prefecture. More than 1,138 women who went to that hospital for ordinary examinations were persuaded by the managing director of the hospital, who had no medical license, to undergo surgical operations promptly because their uteri or ovaries were "rotten" and "in a life-threatening condition." These women, knowing nothing about what is normal and what is not as to their reproductive organs, believed him and lost their healthy uteri and ovaries. One member of the victims league, Konishi Atsuko, recalls that she had to begin their fight against the hospital for compensation by summoning up the courage to utter the word "uterus" in front of people. "Sometimes there were passers-by who, seeing the words 'uterus' and 'ovary' in our handbills, flinched from taking them." [37]

## MIZUKO KUYO AND WOMEN'S GUILT FOR ABORTION

Easy access to and widespread acceptance of induced abortion as a means of limiting fertility do not necessarily mean that people who have resorted to this act have no feeling of guilt. Although abortion is generally acknowledged as "a necessary evil," and some women claim that they feel no guilt for the aborted fetus because there was no other choice, there are women who condemn themselves for not having been more careful about contraception and feel sorry for their "unborn babies."

As I mentioned above, the two major religions in Japan, Buddhism and Shinto, are generally not as vociferous against abortion as is the Catholic Church or fundamentalist Protestant churches. Moreover, some Buddhist temples started a new business exclusively targeting women with abortion experiences in the period after World War II. These temples constructed large statues of Jizo, the guardian of children, or Kannon, the goddess of mercy, or stone monuments of requiem for babies, and have been campaigning vigorously to persuade women with abortion experiences to visit the temples and pay money for kuyo (requiem services) for mizuko (the aborted fetuses). In some temples, the women also buy a small Jizo statue of their own and erect it in rows on the temple ground. For women who cannot visit the temples, they also sell small statues or memorial tablets by mail order, which these women then keep on hand to pray to for the souls of the aborted.

The logic these temples give to explain why such requiem services are necessary is that the soul of a *mizuko*, if not appeased, cannot enter Nirvana and haunts its mother, bringing many evils to her and her family. Large advertisements for these temples appear in newspapers. One such advertisement warns the reader, "Why does a person, wishing happiness and prosperity for her descendants, neglect *mizuko* alone? Lest the grudge of the little aborted soul turn into evil destiny causing woes and misfortunes, you must apologize to *mizuko* for your misdeed, have a requiem service for the soul, and pray to Mizuko Kannon so the soul can peacefully enter Nirvana. That is the shortest way to get rid of *mizuko*'s evil curse, change misfortunes into good fortunes, and live a happy life."[38] In the pamphlet of a Chichibu-area temple that is very famous for *mizuko kuyo*, there is a long list of evil curses due to *mizuko*: "neuroses among young men and women, children's insubordination to parents, epilepsy, weak eyesight, nocturnal enuresis, chronic rhinitis, diseases of the uterus and ovaries, *toko kyohi* (children who will not go to school), sons and daughters who will not marry, breast cancer, lumbago, heart disease, body ache."[39]

These and many other misfortunes are summoned up under the name of retribution for the sin of abortion, and many women who feel guilty about past abortions and have some trouble at home easily succumb to such threats.

## THE PILL AND JAPANESE WOMEN

In Japan oral contraceptive pills have never been formally approved for contraceptive use. Soon after the contraceptive pill was approved in the United States in 1960, it appeared on the Japanese market as an over-the-counter drug to change the menstrual cycle or to treat menstrual disorders. There may have been some women who knew about its fertility effect and used it as oral contraceptive. In 1972, however, the Health and Welfare Ministry designated the pill a prescription drug and withdrew it from the drugstores. The government, which had been severely criticized and repeatedly sued for compensation for such drug-related scandals as the thalidomide and quinoform cases in the 1960s, may have wished to prevent further lawsuits by banning free contraceptive use of the pill. According to Coleman, a high official of the Health and Welfare Ministry expressed his fear of anticipated nationwide uproars if serious side effects of the pill emerged. This official stated that "It would be unwise to take chances like that" and that "Abortion affects only the lower half of the body, but the pill has effects all over the whole body." [40]

Currently, although the pill cannot be dispensed or advertised for contraceptive purposes, the law does not prevent physicians from prescribing it to patients under the pretext of therapeutic purposes. Accordingly, it is an open secret that Japanese women can take the pill, if they wish, as an alternative method of contraception. Nevertheless, the pill is chosen by only a small fraction of women, and its use rate has been declining in recent years (see Table 4-3).

The most important reason why the pill is so unpopular in Japan is the widespread fear of side effects from taking synthetic hormones daily for a long period. This is quite understandable because the oral contraceptives currently used in Japan are the old-type pills that contain higher doses of hormones and are more likely to have various adverse effects than the low-dose pills widely used in other countries. In the Mainichi family-planning surveys conducted in 1977 and 1979, 75.4 percent and 79.6 percent, respectively, of the respondents replied that they had no intention of using the pill in the future, while those who answered affirmatively were only 2.7 percent and 3.1 percent, respectively. [41]

In 1991 it was reported that the Health and Welfare Ministry was preparing to permit manufacturing of and physicians' prescription of the low-dose pill for contraceptive purposes in the very near future. [42] One year later, however, the ministry decided to suspend this plan because "liberalization of the pill at this point of time will lead to unfavorable results such as prevalence of AIDS in Japan." [43] This decision evoked criticism that postponing approval on the pretext of AIDS prevention was missing the point, and it was suspected that the true reason was the government's unhappiness over the declining birthrate. No strong protest occurred among Japanese people, however, and many of them seem to be still doubtful about the safety of the pill. In the Mainichi surveys in 1986, 1990, and 1992, questions concerning the pros and cons of the low-dose pill were asked. The results show that nearly half of the respondents are undecided about the issue, and the rates of pill supporters are declining steadily (see Table 4-5).

There are people who think liberalization of the pill is necessary, especially as a means to reduce the abortion rate. However, even the people supporting the pill are not eager to try it personally. In 1992, when asked about their personal intention to use the pill, 63.0 percent of the pill supporters replied they did not want to use even the low-dose pill, while only 6.9 per-

TABLE 4-5   *Opinions about Liberalizing the Manufacturing and Contraceptive Use of the Low-Dose Birth-Control Pill*

|  | 1986 (%) | 1990 (%) | 1992 (%) |
|---|---|---|---|
| Good opinion | 35.4 | 28.9 | 22.7 |
| Not good opinion | 12.6 | 21.3 | 20.2 |
| Cannot decide | 48.0 | 48.0 | 54.2 |
| Others | 4.0 | 1.8 | 2.9 |

SOURCE: Mainichi, *Kiroku nihon no jinkō*, rev. ed. (1992): 66.

cent answered that they would consider using it.[44] The reasons cited by those opposing liberalization of the pill are given in Table 4-6.

Besides the reasons cited in Table 4-6, I would add a sense of "unnaturalness" regarding the pill. There were many women who told me they did not like the idea of keeping a woman's body in an artificially produced state of pregnancy in order to prevent contraception, even if the side effects were kept to a minimum. As the Japanese preference for rhythm methods demonstrates, many people prefer the methods that interfere least with the natural rhythm of the woman's body, and the pill is in exact opposition to their inclination.

It is interesting to note that there has been no explicit organized effort by women to make the pill more easily available except one that occurred in the early 1970s. This action involved a women's group named *Chu-pi-ren* (Women's Union for Liberalization of Abortion and the Pill) that fought in a rather flamboyant manner demanding free contraceptive use of the pill. Under their highly colorful leader, Misako Enoki, *Chu-pi-ren* used various shock tactics in their attempts to bring this issue to the attention of the Japanese public. These included disruptive actions at the workplace of an exhusband who had been neglecting payment of alimony to his divorced wife.[45] The media ridiculed the movement unsparingly, and the then-burgeoning Japanese women's liberation movement was put at considerable disadvantage by being identified with this group and forced to share much of its notoriety. Apart from this group, and to some extent due to the negative impression the brief activity of *Chu-pi-ren* left on the Japanese public, including feminists, demands for liberalization of the pill have never appeared on the agenda of the Japanese feminists.

On the contrary, many of the activists in the Japanese women-and-health

TABLE 4-6 *Reasons for Not Approving Liberalization of the Low-Dose Birth-Control Pill*

| Reasons | 1990 (%) | 1992 (%) |
|---|---|---|
| It has to be taken daily to be effective | 8.6 | 8.3 |
| Getting a physician's prescription is troublesome | 4.6 | 2.5 |
| Fear of side effects even in low doses | 70.3 | 67.7 |
| Content with the existing methods | 16.5 | 14.7 |
| It will encourage immoral sexual activity | 34.8 | 21.9 |
| Women alone have to bear the burden | 20.6 | 19.7 |
| It cannot prevent AIDS | — | 18.8 |
| Others | 3.8 | 3.8 |

SOURCE: Mainichi, *Kiroku nihon no jinkō*, rev. ed. (1992): 66.

movement clearly stand against the pill. A group that was then working for establishment of Japan's first women's health center in Osaka published a book on the pill and contraception, entitled *The Pill—We Don't Choose It*, in 1987. The women of this group share the negative attitude of American women-and-health activists toward the pill as expressed in the 1984 edition of *The New Our Bodies, Ourselves*.[46] The Osaka group explains why they do not choose the pill:

> I want to choose a method that is as natural as possible and doesn't change the rhythm of my body. I have no mind to take the pill. It suppresses ovulation using hormones and causing side effects. I hate the idea of exposing my body to such an experiment for reasons such as "It may be better than having an induced abortion" or "Its contraceptive effect is very high."[47]

> I don't have sex every day and don't need contraception every day, either. Nevertheless, if I must take a pill every day, I feel my whole life will be revolving around the pill at the center.[48]

> I think the pill is the least communicative of all contraceptive methods. While the man can be free of all troubles, the burden of taking it constantly falls one-sidedly on the woman. The same is true about a men's pill if there will ever be one. However sympathetic a woman or man may be, such one-sided relationships will eventually lead to that of the oppressor and the oppressed.[49]

> If there is enough communication and sympathy toward each other between a man and woman, condoms are enough for effective contraception.[50]

Nevertheless, when the Health and Welfare Ministry decided to suspend the liberalization of the low-dose pill in March 1992, many feminists joined in the criticism of this decision.[51] As Ashino Yuriko, an activist for women's reproductive health and rights and a member of the Japan Family Planning Association, argues, although many Japanese feminists do not regard the pill as the best means of contraception, still they hold the view that Japanese women should be given as many contraceptive alternatives as possible, including the pill, so that they can judge for themselves and make the decision on their own. The postponement of pill approval under the pretext of AIDS prevention was thus criticized as an infringement of this fundamental right of women.[52]

THE ANTIABORTION MOVEMENT AND WOMEN'S
REPRODUCTIVE RIGHTS

Unlike women in other countries who have had to fight a long battle for their fundamental right to have safe and legal abortions, postwar Japanese women have thus far enjoyed the "liberty" of having legal abortions whenever they need them. But the fact that this "liberty" was not won through women's struggle but was decreed from above as a national policy has left some undesirable aftereffects on Japanese women. They have not been very enthusiastic either about obtaining knowledge of alternative methods of fertility control or about changing their relationships with the men in their sexual lives. Often they have seen unwanted pregnancies and induced abortions not as results of body politics between men and women or between women and Japanese society, but merely as "bad luck" or "carelessness." And the women, who cannot conceive of sharing their feelings of guilt for abortion with the men responsible for the unwanted pregnancies, have carried the burden alone and have been frightened by the shadow of *mizuko*'s evil curse. It has been very hard for them to accept the idea that women can claim reproductive rights to protect their own bodies from unsafe and harmful means of fertility control and the idea that women should decide for themselves when, how, and whether to have children.

The liberty given to women by the state for its own political reasons can be modified or withdrawn as the circumstances change. Both the number of births and the birthrate in Japan have been declining constantly since the mid 1970s, while high economic development since the mid 1960s has made Japan one of the richest countries in the world. In such circumstances, there have been at least two attempts to eliminate the "economic reason clause" from the

Eugenic Protection Law, one in the early 1970s and another a decade later. Since more than 99 percent of current abortion cases are legalized by this clause, its elimination actually means placing a ban on induced abortion.[53] In both cases, the *Seicho no Ie* (Home of Life), a religious organization founded in 1930, played the central role in the antiabortion campaigns, both politically and economically.

The religious creed of this organization is very eclectic, cnsisting of elements borrowed from Buddhism, Shinto, and Christianity, and there have been rumors of close contact between *Seicho no Ie* and the Moral Majority and the "right-to-life" movements in the United States.[54] Members of the political arm of *Seicho no Ie*, together with other conservative members of the Liberal Democratic party, tried to push through reforms to the Eugenic Protection Law in 1972–1973 and 1982–1983. They claimed that Japan no longer needed to permit murder of innocent fetuses due to economic reasons, and launched nationwide campaigns under the slogan of "reverence for life." During the second and larger campaign in 1982 and 1983, they held assemblies "to protect the lives of fetuses," funded TV advertisements, published a book entitled *Is a Fetus Not a Human Being?*[55] and launched a petition campaign that aimed to collect ten million signatures. In February 1983, *Seimei soncho kokkai giin renmei* (Federation of Diet Members Who Revere Life) was formed and more than 300 Diet members joined.[56]

Interestingly, it was these political moves that awakened Japanese women to the issue of their reproductive rights. On both occasions, women fought against the attempts to change the law and succeeded in defeating them. During the first campaign, women in the antireform movement coined the famous slogan, "*Umu, umanai wa onna ga kimeru*" (it's women who decide to bear or not to bear). In the 1982 campaign, activists from the women's liberation movement were joined by various citizens' groups, traditional women's organizations, trade unions, and politicians. More than sixty groups participated in the formation of the "82 Antiabortion Law Reform Coalition" in August 1982.[57] In March 1983 seven women students conducted a one-week hunger strike in front of the Health and Welfare Ministry. Also, a national conference and a demonstration of more than two thousand people were held in the same month.[58]

Through these movements many Japanese women came to realize, almost for the first time, what a vital role the Eugenic Protection Law had been playing in their lives and how ignorant they had been on matters concerning their bodies. During and after these experiences, Japanese women-and-health movements began to take shape, and the issues concerning the woman's body, sexuality, and reproduction became important parts of the feminists' agenda. Some women activists are now trying to draft their own abortion bill, in which the right is not granted from above, but comes from below, a product of women's hands.[59]

At the end of 1989, however, the Health and Welfare Ministry announced its intention to shorten the period for legal abortion from twenty-three weeks to twenty-one weeks of pregnancy. The reason given was that there had been one reported case of a premature baby born at twenty-three weeks surviving for more than six months due to technical improvements in perinatal medicine.[60] Although the two-week shortening does not immediately threaten women's vested rights to a legal abortion, there were fears that the teenage girls who are apt to postpone application for abortion to the last minute would be affected by this step. In spite of the protest and demands from the women-and-health activists, feminist ob-gyns, and various women's groups that such an important issue must be discussed fully in the Diet and that opinions of women should be consulted before making any decision, the alteration was rushed into implementation by means of a notification issued by the vice-minister of health and welfare in March 1990, and it went into effect on 1 January 1991. As Dr. Yuriko Marumoto, an ob-gyn, points out, increasing anxiety by the government over the declining birthrate was probably the hidden motivation for this move.[61]

Immediately after the March action, in June 1990 the major newspapers in Japan sensationally reported that the birthrate dropped to 1.57 per thousand in 1989. This news caused such a furor in political and economic circles and the media that a new phrase, "1.57 shock," was coined. The low birthrates were said to be mainly the result of better education for women and an increase in the number of women entering the work force, which caused women to marry later and to bear fewer children. The ominous prospects of an aging society, labor shortages, and decline in the Japanese economy were emphasized repeatedly by political and economic leaders—some of them even criticized the "selfishness" of women who would not bear children. Nationwide pronatalist campaigns were launched during 1990 and in the following two years. Thus, Japanese women found themselves bombarded by both open and hidden calls to have more children for the future of Japan.[62]

Against such campaigns, voices of anger were raised immediately not only by feminists and activists but by ordinary housewives and working women. Indignant letters from women poured into the newspapers. These asserted that the decline in the birthrate was an inevitable result of and the price to be paid for post–World War II Japanese society, which consistently placed a priority on efficiency and economic development, leaving the burdens of raising "good-quality" children and domestic labor entirely to women. For example, a woman aged twenty-nine and working at a part-time job wrote in a letter to the Yomiuri Newspaper: "It is miserable for a grown-up woman to live without economic independence. So I decided that one child was enough for me. I don't want to spoil the life either of my child or myself. . . . Why should women bear children for the aged and the state? Never, for anything! If they think they need more children, let them use the military budget or something for that. But it's a mistake to reproach women for the decline of the birthrate. I want to say to the state, 'Stop exploiting women forever! We won't be duped any more!' and live my life free from regret." [63]

Although there was no mention of "women's reproductive rights" in this or other letters from women, it seems that the basic idea that they should have the ultimate control over their reproductive ability is now shared by more and more women. As the threat of antiabortion movements in the early 1970s and 1980s awakened some Japanese women to the issue of women's bodies and women's rights, the recent controversy over the falling birthrate has served as another opportunity for more Japanese women to think about such matters.

## CONCLUSION

Whether or not there is access to safe, effective, and legitimate means of fertility control is of vital importance for women, and the right to legal abortion is an indispensable part of it. In the case of Japanese women, this right was given from above, without any movement or struggle of their own, as the result of a turnabout on population policy by the state after the defeat in war. Partly because of immediate necessity and partly because of traditional permissiveness toward abortion in Japanese society, including in religious circles, induced abortion took root deeply in the lives of Japanese women in the post–World War II period. Although contraception has gradually become the primary means of fertility control since the 1960s, abortion still plays an important role as the backup for failure in contraception stemming from careless or inaccurate use of condoms and the Ogino rhythm method. Japanese women have not been very eager to get knowledge about effective contraception or very self-assertive on matters concerning their own bodies, and they have remained passive in their relations to both male partners and doctors. Such an attitude can be explained, at least partly, as the unfavorable aftereffect of the legalization of abortion that was attained too easily. Furthermore, resort to abortion often leaves a vague feeling of guilt in some women in spite of its legitimacy, and many of these fall easy prey to the *mizuko* temples.

Despite all this, from the 1970s on we can trace a small but growing women-and-health movement and the gradual infiltration of the idea of women's reproductive rights among women in the general population. Through the threat to women's vested right to abortion posed by the antiabortion campaigns in the early 1970s and 1980s, Japanese women begin to see the danger of leaving the decisive power on reproductive matters to persons other than women themselves. Neither Japanese women in general nor women-and-health activists regard the contraceptive pill, which is not officially approved in Japan, as very helpful for the liberation of women. While many of the latter do admit that the low-dose pill must become available as one of the alternatives for fertility control, they share the general populace's traditional support for condoms. They do so because they see condoms, if used rightly, as more conducive to equal and cooperative relationships between men and women.

Recently, Japanese women have been assaulted by the pronatalist campaigns of those anxious to raise the falling birthrate. However, the indignant reactions and uncooperative attitudes of ordinary women to such campaigns suggest that Japanese women are not willing to resume obediently the role of childbearing machines that their grandmothers used to play in the pre–World War II period. On the other hand, it is still premature to state that they have succeeded in securing the right to control their own bodies in their relations to men and the state. The idea that reproductive rights are fundamental human rights for women is not yet generally accepted in Japan. However, I hope that the current controversy over the declining birthrate and the new attitudes perceivable among women will be a good start toward achieving this recognition.

NOTES

1. Margaret Sanger, "The Morality of Birth Control," *Birth Control Review* 6, no. 2 (1922): 12.

2. See for example, Onshi Zaidan Boshi Aiiku-kai, ed., *Nihon saniku shiryo shūsei* (Collections of manners and customs of birth and child rearing in Japan) (Tokyo: Daiichi Hōki, 1975). See also Gorō Achiba, "*Nihon sanji seigen-shi ni tsuite*" (History of birth control in Japan), *Igakushi Kenkyu*, no. 23 (1967): 9–22.

3. Hiroshi Kitō, *Nihon nisennen no jinko-shi* (Two thousand years of population history in Japan) (Tokyo: PHP Kenkyujo, 1983).

4. Ayatoshi Kure, *"Datai ron"* (On abortion), *Kokka Igakukai Zasshi*, no. 239 (1907): 1–11.

5. Miho Ogino, *"Jinkō ninshin chūzetsu to josei no jiko kettei-ken"* (Abortion and women's reproductive rights), in Hiroko Hara and Kaoru Tachi, eds., *Bosei kara jisedai ikusei-ryoku e* (From motherhood to the nurturing ability of the next generation) (Tokyo: Shinyōsha, 1991).

6. Jinkō mondai kenkyu-kai, ed., *Jinkō no dōkō: nihon to sekai 1990* (Population trend: Japan and the world, 1990) (Tokyo: Kōsei Tōkei Kyokai, 1991), 9.

7. *Kindai nihon sōgō nenpyo* (General chronological table of modern Japan), 2d ed. (Tokyo: Iwanami Shoten, 1984), 324.

8. Jinkō mondai kenkyu-kai, ed., *Jinkō no dōkō*, 9.

9. Shinichi Sano, *Sei no ōkoku* (Kingdom of sex) (Tokyo: Bungei Shunju, 1981), 304; and Tenrei Ohta, *Nihon sanji chosetsu hyakunen-shi* (One hundred years of birth control in Japan) (Tokyo: Ningen no Kagaku-sha, 1976), 359.

10. Sano, *Sei no ōkoku*, 306–9.

11. Ogino, "Jinkō ninshin chūzetsu to josei no jiko kettei-ken," 119.

12. Samuel Coleman, *Family Planning in Japanese Society: Traditional Birth Control in a Modern Urban Culture* (Princeton: Princeton University Press, 1983), 4.

13. Mainichi Shinbun-sha Jinkō Mondai Chosa-kai, ed., *Kiroku nihon no jinkō: shosan eno kiseki* (Japanese population: The way to low birthrate) (Tokyo: Mainichi Shinbun-sha, 1990), 345.

14. Yasuo Kon's word in Yukku-sha, ed., *Onna, ninshin chuzetsu* (Women, abortion) (Tokyo, Yukkusha, 1984), 135.

15. For a more detailed analysis of the attitudes of various religions to abortion in Japan, see William R. LaFleur, *Liquid Life: Abortion and Buddhism in Japan* (Princeton: Princeton University Press, 1992).

16. Emiko Ochiai, "Aru sanba no nihon kindai" (Modern Japanese history of a certain midwife), in Miho Ogino, *et al.*, *Seido to shiteno onna* (Women as an institution) (Tokyo, Heibon-sha, 1990), 305. See also Coleman, *Family Planning*, 47–48.

17. Mainichi, *Kiroku nihon no jinkō*, rev. ed. (1992), 54.

18. Kōsei-shō (Daijin Kanbō Tōkei Jōhō-bu), *Heisei 3-nendo Yūsei hogo tōkei hōkoku* (1991 eugenic protection statistics report) (Tokyo, Kōsei Tōkei Kyokai, 1992), 42–43.

19. Jinko mondai kenkyu-kai, ed., *Jinkō no dōkō*, 76.

20. Teruko Inoue and Yumiko Ehara, eds., *Josei no dēta bukku* (Women's data book) (Tokyo: Yūhikaku, 1991), 117.

21. Atsumi Ishihama, *Jūdai no ninshin to chūzetsu* (Pregnancy and abortion of teenage girls) (Osaka: Medika Shuppan, 1989), 17.

22. Inoue and Ehara, *Josei no dēta bukku*, 55.

23. Hiroyoshi Ishikawa, *et al.*, *Nihon-jin no sei* (Sexual lives of the Japanese) (Tokyo: Bungei Shunjū, 1984), 111, 139.

24. *Ibid.*, 220.

Women's Reproductive Rights • 93

25. Mainichi, *Kiroku nihon no jinkō*, 78.
26. Ishikawa, *et al.*, *Nihon-jin no sei*, 138.
27. Coleman, *Family Planning*, 33, 45.
28. Sano, *Sei noōkoku*, 240.
29. Coleman, *Family Planning*, 117.
30. "35-nin no mizuko ga migite no hashi ni notte iru" (Thirty-five *mizuko* sit on the chopsticks in my right hand), *Shūkan Josei*, 24–31 August 1976, 26–30.
31. Mainichi, *Kiroku nihon no jinkō*, 78.
32. Coleman, *Family Planning*, 101.
33. *Gurūpu waifu* (Group wife), *Sei—tsuma-tachi no messēji* (Sex: Messages from wives) (Tokyo: Komichi Shobō, 1984), 28–29.
34. Yukku-sha, ed., *Onna, ninshin chūzetsu*, 74, 76.
35. *Ibid.*, 77.
36. Mainichi, *Kiroku nihon no jinkō*, 66–68.
37. "Jibun no karada jibun no mono ni shite imasuka" (Do you feel your body belongs to you?), *More*, June 1986, 164–66. See also Fujimi Sanfujin-ka Byōin Higaisha Dōmei, ed., *Wasurenai Fujimi Sanfujin-ka Byōin jiken* (We will never forget the Fujimi Ob-Gyn Hospital case) (Tokyo: Bansei-sha, 1990).
38. An advertisement of Daikannon Temple in *Yomiuri Shinbun*, 2 May 1991.
39. Shakai Hyōronsha henshūbu, ed., *Onna no sei to chūzetsu: yūsei hogohō no haikei* (Women's sexuality and abortion: Background to the Eugenic Protection Law) (Tokyo: Shakai Hyōron-sha, 1983), 65.
40. Coleman, *Family Planning*, 36–37.
41. Mainichi, *Kiroku nihon no jinkō*, 69.
42. *Asahi Shinbun*, 31 May 1991.
43. *Yomiuri Shinbun*, 18 March 1992, 1.
44. Mainichi, *Kiroku nihon no jinkō*, 69–71.
45. For more details about *Chu-pi-ren*, see Yoko Akiyama, *Ribu shishi nōto* (A note on my experiences with women's liberation) (Tokyo: Inpakuto Shuppan-kai, 1993).
46. Boston Women's Health Book Collective, *The New Our Bodies, Ourselves* (New York: Simon and Schuster, 1984).
47. Onna no tameno kurinikku junbi-kai, ed., *Pill—watashi-tachi wa erabanai* (The pill: We don't choose it) (Osaka: Onna no tameno kurinikku junbi-kai, 1987), 118–19.
48. *Ibid.*, 113.
49. *Ibid.*, 127.
50. *Ibid.*, 130.
51. Women's Center Osaka, ed., *Onna no tameno kurinikku nyūsu* (Women's clinic news), nos. 84–86, April–June, 1992.
52. *Mainichi Shinbun*, 19 April 1992.
53. Kōsei-sho (Daijin Kanbō Tōkei Jōhō-bu), *Heisei 2-nendo yūsei hogo tōkei*

*hōkoku* (1990 eugenic protection statistics report) (Tokyo: Kōsei Tōkei Kyokai, 1991), 21.

54. Concerning *Seicho no Ie*, see Coleman, *Family Planning*, 62–64; and Sandra Buckley, "Body Politics: Abortion Law Reform," in Gavan McCormack and Yoshio Sugimoto, eds., *The Japanese Trajectory: Modernization and Beyond* (New York: Cambridge University Press, 1988).

55. Nihon kyōbunsha, ed., *Taiji wa ningen de nainoka* (Is a fetus not a human being?) (Tokyo, Nihon Kyōbun-sha, 1982).

56. Nihon Kazoku Keikaku Renmei, ed., *Kanashimi o sabakemasuka* (Can you judge a sorrow?) (Tokyo: Ningen no Kagaku-sha, 1983), 266.

57. *Agora 28: Umu umanai umenai* (*Agora* no. 28: To bear, not to bear, cannot bear) (Tokyo: BOC Shuppan-bu, 1983), 269.

58. *Ibid.*, 226, 269–88.

59. Gurūpu Onna no Jinken to Sei (Group Women's Rights and Sex), ed., *Ripurodakutibu herusu wo watashitachi no teni* (Reproductive health as our fundamental right) (Tokyo: Gurūpu Onna no Jinken to Sei, 1990).

60. *Yomiuri Shinbun*, 17 December 1989.

61. Yuriko Marumoto and Keiko Ochiai, "Chūzetsu kikan tanshuku de naniga okoruka" (What will happen as the result of shortening the period for legal abortion?), *Fujin Kōron*, October 1990, 280–87.

62. For further details, see Miho Ogino, "Japanese Women and the Decline of the Birth Rate," *Reproductive Health Matters*, no. 1 (May 1993): 78–84.

63. *Yomiuri Shinbun*, 3 July 1990.

# 5

## Women Workers in Japan: Past, Present, Future

### EIKO SHINOTSUKA

THIS is a survey of the transitions that women workers in Japan, especially in the "Japanese-style management" system, have undergone since World War II and women's economic status today. Japan's economy has been relatively strong since the latter half of the 1980s. This can be attributed to many factors, one of which is Japanese-style management.

The population shifts expected in Japan in the twenty-first century will have a strong influence on its women workers. According to estimates made in 1992 by the Ministry of Labor's Employment Policy Research Committee, Japan's total working population will peak in 1995 and then decline. In the year 2000 the total number of male and female workers over age fifteen is predicted to be 66.97 million; in 2010 it is predicted to be 64.87 million. Thus, a decline of 2,100,000 workers is forecast between 2000 and 2010.[1] Confronted with this specter of a definite labor shortage in the immediate future, the government's policies affecting working women—such as the Child Care Leave Law—have finally become more full-scale and concrete.

My analysis will focus on the following three areas: first, the transitions undergone by women workers since World War II; second, the connection between women workers and the "Japanese-style management" system or "Japanese-style labor customs" that have formed the backbone of Japan's economic strength; and third, the various policies that affect working women, how they have been made more concrete, and the debates being waged about them.

## WOMEN WORKERS AND SHIFTS IN THE INDUSTRIAL STRUCTURE

Table 5-1 illustrates long-term trends relating to women workers as seen in the Management and Coordination Agency's *State of the Nation Survey*.[2] Because this survey was first taken in 1920, the table provides an overview of more than seventy years of changes, including some data from before World War II. When the war ended in 1945, the Japanese economy was in a state of confusion. Five years later, there were 13.9 million women workers, 60 percent of them working in primary industries. The smallest number, only a little over 10 percent, worked in secondary industries, and 25.6 percent worked in tertiary industries. It is important to note here that the percentage of women employed by each level of industry had not changed significantly since 1920.

By 1980, however, Japan's industrial structure had changed dramatically. Because industrial policy had shifted away from agriculture and toward manufacturing, there had been a marked decrease in the number of people employed in primary industries. During this time there was also a large population shift, from farming villages to urban areas. Also, in 1960, the Ikeda cabinet initiated its "income-doubling plan." Japan's economy began gearing up to embark on its high-growth period.

The period from the end of World War II through the period of high economic growth, when Japan's economy grew between 10 percent and 20 percent annually, until 1973, the year of the first oil shock, can be regarded as one discreet period in Japanese economic history. Japanese-style management, which was already being practiced by Japan's largest companies before the war, spread to medium-sized companies and to companies outside the manufacturing sector. There was a great demand for labor. The labor shortage was particularly severe in manufacturing, where there was a great need for young men with technical skills and technical knowledge.

During this period, women became part-time workers in the manufacturing industry. The majority were housewives; when business was good and their labor was needed, they joined the work force, and when business slowed down, they were laid off and returned to their households. Thus, because unemployed women workers did not remain in the job market during difficult economic times, a high level of total employment could be maintained at all times (during the 1960s and 1970s Japan's unemployment rate was around 1 percent). With the oil shocks in 1973 and 1978, however, Japan's high growth rate was cut in half, and its economy underwent intense structural changes. The ten years from the latter half of the 1970s through the first half

TABLE 5-1  *Japanese Workers*

| Year | Total Workers, by Industry | | | | Percentages of Women, by Type | | |
| | Total | Primary | Secondary | Tertiary | Employees | Self-employed | Employees in family business |
| --- | --- | --- | --- | --- | --- | --- | --- |
| 1920[1] | 100.0 (27.3) | 53.6 | 20.8 | 25.7 | — | — | — |
| 1950[2] | 100.0 (35.6) | 47.0 | 21.3 | 29.8 | 26.3 | 12.5 | 61.2 |
| 1980 | 100.0 (55.7) | 10.4 | 34.8 | 54.6 | 64.3 | 11.6 | 24.1 |
| 1990[3] | 100.0 (62.5) | 7.2 | 33.6 | 59.8 | 72.3 | 10.7 | 16.7 |

NOTE: Figures are in percentages except those in parentheses, which represent millions of people.
[1]For this year, people over fourteen years; for other years, people over fifteen years.
[2]Okinawa is omitted in 1950.
[3]1990 figures only are from Management and Coordination Agency, *Annual Survey of the Labor Force.* Figures for other years are from the agency's national census.

of the 1980s are thought of as a painful period of slow growth for the Japanese economy. The oil shocks put economic pressure on management. To save on personnel costs, strong efforts were made to invest heavily in robots and to make use of nonregular workers, whose terms of employment were easily adjustable.

These changes in the industrial structure had a large impact on women workers in other ways as well. First, up to this point it had always been said that the lifetime employment system, with no layoffs, was the heart of Japanese-style management, but that myth was shattered by the oil shock. Even regular male employees now had to accept a change in status in the form of temporary transfers, reassignment, or forced early retirement. Furthermore, the annual increase in wages, which had been 10 percent during the high growth period, was suddenly only half that much. Under these circumstances, the participation of women in the labor force, which had heretofore been looked upon as merely supplementary, became more central. Second, as labor saving took hold in the manufacturing industry, the number of jobs suitable for women in the service and sales industries increased.

As a result of all these factors, supply and demand conveniently converged. Having learned a lesson from the oil shocks, companies were eager to make use of employees whose terms of employment were more easily adjustable, while women (chiefly housewives) were eager to earn a little money while they could. The number of women employed as nonregular (mostly part-time) employees thus increased, chiefly in the tertiary industries.

## How Women Work and Think about Work

In all societies, no matter how they are structured, women are saddled with a particular role in the household based on their gender. In all countries, including Japan, housework and child rearing act as fetters on women when it comes to their participation in society. Japanese women were first given the right to vote on 17 December 1945, immediately after Japan's defeat in the war. In addition, the new constitution guaranteed equality for women in education, economic matters, and all other aspects of society. But because these rights were something bestowed on them from above rather than something women had secured for themselves, there was a huge gap between the letter of the law and actual practice. And more than anything else, neither men nor women had any real sense of what equality of the sexes meant.

Despite the fact that there has been consistent progress in women's access to and attainment of higher education since the war, there have been no major

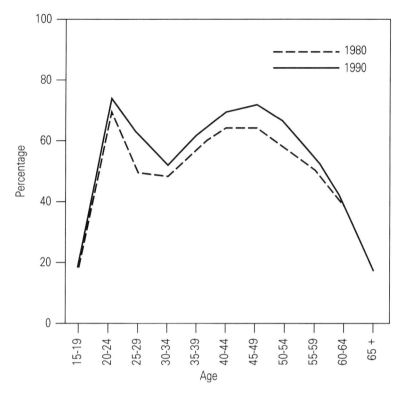

FIGURE 5-1    *Percentages of Women Workers by Age*
SOURCE: Bureau of Statistics, Management and Coordination Agency, *Survey of the Labor Force.*

shifts in the percentages of women workers by age. As Figure 5-1 shows, the graph representing the percentage of women workers in Japan by age continues to form the letter *M*. It is interesting to note that this is also true of Korea's women workers. There were no fundamental changes between 1980 and 1990 except that the dip in the middle moved up slightly and shifted from the 25–29 to the 30–34 age group. American women workers broke out of the *M* pattern in the 1970s and began following the same plateau pattern as men workers. In other words, American women don't leave the workplace because of childbirth and child rearing. In Japan, however, the work pattern of more than half of all women continues to show that childbirth and child rearing are regarded as the most important roles for women, with work in the workplace treated as secondary.

Figure 5-2 categorizes the percentages of women workers shown in

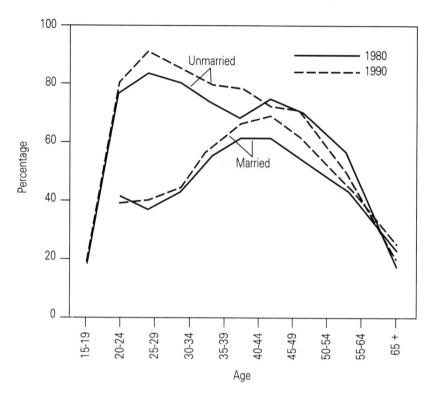

FIGURE 5-2   *Percentages of Women Workers by Age and Marital Status*
SOURCE: Bureau of Statistics, Management and Coordination Agency, *Survey of the Labor Force.*

Figure 5-1 into unmarried and married. Only 40 percent of married women in their twenties and early thirties are employed. The increases in women workers over the past ten years have come in the categories of unmarried women and middle-aged women who have finished bringing up their children.

What sustains percentages like these is undoubtedly the Japanese view of women's work: Japanese women, much more so than women in other industrialized nations, have had a division of labor by gender deeply ingrained into their consciousness from the time they were very young. No matter what kind of sampling is taken, a variety of studies have found that more than half of their respondents prefer that women quit work when they get married and have children and return to work when they are finished raising their children. In one such survey, taken by the prime minister's office in 1987 and again in 1992, the responses of unmarried and married respondents regarding their preferred working pattern did not differ significantly from each other in either year. But the number of both unmarried and married respondents who cited a desire to work continuously throughout their lives did show an increase in 1992 (more than 25 percent versus 20 percent in 1987).

Figure 5-3 shows the results of an international survey that was conducted independently by Japan. The two countries with the highest percentage of young people who agree with a division of labor by gender that calls for men to work outside the home while women stay home are the Confucian countries, Japan and Korea. The figures show that between 1983 and 1988 in Japan there was an increase in the percentage of people opposed to sex-role differentiation. But it is also important to note that a remarkably high percentage of Japanese, one in four, did not respond to this question. This is evidence of the lack of assertiveness of Japanese and the tendency to agree with either side of a question depending on the context in which it is asked.

## WOMEN WORKERS AND JAPANESE-STYLE MANAGEMENT

When the economic struggle between Japan and the United States intensified in the latter half of the 1980s, Japanese-style management once again became a topic of discussion and was suggested to be the foundation of the special system underlying the Japanese economy. I say "once again" because Japanese-style management was also viewed internationally as being the cause of Japan's high economic growth after the war.

James Abegglen was among those who researched the topic at that time.[3] He sought to find the secret behind the economic growth that allowed Japan to rise from the destruction of World War II like a phoenix from the ashes. After a close observation of Japan's factories, Abegglen concluded that Japanese management was totally different from that of other advanced nations, and he cited the following three characteristics as the pillars of its existence: (1) the lifetime employment system, (2) the seniority-based wage system that sustains the lifetime employment system, and (3) the enterprise unions that minimize labor disputes.

A variety of counterarguments and objections to Abegglen's proposed theory of Japanese-style management were raised. Consolidating the opinions of many researchers, who said that there was a subtle difference between labor practices in Japan and those in Europe and the United States, the sociologist Tominaga Ken'ichi wrote, "The phrases 'Japanese-style management' and

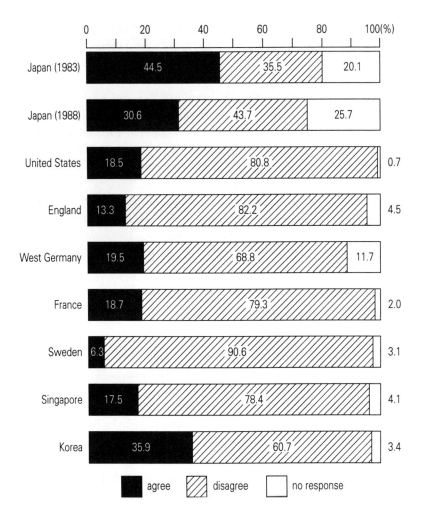

FIGURE 5-3 *Opinions about Sex Roles, Males and Females Aged 18–24*
NOTE: Responses to: Men should work outside [the home] and women should
stay home.
SOURCE: Mariko Bando, *Survey of the World's Youth*, Youth Policy
Headquarters, Management and Coordination Agency (1991) p. 21.

'Japanese-style labor relations' indicate that even now, after the war, Japanese society is not yet completely modernized. In Japanese-style management, the basic structure of the social relationship between management and labor is paternalistic, and in actual practice it is characterized by a harmony of feeling."[4]

As modernization proceeds, however, the survival of Japanese-style management becomes endangered. Economic friction with the United States is probably another reason for this. And what will become of Japanese-style management when the women workers who are the subject of this essay come to participate in the job market as real principal workers? What will happen when young people who have been raised in the era of individualism become the top managers in the Japanese economy? Surely Japanese-style management is destined to disappear once Japan completes its modernization.

To understand the position of women workers in the Japanese-style management system, it is necessary to examine the peculiar development of Japanese capitalism. In 1868, after 265 years of isolation under the Tokugawa shogunate, Japan was forced by foreign pressure to open its doors to the outside world, and the Meiji Restoration took place. Having just awakened from a long, tranquil sleep as an isolated nation, Japan needed first of all to create a modern state system. But Europe and the United States had already had their industrial revolutions and were well along the road to industrialization. Japan's Meiji government began by planting the roots of capitalism.

Japan's capitalist economy got its start by borrowing both technology and human resources from Europe and the United States. Japan had neither the capital nor the skilled workers needed to get started immediately in heavy industries like shipbuilding and ironworking. Thus it began with light industries like silk-reeling and textiles.

The Meiji government established Japan's first government-operated modern factory, the Tomioka Silk-Reeling Mill, in Gumma prefecture in 1872. Recruiting women workers was extremely problematic. Up to that time women had been taught that their place was in the home. Furthermore, for women brought up under feudalism, nothing would have been more unthinkable than working under one of the foreign experts the government had brought in. Along with fifteen other women from her hometown, Wada Ei (1857–1929), daughter of a former samurai from Matsushiro in the old province of Shinshu, went to work at the Tomioka mill and set out to learn the technology. Later, when a private mill was opened in Nagano prefecture, she was invited to teach the technology there. Today, the valuable record she kept of her experiences at the Tomioka Silk-Reeling Mill is the most valuable tool we have to help us understand women workers during the early days of capitalism in Japan.[5]

The Meiji Restoration's "increase production and promote industry" policy called first for the production and exporting of light industrial goods in order to earn foreign capital. The foreign capital would then be used to purchase the materials needed for heavy industry, and heavy industry would thus be launched in Japan.

The initial establishment of the Japanese-style management system came at this time, when heavy industry was first being promoted. The principal workers shifted from women, as at the start of capitalism, to men, who were now sought for their technical skills. In order to have them master the technology borrowed from Europe and the United States, the companies wanted the skilled male workers as permanent employees; thus, the lifetime employment and seniority-based wage systems were initiated.

This does not mean that women workers were not needed when Japanese-style management came into being. This is made clear by the journalist Yokoyama Gennosuke (1871–1915), who published the results of his survey of workers in Japan during the sudden rise of capitalism in *Japan's Lower Classes* (1899).[6] It was natural that women accounted for over 70 percent of the workers in spinning mills, an industry considered to be woman oriented, but even in the male-oriented ironworking industry women constituted over 60 percent of the workers.[7] Women workers were more numerous than male workers at the ironworks because they did supplemental, unskilled jobs (this was also true in glass factories, among others) while men supplied the skilled labor.

When Japanese-style management thus took hold in Japan at the same time as capitalism, during the Meiji period, women workers were placed outside the structure from the beginning. The lifetime employment system, which was designed to lure skilled workers to companies, as well as the seniority-based wage system, which was designed to keep them there, were ultimately directed only at male workers.

Before the war, the family system was an important pillar of Japanese society. Within that system, the important work required by women was to enter a household as a wife and produce children to ensure the continuity of the family. Women who married but could not produce children were unilaterally divorced by their husbands. According this status to women was a remnant of the warrior family system of the feudalistic Edo period. The status of women in the succeeding Meiji period was a natural extension of that system, which had as its principal textbook *The Great Learning for Women*, a Confucian manual of ethics that preached male dominance over women. During the Meiji period, when the policy of "increase production, promote industry" was being implemented, companies were concerned exclusively with male workers with technical skills. The view of women was that they really belonged in the home and worked only in exceptional cases, because of poverty.

After the war, men and women were guaranteed equal rights in the Constitution in the name of democracy, and during the high economic growth period Japanese-style management again became a fixture and gained worldwide renown. However, even at that time, it was virtually unheard of for women workers to be accorded a place of importance in the Japanese-style management system.

## WOMEN WORKERS AND THE REFORM OF THE LABOR STANDARDS LAW

As part of the postwar democratization, the Ministry of Labor was established in September 1947. Thus, whereas before the war labor policy had been handled by the Ministry of Welfare, now it was under the jurisdiction of a separate agency. Before that, on 5 April 1947, Law No. 49, the Labor Standards Law, which had been drafted at the Ministry of Welfare, went into effect. Chapter 6 of the Labor Standards Law deals with women and minors. The law takes the stance that women and minors require special consideration for health reasons and suggests that it is therefore the duty of a democratic state to "protect" them by establishing special provisions for them.[8]

The following items were included as the chief "protection provisions" for women. First, limits were placed on the amount of overtime work that could be done by women over eighteen years who worked 8 hours per day: They couldn't be made to work more than 2 hours of overtime per day, 6 hours per week, and 150 hours per year. Second, women could not be made to work on holidays. Third, women could not be made to do late-night work (between the hours of 10 PM and 5 AM). Fourth, women could not be made to work for six weeks before or six weeks after childbirth. And fifth, employers could not force a woman to work during menstruation if it presented a hardship for her to do so and if she requested menstrual leave.[9]

The 1947 Labor Standards Law incorporating these protection provisions for women remained in effect for nearly forty years, from its enactment, through Japan's high economic growth period in the 1960s, until the enactment of the Equal Employment Opportunity Law for Men and Women in April 1986. And, as will be discussed below, even after the establishment of the Equal Employment Opportunity Law, the protection provisions in the Labor Standards Law still have not been fully reconsidered primarily because of the strong views held by many women who feel that the position of all women workers should be protected by law.

The concepts of protection and equality are diametrically opposed. With the promulgation of the new Equal Employment Opportunity Law, there was a call for reform of the protection provisions in the Labor Standards Law. As a result, in April 1986, when the Equal Employment Opportunity Law was promulgated, the Labor Standards Law was also revised in the following ways. First, the provisions listed above regarding overtime work, work on holidays, and late-night work were declared not to apply to women in managerial positions and women who belonged to any of fourteen occupational categories determined to require specialized knowledge or technical skills.[10] Such women were to work on a basis of total equality with men.

As of 1990, 18.34 million women were employed in Japan. One percent of these women, or 180,000, were in managerial positions (7.2 percent of all men employed were in management). When the number of women and men managers are combined, women constitute 7.7 percent of the total.[11]

On the other hand, there are more women in positions requiring specialized knowledge or skills than in management: 13.8 percent of all women employed, or 2.53 million (11.3 percent of male employees fall into this category). However, if this calculation is restricted to the fourteen categories of women workers cited as exclusions to the Labor Standards Law protection provisions, the proportion of women in positions requiring specialized knowledge or skills would probably fall to fewer than 10 percent (there are no exact figures). Thus, fewer than 5 percent of all women employees work on a totally equal basis with men due to the enactment of the Equal Employment Opportunity Law, even including managers and those with specialized knowledge or technical skills.

The second reform in the Labor Standards Law brought about by the passage of the Equal Employment Opportunity Law involved preserving, for the time being and with a few minor changes, the protection provisions of the Labor Standards Law. The reasoning behind this was that the Japanese workplace is not presently set up in such a way that the vast majority of women can work on an equal basis with men.

The provision prohibiting more than 150 hours per year of overtime work was left unchanged, but the 2 hours per day and 6 hours per week limits were relaxed.[12] Although the overall total of 150 hours was left unchanged, it has now been made somewhat flexible in the case of exceptionally busy times in some occupations. The phrase "menstrual leave" was also removed from the protection provisions of the Labor Standards Law. However, a "measure concerning women for whom it is an extreme hardship to work during menstruation" was left in the law. In reality, women can still ask for menstrual leave, so from the point of view of the companies there has been no real change in this provision.[13]

Finally, a change was made in the maternity leave policy. Traditionally, if a woman so requested, a company had to allow her to take off at least six weeks before and after childbirth. The amount of leave allowed after childbirth was expanded to eight weeks. However, the law does not specify whether this leave is paid or unpaid. Most Japanese workers are enrolled in health insurance unions, and under Japan's national health insurance system workers are guaranteed 60 percent of their salary when they are on disability leave.[14] This reform in the maternity leave provision of the Labor Standards Law was justified on the grounds that, although the promotion of protection for mothers is exceptional, it is considered not to run counter to equality in employment or to the spirit of equality extolled in the Equal Employment Opportunity Law. As will be discussed below, the establishment of the Child Care Leave Law in May 1991, which allows women to return to the workplace, is similarly considered to be in keeping with the goal of achieving equality in employment. Thus, the protection provisions in the Labor Standards Law treating women workers as "different" from men remained in effect for forty years after World War II, and even in 1992, after the April 1986 passage of the Equal Employment Opportunity Law, they are still in existence.

It is undeniable that Japan lags significantly behind other industrialized nations in the area of equal opportunity in employment for women. This is undoubtedly because the surprising strength of the postwar Japanese economy depended on "Japanese-style management, the heart of which was a relatively homogeneous work force of young and middle-aged men that provided the only possible route to attain the needed level of efficiency."[15]

## THE PRESENT STATUS OF WOMEN WORKERS

Under Japanese-style management, the number of women workers has increased, but their economic status has improved little. The reasons for this will be examined below.

*The increase in married women workers*

During the period of high economic growth, the majority of women workers were unmarried. Referred to by a made-in-Japan English expression, "OL" (office lady), the majority of these women worked as assistants, pouring tea and doing a variety of other menial tasks. Under Japanese-style management, in which men were the principal workers, it was customary for OL's to quit work when they got married.

However, the period of high economic growth ended, and the latter half of the 1970s marked the beginning of a period of stable growth, and, as the number of service industries increased, married women assumed a growing importance in the work force. Some of the factors contributing to these developments included the growing predominance of the nuclear family and the accompanying decrease in the number of children per family, the decrease in the amount of time needed for housework due to the widespread availability of electrical appliances, the fact that the number of women seeking higher education had shown its first significant increase since after the war (when the number of men seeking higher education had begun to increase), and the widespread use of part-time labor. In 1990 married women constituted close to 60 percent of all women workers; in about 30 years the percentages of married and unmarried women workers had reversed themselves.

*Increase in part-time workers*

A structural change has taken place in the Japanese economy since the oil shocks. In particular, in the work force there was an increase in the number of irregular workers, whose terms of employment were easily adjustable, as opposed to regular workers. This trend manifested itself in the form of a greater increase in the number of women workers than in the number of men workers (the principal workers).

The proportion of women workers compared to men workers is about 60 percent, but in the fifteen years after 1975 the number of women workers increased about twice as much as did that of men. That increase, however, is attributable to an increase in the number of temporary workers. While the increase in temporary male workers was 42.6 percent during this period, the increase in temporary women workers was 253.0 percent, or more than two and a half times greater. In 1990 the number of temporary women workers had climbed to 5.01 million, or about 30 percent of all women workers. These temporary workers are made up of part-timers and seasonal employees. The overwhelming majority of temporary women workers are part-timers.

In the *Special Report on the Labor Force* of the Statistical Bureau of the Management and Coordination Agency, part-time workers are defined as "those considered by the company to be part-time workers."[16] According to this March 1991 survey, there were 4.91 million part-time women workers, of which the overwhelming majority, or 4.2 million (85.5 percent), were married. By age, 38.7 percent were between thirty-five and forty-four, and 31.4 percent were between forty-five and fifty-four, with those two age groups accounting for about 70 percent of the total. Most had returned to the workplace after raising children.

*Differences in wages*

As principal workers, men work under the lifetime employment system. The working pattern of women contrasts markedly with that of men: Most women stop working to marry and have children and return to work after raising their children (see Table 5-1, which illustrates this M-shaped pattern). For this reason, there is a large difference in the average wages earned by men and women.

Since the period of high economic growth, the differences have lessened. However, since the latter half of the 1980s, that is to say, since the enactment of the Equal Employment Opportunity Law, there has been no significant decrease in the differences in wages. Koike Kazuo presents evidence that, he asserts, illuminates the reasons for wage differences by sex.[17] His data are in the form of an international survey of wage differences between men and women in four countries: Japan, France, West Germany, and England. The survey, which was done in 1972, 1973, and 1975, was limited to the manufacturing sector, which he separates into two occupational divisions: production workers and white-collar workers. In both categories, the difference in wages in Japan is the greatest. Koike makes two points regarding this. One is that there is a difference in wages not only in Japan but in all countries. The other is that Japan's disparity occurs particularly among workers above age thirty and is a result of the seniority-based wages received by Japan's male workers. To explain this last point, we must consider the wages earned by men and women according to years of service. Men's wages clearly fall into a pattern based on seniority. On the other hand, women's wages show a seniority curve until around age thirty, but thereafter, even if their years of service increase, there is no clear ascent of the curve.

### Part-time workers' wages

Part-time workers are usually paid on an hourly basis. Koike says that "part-time wages in Japan do not appear to be particularly low." [18] He bases this on a comparison of the hourly wages of part-timers and regular employees. In companies with over one thousand workers, part-timers earn only 70 percent as much as regular workers, but in companies with between ten and ninety employees, they are paid 90 percent as much. However, Japanese workers receive a bonus in addition to their salaries, and the fact that this causes a significant disparity in the wages earned by regular and nonregular workers must not be overlooked.

In 1990, part-time women workers worked 6 hours per day, or 1.5 hours less than their regular-employee counterparts, who worked 7.5 hours per day (including overtime). There has been absolutely no change in these figures over the past twenty years. The number of days worked per month by part-timers (22) has also shown no change over twenty years; regular workers averaged less (20.7 days), and this figure has been decreasing over time. At 712 yen per hour, part-timers earned 60 percent of the regular workers' hourly rate of 1,181 yen. Part-time women workers received only 15 percent as large an average annual bonus as regular workers, 86,500 yen compared to 567,100.[19] Thus, misinterpretation is inevitable if comparisons are made between Japan and Europe using only hourly wage rates as a basis. These workers are called part-timers, but their daily working hours are only one to two hours shorter than those of full-time employees, and their total monthly hours are longer. And yet, the fact that they have a different status from regular workers is evident in their low bonuses, which create a large disparity in their annual earnings. Under these conditions, companies stand to save a lot in personnel costs by using part-time workers. Two part-time workers can work in the place of one regular worker.[20]

Japanese part-timers aren't distinguished merely by their shorter work hours, as are European. Another by-product of Japanese-style management is that the logic of "the traditional family" applies in the workplace." [21] There is a big difference in the amount of an employee's bonus according to whether that employee is member of the family, that is, a regular employee. A distinction is thus made between "family members" and "outsiders," and part-time workers are outsiders. Although part-time workers are also supposed to be covered by the Labor Standards Law, they have not been made a part of employment policies to date.

## THE EQUAL EMPLOYMENT OPPORTUNITY LAW:
## LIMITATIONS AND PROBLEMS

Although the Japanese workplace is very gradually becoming accustomed to the Equal Employment Opportunity Law, enacted on 1 April 1986, there is still not much evidence of its having had the effect of advancing the cause of women's equality with men. The biggest reason for this is that although the law states that when a company employs a woman it cannot discriminate against her, this provision has met with great opposition from companies, thus rendering the law incomplete.

It is not the "prohibited" provisions of the law that companies oppose so strongly; rather, they have contested the "endeavor" provisions, which contain sections on recruiting, hiring, assignment, and promotion. These matters indisputably form the core of a personnel management system that overemphasizes men, a system that is, in turn, the core of the Japanese-style management system. It is probably only natural that companies resist the idea of treating men and women equally in these four areas. The climate is simply not right for Japanese companies to reach a consensus on giving entirely equal treatment to men and women in these four areas; such an action would shake the very foundations of Japanese-style employment customs.

On the other hand, the "prohibited" provisions included in the law relate to discrimination against women in such areas as retirement, resignation, dismissal, welfare, and education and training. Even before the promulgation of the Equal Employment Opportunity Law, discrimination in these areas (particularly discriminatory retirement practices) had been prosecuted in court cases, and rights had been won by women on the grounds that such discrimination is in violation of "public order and good morals" as defined in Article 90 of the civil code. So the companies concluded that there was already a kind of national consensus on these "prohibited" provisions that sex discrimination was illegal.

Still, the Equal Employment Opportunity Law had a great impact on companies. Previously, Japanese-style management did not have the concept of equality between the sexes. But from this point onward, companies had to incorporate the concept into their operations. So they groped for a way to incorporate women without making any changes in the efficient system centered on young men and men in the prime of life that traditional Japanese-style management had always maintained.

As a result, the system of separate personnel tracks that had always existed in Japan was reexamined and put back into practice. The "acid test" for determining track assignments consisted of a series of questions asked of women when they were hired, such as, Do you aspire to a management job? Will you accept a transfer? and Will you continue to work after marriage. Women who replied that they would work as men did were hired as managerial workers and treated like men. Women who said that they would be satisfied with the traditional role of assistant were hired as menial workers and were thus assigned to a different track from the time of their entrance into the company.

Recently, however, some have suggested that this division into two tracks at the time of hiring is problematic, and so there is now a tendency to allow a transfer from menial work to managerial work after the employee has joined the company. In addition, an increasing number of companies have created a third, intermediate track; namely, professional work (managerial workers who don't have to accept transfers).

However, the companies adopting the track system have tended to be only the larger companies, and the type of industries adopting it have generally been only the finance and insurance industries. Since a large proportion of women tend to work in small and medium-sized companies, it is clear that adopting a track system of employment has been the response of Japanese-style management, which centers on the large companies.[22] According to one survey, even in the finance and insurance industries, which have a high rate of adoption of the track system of personnel management, only 3.7 percent of women employees were professional workers.[23]

## WOMEN MANAGERS UNDER THE EQUAL EMPLOYMENT OPPORTUNITY LAW

How effective has the Equal Employment Opportunity Law been in improving the use made of women workers? We will consider this point by examining the statistics available on women managers. The only major survey of women managers was done in November 1989 by the Japan Institute of Women's Employment.[24] Although its results could be considered predictable, they nevertheless elicited many cries of surprise. Of the companies surveyed, 75 percent had no women managers (women holding the position of section chief and above). Of women managers, 79.6 percent were age forty and above, and 59.3

percent were not married. One-third of the 34.3 percent who were married were childless. Fully 70 percent of those who were married with children said, "The children are being taken care of by my parents."

The findings of three 1990 surveys regarding women managers conducted by various Japanese government agencies can be summarized as follows. Women managers constitute only 1 percent of women workers (male managers constitute 7.2 percent of male workers). But when the study is limited to relatively large companies with more than one hundred employees, the percentage of men in managerial positions rises to 1 in 4, while the proportion of women remains at 1 percent. When you include small and medium-sized companies with more than thirty employees, however, the number of women in managerial positions rises to 9.6 percent. Thus, more progress in the area of promoting women to managerial positions has been made in small and medium-sized companies than in large companies. The reason is that aspects of the traditional Japanese-style management system such as seniority-based wages and a male-oriented promotion system are not as firmly entrenched in small and medium-sized companies, thus enabling them to promote their women workers to managerial positions more readily than do large companies. Thus, the differences between Japanese companies of different sizes are also apparent with regard to the promotion of women.

## THE LABOR SHORTAGE AND POLICIES REGARDING WOMEN WORKERS

In spite of the passage of the Equal Employment Opportunity Law, progress in its actual application to women workers seemed to be proceeding at a snail's pace. But beginning in the early 1990s, the winds of change began to blow. This is because a labor shortage has become a major concern for companies, and illegal alien workers became a major social problem in Japan. But the Japanese government, having observed the problems caused by alien workers in Europe and the United States, adopted the stance that as a rule foreign workers would not be permitted in Japan. Then the government unveiled a strategy to cope with the labor shortage by making use of women and older people who were not employed but would like to be.

In the midst of this initiative, the Child Care Leave Law was proposed to deal with the problem of child raising, which was making it difficult for married women to continue to work. It was passed readily in May 1991 and went into effect in April 1992. The underlying purpose was of the law was to use women workers to cope with the labor shortage. Moreover, it was also intended to somehow put a stop to the continuing decline in the birth rate (in 1992 the fertility rate was 1.5). As of 1990, however, only 21.9 percent of companies with over thirty employees had put into effect a system of child-care leave. Since the Child Care Leave Law does not guarantee pay during the leave, many are dubious about the extent to which it will be used.[25]

In July 1991, when the labor shortage became particularly severe, an administrative inspection by the Management and Coordination Agency resulted in a call for "a reexamination of the women protection provisions in the Labor Standards Law."[26] As mentioned in the previous section, for the companies who were trying to put women workers to use due to the labor shortage, the protection provisions presented a notable obstacle, and thus this initiative by the government was in response to the companies' demand for the immediate relaxation of the restrictions. There had been furious debate about the relaxing of the women protection provisions of the Labor Standards Law after the Equal Employment Opportunity Law was established.

On the other hand, to encourage women's participation in the labor force, the Ministry of Labor announced that the women protection provisions in the Labor Standards Law would be abolished in 1994.[27] The official position can be found in a statement by the Advisory Committee on Policy for Women Workers (March 1992) of the Ministry of Labor: "Hasn't the time come for us to grasp the trends in working conditions for all workers and test a new vision that includes setting up a legal framework that is the same for both men and women by abolishing restrictions on work hours and late-night work?"[28]

Seeking equality of the sexes while leaving in place the women protection provisions of forty years earlier would certainly impede the opening of the door to women. Some Japanese feminists have strongly opposed the abolition of the protection for women workers in the Labor Standards Law, however. If the "protection" for women workers in the Labor Standards Law is to be reformed completely, the "endeavor" provisions should be changed to "prohibited" provisions in the Equal Employment Opportunity Law. The fact that the statement from the Advisory Committee on Policy for Women Workers (1992) didn't touch on that issue is cause for concern.

## WOMEN WORKERS AND THE TAX SYSTEM

Due to the labor shortage, it has finally begun to seem that expectations regarding an improvement in the status of women workers might actually be met. However, simply passing an Equal Employment Opportunity Law and a Child Care Leave Law is not enough to bring about a true expansion of the role of women workers. One additional major government policy initiative is needed to bring this about, that is, the casting off of Japanese-style management. The only way to do that is to shift women workers from their role as assistants to a role as principal workers. Until the following statement by the Ministry of Labor's Employment Policy Research Committee (1992), however, the government had never expressed the view that women should be principal workers: "From this point onward, the demonstration of women's desire and ability to work will be more crucial than ever to the maintenance of the vigor of society as a whole. Thus, we need to examine more closely the relationship between women workers and the tax and pension systems with the goal of enabling women to assume the status of *principal workers* in our society" (emphasis added).[29]

This statement reflects the fact that Japan's tax system hinders women from becoming principal workers. Japan's tax system is based on tax assessment of individuals. If the head of household has a dependent family or spouse, they are exempt from tax as long as their annual income is less than 1 million yen (a salary income exemption of 650,000 yen and a basic exemption of 350,000 yen). If their income exceeds the limit, they must pay income tax and social insurance fees. In addition, the head of household's (husband's) tax liability increases because he no longer receives the spouse exemption that had hitherto been subtracted from his income. Moreover, many companies independently pay a special spouse allowance (10,000 yen on average), so the husband's income is reduced by that amount as well.

Under a system of taxing workers based on the assumption that the head of household will work outside the home and the spouse will take care of the household, a husband and wife will maximize their joint income if the spouse works but stays within the maximum earnings allowed under the dependent family member exemption clause (that is, within the amount allowed so that the spouse exemption can still be received). Thus, it is clear from many surveys that the wages earned by working housewives have been affected by the 1 million yen spouse exemption ceiling.[30]

This phenomenon is not restricted to the tax system. It is also true of other social-security programs, such as the pension system. When both members of a couple work, they each contribute individually to the pension fund, but when the husband works and the wife stays home no contribution is required of her, thus creating a seemingly unfair relationship between contributions and benefits.

A tax system with this type of spouse exemption has the ultimate effect of reducing the opportunities for real employment for women. If further increases in the number of married women workers are anticipated, radical reforms are needed in the tax and social-security systems on which Japan's economy is based, converting them from being family centered to being individual centered.

Until now, policies to promote working by women have centered on aspects of labor administration that affect women workers directly, such as the establishment of day-care centers, a rehiring system, and a child-care leave system. Only a very small number have called for reforms of economic policies, suggesting that women be given the status of principal workers and questioning the structure of the tax system and the social-welfare system.

But there are finally some signs of change in this area as well. In the 1992 edition of the *White Paper on Labor Relations*, the Japan Productivity Center, an organization (supported in part by the Ministry of International Trade and Industry) that researches the traditional pattern of labor participation, suggested for the first time that women be made principal employees and the tax system be reformed.[31] This is a truly epoch-making development.

In 1993, however, Japan entered a period of economic recession, and in response many companies initiated reductions of their professional staffs, beginning with their women employees. Women graduating from college that year faced a nearly impenetrable job market, one that didn't appear to reflect the passage of the Equal Employment Opportunity Law of 1986. As mentioned earlier, that law does not in fact prohibit differential treatment of women with respect to recruiting, hiring, assignment, and promotion; it contains only "endeavor" provisions. With the recession and consequent decrease in the number of new positions, instances of male employees and male candidates for employment receiving preferential treatment have become more prevalent than ever. It thus appears that Japanese companies are not yet prepared to accept women workers into their system. Despite the recession of the early to mid-1990s, a labor shortage is anticipated to intensify in Japan in the twenty-first century: Can Japan really remain competitive in the world economy without fully utilizing the capabilities of its women workers?

## NOTES

1. Employment Policy Research Committee, Occupation Stabilization Bureau, Ministry of Labor, *Rodoryoku jukyu no tembo to Kadai* (1992).
2. As of 1992, the results of the 1990 state of the nation survey had not yet

been completely tabulated, so for Table 1 I took the figures for that year from the Management and Coordination Agency's 1990 *Annual Survey of the Labor Force.*

3. See James C. Abegglen, *The Japanese Factory* (Glencoe, Ill.: Free Press, 1958).

4. Tominaga Ken'ichi, *Nihon no kindaika to shakai hendo* (Modernization and Social Change in Japan) (Tokyo: Kodansha Gakujutsu Bunko, 1990), 325.

5. See Wada Ei, *Tomioka nikki* (Tomioka Diary) (Tokyo: Chukō Bunko, 1978).

6. Yokoyama Gennosuke, *Nihon no kaso shakai* (Japan's Lower Classes) (Tokyo: Iwanami Bunko, 1899).

7. *Ibid.*, 202.

8. Matsumoto Iwakichi, *Rodo Kijun Hō ga yo ni deru made* (Before the Enactment of the Labor Standards Law) (Tokyo: Rōmu Gyōsei Kenkyūjo, 1981), 340.

9. Matsumoto, *Rodo Kijun Hō ga yo ni deru made*, 239, summarizes the factors leading to the incorporation into the Labor Standards Law of menstrual leave, Japan's unique form of women's protection (no similar clause can be found in the labor laws in existence at that time in other countries), as follows: (1) When the prewar Factory Law went into effect, it was observed that women workers in certain types of jobs were not able to function properly during menstruation, and the opinion was advanced that some provision needed to be made for this; (2) There was a precedent for this because similarly, during the war, when students were mobilized and girls from good homes were made to work in munitions factories as part of the girls' volunteer corps, they were given menstrual leave; and (3) The first problem that arose regarding postwar protection of laborers related to the banning of women miners (March 1946) by GHQ. A controversy arose in reaction to this, with some opposing the ban on the grounds that Japan needed women workers in the mines to aid in the revival of the economy. At that time, a provision stating that "until the ban on women miners takes effect, such workers wil be guaranteed menstrual leave" was inserted. Thus it was that as a result of all these precedents, a menstrual leave provision that had no counterpart in the laws of other countries found its way into postwar Japan's Labor Standards Law.

10. "Managerial positions" are defined as positions at the head of the smallest organizational unit formed to accomplish a task (there must be more than one person under the head) or positions in which people have a higher job status than others and issue orders. This usually means people in the position of section chief or higher. The fourteen specialized occupations are certified public accountant, doctor, dentist, veterinarian, lawyer, level 1 architect, pharmacist, real estate appraiser, researcher, systems engineer, newspaper reporter or editor, correspondent, designer, and producer or director.

11. Management and Coordination Agency, *Annual Survey of the Labor Force* (1990).

12. In industrial work (manufacturing, mining, construction, shipping, freight, and electricity and gas), the maximum overtime permitted was 6 hours per week, and

working on holidays was prohibited. In the agricultural, forestry, and marine-products industries, there were no restrictions whatsoever (including the 150-hour annual overtime restriction). In nonindustrial work (except the above-mentioned categories), the maximum overtime permitted in the hotel, restaurant, and service industries was 12 hours every 2 weeks, with others restricted to a maximum of 24 hours every 4 weeks. Work on holidays by the former was prohibited, while the latter were allowed to work on 1 holiday every 4 weeks.

13. This change came about as follows. Up to this time, under the Labor Standards Law women were allowed to request menstrual leave if "the work was injurious to their physiology," regardless of "whether or not the work presented a hardship." With the reforms, however, "a woman cannot be made to work during menstruation if doing so represents an extraordinary hardship for her and if she has requested menstrual leave."

14. Under national health insurance, if a company has more than five employees (in the case of juridical persons, more than one employee), it must be enrolled in the system. Under the Labor Standards Law, it was decided that maternity leave "would not be treated in the same way as absence from work."

15. Japan Productivity Center, 1992 nempan roshi kankei hakusho (White Paper on Labor Relations) (Tokyo: Japan Productivity Center, 1992), 107.

16. Statistical Bureau, Management and Coordination Agency, Rodoryoku tokubetsu hokoku (Special Survey of the Labor Force) (Tokyo: Ministry of Finance Printing Bureau, March 1991).

17. See Koike Kazuo, Shigoto no keizaigaku (The Economics of Work) (Tokyo: Toyo Keizai Shimpōsha, 1991), 142.

18. Ibid., 158.

19. Ministry of Labor, Basic Survey of the Wage Structure (Tokyo: Ministry of Finance Printing Bureau, 1990).

20. If you use the 1990 Basic Survey of the Wage Structure to calculate the annual income of part-time and regular women workers, the results are as follows. Part-time workers earn a total of 1.18 million yen (712 yen/hour × 5.9 hours/day × 21.7 days/ month × 12 months/year plus a bonus of 86,500). Regular women workers earn 2.8 million yen (average monthly salary of 186,100 yen × 12 months/year plus a bonus of 567,100). Thus part-time workers earn 42 percent as much as regular workers. See also Shinotsuka Eiko, Nihon no joshi rodo (Japan's Women Workers) (Tokyo: Toyo Keizai Shimposha, 1982).

21. Mito Tadashi, Ie no ronri 1, 2 (The Logic of the Ie [Household]) (Tokyo: Bunshindō, 1991).

22. As of 1990, women workers (other than in agriculture and forestry) totaled 18.23 million, with 37 percent employed by companies with 1 to 29 employees. Therefore, about half were employed by companies with fewer than 100 employees. By contrast, of the 29.84 million male employees, 30.6 percent were employed by com-

panies with 1 to 29 employees and 15.6 percent were employed by companies with 30 to 99 employees.

23. According to a September 1987 survey done by the Japan Institute of Women's Employment and published in the *Report of the Committee for Research on Separate Track Employment Practices* (June 1991), only 3.7 percent of 55,600 women employees were professional workers in 148 banking, insurance, security, and trading companies listed on the first and second sections of the Tokyo, Nagoya, and Osaka stock exchanges. Of the companies' 820,000 male employees, 99.0 percent were professional workers.

24. Japan Institute of Women's Employment, *Report of the Results of the Survey of Women Managers*, April 1990. This was a 1 November 1989 survey of women managers (437 women at 818 companies with the title of section chief or above). A total of 2,027 companies listed on the Tokyo, Osaka, and Nagoya stock exchanges were surveyed.

25. Child-care leave may be taken by either the mother or the father. But because the mother usually earns less money, under the system established by the Child-Care Leave Law, in which payment of salary while on leave is not guaranteed, it is usual for the mother to go on leave. Although the spirit of the law intends to do away with occupational sex roles, there is a strong danger that the lack of a guarantee of salary payment while on leave will result in an even greater tendency for women to take the role of exclusive child rearer.

26. Rengo (Japan Trade Union Confederation), *1993 Women's Activity Survey* (Tokyo: Rengo, 1993), 178–89.

27. *Nihon keizai shimbun*, 1 June 1992, morning edition.

28. Advisory Committee on Policy for Women Workers, Women's Bureau, Ministry of Labor, *Joshi rodo no doko to kongo no seisaku kadai* (Trends in Women's Labor and Future Policy Viewpoints), March 1992, 15.

29. Employment Policy Research Committee, *Rodoryoku jukyu no tembo to kadai*, 19.

30. Ministry of Labor, *General Survey of Part-Time Workers* (1990); Japan Institute of Labor, *Research Survey on Part-Time Labor* (1989); and Labor and Economy Department, City of Tokyo, *Research on Part-Time Workers and Survey of Workers' and Employers' Consciousnesses* (1990).

31. Japan Productivity Center, *1992 nemban roshi kankei hakusho* (1992), 123–25.

# 6

## Obstacles and Opportunities: Women and Political Participation in Japan

### KIMIKO KUBO *and* JOYCE GELB

---

AT first blush, women in Japanese politics have made great progress in recent years. The Lower House election of July 1993 particularly seemed to bring positive results for Japanese women. After a new coalition government took power, three women were appointed to the cabinet by Prime Minister Hosokawa, the first time that such a large number served simultaneously. There have been six female cabinet appointees since 1960, although three served only briefly. Hosokawa also appointed the first woman, Hisako Takahashi, to the fifteen person Supreme Court. During the last decade, as well, Japan for the first time had a woman, Takako Doi, as chair of a major political party (the Socialist party, JSP, from 1986 to 1991). Takako Doi was later named speaker of the Lower House by the reform coalition in 1993. The number of women members elected to the Diet and particularly to municipal level legislative positions increased rapidly, especially when compared to a decade before. Women have won two mayoralties and three women have been appointed as prefectural lieutenant governors. The voting rates of women exceed those of men.

Yet, despite this apparent and in some ways real progress made by women, their political consciousness and representation in the political decision-making process is still very low in comparison with many other industrialized, democratic nations. According to a survey conducted by the Interparliamentary Union in Geneva in June 1991, Japan ranked lowest among industrialized nations (in 110th position) with regard to national parliamentary representation in the Lower House.[1]

Although Japanese women have never equaled their all-time record, set

120

in 1946, of thirty-nine women (8 percent) in the Lower House,[2] activism and efforts to gain empowerment have continued at all levels of politics.[3]

After providing a brief introduction of the history of women's suffrage in Japan, we will assess the role of women in politics at the national and local levels. We will analyze the reasons for low representation by women in elective politics. Efforts to increase the representation of women in politics will be evaluated. We will provide a brief portrait of the role women who have been elected at the local and national levels play in their respective legislatures. Finally, our conclusion will provide a look at the future possibilities for women in politics in Japan, at both legislative and executive levels, particularly in the light of the 1993 reform coalition victory in the Lower House elections.

Our analysis focuses on the role of women in politics within two contexts: first, that of Japanese culture, and second, the obstacles erected by the complex political system. Japanese culture tends to mitigate constitutional guarantees of gender equality by emphasizing women's roles as wives and mothers. Despite Japan's formally democratic system and its emphasis on high voting participation by women as well as men, women are often thought to be politically unaware and unsuitable for political office.[4] The political system has been based on the one-party dominance of the Liberal Democratic party (LDP), a weak opposition (though a variety of factors, to be discussed below, led to its takeover of the less-powerful Upper House in 1989 and the Lower House in 1993), and factionalism, both within parties and at the electoral-campaign level. The LDP's rural, conservative, corporate base has generally been inhospitable to women candidates. Under these circumstances, it is understandable that women have had limited success in gaining representation to both Houses.

Representation at the local level has not accurately reflected women's activism in community politics, although at the municipal level an increase has recently occurred. Prior to the early 1990s, women's local participation, primarily voluntary, in grassroots issue-oriented community groups was viewed as more compatible with home and motherhood than party and electoral politics. We will examine the extent to which this is changing.[5]

A landmark 1981 study of "political women in Japan" sought to investigate the sources of women's involvement in politics and the constraints they faced.[6] Pharr found that for most women political activism was viewed as unacceptable behavior and that its costs were extraordinarily high.[7] We will examine to what extent women's interest in electoral political activity will find increasing receptivity and result in greater representation in the political system.

This article is based primarily on former conditions that have affected women's political role in Japan. Significant changes appear to be occurring with regard to partisan politics and the system of electoral representation utilized. At the time of this writing, no one can predict the outcome, given the uncertainties regarding the future of the reform governing coalition, enduring partisan realignments, changing leadership patterns, and the specific type of electoral system to be institutionalized. Assessment of the role of women in politics is made even more challenging by uncertainty regarding the shape and structure of Japanese politics toward the close of the twentieth century.

A BRIEF HISTORY OF WOMEN'S SUFFRAGE

The movement to win suffrage for Japanese women began in 1878. In that year, a woman, the breadwinner of a household, Kita Kusunose, filed a request to vote with a prefectural government. This action, part of a larger movement to gain equal rights for women, gained momentum and was known as *Jiyu-minken Undo*.[8]

But the movement soon hit a snag. In 1889 the Japanese Constitution was promulgated and, as the electoral system took shape, women's political activities were banned across the board by Article 5 of the Peace Preservation Law. In 1905 women socialists began a movement to appeal for revision of the Public Order and Police Law, which prevented women's political organization and participation. But the movement did not succeed. In 1919 women activists, including Raicho Hiratsuka and Fusae Ichikawa, organized the New Women's Association, the first organized women's movement in Japan. (Even before this, in 1870, Hideko Fukuda was speaking out for women's equality and independence as part of the Democratic Rights Movement.) Ichikawa and others stepped up their activities to seek revision of the Public Order and Police Law and finally won freedom to take part in political rallies and debates in 1922.

In 1924, Ichikawa and Ochimi Kubushiro organized the Women's Suffrage League of Japan. It continued its activities until 1940, when it was forced to disband during World War II.

Japan surrendered in August 1945, and in December of that year women won suffrage for the first time. In the Lower House election of 1946, Japanese women exercised the franchise for the first time in history. A historic number of women ran for office and were elected. Thirty-nine women (8.4 percent) were elected to the Lower House. At this time, voters in some districts (depending on the size of the constituency) could write in the names of two candidates, perhaps explaining the relatively high representation of women. Apparently women voters, especially in many urban areas, were willing to cast one of their two or three votes for women candidates.[9] But in the following year, the election system was altered to medium-sized electoral districts, in which each voter cast a single vote for a single candidate, and only fifteen women were elected (3.2 percent). Under this latter system, because usually more than one candidate from each party ran for election in Lower House elections and also in 150 of those in the Upper House, competition for electoral support within the same district, within and between parties, has been extremely intense.

In 1946 the turnout of women voters was 67 percent, compared to 79 percent for men. This gap has steadily narrowed in the postwar period, so that today female voting participation is higher than that of men. The new constitution of November 1946 guaranteed equal rights, including suffrage, to men and women. Article 14 of the new constitution provided for the equality of all people under the law and for an end to discrimination in politics and social relations based on sex.

RECRUITMENT AND MOBILIZATION OF WOMEN AT
THE NATIONAL LEVEL: THE DIET

In 1993 there were fifty-two women members in the Parliament: thirty-seven (15.1 percent) in the Upper House and 14 (2.7 percent) in the Lower House (see Table 6-1 and Figures 6-1 and 6-2). The Japanese Diet is divided into two Houses: the more-powerful House of Representatives (Lower House) and House of Councillors (Upper House). Prior to the reform era that began in 1993, the term of office for Lower House members was four years and the number of seats was 511. In the postwar period there have been five major parties in Japan, including the dominant Liberal Democratic party (LDP), Socialist party (now called the Social Democratic party of Japan, or SDPJ; formerly JSP, Japan Socialist party), Komei party (associated with the Buddhist movement Soka Gakkai), the Communist party (JCP), and Democratic Socialist party (DSP). Recently, Rengo, a trade-union coalition (now known as the Democratic Reform party) backed candidates for election. In 1992, the New Japan party (JNP) was formed in order to challenge the dominance of the LDP, and in 1993 defectors from the LDP formed two additional new parties. Their ostensible goal was reform of the political system, and a "reform" coalition comprised of seven parties was victorious in 1993.

The Upper House has 252 seats. From 1983 until 1994, 100 have been elected through proportional nationwide representation (in effect meaning a vote for a party, not an individual) and 152 elected in prefecture-wide multi-member constituencies. During this period, the term of office was six years, with half of the members elected every three years. Each voter elected one rep-

TABLE 6-1  *Number of Women Members of the Diet, August 1993*

| Party | Upper House (Total members-252) | Lower House (Total members-511[1]) | Total (Total members-763) |
|---|---|---|---|
| LDP | 7 | 2[2] | 9 |
| SDPJ | 18 | 3 | 21 |
| Komeito | 5 | 2 | 7 |
| JNP | 1 | 2 | 3 |
| JCP | 4 | 2 | 6 |
| DRP[3] | 2 | 0 | 2 |
| Indep. | 1 | 3 | 4 |
| Total | 38 | 14 | 52 |
| (%) | 15.1 | 2.7 | 6.8 |

[1]Total number of seats for the Lower House were 512.

[2]As a result of the 1993 Lower House election, only one LDP woman (who had the LDP's official endorsement) was elected. After the election, another woman who had run as an independent joined the LDP.

[3]The former name of DRP (Democratic Reform party) is Rengo-Sangiin.

SOURCE: Information collected by Kimiko Kubo, Fusae Ichikawa Memorial Association. Some of this material appeared in a somewhat different version in the semiannual *Japanese Women*, published by the Ichikawa Association (Tokyo: 1990–1994).

resentative to the Lower House and selected one Upper House representative in prefecture-wide elections. The electoral system of multimember districts (three to five representatives per district) for the Lower House, coupled with a single nontransferable vote for each voter, contributed to factional divisions within the parties and a candidate-oriented campaign process. Factions channel patronage and financial support to their members.[10]

In the Lower House, the number of elected women in 1994 was 2.7 percent, far below the 1946 cited above. Since that time, women's representation has hovered between 1.2 percent and 3.2 percent. In 1990 the number of women candidates was sixty-six and they accounted for just 6.9 percent of all candidates. The LDP had only one woman candidate, as did the DSP; the Socialist party, eight; and the Communist party, twenty-nine. Other parties and independent candidates accounted for twenty-six.[11] Twelve women were elected: nine represented the JSP; two, the Communist party; and one, the Komei party. From 1980 to 1993 the LDP, the ruling party, did not have a single woman in the Lower House. In 1993, two LDP women candidates were victorious (one independent joined the LDP after the election). In that year, more women ran as candidates (7.3 percent) and two more were elected to the

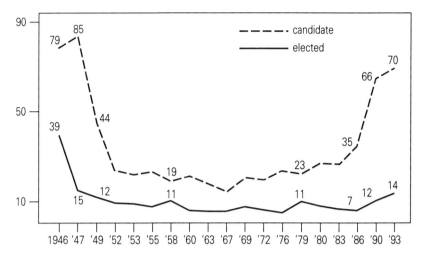

FIGURE 6-1  *The Number of Women Candidates and Women Elected (Lower House Elections, 1946–1993)*

SOURCE: Information collected by Kimiko Kubo, Fusae Ichikawa Memorial Association. Some of this material appeared in a somewhat different version in the semiannual *Japanese Women*, published by the Ichikawa Association (Tokyo: 1990–1994).

Lower House. Both LDP women came from politically prominent dynasties. Particularly noteworthy was the election of Makiko Tanaka, daughter of the former prime minister whose corrupt practices helped to cause voter cynicism regarding the government, whose husband also served as an LDP member of the Diet. But as a political "insider" whose campaign issues and style were unusually outspoken, she appeared to represent a new kind of woman politician in Japan.

The LDP especially has tended to give priority to incumbents in making nominations; most of its members are personal supporters of Diet members, making it difficult for women to gain influential party posts. The obstacles to victory for women seeking Lower House office remain significant and the strong showing of 1946 has never been repeated.

As suggested above, the Upper House elected over one hundred candidates by proportional representation from the nation at large from 1983 to 1994. Under this system, the position of the candidate on the party list determines the vote; actually, it is the party that is being selected. The LDP, in particular, has created almost insuperable barriers for women to run for office and to be ranked highly in this system (although all parties in Japan

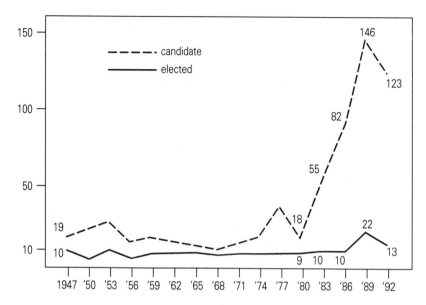

FIGURE 6-2 *Number of Women Candidates and Women Elected (Upper House Elections, 1947–1992)*

SOURCE: Information collected by Kimiko Kubo, Fusae Ichikawa Memorial Association. Some of this material appeared in a somewhat different version in the semiannual *Japanese Women*, published by the Ichikawa Association (Tokyo: 1990–1994).

have similar policies). In 1986 the LDP set onerous obstacles for inclusion on the party list: recruitment of at least two thousand new party members (paying dues of 4,000 yen each); submission of a list of supporters numbering at least one million group supporters (*Koenkai*) to LDP; and holding of at least two public meetings in each of the forty-seven prefectures.[12]

Nonetheless, LDP women have gained office most significantly through the proportional representation system, and generally they have endorsed more women running for the Upper than the Lower House, especially since the replacement of candidate-based elections by proportional representation in the 1980s. In most elections the LDP and other parties have tended to recruit publicly known figures (entertainers, television personalities, and the like), and representatives of large organizations. If placed high on the party list, they have been able to gain victory.

In 1947 the first Upper House election was held and ten women (4 percent of the total) were elected, two from local districts and eight from the national constituencies. In 1989, twenty-two women were elected to office, including six former office holders who were reelected, the highest number ever (17.5 percent). They included ten from local districts and twelve through the proportional representation system.[13] Women candidates were 22 percent of the total of 146, far more than the usual 3 to 16 percent.

The 1989 election was unusual due to the importance of several issues, including the 3 percent consumption tax, the "Recruit" scandal (related to corporate bribery of electoral officials), the prime minister's "sex scandal," and the involvement of Takako Doi as the first female head of a Japanese political party (the Socialist party). Increased political awareness appeared to herald a new era for women in national politics in Japan (the so-called "Madonna" boom).[14] The Socialist party alone put forth twelve women candidates, of whom eleven were elected.[15] It appears that consumer-related issues played a particularly important role capturing the interest of female candidates and voters.[16]

In July 1992, however, the number of female candidacies for the Upper House declined. One hundred twenty-three women ran for office and only thirteen were successful. Perhaps disillusionment set in when women candidates who promised tax and other reforms were unable to deliver. One successful candidate, lawyer Toshiko Hamayotsu of the Tokyo district, representing the Komei party, particularly sought women's votes by stressing educational and health-related issues in order to attract mothers and housewives.[17] Other women who were identified with the women's movement were elected on the Socialist party ticket through the proportional representation system, including attorney Masako Owaki and Sachiko Kawahashi (former director of the Office for Women's Affairs of the Prime Minister's Office and former division chief of the Women's Bureau of the Labor Ministry), and former assemblywoman Kimiko Kurihara, one of the rare women elected directly from the town level to the Diet (from the Hiroshima district). The latter's campaign emphasized peace issues, opposing the overseas deployment of Self-Defense Forces as part of the United Nations Peacekeeping Operation. The governing Liberal Democratic party put only a small number of women (four) on its national, proportional representation list and ranked them low on the party list, and the Socialist party fielded just five women candidates out of the total number nominated. (Out of twenty-seven candidates, the LDP ranked women at positions sixteen, twenty-one, twenty-three, and twenty-six, and only number sixteen was elected. The Socialist party ranked women at two, four, fifteen, twenty-one, and twenty-three out of twenty-five candidates, and only numbers two and four were elected.) In the Komei party, similar patterns were evident, illustrating the importance of position on the party list for victory in the proportional elections. The newly formed New Japan party (to be discussed further below) appeared to attempt to utilize women's candidacies in at least a symbolically significant way; with sixteen candidates, it ranked women at two, seven, eleven, twelve, fourteen, and fifteen. The number two ranked woman won one of the four seats this party captured in the 1992 Upper House elections.

As suggested above, in the 1970s and 1980s especially, the LDP and other parties selected women for the Upper House through the proportional representation system who were well-known actresses, television personalities, and entertainers, or women who had the support of large groups, such as the Japanese Nursing Association or Japanese Women's Pharmacists Association. Others have been supported by big corporations, have served as successors to their late husbands, and, since 1980, have been career bureaucrats. From the local districts, women representatives included a former director of the Women's Bureau of the Ministry of Labor, whose husband had been a long-time LDP politician, and an Olympic medalist.

Particularly in the case of the formerly dominant LDP, connections to party factions prove crucial in order to obtain an official endorsement and to get a high rank on the list. The LDP has consisted of six factions; each has had Diet representatives, each of whom have had their own supporter groups (*Koenkai*), including local assembly members in their own electoral district. So when seeking election to the Diet or local assembly on the LDP ticket, the first choice is which faction to approach for assistance. The factions have been operative when candidates are recruited, endorsed, ranked for the proportional representation system, and on all other political matters. As LDP has been managed by this system of factions, it is difficult for women to be regarded as potential candidates.

A good example of the power of factions occurred in the 1992 Upper House elections. Ms. Ritusko Nagao, former director of the Social Welfare Bureau's Health and Welfare Department, decided to run through the proportional representation system on the LDP ticket without support of any faction. As a result, she was ranked twenty-third (out of twenty-seven) on the party list and lost the election, at least partially due, it has been suggested, to her low ranking.

The Komei party, affiliated with the Nichiren Shoshu sect of Buddhism, has tended to recruit activists or executives of the Buddhist movement (Soka Gakkai). But especially since the adoption of proportional representation in the Upper House in 1983, the party has sought to change its image by recruiting scholars or international experts, some of whom were women who were not members of Soka Gakkai or the party. The Komei party appears to be trying to recruit more women candidates, and because of its strong organizational structure, women's chances for electoral victory may be enhanced. In the 1992 Upper House election, Toshiko Hamayotsu, a member of the Komei party, ran and was elected from the Tokyo district in which the party had a woman candidate after a thirty-year absence. Setsuko Takeda, member of the Komei party and chair of the Association of Working Women, which is affiliated with the party, was elected for the first time. Wakako Hironaka, an essayist (named director general of the Environmental Agency in the 1993 coalition cabinet), was asked to run as a nonparty member in 1983 and was elected twice through this system. The latter two women were elected through the proportional representation system.

The SDPJ is regarded as the labor-union dominated party. It, too, has factions that are based on its support groups, primarily unions. Since women were rarely promoted to executive posts within the union, they were rarely recognized as potential candidates. Similarly, few women were nominated to executive posts in the party itself. In recent years, union membership has been declining and as a result, in order to appeal to a broader constituency base, the SDPJ has tended to recruit more citizen-oriented candidates, including women. The party has even encouraged and supported the candidacies of women who are running as independents. Women nominees since the mid-1970s have included scholars, activists, lawyers, and journalists. In the 1993 Lower House election, the SDPJ vote declined precipitously as new opposition parties may have provided more promising alternatives to voters.

Ms. Doi, a constitutional scholar who was the head of the Socialist party from 1986 to 1991, although not initially associated with the women's movement, proved to be a force encouraging women, regardless of party and including independents, to run at all levels of the political process. It is possible that her impact in this regard was greatest at the local level, to which we now turn.

## RECRUITMENT AND MOBILIZATION OF WOMEN AT THE LOCAL LEVEL

In Japan local legislative government is divided into three tiers: town and village, city and ward, and prefecture. In the first postwar unified elections in 1947, 22 women (0.9 percent) were elected in the prefectural assemblies, 94 in the city and ward assemblies (1.2 percent), and 677 (0.4 percent) in the town and village assemblies. Little change has occurred since then. From 1951 to 1971, the number of Japanese women in local government dropped from almost one thousand to six hundred. The sharp drop is attributed to the reduction in the number of seats in town and village assemblies following enactment

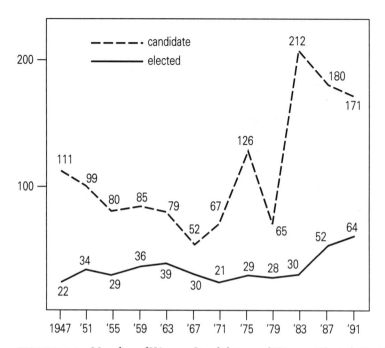

FIGURE 6-3  *Number of Women Candidates and Women Elected (Unified Local Elections, Prefectural Assembly, 1947–1991)*
SOURCE: Information collected by Kimiko Kubo, Fusae Ichikawa Memorial Association. Some of this material appeared in a somewhat different version in the semiannual *Japanese Women*, published by the Ichikawa Association (Tokyo: 1990–1994).

of a law in 1953 to promote the amalgamation of towns and villages. As of 1991 there were 82 (2.3 percent) women in prefectural assemblies, 1,157 (5.7 percent) in city and ward assemblies, and 791 (1.8 percent) in town and village assemblies. When we take a closer look, it was just after Doi's chairpersonship that female members in local assemblies rose, though still at a low rate. The total number of women in local assemblies increased to 2,030 (3.1 percent), up from 1,420 (2.1 percent) in 1987 (see Figures 6-3, 6-4, and 6-5).[18] In 1993 women did not represent a thick wall of representation, but rather only a few scattered dots. Some have suggested that one reason that more women are running for local assembly office is that fewer men are interested in the relatively small salary paid.[19] Conversely, for women accustomed to community level volunteer work for no pay, even a small salary is better than none.

Of the forty-seven prefectural assemblies, 34 (72.3 percent) have women

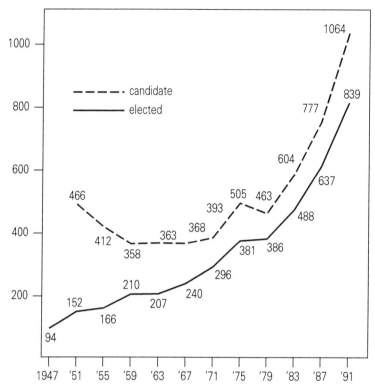

FIGURE 6-4    *Number of Women Candidates and Women Elected (Unified Local Elections, Municipal Assembly, 1947–1991)*
SOURCE: Information collected by Kimiko Kubo, Fusae Ichikawa Memorial Association. Some of this material appeared in a somewhat different version in the semiannual *Japanese Women*, published by the Ichikawa Association (Tokyo: 1990–1994), and the *Local Assemblies: Handbook of Data on Japanese Women in Political Life*, published by the Ichikawa Association (Tokyo, 1991).

members, and 17 of the 34 have only one woman member. At the city and ward level, 497 assemblies (73.2 percent) have women members, 208 (41.9 percent) have only one woman member, and 129 (26 percent) have two female representatives. This means that 70 percent of the city and ward assemblies have fewer than two women representatives. At the town and village level, where representation of women remains weakest, perhaps because this is the most rural and conservative tier, only 23.3 percent of assemblies have women members; 465 (77.4 percent) have only one woman. In small communities, people are tied very closely to traditional groupings and sex roles. Especially in

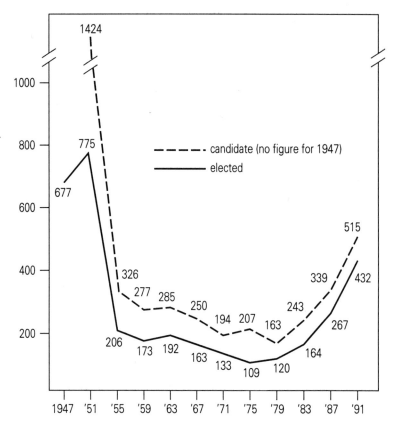

FIGURE 6-5   *Number of Women Candidates and Women Elected (Unified Local Elections, Town and Village Assembly, 1947–1991)*
SOURCE: Information collected by Kimiko Kubo, Fusae Ichikawa Memorial Association. Some of this material appeared in a somewhat different version in the semiannual *Japanese Women*, published by the Ichikawa Association (Tokyo: 1990–1994), and the *Local Assemblies: Handbook of Data on Japanese Women in Political Life* (Tokyo: Ichikawa Association, 1991).

the town, village, and small city assemblies, the post of assembly member has been regarded as an honorable post (*meiyoshoku*) that should be taken by the boss or leader of the community, such as the president of a neighborhood network, shop-owners group, and voluntary firefighters. They have been expected to have a pipeline to or network with the upper levels of the political system, including the prefecture, Diet, and national government in order to get subsidies and budget for their community. Women, excluded from these traditional networks and contacts, have had few opportunities to run and be elected. For example, women are the primary workers in agriculture (over 60 percent), but their membership in agricultural cooperatives (e.g., the National Federation of Agricultural Cooperative Associations) is still very low (12.1 percent). Their husbands, who work outside the community, are still official members of the cooperatives, thus denying women a local base of activism. Rural women have few avenues of access to community decision-making structures, which are among the major routes to local assemblies, unlike their urban counterparts. The highest number of women representatives are found in large metropolitan areas, with Tokyo having by far the largest representation (12.2 percent), followed by Kanagawa (7.9 percent), and Osaka (8.1 percent).[20] As of 1991, only one-third of assemblies in Japan had female representatives, and most of those had only one woman office holder.

### REASONS FOR LOW REPRESENTATION OF WOMEN

In Japan it is said that successful candidates need to have three *bans* in order to win elections: *ji-ban* (ground, organization), *kan-ban* (signboards, signifying being well known or having widespread popularity), and *ka-ban* (bag, money). It is not easy for Japanese women to obtain these three *bans*, as they face deep-rooted traditional stereotyped sex-role obstacles to active participation even before running for election. These exist both in terms of their traditional family roles and their roles in the political parties.

With regard to domestic roles, recent surveys have revealed that the average time Japanese men spend in domestic activity is only twenty-four minutes a day, so women must continue to play the dominant role as wife, mother, daughter-in-law, or daughter.[21] They are expected to be the care giver for their children and aged parents and in-laws. So, while they may have some time to participate in local activities, many women may feel it is very difficult to run for office and be a member of an assembly, which requires long hours of work.[22] As an example, one Tama City representative indicated that she spends four to five months per year attending assembly sessions and committee meetings, including study tours. Sessions sometimes run into late evening hours. Combined with the continuing role Assemblywoman Sumita is expected to play as community leader, this type of schedule may pose difficulties for young women with family responsibilities.[23]

The pull of traditional attitudes and values makes women hesitate to enter the political world; several interviewees indicated that their husbands were initially opposed to their entrance into elective politics.[24] Interviews conducted by the Ichikawa Association before the 1987 elections with five major political parties similarly confirmed that the families of female candidates sometimes oppose the idea of women running for political office. The average age for women in local political office in Japan is an advanced 50.4, indicating the continuing obstacles to office holding for mothers of young children in Japan.[25]

With regard to party attitudes, the proportion of women members in the major political parties varies from 6 percent to 44 percent, but they are not given opportunities to run for office as candidates. In contrast to some other countries, women's sections of party organizations play only a limited role in recruitment or access to decision making. Although the LDP and Komei party have the largest number of women members (40 percent and 44 percent, respectively, as compared to the JCP's 38 percent, SDPJ's 16 percent, and DSP's 6 percent), as we have suggested, this does not translate into nominations or political influence. Rather, they are expected to back up party activities and voter mobilization through preparing meals, making telephone calls, mailing campaign leaflets, and the like during campaigns for male candidates. So their contributions to the party are unfairly overlooked when recruitment for candidates is undertaken.

The numbers of women in the SDPJ have increased significantly, from 5,700 in 1985 to 19,449 in 1992 (the major increase came about in 1989–1990).[26] The SDPJ made special efforts to recruit member's wives as auxiliary members, with nonofficial status, reduced fee payments, and the right to vote to elect the chairperson and attend party conventions as observers. In 1987 women began to organize women's groups to support Doi at the prefectural level; in 1993 such groups existed in forty prefectures. At their peak, they included some thirty thousand members. Since Doi's resignation as party chair in 1991, however, the SDPJ appears to be losing women members and supporters, resulting in a decline in candidacies as well.

## ACTIVITIES OF WOMEN REPRESENTATIVES IN THE DIET

Despite their limited numbers, women members of the Diet helped to pass such legislation as the Equal Employment Opportunity Law in 1985 and the Parental Leave Act in 1991. Since its adoption they have tried to revise the Equal Employment Law, widely viewed as ineffective, and promulgate new laws regarding leave for care of the elderly. Eighty-four percent of those who care for their families are women, but only 14 percent of employers with more than three hundred employees as of 1990 provided leave for such care givers. The SDPJ, Komei party, and DSP have outlined a draft of a bill for "elder care." As of 1993 there is no agreement on how long, how often, for whom and whether it is to be paid or unpaid.

From the 1950s to the 1970s, the Diet Women's Association played an active role in the passage of the Prostitution Prevention Law, the enactment of the Inebriates Control Law, and action to prevent the closing down of the Women's and Minor's Bureau in the Department of Labor, among other issues. During this period, there were few women in the Diet, and they sought to impact women's policy by organizing a support group of women. Recently, however, as women's numbers have increased, the (former) opposition parties in particular began to compete with each other concerning women's issues. Gender based cross-party coalitions have been difficult in a system that insists on strict loyalty to party policy. Hence, women may be more likely to be active on women's issues within their own party. A second group, the Diet Members Association (with both male and female support), was formed in 1978 during the UN Decade for Women. While it still exists, it is not so active today, partially because of a lack of leadership. Strong leaders like Fusae Ichikawa (independent) and Sumiko Tanaka (JSP) left the Diet in the early 1980s. But in 1990 the Earth Environmental Protection Diet Women's Group, in which forty-one women members from all parties participated, was established. This group submitted a declaration and appeal to the prime minister regarding environmental concerns. They have also lobbied for reform of Diet procedures. So, single-issue networks sponsored by women are organized from time to time, although today they may be less oriented specifically to women's interests than before.

During the 120th session of the Diet, from January to June 1992, the thirty-five Diet women in the Upper House took part in such standing committees as Education, Labor, Health and Welfare, and Audit and the Committee on the Budget. They attended 90.9 percent of all committee hearings to which they belonged as members. In the Lower House, they attended 86.7 percent of committee meetings.[27] Though women from all parties attended committee sessions equally, members of the LDP spoke least often at them.

Women Diet members questioned and commented regarding the enactment of a care-giving leave law, part-time workers protection law, review of revision of the Equal Employment Opportunity Law, sex discrimination in wages and promotions in national universities, ratification of aspects of the ILO convention dealing with discrimination in the labor force, and sex discrimination in the Imperial House Law (which bars women from being emperor). In addition, Diet women have asked the government to set up an agency in the Diet to investigate the "comfort women" of Korea and other countries who were forced into prostitution for Japanese soldiers during World War II. They have worked together with women's groups in publicizing what has become a major political issue.

## EFFORTS TO INCREASE WOMEN'S REPRESENTATION IN LOCAL GOVERNMENT

Since 1985, International Women's Year (IWY), when women were encouraged to enter fields on a basis equal to that of men, the representation of women running for both local office and the national Diet has increased gradually. During the International Decade for Women (1976–1985), an IWY Liaison Group was formed to carry out the goals of the IWY, which included a larger role for women in the political process. The Liaison Group, organized under the leadership of the late Fusae Ichikawa, was the most influential group pressing the government to ratify the UN Convention on the Elimination of All Forms of Discrimination against Women in 1985 (this, in turn, led to the passage of the Equal Opportunity Law). One of its efforts was to urge the political parties to nominate more women candidates for the Diet and local assemblies. The recent appointments of women to lieutenant governor positions in three prefectures were more than likely influenced by such pressure. In the 1990s, the group has sought to elicit views regarding electoral reform and increased representation for women in the Diet through dissemination of a survey of all women Diet members.

Among other sources of new representation for women are consumer environmental and educational groups that decided to enter electoral politics in order to realize their policies in the decision-making process. Also, some feminist activists have entered the electoral arena. And the political parties have sought to recruit women for national and local nominations to office with a bit more enthusiasm. Ms. Doi, as head of the Socialist party, played a key role by seeking to change the image of her party from one that was labor-union dominated to one more broadly representative of a wide range of citizens, including women. Her charismatic character encouraged more women to run for electoral office and helped to gain support for such candidates by developing networks for election campaigns. This approach inspired other parties to recruit more women in order to compete more effectively.

Under Doi, support for women candidates took the form of campaign funds. In the 1987 local elections, for the first time women were given 1 million yen for prefectural elections and big cities of more than one million people. They were given 500,000 yen for city and ward assemblies, and

300,000 yen for town and village assembly contests. While this is a small amount in relation to total election costs, it did provide aid for women to prepare the first stage of a campaign effort. The Democratic Socialist party also helped women candidates by providing campaign funds. The Communist and Komei parties provided equal support to male and female candidates. In the case of the Komei party, the candidate provides the equivalent of two months of Diet or assembly salary, the rest of the funds are provided by the party. In the case of the Communists, the candidates themselves pay nothing as the party bears all campaign costs, including "political activity expenses" (actually voluntary assistance to assist with care for children and the elderly). Perhaps this assistance with funding and support for domestic responsibilities and the effort to field women candidates accounts for the fact that Communist party female representation at the local level has increased most rapidly; almost 40 percent of the women members of local assemblies represent the JCP. The Komei party increased its share of representation from 0.6 percent in 1967 to 10.6 percent in 1991, while the SDPJ decreased slightly from 1975 to 1991 (from 14 percent to 12.2 percent).[28] Perhaps the most striking progress in recent years has been made by those who identify as "others" (twenty-nine of the thirty are members of the Seikatsu Clubs, to be discussed below). Two other facts are notable, the numbers of female LDP-affiliated local representatives has continued to decrease (from 12 percent in 1967 to 2.6 percent in 1991), and the number of "independent" female candidacies, while half the 1967 number, is over one-third, second only to those of the Communists. However, many of these "independents" subsequently join the ranks of the LDP once elected. They prefer to eschew the party label when running for office, as part of their campaign strategy is to draw votes from as broad a base as possible. And, because at the local level people are tied closely to *chien* (community networks) and *ketsuen* (family networks), party identification may be shunned for campaign purposes.

A survey distributed to the parties by the Ichikawa Memorial Association in 1991 elicited the response from the LDP that 338 local assemblywomen (or 47 percent of all independents) were conservative independents working with the LDP.

Though Japanese women lack a support system such as that provided by the NWPC, Emily's List, and Women's Campaign Fund in the United States, nonetheless, as discussed earlier, an International Women's Year Liaison Group was established in 1975 and now includes fifty-two nationwide women's organizations. This group continues to ask the political parties to include more women candidates in each election. One possible result of this process has been the selection of three women as prefecture-level lieutenant governors, in Tokyo, Okinawa, and Ishikawa prefectures. The Alliance of Feminist Representatives was founded in 1991 by Mariko Mitsui and Satomi Nakajkima. It claims a membership of 167, including eight Diet members, none of them from the LDP, ninety-three local assemblywomen, and twenty-seven citizens. It has also pressed for greater inclusion of women as candidates. Most members are independents or are affiliated with the SDPJ, although a few women from other parties are also involved. While the group's base is in the Tokyo metropolitan area, its members are from all over Japan. The alliance has endorsed the idea of a quota system in order to increase women members at the local and national levels.[29] These two groups have particularly pressed for women to be nominated as candidates high on the party lists in order to guarantee election under the proportional representation system operative in the Upper House.

In 1992 the newly established New Japan party decided to institute a quota system that ensures that women make up at least 20 percent of its executive committee. They sought to help to increase women's political participation by holding a series of lectures and training seminars on women in politics in early 1993. It is not clear how powerful this new party—a dominant force in the coalition government established in 1993, with its head as prime minister—is likely to become. But it does seem significant that a party whose aim is to make changes in Japanese politics, amid numerous cries for reform in what is increasingly viewed as a corrupt system, cannot ignore women's representation in its effort to mobilize new voter constituencies, at least as part of its campaign strategy.

In the local communities there are some women's groups that help women to run for office; they are on the increase although they are still few in number. Participation in women's groups, organizations, and networks helps to increase women's role in the public sphere.

## COMMUNITY GROUPS IN ELECTORAL POLITICS

Two different groups of women have mobilized for greater inclusion in the local political process. The first are essentially working women motivated by feminist ideology, represented by the women who organized the Alliance for Feminist Representatives mentioned above. The second and larger group grew out of a housewives movement at the community level. Women began to have more time for themselves as electronic and other labor-saving devices found their way into their homes.[30] Many of them used their newly found time to take part in consumers movements and other citizens activities. As they did so, they recognized that simply taking part in citizen politics would not change the political system. They began to send their representatives to public office.

Women were more likely to be "full-time citizens" of their communities, as opposed to men whose work commitments made them "part-time citizens." Some contend that the housewives spearheaded a movement reflecting a more balanced, integrated, and democratic perspective in the conservative world of local politics, bringing a new spirit of democraticization and modernization to local administration.[31] As a result of their newfound mobilization, women accumulated experiences in equal-rights movements and citizen-based activities. For many, the International Women's Year and subsequent UN Decade for Women provided the impetus for more active participation in political activities. During this period, a nationwide campaign encouraged women to leave their homes and "participate in society."[32]

For example, the Tokyo-based Seikatsu Clubs began in 1965 when a women's consumer cooperative organized to buy safe and inexpensive consumer commodities (including milk) for its members.[33] The ensuing movement devoted itself over the next twenty years to issues concerning the environment, workers collectives, and the empowerment of women.[34] In the mid 1970s the club's "soap" movement organized in Kanagawa, Chiba, Saitama, and Hokkaidō prefectures in an effort to gather petition signatures to endorse the use of natural detergents. While the mobilization was not entirely successful, they did collect about 300,000 signatures.[35] Because of the recognition that lack of experience and representation in the political process contributed to defeat, the club's members sought a more active role in organized politics. Local "networks" and group members collected election funds through contributions by members of the club, and group volunteers provided campaign support. Candidates and elected members were viewed as "delegates" by club members; they were to be accountable to the group.[36]

In 1975 a housewife became the first Seikatsu Club member to be elected in Tokyo's Nerima Ward. She campaigned on the slogan "political reform from the kitchen." This club had elected thirty members (or "delegates") to local office by 1993. In 1987 women members of Seikatsu Clubs in Kawasaki and Yokohama ran for office. They were supported by the Kanagawa Network Movement (NET), which had been established in 1984 to work for political representation and support political activity. Of the twenty-four who ran, fourteen women were elected in 1987 to the local assemblies in Kanagawa, including three at the prefecture assembly level, and members were also elected in the greater Tokyo area.[37] By 1993, twenty-nine women were elected to local and prefectural office in Kanagawa prefecture.[38] In 1993, almost thirty years after the movement began, there were fourteen Seikatsu Clubs with over 200,000 members in twelve prefectures. In seven of these prefectures, clubs (organized into seventy networks or political organizations) send delegates to local and prefectural assemblies. They have been most successful at the city assembly level in Tokyo, Kanagawa, and Chiba prefectures (thirty, twenty-nine, and ten members, respectively).[39] In an effort to increase participation and encourage rotation of office-holding by members, the Seikatsu Clubs limit their representatives to two terms in electoral office. Some have argued that this practice will prevent elected representatives from gaining seniority, experience, and expertise in the political system they are seeking to influence.

Though in Japan local autonomy is almost nonexistent and local assemblies do not deserve "high marks for local democracy," while local governments usually do very little, "occasionally they can do a great deal."[40] This is particularly true, according to Reed, in regard to gubernatorial and mayoral leaders; a dynamic chief executive may activate local government and provide a source of flexibility, innovation, and citizen responsiveness.[41] In this context, the November 1992 election of Japan's second woman mayor in Zushi, Kanagawa prefecture (the first was in Ashiya, Hyōgo prefecture), is perhaps notable. Ms. Mitsuyo Sawa had been a major activist since 1984 in the citizen's group that had protested against the construction of housing for the U.S. military, in order to protect the environment in the Ikego forest. During her second term in the Zushi city assembly, Ms. Sawa was elected with 26 percent of the vote, running against five male candidates.[42] Her victory was made possible by the existence of a local citizen-action movement and a strong record of support for issues such as local services for the elderly and protection of the environment. She received campaign contributions from all over the country totaling 12 million yen from over nine hundred people to defray her campaign expenditures of 10 million yen.[43] In other cities, including Kawanishi, where two female members of the "Life-Style" School and Women's Association for Restructuring Japan were elected to the municipal assembly, and Ashiya, where a woman attorney with a strong commitment to educational policy reform was elected Japan's first woman mayor, similar trends have been in evidence. These women have been affiliated with consumer and citizens groups other than the Seikatsu movement. In Kawanishi, for example, women also became active on issues related to defective products, environmental protection, and antinuclearism, and their community activism made them well known when they sought electoral office.[44] In a number of other local areas, candidates representative of and supported by community-based housewives' groups committed to environmental and consumer issues, as well as parent-teacher associations,[45] who espouse a non-partisan or independent political stance, have also been elected.

Nonetheless, efforts to mobilize women at the local level elsewhere have been less successful. In Nagoya, for example, Ling and Matsuno report that women were afraid to join the local network because their husbands' companies might not like the environmental focus.[46] There is considerable concern about the coop movement as "leftist politics," outside the predominant conservative mainstream. It may be difficult for those women who are elected as "independents" to gain influence among party elected politicians. They are usually organized into small factions and may be isolated from the decision-making process, which, as noted above, has limited autonomy in a highly centralized political system. On the other hand, recent trends indicate that women assembly members have begun to organize "women-only" factions to work for women's issues, now that their numbers have increased and they have at least one additional female member to work with in some areas. A survey conducted in October 1991 by Kimiko Kubo of the Fusae Ichikawa Memorial Association found that 12 out of 111 assemblies that had more than two women independents had a women's faction.

Thus far, efforts to elect community activists to the national legislature have not been successful. Even the well-organized Seikatsu Clubs currently have only two representatives at the subnational prefectural, as opposed to municipal, level. While not allied with the feminist movement, these clubs are committed to collectives that may foster economic independence and empowerment for women, egalitarian values, and the restructuring of Japanese society. The ultimate contribution of such groups and others who participate in consumer and environmental politics may be to question the role of women solely as housewives and mothers and to seek social change through the development of alternative options and choices for women.

## WOMEN IN OTHER POSITIONS

Women have played only a limited role in the all-important bureaucratic structure, which many view as politically dominant in Japan. A few have been appointed to direct the Ministry of Labor's Women's Bureaus, and have used this institutional base as a stepping stone to higher office, including ambassadorships. The directorship of this ministry (known as the Women's and Minor's Bureau until 1984) is the only one that has been occupied by women since 1947 (except for the period from July 1990 to October 1991). As one of the ministry's intended roles was to raise the status of women as part of the process of democratization after World War II, it was the only one to hire women officials who passed the higher level public-service personnel examination. Some forty years later, some of them were positioned to seek higher office. Directors of the Women's Bureau have served as ambassadors to Kenya, Sweden, and Uruguay. Other women who held lower-level agency positions have gained higher-echelon roles as well.

As of January 1993, only four women served as directors in ministries: in the departments of Labor, Education, Health and Welfare, and International Trade and Industry. In addition, eight women who had been director or division chief in their ministry ran for the Diet as of 1993 (four from the Labor Ministry, three from Health and Welfare, and one from the Economic and Planning Agency). Six were elected: four on the SDPJ ticket and two on the LDP ticket.

In December 1992, Mayumi Moriyama (widow of a prominent LDP politician), a successful career bureaucrat, former director of the Women's Bureau of the Labor Ministry, and longtime LDP member of the Upper House (elected three times), became the seventh woman to serve in the cabinet and the first woman minister of education. Moriyama had previously served as chief cabinet secretary in 1989, when the LDP sought to counter the appeal of Ms. Doi as head of the Socialist party by appointing two women to the cabinet. After serving for six months, after the Lower House election, both women were summarily dismissed. The most recent Moriyama appointment was apparently motivated by the need to develop a new image for the Miyazawa cabinet, whose reputation had been greatly tarnished by allegations of corruption among prominent party leaders and whose popularity ratings were on the decline. In her first cabinet position, Moriyama was notable for her symbolic role in seeking to gain entrée to such male preserves as sumo wrestling and golf courses.[47] As an established member of the Conservative party, she spoke out against sex discrimination in these manifestations of traditional Japanese culture.

In August 1993, Prime Minister Morihiro Hosokawa appointed three women to his twenty-one member coalition cabinet: Ryoko Akamatsu, former director of the Women's Bureau of the Ministry of Labor and former ambassador, as minister of education; Manae Kubota, SDPJ Diet Upper House member and first head of the Prime Minister's Office of Women's Affairs, as director general of the Economic Planning Agency; and Wakako Hironaka, Komei member of the Upper House, as director general of the Environment Agency. An assumption widely shared was that Hosokawa sought to present a fresh image to the voting public by appointing an unprecedented number of women to his cabinet (albeit to the same positions they had held in previous cabinets).

Despite this real progress, at the upper echelons of power women comprised only 0.8 percent, or sixty-seven, of the 8,479 bureaucrats of section-chief rank or above in 1990, with the numbers decreasing as rank got higher. Their general representation in the civil service rose only slightly from 1975 to 1990, from 14 percent to 15 percent.[48] The number of women serving as director general or in similar positions increased from 0.1 percent to 0.6 percent (from one to nine); at the section-chief level, their numbers went from 0.3 percent to 0.8 percent (nineteen to fifty-eight).

In 1991, women comprised 5.5 percent of the nation's judges (up from 2.1 in 1977), including 13.8 percent of vice-justices and two presiding judges.[49] The first female Supreme Court judge was appointed in 1994, while a woman served as High Court judge for the first time from January to December 1987. The number of female attorneys has increased as well, reaching about 6 percent in 1992.[50] Perhaps the judicial and legal professions have been a bit more hospitable than other public service areas to women because admission to them requires passing a gender-neutral examination. Remaining barriers to civil-service employment fell a bit when the government decided to admit women to the Defense Academy in 1992.

FUTURE TRENDS

What is the likely future for the participation of Japanese women in politics? While in 1989 women helped to decisively defeat the Liberal Democratic party, supporting the opposition and handing the LDP a stunning defeat in the Upper House, confidence that politics can be changed and that women can be the architects of such change may be less apparent now. The rapid increase of women representatives both at the national and local levels seem to be due to Doi's assumption of the chairpersonship of the Socialist party and to easily understood issues such as the consumption tax and the prime minister's sex scandal. These results were made possible by a long period of preparation, especially the exposure offered by International Women's Year and the UN Decade for Women. During this period, women had many opportunities to open their minds to the broader world because the national and local government and women's organizations worked in a more international arena and raised issues concerning enhancement of women's political status.

Today, local-level politics may hold out more promise for aspiring women politicians than seemed possible some years back. While the numbers and percentages are still very small, they will keep on increasing gradually even in those rural areas where urbanization and modernization are occuring. Indicative of possible change even in rural Japan was the election in January 1994 of a woman, Fumiko Kira, as mayor of a small village in Kōchi prefecture— the first such female victory at the village level. The Seikatsu Clubs have had a rapid political rise and are likely to continue to increase their numbers, at least at the local level. Because their activities are based in the consumer-cooperative movement, they have an additional source of strength that they have mobilized effectively.

At the national level, some Japanese media have referred to women representatives newly elected in 1989–1990 as part of a "bubble effect," which, like the Japanese boom economy, seemed to disappear quickly. Efforts to increase both quantity and quality in the future will be of importance. The recruitment of more women with political agendas, such as those in the Seikatsu Clubs or the Alliance of Feminist Representatives, might make women's legislative role more meaningful than it has been to date.[51]

While some women activists in Japan believe that the younger generation of women are apolitical and indifferent to politics recently gathered survey data suggest that some changes related to "politicization" among women may be taking place.[52] In fact, however, most women who are seeking and winning political office are in their late forties and fifties, similar to trends described by Hagardine in the 1970s.[53] Japanese women may enter the electoral arena only after their children are raised, in contrast to single-issue and more loosely structured voluntary activity, which can be balanced with housewives' responsibilities. A 1989 survey found that 6.1 percent of women from ages thirty-five to forty-five said they wanted to be politicians.[54] This number, however small, seems somewhat significant among a generation believed to be indifferent to politics.[55]

Japanese women's attitudes toward politics are characterized by ambivalence and also new consciousness around some issues. In a 1990 prime minister's survey, 60.5 percent of women respondents said they were interested in politics, compared with 81.3 percent of male respondents. Women are also less likely than men to engage in political activity other than voting (attendance at political party Diet member meetings: men 29 percent; women 15 percent). Other surveys indicate that women are far less sure of their political ideologies than men.[56] However, nearly half (49.8 percent) of women indicated that they thought women's views were not represented in government, compared to 39.5 percent for men, although for each group there were more favorable assessments of women's representation than had been the case three years earlier).[57] A "gender gap" of sorts seems to be emerging on this issue, particularly between young women and young men.

Of female respondents, 64.3 percent also said they wanted to see more women hold public office. These attitudes mark a strong departure from earlier studies by Hagardine and Pharr, who reported hostility to women politicians and female political activism by the male and female public as well as opinion leaders, based on survey data primarily from the 1970s.[58] With regard to the emergence of possible gender-based distinctions among Japanese men and women surveyed, women indicate a far higher interest than men in environmental issues and taxation and a lesser interest in issues related to defense. Fewer women express conservative (35 percent women, 44 percent men) and radical ideologies (13 percent women, 22 percent men) than their male counterparts, according to a 1992 survey.[59] Finally, women support the LDP less than men (36 percent to 44 percent) and are far more likely to support "other" or "no party."[60] This data appears to suggest that while Japanese women are still groping for political identity and ideology, they are not likely to be more conservative than men, and in fact hold a different set of views on a number of issues that may provide potential for future political mobilization.

There have been several significant indications of increased political and electoral interest among women. On 3 February 1993, the New Japan party began a Political School for Women and held their opening lecture (of twenty, in a year long series) in Tokyo. More than 600 inquiries were received about the program (495 from women, 123 from men), and 147 applied for the entrance examination by submitting a paper entitled "Women and Politics." Fifty-eight women and twelve men were selected. Most successful participants were from metropolitan Tokyo, but some came from as far away as southern Kyūshū. Entrants paid a tuition fee of 200,000 yen (about $1,500)! The average age of entrants was 38.2.[61] The extraordinary outpouring of interest in gaining expertise in running for office is evident from the large numbers who were willing to spend their time and money. A May 1993 symposium on women and politics in Tokyo attracted 500 women as well. The evolving role of the New Japan party, seemingly providing a new channel for influence in a scandal-ridden political system, may offer some encouragement to those who want to change politics. In addition, because such "training schools" open to the public have not existed in Japan, a new trend may be beginning. Women participants may seek advice on running campaigns for office, may wish to use their new expertise to develop other types of political activities, or may wish to establish networks with the New Japan party or other parties.

The impact on women resulting from the coalition government elected in 1993 is still unknown. In visible terms, women have gained increased representation in the cabinet due to the effort to create a fresh, reform image. And former SDPJ leader Takako Doi became the first speaker of the Lower House. This position has in the past been rather symbolic, so it will be interesting to analyze the extent to which it can be used both as a role model to encourage women and a focus for active policy-making. (There is also some feeling that Doi's appointment was a way to prevent a leader with great popularity and outspoken views from attacking the government from the outside, as well as to gain support for electoral reform).[62] The future of these governmental arrangements may be tenuous because the SDPJ is a left-oriented party in a conservative coalition, with apparently declining popularity.

On the positive side as well, two more women were elected to the Diet, largely because female nominees from the new parties helped to compensate for losses by the SDPJ. Many women for the first time find themselves to be part of the governing group in Japan.

Still, policy-making in the Japanese system remains concentrated in the bureaucracy, and women are newcomers at negotiating effectively with it. Women played a limited role in creating the change that brought about the coalition success, so their future role in it is by no means assured. There is concern among women as to the possible effect on future candidacies of the proposed adoption of a single-member district electoral system for the Lower House.[63] And, it is not clear how, and with what success, the LDP, a past master of electoral support, will fight back to counter the new governing coalition. The latter may prove to be unstable.

In the short run, at least, the underlying features of Japanese politics and culture described above remain significant obstacles to enhanced political power for women. The power of women as voters may be improved by the instability of the political system, and it is possible that this could produce concessions if women organize strategically to make demands. Efforts to increase the number of women in national and local politics may require the adoption of quota systems within the parties, similar to those recently adopted by the New Japan party, and the willingness of parties to establish meaningful support systems for women candidates, such as those provided by the Communist party.

In the long run, political opportunities will be most affected by education and changing social patterns which may have the effect of eliminating or moderating traditional sex roles and values. More women in the bureaucracy, political parties, and labor unions will serve as role models and may help still other women to enter the political arena. A reformed and less expensive system of nomination and campaigns would also greatly facilitate the entrance of more women into elective politics in Japan.

NOTES

1. Kimiko Kubo, *Women's Outlook* (Tokyo: Fusae Ichikawa Memorial Association, no. 423, 1992), 1.
2. They have long since surpassed the 1947 total of 4 percent (or 10 of 250) in the Upper House.
3. Yuriko Ling and Asusa Matsuno, with Jill Bystydienski, in Bystydienski, ed., *Women Transforming Politics: Worldwide Strategies for Empowerment* (Bloomington: Indiana University Press, 1992), 55–63.
4. Eileen Hagardine, "Japan," in Joni Lovenduski and Jill Hills, eds., *The Politics of the Second Electorate* (London: Routledge and Kegan Paul, 1981), 316.
5. This section is drawn from Kimiko Kubo, "Japanese Women's Participation in Politics" (paper presented at the International Seminar on Women and Elections, Seoul, Korea, 6–7 October 1989).
6. Susan Pharr, *Political Women in Japan* (Berkeley: University of California Press, 1981), 168–69.
7. *Ibid.*
8. Hagardine, "Japan," 299.
9. Gerald Curtis, *The Japanese Way of Politics* (New York: Columbia University Press, 1988), 260.
10. Hagardine, "Japan," 299.
11. Kimiko Kubo, "Japanese Women's Participation in Politics" (paper presented at the Fourth Interdisciplinary Congress on Women, Hunter College, New York, 3–7 June 1990, 7.
12. Curtis, *Japanese Way*, 188; and Kubo, interviews reported in *Women's Outlook* (Tokyo: Fusae Ichikawa Memorial Association, no. 428 1992), 6.
13. This brought the total number of women in the Upper House to thirty-three, including the eleven elected previously.
14. Asako Murakami, "Politics Loses Some of its 'Madonna' Touch," *Japan Times*, 10–16 August 1992, 4.
15. Merry White, *Challenging Tradition: Women in Japan* (New York: Japan Society, 1991), 19.
16. *Ibid.*
17. *Ibid.*
18. *Local Assemblies: Handbook of Data on Japanese Women in Political Life* (Tokyo: Fusae Ichikawa Memorial Association, 1991), 10.

19. Yuriko Ono director, Women's Bureau Komei party, interview by Kimiko Kubo, May 1992, at Diet members building.

20. The salary is set by each local assembly and is related to population. In small districts the remuneration may be very unattractive to men who are major breadwinners for their families.

21. Including ten minutes for housework, one minute for nursing, three minutes for child rearing, and nine minutes for shopping. Data collected by Kimiko Kubo from the Management and Consulting Agency, Tokyo, 1991.

22. Prefectural assemblies meet an average of 70.4 days per year; town and village assemblies an average of 30.6 days, plus a few additional days for special sessions. National Association of Chairmen of Prefectural Assemblies, July 1992; Japan National Association of Chairmen of Towns and Villages, July 1992.

23. Ms. Keiko Sumita, interview by Kimiko Kubo, January 1993.

24. Interviews, Emiko Iwai, Kawanishi City, and Mitsuko Watanabe, Kanagawa, by Joyce Gelb, October 1992.

25. Kubo, "Women's Participation," 9.

26. Data collected by Kimiko Kubo from the SDPJ, 1992.

27. Data collected by Kimiko Kubo from Diet records, 1992.

28. *Local Assemblies: Handbook*, table 5, 15. Put another way, responses to FIMA's 1991 survey indicate that 19.3 percent of the JCP's members are women, compared to 8.3 percent for the SDPJ, 6.5 percent for Komei, and 1.6 percent for DSP. The LDP did not respond to the survey.

29. "Alliance Seeks Larger Political Role for Women," *Japan Times*, 9–15 March 1992, 4.

30. Much of the following is drawn from Kubo, "Women's Participation," and interviews conducted by Gelb in Japan, 1992.

31. See Nishiyama, quoted in Ling and Matsuno, *Transforming Politics*, 62; and Kubo "Women's Participation," 12.

32. Chizuko Ueno, quoted by Ling and Matsuno, *Transforming Politics*, 57.

33. *The Seikatsu Club* (Tokyo: Seikatsu Club Consumer's Cooperative, 1989?), 4.

34. *Ibid.*, 6. The collectives began by asking workers to pay a certain amount of money to club members who worked for the club. At the next stage, they organized collectives for welfare and other issues in which they invested money worked together and shared income from services provided. Most recently, this approach has been utilized to assist women to own small businesses.

35. *Ibid.*, 10. The movement did succeed in Chiba prefecture and led to an effort to elect a member to the assembly soon thereafter.

36. Kubo, "Women's Participation," 10.

37. Katsumi Yokota, *I among Others* (Kanagawa: Seikatsu Club Seikyo Kanagawa, 1991), 20; and *Seikatsu Club*, 14.

38. Interview, Mitsuko Watanabe, Yokahama, by Joyce Gelb, October 1992.

39. Only two Seikatsu members serve in prefectural assemblies. The total number of members nationally was seventy-nine as of January 1993.

40. See Steven Reed, *Japanese Prefectures and Policy Making* (Pittsburgh: University of Pittsburgh Press, 1991), 167–68.

41. *Ibid.*, 168–70.

42. "Military Housing Foe Elected Mayor of Zushi," *Japan Times*, 9 November 1992, 2.

43. Interviews, Sawa's campaign managers (Haruka Kopayashi and Shigiko Uchida), Diet members' office, December 1992.

44. Interview, Emiko Iwai, Kawanishi, by Joyce Gelb, October 1992.

45. Ling and Matsuno, *Transforming Politics*, 56.

46. *Ibid.*, 61.

47. Interview Yayori Matsui, *Asahi Shimbun*, October 1992.

48. Data collected by Kimiko Kubo, National Personnel Authority, 1990.

49. Data collected by Kimiko Kubo from the Supreme Court, 1991.

50. Data collected by Kimiko Kubo from the Japan Federation of Bar Associations, 1992.

51. Sumiko Iwao, *The Japanese Woman* (New York: Free Press, 1993), 236–41.

52. Interview, Tokyo, by Joyce Gelb, October 1992.

53. *Local Assemblies: Handbook*, table 7, 16; Hagardine, "Japan," 315.

54. "Survey on Political Consciousness" in *Nihon Keizai Shimbun*, 10 July 1989, 5.

55. Kubo, "Women's Participation," 13–14.

56. This survey material is from Zaidan Hojin Akarui Senkyo Suishin Kyoka (Association for Fair Elections), 1992, collected by Kimiko Kubo.

57. "Japanese Women Today," *About Japan*, no. 5 (Tokyo: Foreign Press Center, 1991), 38.

58. Hagardine, "Japan," 313–14.

59. Association for Fair Elections, 1992.

60. *Ibid.*

61. These observations are by Kimiko Kubo, who attended as a reporter.

62. Mutsuko Fukushima, "Doi's Acceptance of Job to Tame SDPJ's Leftwing," *Japan Times*, 16–22 August 1993, 7. See also Takashi Kitazume, "Electoral Reform Bills to Test Strength of Coalition Government," *Japan Times*, 23–29 August 1993, 5.

63. A 1991 survey conducted by the IWY Liaison group of all women Diet members found that thirty-four of the forty surveyed opposed adoption of such a system, saying it would make election of women to the Lower House more difficult. Discussions in fall 1993 centered on the dimensions of electoral reform: the combination of proportional and single-member constituencies, the total number of votes and their division, the vote per consitutent, and the like. As of 1994, the new allocation of seats will be 300 in single-member districts and 200 through proportional representation.

# 7

## A Short History of the Feminist Movement in Japan

SANDRA BUCKLEY

CHIYO Saito is the founding editor of *Agora*, the longest-running feminist journal in Japan. In a commemorative issue of the journal she commented that "it is not so simple for a foreign feminism to take root as the basic ideology of a movement in another country. I think that we have reached a stage where we need to look more closely at the various origins and currents of [Japanese] feminism."[1] In the same article she also referred, good humoredly, to the number of times she has attempted to explain to foreign feminists (especially Americans) that Japanese feminism developed out of distinct indigenous conditions and was not one more import from the United States. This survey maps the history of postwar Japanese feminism in both its national and international contexts, recognizing the long national history of women's action for social and political reform, dating back to the beginnings of the modernization process in the late nineteenth century, and the specific internal economic and political conditions of postwar Japan.[2] By tracing the points of intersection of the postwar trajectories of policy development in such diverse areas as employment practices, consumer affairs, abortion access, education, welfare, contraception, elderly care, and prostitution, it is possible to begin to identify the shifting priorities and objectives of the Japanese state industrial complex and the impact of these shifts on the positioning of "Woman." The constant and detailed attention to the construction and reconstruction of "Woman" in policy-making foregrounds the centrality of the management of women's bodies and female sexuality to the maintenance of the dominant economy/ reality that is contemporary Japan. In the process of constructing a narrative of the development of Japanese feminism over the postwar period, it should

150

become evident how often the issues of past and present collapse into a complex loop of ideological formations and reformations. This process reflects the tenacity of the discursive practices that constitute and sustain both the organization of the body politic and the politics of bodily organs—especially when that body is female.[3]

WOMEN AND ECONOMIC RECOVERY: LOCAL AND
NATIONAL STRATEGIES

The decisions faced by Japanese women over the war years were difficult ones. Those who voiced their opposition to the war effort went to prison for their beliefs. Some died there. Others remained silent, while still others calculated the war effort to be an opportunity to gain certain improvements in the status of women and chose to collaborate. Postwar feminism in Japan has demonstrated a high level of tolerance and understanding toward the complexity of the choices faced by women in wartime. In the period immediately following defeat the emerging organizations were often closely linked to prewar women's action groups, and the leaders were also familiar figures. Fusae Ichikawa was the most notable of these. In addition to founding the Women's Committee for Postwar Policies (1945), she was active in the founding of the New Japanese League of Women (1945). Kikue Yamakawa, a prominent left-wing feminist of the prewar years, helped found the League of Democratic Women (1946) and was the first head of a new Women's Bureau within the Ministry of Labor (1947). In 1948 the Housewives Association and the first National Women's Congress were launched. The Association of Women in Agriculture was founded one year later. In 1950, Ichikawa's New Japanese League of Women amalgamated with the Japanese League of Women Voters, and the National Federation of Rural Women's Associations came into being the following year. The influential League of Regional Women's Associations was founded in 1952 and held its first national congress in 1953.

The Occupation period was seen to represent a once-only opportunity to push for the passage of the rights denied women in the prewar decades of modernization, and this period is often referred to as the first wave of feminism. To the extent that women's demands were perceived to be consistent with the goals of SCAP (Supreme Command for the Allied Powers) administration, there was an official willingness to consult and cooperate with key proponents of women's rights. Women and the Left were identified by the Occupation command as potential allies in reforming the political and social fabric of Japanese society. The mobilization of the women's vote was considered crucial for a successful outcome to the first postwar democratic elections scheduled for April 1946. This led to a comprehensive registration and information campaign targeted at eligible women voters. In a similar vein, SCAP pursued an aggressive policy for constitutional reforms aimed at the dismantling of the traditional household (*ie*) structure. While this remained a primary focus of much immediate postwar legislative reform for both SCAP and women's groups, the majority of Japanese women were preoccupied with the day-to-day struggle to survive in the face of food and fuel shortages.

The women's groups and congresses that formed over the Occupation period represented a general trend toward large national organizations committed to SCAP policies for the democraticization of Japan. They also shared a basic concern with issues central to women's struggle to protect and nourish their families over the immediate postwar years. Both jointly and independently these organizations lobbied SCAP and the government for improvements in food supplies, health care, welfare support, and unemployment benefits. The emergence of the women's agricultural groups represented the increased difficulties experienced by rural women faced with pressures to re-establish food crops with a dramatically diminished rural work force, limited financial aid, and a seriously damaged infrastructure. A priority for all of the women's organizations was to establish strong overseas links, and consequently there was a considerable traffic in Japanese women's delegations to international congresses focusing on the economic and political status of women; e.g., Moscow World Economic Conference (1952), International Council of Democratic Women (1955), World Congress of Women Workers (1956). The national federations that characterized the late forties and the fifties were consistent with a SCAP strategy of coordinating reform through the instrument of national, centralized bodies rather than smaller regional groups. The Occupation forces believed that well-funded and effectively structured national organizations would be better suited to sustaining a high level of politicization and action among women. The official end of the Occupation in 1952 and the changing trends in the economy and work force by 1955 witnessed a significant shift in the structure, constituency, and agenda of new women's organizations.

Both the National Congress of Working Women and the National Congress of Trade Union Women were inaugurated in 1956, only two years after the Omi Kenshi Silk Mill strike—the first major labor action by women workers in the postwar period. Delegates from Japanese women's groups also became actively involved in key international labor organizations from the mid 1950s, leading to the establishment of the Japan Women's Union in 1959. These developments reflected the rapid return of women to the work force in the wake of the restructuring of the industrial base and the associated increase in labor demand in the expanding tertiary and secondary sectors. However, just as in the 1910s and 1920s when economic development had similarly favored the entry of increasing numbers of women into the work force, a discourse of motherhood and the family was quick to surface through the 1950s in opposition to the emerging women's labor movement. Thus, at the same time that Japan saw the beginnings of an organized women's labor movement, there was also a parallel growth in the number of organizations concerned with the status of motherhood and the family. The All-Japan Congress for Antiprostitution Reforms met in 1954 and established a rigorous campaign platform culminating in the passage of antiprostitution legislation in 1956. While the group's stated goal was the elimination of the exploitation of prostitutes, this was widely perceived to be a very conservative organization concerned primarily with the protection of the family through the elimination of "immoral" practices. The Congress for Mothers met for the first time in 1955, and other organizations (government and nongovernment) developed around questions of the quality of life (e.g., the National Federation for the Improvement of Life-Style [1953] and the National Congress for Women's Action of the Japanese Union for Equal Standard of Living [1957]), and these too were keenly focused on the status of the family.

These two divergent streams of women's activity were characterized by the "promotherhood" and "prowork" polarization of the 1950s "housewife debate," an exchange of views around the question of women's proper role that was carried in the popular women's magazine *Fujin koron* (Housewives' Forum). However, by the mid 1950s the situation could not be reduced to a simple choice of motherhood or work. More and more women were working full-time prior to marriage and attempting to return to work after a period of child rearing. The primary motivation for work after marriage was economic, and throughout the 1950s women's income, however small, remained crucial to household budgets.

Other factors were also becoming relevant to women's employment decisions toward the late 1950s. The continuing trend toward nuclear households contributed to the desire of younger women to maintain a workplace network of support rather than remaining isolated in the often barren environment of postwar urban residential development. Another factor was the dramatic fall in postwar birthrates and an associated reduction in the period of active childbearing. Profamily advocates blamed the downturn in births exclusively on the increased participation of women in the work force, but another significant factor was a general reaction among women to the hardships of the war and the Occupation period that translated into a preference for smaller, more economically viable households. Such choices were also clearly linked to the conditions of life in the new urban environment of high-density apartments and company housing. It is also true that many women who were in their thirties by the mid 1950s had wartime work experience. This may be one more reason why this generation rejected any stigma attached to working women and led the trend toward reentry into the work force after child rearing. By the late 1950s the patterns that would continue to escalate over the next three decades were well underway—the increased participation of women in the work force, a shift to nuclear households, and a declining birthrate.

Faced with the inevitability of the continued incorporation of women into the work force and rapid changes in the profile of the contemporary family, the proponents of the "promotherhood" side of the "housewife debate" found themselves redefining the terms of the debate in an attempt to regain lost ground. By the 1960s the debate itself was renamed the "domestic work debate" and the differences between this stage of the ongoing conflict and the terms of the earlier "housewife debate" were indicative of the different issues faced by women in these two decades.[4] The reaction of the readership of *Fujin koron* to the "housewife debate" in the mid 1950s was generally more sympathetic toward the defenders of motherhood than the prowork advocates. However, the late 1950s emerged as a period of transition during which the economic and social reality represented by the statistics for women's gradually increasing work-force participation came to increasingly belie advertising images of happy full-time mothers living in modern "Westernized" domestic bliss. The need for women to work to supplement income in an increasingly consumer-driven socioeconomic environment continued to grow over the 1960s. This, together with the government's active encouragement of female work-force participation as part of its rapid economic growth strategy, led to a relaxation of public criticism of working mothers. The onus shifted to the "promotherhood" lobby to adapt its strategies to better reflect the complexity of the contemporary choices faced by the majority of women. Housework and child rearing thus came to be redefined as "domestic work," and the platforms of such national organizations as the Japan Mother's Congress were reoriented away from an emphasis on the need for the protection of motherhood toward demands for the recognition of the domestic and nurturing role as a form of labor in its own right. Related campaigns worked to achieve a reevaluation of domestic work using strategies that amounted to a public face-lift for the image of motherhood over the 1960s.[5]

The tensions between what were characterized as the "prowork" and "promotherhood" lobbies, a serious oversimplification of the complexity of the debate, remained unresolved and were nowhere more evident than in the government policies of the 1960s. Prime Minister Ikeda introduced his Income Doubling Policy in 1960.[6] Based on a combination of rapid expansion of the domestic industrial base and a parallel growth in domestic consumption of manufactured goods, this was to be the policy base for the ensuing decade of rapid economic growth that would eventually come to be known as "the Japanese miracle." The continued increase in female participation in the work force was crucial to the success of high economic growth, although it was not clearly stated as a policy goal at this stage. The 1963 document "Tasks and Measures for Development of Human Resources" first clearly outlined the central role of women in the new work force. This document attempted to balance the need to maximize women's work-force participation and the equally strong need for women to continue to perform the primary care-giver role within the family. However, the expectation that women could both increase their participation in the work force and continue to carry full responsibility for unpaid domestic work was unreasonable in the absence of any social support infrastructure.

Even as early as 1963 government and nongovernment studies were expressing concern that the family structure was coming under pressure as more and more women struggled to balance their paid and unpaid labor commitments. A White Paper on Child Welfare published in 1963 commented that "a deficiency in the level of nurturing is creating a risk for the children of this generation." It also made a direct connection between "the decline in child welfare" and "women's increased penetration of the work force." This and other documents, however, placed the burden of responsibility and guilt on Japan's women rather than on a system that failed to provide the necessary level of child-care support for working mothers. Other documents followed, with titles such as "Image of the Ideal Japanese" (1966) and "Toward A Better Family Life" (1967). The Motherhood Welfare Law (1964) and the Mother-Child Health Law (1966) also represented government attempts to improve the level of funding and infrastructure support for families but both continued to reproduce the dominant assumption that women's primary role remained unpaid domestic work. On this basis the kind and degree of support was calculated only as a complement to part-time employment. One could go so far as to argue that government policies from the 1970s to the present in the areas of welfare, taxation, pensions, and child care have continued to foreclose any realistic option for ongoing full-time employment for Japanese women. The policy reforms of the 1960s did little in real terms to deal with the hard issues faced daily by a growing population of working mothers.

One unsatisfactory labor-market response to these conditions was a rise in the practice of *naishoku* employment (homework). Women, unable to find adequate day-care for their children but wanting or needing to work, sought contracted homework. The wages for *naishoku* labor were notoriously low but this did not deter growing numbers of women in the absence of any other realistic employment alternatives during their child-rearing years. There was more than a 250 percent increase in *naishoku* workers during the 1960s, with some 2 million women involved in this form of labor by the end of the decade.[7] Surveys of women workers during the 1960s showed that the majority of married women respondents cited household-income supplementation as the primary reason for labor force participation. For the most part, this new category of workers was not protected by unions or other organized labor. Isolated in their homes, the *naishoku* women workers were not in a position to organize to protest the high quotas and low wages that characterized their working conditions.[8]

The other fast-growing category of married women workers over the 1960s were the *paato* (part-timers). This designation of part-time employee excluded women from company benefits, union membership, job security, and equal pay. The category has remained contentious given that the distinction between full- and part-time labor often seems more related to gender than any specific designation of working hours. A female *paato* performing comparable tasks to a male full-time employee would be payed as much as 40 percent to 50 percent less. The wage differential for women has remained high throughout the postwar period, at least in part due to the extremely low wages paid to part-timers and the continual increase in the percentage of female employees falling into this category. By the end of the 1970s the majority of new job openings were part-time positions.

In the early 1960s one Tokyo woman decided to take an initiative aimed at easing some of the pressure faced by Japanese working mothers. Chiyo Saito founded a cooperative child-care network in her district with the aim that women could create a supportive environment for one another while also moving some distance toward solving the ever-present crisis of adequate and reliable child care.[9] This model of neighborhood-based day-care became popular over the 1960s and 1970s but was not without problems in the absence of adequate quality controls. The issue of unregistered day-care centers would come to a head over the "baby hotel" controversy of the 1980s, to be discussed below. Once Saito's child-care project was under way it soon became evident that many of the mothers who were attempting to reenter the work force after the first years of child rearing were lacking not only child-care support but also the necessary training or skills to move back into a work force that was changing rapidly with the introduction of new technologies. Women who had been employed as office workers frequently needed refresher courses in basic office skills or retraining to prepare them for jobs in manufacturing or light industry. As a consequence, the cooperative under Saito's leadership developed the Bank of Creativity—a women's training and resource group. The need for access to adequate and affordable reskilling for women wishing to return to the work force has remained a major concern to the present with municipal and prefectural women's centers together with adult education programs and labor unions now offering a range of outreach programs for mature age female students. For the most part, however, the prevailing trend is for women returning to employment to take up *paato* jobs at a significantly lower level of skills and responsibility than the full-time positions they had occupied prior to withdrawal from the work force.

Saito located the Bank of Creativity activities in the Agora Resource Center. From the early 1970s the center published a journal of the same name. *Agora* continues to be the longest running feminist journal in postwar Japan. Saito is not alone among Japanese feminists in identifying one particular point in Japan's postwar history as the catalytic moment for what is often described as the second wave of Japanese feminism. That moment occured with the convergence in 1960 of two deeply interconnected political movements, the anti-AMPO (opposition to the reratification of the U.S.-Japan Peace Treaty) and the anti–Vietnam War protests. Another leading feminist figure, Aoki Yayoi, recalls the impact of this period of unrest on the development of feminism: "The combination of the anti-Vietnam and anti-AMPO movements sparked off the possibility of a second wave of Japanese feminism as the women who came together around these two issues began to recognize their shared experiences and goals. This all happened at the same time as, but without direct contact with, the beginnings of American feminism."[10]

In many ways 1960 marks the emergence of a new generation of feminists whose priorities and strategies often differed from those of the generation of feminists whose activities spanned the pre- and postwar periods. Two distinct but not always independent structures came to characterize postwar feminism from the 1960s. The first was characterized by the style of large, national organizations and affiliations with government and party structures that had dated from the reemergence of feminism in the Occupation period. The second was, by contrast, committed to a strategy of nonaffiliation, decentralization, and local activity. Bodies such as the National League of Regional Women's Organizations (Chifuren), the Housewives Association, and the Japanese League of Women Voters are representative of the former. The latter trend led to a proliferation of women's organizations across Japan that saw a total of some thirty-seven thousand groups active by the 1970s.

A structure of localized strategies of organization and action has characterized the development of Japanese feminism from the 1960s. This has led some Western feminists to misjudge the capacity of Japanese women to mobilize and lobby on a major scale. Many Japanese feminists on the other hand would argue that it is this fragmented and decentralized nature of the movement that is its greatest strength in a country where the vulnerability of national organizations to government cooptation increases in direct correlation to their rate of growth. It was state pressure to centralize and consolidate that brought prewar women's groups under the jurisdiction of the Ministry of War. This history has left many contemporary Japanese women activists wary of government support, financial or otherwise, and any attempt to establish permanent national coalitions on more than a temporary, one-issue basis.

It was in this context that the *minikomi* system came into being. This informal network of women's communication allowed the many and diverse local feminist groups across the country to remain in close contact while still maintaining the independence of their separate histories and priorities. The flow of information sheets, newsletters, informal magazines, journals, self-help and advise columns, and other varied publications functioned as the central nervous system for the women's movement through the 1960s. While some publications were simple handwritten copied sheets delivered by volunteers, others were professionally printed journals with nationwide subscription lists. Estimates of the total number of publications produced within the *minikomi* vary but by the late 1960s there were as many as forty thousand women's publications being printed and circulated. Larger women's organizations with more substantial infrastructures functioned as regional holding centers that could be accessed from across the country.

One characteristic of the *minikomi* publications was the use of a writing style that not only retained but highlighted the female identity of the writer. In a language in which gender difference permeates every dimension of expression, the decision to avoid the "neutral" or more masculine markings of academic and other public styles of writing was a conscious strategy of revaluing and redefining the language of the "weaker" sex.[11] This particular strategy was not so apparent in the feminist journals of the 1970s and 1980s but remains common in a large number of the *minikomi* publications still in circulation. Today, it is the larger centers, such as the Shinjuku Women's Center in Tokyo and the prefectural Fujin kaikan (Women's Halls) coordinated by the National League of Regional Women's Organizations, that usually hold the most substantial *minikomi* collections. While the total number of publications in production has fallen, interviews with Japanese feminists young and old, rural and urban, leaves no doubt that this communication network still plays a central role in the circulation of ideas and in maintaining the potential for rapid, effective alliances around single-issue campaigns.

This more informal network existed side-by-side with such larger national bodies as the National League of Regional Women's Organizations (Chifuren, founded in 1952) and the Housewives Association (Shufuren, founded in 1948). These two organizations became the leading forces behind the consumer protection movement of the 1960s. Both groups have close links with government agencies and receive regular updates on price and quality controls and expected shifts in policy.[12] Chifuren receives far higher levels of direct financial support from the government and also performs various government administrative duties, including the management of the prefectural Women's Halls. These locations function as resource centers, women's adult education venues, meeting rooms, conference centers, drop-in lounges, counseling clinics, wedding halls, concert halls, and much else. They offer an important publicly funded forum for women's activities at the local level. The Chifuren is also actively involved in lobbying the LDP for policy reforms on issues of direct concern to its female constituency. There is no question that the Chifuren operates in a close working relationship with the dominant party's interests. On those occasions when the LDP has sought female candidates for postings or to run in elections it has often looked to Chifuren. This does not mean, however, that Chifuren's interests and objectives always coincide with those of the LDP. It has frequently been Chifuren in cooperation with Shufuren that has organized the more successful lobbying campaigns against government and industry on issues such as pollution, waste management, price controls, and consumer rights.

Shufuren is also dependent on both industry and government for a good deal of the information needed for its consumer-focused research and lobbying. However, Shufuren has remained more nonpartisan than Chifuren, and this has enhanced the credibility of its many successful campaigns. A major focus of this organization has been in-house testing of consumer products. In the 1960s they repeatedly challenged industry, manufacturing, distributers, and retailers on questions of quality, safety, pricing, and misleading advertising. While much of the funding for the now highly sophisticated testing laboratories comes from government sources, Shufuren has protected its structural autonomy in ways that allow it to continue to maintain a highly adversarial role. It could be argued that the increased influence of these two consumer-oriented organizations in the early 1960s was consistent with a government policy of domestically driven GNP growth. While the actions of the consumer-protection movement were seldom welcomed by the private sector, the increase in consumer confidence fired by the successes of the movement in assuring quality and price control did serve to promote the desired levels of consumption of domestic products in the early 1960s. By the mid to late 1960s the government's support for consumer initiatives for reductions on tariffs on imported goods and increased controls on inflationary pricing of imports coincided neatly with the policy goal of shifting away from domestically driven growth toward the development of export markets and the downloading of labor intensive industry off-shore by the 1970s. The call from Chifuren and Shufuren for the opening of domestic consumer markets to a range of affordable imported consumer goods as disposable income levels increased over the second half of the 1960s again dovetailed conveniently with the government's projected schedule for industrial development.

It would not do justice to the initiatives of either of these two national women's consumer groups to tie their impact and initiatives solely to government priorities. The greatest triumph of the consumer movement in this period was the boycott of color televisions in 1970. A coalition of women's consumer groups organized by Shufuren and Chifuren brought together some 15 million women in a boycott of overpriced domestic color television sets. The action was quick and highly successful and set a precedent for similar actions against both manufacturers and distributers in the 1970s, leading to price or quality reform for products as diverse as makeup, rice, textiles, and canned foods. The culmination of the rapid growth in the politics of consumerism was the passage in 1968 of the Consumer Protection Law. While there are some who might question whether or not these two organizations can be described as feminist, I would argue strongly against any attempt to isolate the actions of the women's consumer groups from a history of Japanese feminism. The national organizations work in close cooperation with the multitude of interest groups represented within the *minikomi* network, frequently linking local initiatives with national policy reform campaigns. The women leaders, scientists and grassroot activists of the consumer organizations provide one of the few consistently effective checks on both industry and government policies in a country where the state-industrial complex operates under few such constraints.

It is also significant that many Japanese women were first politicized through their work within local chapters of the consumer movement in the

1960s, and the successful strategies of lobbying, boycotts, and petitioning that characterized the movement were important tools these women would bring to the feminist campaigns of the seventies.

The change in the popular slogans of the women's movement in the few years from the late 1960s to the early 1970s was indicative of the shift in focus and tone between the feminisms of these two decades. "Let's Contribute to a Richer Tomorrow" gave way to a call for "Solidarity and Action for Women's Independence."[13] As the reality of women's lives looked less and less like the idealized advertising images of a Westernized, hi-tech life of leisure, and as more and more women faced the reality of low wages, no job security, part-time employment, and mandatory retirement on marriage or childbirth, questions of employment equity rapidly gained currency within the women's movement. By the early 1970s, 91 percent of the part-time workers in Tokyo were women over twenty-five, more than 80 percent were married, and more than 70 percent had school-age children.[14] Women seeking an end to discriminatory employment practices found themselves caught in the middle between the interests of government and industry on the one hand and the unions on the other.

Working women were understandably suspicious of the motivation behind an initiative, supported by the Tokyo Chamber of Commerce, for the withdrawal of protective clauses in the 1947 Labor Standards Law. These clauses, while intended to protect women against exploitation, had come to function as a basis for the exclusion of women from certain types of employment. What interest in the withdrawal of these protective clauses did the Chamber of Commerce have? And what was the motivation of the male-dominated unions in mounting a comprehensive campaign to not only protect the existing clauses but to expand the range of the protection in areas such as maternity and menstruation leave and paid time for breast-feeding. Industry clearly recognized the potential financial benefits of unrestricted access to a growing pool of cheaper, part-time female employees. Under the 1947 Labor Standards Law women were excluded from night shifts and excessive overtime. For their part, unions were not unaware of the risk to the status of their full-time male members should industry find itself free to employ larger numbers of women on all shifts and across the whole range of job functions. Women labor activists found themselves caught trying to establish effective and advantageous alliances in an environment where the two major players—industry and organized labor— were each driven by their own independent agendas.[15]

The late 1960s and early 1970s saw a series of well-publicized strikes and court actions that led to some increased awareness of the issue of equal employment and the need for legal reform. Various feminists have pointed out that it was at about the same time that women voters came to outnumber men at the polls that the government became aware of the increasingly large numbers of women attending employment-equity rallies and also began to take the first steps toward addressing women's concerns in the workplace.[16] Although Japan ratified the ILO Convention Number 100 on Equal Pay in 1967, women's groups continued to lobby the government throughout 1968 and 1969 for a closer investigation of gender-based inequities in such areas as differential wages, gender-based retrenchments, and discriminatory retirement policies. The first court cases were brought by women against companies practicing such discriminatory policies in the late 1960s and early 1970s. The courts, however, have proven to be a slow vehicle for either reform or compensation. Tatenaka Shuko's complaint against Tokyo Heavy Metals is a good example. Initiated in 1969, the court case ran until 1980, when she was finally compensated for 15 million yen and reinstated. Some feminists have argued that it was only a public commemorative rally of the ten-year anniversary of her case in 1979 that finally embarrassed the court to settle. In 1969, in response to ongoing lobbying, the Ministry of Labor finally established the Research Group for the 1947 Labor Standards Law with the mandate to bring forward recommendations for reform.

The early 1970s witnessed a series of mixed messages from the government and courts. The passage of the Industrial Home Work Law and the Working Women's Welfare Law marked the first major policy reform aimed at addressing the specific conditions of women's work. Similarly, the granting of maternity leave to public servants (1972), the approval of the Child Allowance Law (1971), and the opening of the first publicly funded day-care center for infants under the age of one (1975) all suggested a growing recognition of a woman's right to work full-time. And yet, several court decisions over the same period found in favor of companies practicing gender-based retrenchment. Rulings on discriminatory retirement and wages policies fluctuated from case to case, leading to a series of regional and national women's protests calling for judicial reform.

The proclamation of the United Nations Decade for Women in 1975 and the subsequent Japan Year of the Woman Conference stimulated new levels of focused lobbying in an attempt to influence the outcome of the ongoing work of the Ministry of Labor's Research Group. Japanese women attending the plethora of international conferences dealing with women's issues in 1975 and the years that followed repeatedly expressed their concern at the extent to which Japanese women's working conditions fell behind those of other industrialized growth economies. Both the Industrial Homework Law and the Working Women's Welfare Law were finally rejected by many women labor activists as no more than Band-Aid measures and largely ineffectual due to the lack of substantive penalties for noncompliance. The most obvious flaw in these fledgling attempts to address women's working conditions was the fact that the fastest growing group was the shadow labor force of part-timers and homeworkers, two areas where either the individual woman worker or her employer often preferred to conceal employment information.[17]

Preliminary findings of the Ministry of Labor Research Group on the Labor Standards Law were released in the early 1970s but it was not until 1978 that the final recommendations were announced. The basic recommendation was for the elimination of all protective clauses on the grounds that they constituted discrimination and locked women out of many job opportunities. Within less than a month women's groups across Japan were organizing conferences and discussion groups to develop strategies for the rejection or modification of the recommendations. The International Women's Year Action Group was the first to call for an organized response. Using its extensive nationwide network of regional action and study groups they were able to mobilize a rapid and comprehensive critique through both the informal channels of the *minikomi* and the mainstream media. The Organization for the Formulation of Our Own Equal Opportunity Act was initially formed as a single-issue campaign group committed to pressuring the government into reopening its deliberations, only this time to do so in close consultation with women's groups. It was the extent of Japanese women's representations to the many international conferences and meetings held in conjunction with the UN International Decade for Women that eventually led the government to sign the 1980 Copenhagen Treaty to End All Forms of Sexual Discrimination.[18] Women's groups developed strategies to maximize the government's sense of potential embarrassment in the international arena if they failed to meet their obligation as signatories. This left five years until the final date for ratification in 1985.

The final result was the passage of an Equal Opportunity Act that rests largely on the good will of the employer and includes only minimal penalties for noncompliance (see Chapter 5 for more details on the act). Feminists were quick to point out that there was little reason for optimism based on the past performance of industry. Early indications suggest that the worst fears of the opponents of the act are being realized as industry shows every sign of interpreting it as an effective deregulation of working hours and a licence to substitute cheaper, nonunionized part-time female workers for male full-time workers wherever possible. In the absence of dramatic changes in the provision of child-care facilities and a significant shift in cultural attitude toward the desirability of full-time mothering, it is likely that women wishing to re-enter the work force will continue to have only two serious options—part-time employment with the average wage of 580 to 600 yen per hour, or contract homework (averaging 380 to 400 yen per hour.[19] There is no indication that the on-going annual increase in married women's part-time labor force participation will subside in the near future.[20] The majority of women surveyed clearly identify economic need as the basis for their choice to reenter the work force. In 1982 it was estimated that 24,000 local day-care centers were needed to meet demand, but at the time there were only 4,739.[21] One response to this major shortfall was the emergence of "baby hotels." These care centers were unregistered and frequently understaffed, poorly equipped, and unhygienic. As early as 1981 the government mounted a special investigation into the rapidly emerging problems of outbreaks of disease and accidents in the baby hotels. By 1983 some 13,000 infants were officially estimated to be enrolled in the 527 known baby hotels. Only 22 percent of these met government requirements for registration.[22] Those who could not gain access to public day-care facilities and either couldn't afford or rejected the option of a baby hotel often fell back on the extended family model.

Women's groups have organized extensively since the early 1980s to pressure the government for both improved child-care facilities and a satisfactory Child-Care Law. Both part-timers and homeworkers are seldom in a position to organize labor action or to develop their own lobbying groups. Isolation, long working hours (including unpaid domestic work), and vulnerability all work against organized action. Extensive lobbying by several major women's groups focusing on all political parties in 1981 and 1982 resulted in the passage of a Part-Time Labor Law in 1983. Although the law was generally seen to take reasonable steps to improve the conditions and security of part-timers, there was minimal implementation. In 1988 a Council of Part-time Workers' Issues was established within the Ministry of Labor to monitor implementation and investigate complaints.

The passage of a Child-Care Law took much longer, and even when it was finally approved in 1991 it met with harsh criticism for its failure to secure the employees reentry to the same or equivalent position over the period of the leave or requirements for paid leave. By 1991 only 20 percent of companies had introduced any form of child-care leave.[23] Equal access to child-care leave has become a key demand of women's groups and the Equal Access Child-Care League has mounted nationwide campaigns for the increased participation of fathers in the child-rearing process. Ironically, while the Ministry of Labor was coordinating with feminist activists and scholars to formulate and monitor procedures to improve the working conditions of women, as recently as 1987 it was still possible for the minister for education to state publicly that it was preferable for women to remain at home for the period of their children's compulsory education.[24] A document published at about the same time entitled "Education for the Twenty-first Century" also stated that women should seek their satisfaction in life from their nurturing role in the family rather than in the work force.[25] The famous media debate over the "Agnes-chan incident" exemplified the continuing pressure on women to devote themselves full-time to child rearing. Agnes Chen (affectionately known by her fans as Agnes-chan), a popular television personality, was severely criticized by a leading spokesperson of the promotherhood lobby when she was reported in the media to be taking her small child to the workplace with her.[26] The debate that ensued over Agnes' action revisited much of the same ground as the Taisho "motherhood debate" and the 1950s "housewife debate," with feminist groups and women's labor organizations rallying yet again to defend the right of women to work. Statistics released in the following year in a major Japanese medical journal indicating significantly higher rates of miscarriage in working women fueled further sensational headlines. However, as the debate raged in the popular media, feminist journals, and books, more and more women were making the choice to return to the workplace on a part-time basis over the second half of the 1980s. By 1990, one in three working women were in part-time positions.[27]

One other trend that has developed in close association with the dramatic increase in part-time workers has been the emergence of a new category of elderly women workers. A 1991 survey indicated that 41 percent of women aged fifty-nine to sixty-nine are actively participating in the work force, usually in low-skilled, part-time positions.[28] The need for older women to return to the work force or, in some cases, to enter the work force for the first time, is a direct result of the "graying" of Japan. Inadequate welfare and pension provisions for the elderly impact seriously on the quality of life that Japanese can look forward to in their old age. The Ministry of Health and Welfare has predicted that by 2015, 20 percent of the population will be over sixty-five-years old and there will be some 5.5 million elderly Japanese living alone.[29] Two-thirds of these single elderly will be women, given their present longer life expectancy. In the absence of adequate government facilities, the burden of care for the increasingly high number of infirm elderly falls on the shoulders of women, in addition to the child-care function. It is estimated that 90 percent of care givers for the elderly are women.[30]

The issue of the increasing number of elderly women as a proportion of the population directly affects patterns of women's employment. There is, as already noted, a trend toward elderly women seeking employment to supplement inadequate welfare and pensions. Given that the gender wage differential is even higher for employees over fifty-five, an increase in the numbers of elderly women entering the work force is attractive to employers.[31] This has only further reinforced the trend toward transforming positions from full-time to part-time status. Another effect is related to child-care needs. Since the mid 1980s more than 40 percent of families with school-age children have been living in three-generation households. However, Ministry of Health and Welfare surveys consistently show that as many as 60 percent of families would take up this option if possible as a means of dealing with the problem of child care and thus freeing the mother to work.[32] From the government's point of view the three-generation household where grandparents can assist in child care and the mother in turn acts as primary care giver for the grandparents offers obvious advantages in terms of the future welfare bill.[33]

Women's groups have expressed concern over this double-edged strategy on the basis that it essentially precludes the mother from full-time employment, locking her into part-time work in addition to an increased burden of unpaid domestic work—a lifetime of care giving to children and the elderly. The preference of most feminist organizations has been to continue to promote a family-leave policy allowing both parents access to paid or unpaid leave with a guarantee of position. Elderly women and professional care givers have actively campaigned since the mid 1980s for independent (nonspousal) pensions for women, higher welfare and pension budgets, increased and improved government care facilities, and better legal protection of the rights of the elderly to self-determination rather than dependence on government or family. Over the last several years the Women's Association for Improvement in an Aging Society and the Forum of Women Directors of Homes for the Elderly have done much to focus new attention on welfare, health care, and work-force reentry issues (salary, conditions, work hours, pension access) from the perspective of the elderly.

In addition to its obvious impact in the area of Japanese women's employment, the UN Decade for Women and Development also played an important role in stimulating a new level of awareness among Japanese women of the relationship between their lives and the conditions of the lives of women in the Third World and throughout Asia.[34] From the early 1960s Japanese women's organizations began sending delegations to the annual Conference of Asian and African Women. The women most involved in the protests against U.S. bases in Japan formed some of the strongest early alliances with the women of Southeast Asia. Vera Mackie writes of this link, "In the 1950s Japan's economy benefited indirectly from the Korean War, and in the '60s from the Vietnam War. Within Japan, the people affected most directly by this relationship lived near American bases or the proposed Narita airport. The women of Kitafuji and the farmers of Sanrizuka (Narita), for example, expressed solidarity with the peoples of Asia and described their own struggles as 'guerrilla warfare.'"[35] There has continued to be close regional cooperation in campaigns to both monitor and protest the presence and activities of U.S. forces in the region with a particular focus on nuclear arms and submarines. Japanese women's groups worked closely with organizations across Asia in coordinating peace petitions to the U.S. government calling for an end to the Vietnam War.

At the height of the anti–Vietnam War and anti-AMPO demonstrations a coalition of the five largest national women's organizations played a key role in mobilizing large numbers of women to demonstrate and lobby. Women were also active in the left-wing and student organizations central to the antigovernment protests. The peace movement in Japan has been closely linked to a deeply rooted antiwar platform among women's groups throughout the postwar period. While SCAP had promoted an antiwar platform among women's groups it had discouraged any antinuclear rhetoric as potentially anti-U.S. This was a serious source of difference between the Occupation command and women's organizations. From the late 1940s major women's groups cooperated to petition both the U.S. government and the Occupation command for the demilitarization of Japan, including the removal of all U.S. forces and military infrastructure. In 1952, the same year that the Occupation officially ended, the Japan Women's Council officially declared an antinuclear and peace platform. During the 1960s questions of the return of Okinawa, the presence of U.S. military bases on Japanese soil, U.S. nuclear submarine access to Japanese maritime space and port facilities, Japanese government support for U.S.

involvement in Vietnam, and other military issues were the objects of constant protest and lobbying by women's groups across the country.[36] Organizations as diverse as the YWCA, Japanese League of Women Voters, National League of Regional Women's Organizations, the Women's Bar Association of Japan, and the Christian Women's Temperance Union each independently declared their opposition to nuclear armaments and a firm commitment to the protection of what is frequently labeled the "Peace Constitution." Over the 1960s Japanese feminists petitioned leaders on both sides of the Pacific and sought antiwar coalitions with Asian, European, and U.S. women's groups to maximize pressure on both the Japanese and American governments on a range of defense issues.

One of the most well-known ongoing antimilitary campaigns was mounted by the local women's groups of the rural communities surrounding Mt. Fuji. This region has been used for military training and war games since early in the century. In her work *The Women of Kitafuji*, Ando Toshiko describes passionately the struggle the women of this region mounted when the noise and intrusion of postwar U.S. military and Japanese Self-Defence Force exercises began to encroach seriously on the fabric of their daily lives.[37] Vera Mackie writes of these women, "it is the 'grandmothers' who lead the movement— their sons are engaged in wage labour, while their daughters are responsible for child care and farming. Years before Greenham Common, these grandmothers were occupying huts on the military practice grounds and employing various forms of active and passive resistance. The women of Kitafuji continue to provide inspiration for peace activists."[38]

An uncompromising commitment to peace found its strongest and earliest expressions within the women's movement in the 1960s but has now taken root as one of the defining principles of Japanese feminism. The Mothers Congress emerged as perhaps the strongest continuous antiwar and antinuclear voice in postwar Japan. At the time of the formation of a nationwide coalition of women's groups to protest the AMPO treaty reform in 1960, the Mothers Congress played a central organizing role in mobilizing the women's protest. While the often conservative position adopted by the congress on issues of women and work and motherhood have at times been at odds with the agendas of some feminist organizations, it has continued to receive support and recognition for the success of its regular peace conferences. Another key organization in the peace movement has been the Women's Liaison Group against War, which also coordinates both lobbying and conference activities as well as the high profile "speech marathon" that takes place each year outside the

Shibuya station in downtown Tokyo—a frequent site for public speeches by right-wing, promilitary activists. The speech marathons began in 1981 and are now a popular annual event drawing considerable media attention.

In the mid-1980s a coalition of women's groups was extremely effective in coordinating major protests that delayed the passage of the LDP challenge to the 1 percent of GNP limit on defense spending (finally approved by Prime Minister Nakasone in 1986). Similarly, a nationwide coalition of forty-nine women's groups campaigned against the PKO (Peace-Keeping Operations) Bill with its proposal to allow Japanese Self-Defense Forces to be mobilized on overseas missions under the UN flag (it was approved in 1992).[39] Japan's commitment to the U.S. policy in the Gulf War also prompted strong protest, including a major street demonstration in the Ginza. Though in each of these cases the amendments were finally passed into law, the actions of the women's protests and their continued monitoring of defense-policy issues has seriously restricted the conservative agenda for an expanded military role for Japan. In reaction to the passage of the PKO Bill, Japanese women's groups hosted an international conference in Tokyo on the theme "Peace and the Role of Women in Asia." The interest generated by recent initiatives of the peace movement attracted over twenty-seven thousand women to the 1991 Mothers Congress, where peace issues were a central theme.

Other areas in which there has been increased cooperation between Japanese and Southeast Asian women's groups are the attempts to block the continued recruitment of Southeast Asian women into prostitution in Japan and the boom in "sex tours" from Japan to the countries of Southeast Asia. From the mid 1970s Japanese women's groups began forming coalitions with anti-prostitution organizers in such countries as Thailand and the Philippines in an attempt to bring an end to this North-South sex trade. The Tokyo-based Asian Women's Association has been central to campaigns to change public attitudes toward prostitution both in Japan and Southeast Asia. The sex trade is only one of the areas in which this group actively pursues a program of both education, coordinated action, and lobbying. The association came into being in 1977 as the outgrowth of a period of research and ongoing consultations stimulated by the hosting of the 1974 Asian Women's Congress in Japan. *Asian Women's Liberation* is the name of the association's publication, which carries reports and other materials generated around the issues raised at the regular discussion meetings known as Onna Daigaku (Women's University).

While the sex trade remains a major focus of the Asian Women's Association's activities, other central concerns have become the exploitation of female labor by Japanese subsidiaries operating in Southeast Asia and the impact on the lives of women and children in the region from environmentally destructive Japanese development projects. The "downloading" of labor intensive and "dirty" (polluting) industries from Japan to the countries of Southeast Asia was central to a national reorientation toward the service and information sectors and high-tech, sunrise industries. In the "recipient" countries of Southeast Asia the effect was the creation of large numbers of low-paid, low-skilled factory jobs. Local labor-brokers actively recruited young, poorly educated, rural women into the new factories, where working conditions were frequently in breach of the most basic ILO guidelines. At the same time, in Japan jobs in the manufacturing industry declined dramatically while new opportunities for work in the service and information industries were characteristically part-time and underpaid. The highly computerized nature of these two industries also led to an increase in homework contracts. The subsequent fragmentation and decentralization of Japanese women workers further weakened any potential for collective bargaining or other forms of labor organization. The nature of women's work in both Japan and Southeast Asia was thus dramatically redefined by the new priorities of Japanese capital over the 1970s.

Many of the questions surrounding Japan's impact on the lives of the women of Southeast Asia have gained wider public recognition since the late 1980s due to a series of cases that have attracted widespread media coverage. These cases have been typified by the physical abuse of illegal women immigrant workers in the entertainment and bar industry, and this abuse has frequently involved varying levels of police corruption.[40] Several instances of forced repatriation of illegal workers in 1990 and 1991 also drew the anger of such groups as the Asian Women's Forum, Asian Women's Association, the Women's Action Group, and the Resource Center for Filipino Issues. In each instance women made up as much as 90 percent of the deportee group, and the majority of the women were bar workers. Women's groups protested that the authorities were concentrating on prostitutes and bar workers and ignoring the illegal male workers who make up a rapidly growing proportion of the day laborers in Japan. The Philippines is the source of the largest proportion of both male and female illegal workers, but an increasing number of Thai women are also finding their way into the bar world. Feminists argue that the government is avoiding the issue of illegal workers because any tightening of regulations would affect the number of foreign unskilled male workers available to perform the range of manual and dirty jobs that fewer and fewer Japanese workers are willing to accept. It would be impossible to offer an amnesty only to male illegal workers, but to extend amnesty to illegal women workers is seen by conservatives as tantamount to sanctioning prostitution.

Until recently, much of the activity of Japanese women's groups in relation to the illegal women workers focused on an antiprostitution campaign. The Temperance Union and the Antiprostitution Association have been particularly active. This approach to the problem has lead to some considerable tension around moral issues. The Women's House of Help was established in 1986 by the Temperance Union and has worked hard for the human rights of illegal Asian women workers, but the union remains committed to the abolition of prostitution. The name of one other action group, Stop the Flow of Filipino Women, has caused some uneasiness among the Filipino women themselves. The prostitutes are seeking safety and support, not the elimination of their source of income. Filipino women have now begun to take the initiative in organizing their own support groups based on such issues as protection from violence, improved working conditions, legalization of their status, and protection from deportation. Filipino women who have married in rural Japanese villages where there is a shortage of eligible Japanese brides have also formed support networks to deal with a diverse range of issues—isolation, abuse, divorce, custody of children, the right to remain in Japan after divorce, and citizenship. Some of these areas of concern overlap with the interests of prostitutes (both in Japan and Asia) who have mothered children by Japanese fathers. There is now an Association of Filipino Brides and a "community" newspaper published out of Tokushima prefecture.

The "comfort women" issue has also prompted a new level of cooperation between Japanese and Korean women's groups.[41] Estimates of the number of women forced to serve as prostitutes for Japanese troops during the Pacific War vary from seventy thousand to two hundred thousand. Up to 80 percent of these women were Korean. There were various efforts by Korean and Japanese-Korean women's groups seeking compensation from the Japanese government in the postwar period. However, the government continued to deny any responsibility and argued that the military did not conscript these women directly. A series of embarrassing disclosures by ex–military officials and careful archival research provided the basis for a massive public campaign from 1990 to 1992, with considerable media attention in the form of television documentaries and interviews. Public opinion polls in 1992 indicated a significant shift in attitude in favor of a government statement of responsibility and some offer of compensation. Immediately prior to handing over power to the new coalition government in 1993, the LDP approved the release of an official document acknowledging limited responsibility for the fate of the "comfort women." The issues of compensation and the need for quick action if the victims themselves are to benefit in their own lifetimes remain unresolved.

## FROM SEXUAL LIBERATION TO A DISCOURSE OF SEXUALITY

Nineteen seventy is frequently given as the year that the *ribu* ("lib"—as an abbreviation of women's liberation) movement began in Japan. It is important to distinguish here between *ribu* and the feminist movement. The Japanese feminists I've interviewed always insist on this distinction, pointing out that while feminism has a long history in Japan, the *ribu* movement emerged in the specific circumstances of the 1970s. It was most closely associated with the life and work of Tanaka Mitsu and the publication *Ribu Nyuusu* (Lib News).[42] This movement shared much more in common with the American women's liberation movement, but Japanese women saw it as distinct from its American counterpart and even recognized certain risks in allowing the media to conflate the two movements. One well-known feminist remembers the period in this way:

> Even the second wave of Japanese feminism in the late 60s and 70s, although it took the same name of "women's liberation" and was accused in the media of copying the American women, in fact had its own quite distinct origins in Japan. Tanaka Mitsu, one of the early leaders of this second wave, said to me once that she can still remember her own sense of amazement when she discovered the existence of women's liberation in America. She had already found her own identical goal before this. . . . Unfortunately American feminism, or Women's Lib as it was called then, was introduced to Japan through the mass media. The women in the movement were presented as eccentrics. The media focused on such isolated events as bra-burning ceremonies and the violent protest at the Miss America quest. That was Japan's first exposure to the American movement. Japanese feminists were not anxious to be identified with all of this given the media environment of the day. They were wary of giving the media any excuse to represent them in the same light.[43]

Indeed many feminists were openly critical of Chupiren (Pink Helmet Brigade), the Japanese women's group that incorporated some of the more exuberant strategies of the American movement while implementing them in its own quite distinctive way. There was a real concern that the media would grab at any opportunity to sensationalize the "dangers" of feminism. Such fears appear to have been well grounded when one looks at the headlines and general coverage of feminism in the mainstream media of the early to mid 1970s. One headline in the usually staid *Asahi Shimbun* read, "They're Invading the Empire of Men: Groups Forming in Every Region."[44] Under the leadership of Enoki Misako, Chupiren took up a strategy of high-profile events, including the occupation of public and corporate buildings to demand the legalization of the contraceptive pill, surrounding the offices of individual politicians in their reknowned pink helmets and chanting loud slogans, and various methods for publicly embarrassing husbands whose alimony payments were in arrears (e.g., appearing in the husband's office in large numbers with banners and pink helmets). Their actions received wide coverage in the general media up until the collapse of the group in 1977.

An important dimension of the development of *ribu* feminism over the 1970s was a new focus on female sexuality. The journal that became a key voice for this aspect of women's self-discovery was entitled *Onna Erosu* (Women Eros). A total of seventeen volumes were published between 1973 and 1982. The journal took a special theme approach with topics including "Liberation from What?" "The Construction of Images of Woman," "The Work of Erotic Desire," and "Thoughts on Prostitution." Questions central to women's identity within the family and marriage dominated many of the issues. In a review some years later one Japanese feminist who had been an avid reader of the journal recalled how important it had been to her that the language used in *Onna Erosu* was less stiff and academic than that of the U.S. feminist works translated into Japanese or the publications of the growing number of Japanese academic feminists.[45] The frequent use of the feminine first-person pronoun (*watashi*) and the sense of familiarity created by a more colloquial or informal language was a direct carry over from the style of the *minikomi*.

The one conspicuous absence in *Onna Erosu* was the voice of the emerging lesbian community. The 1970s saw the first signs of an organized and public lesbian movement in Japan. Lesbian groups and centers that formed over this period ranged in size from smaller local solidarity groups, communal houses, and lesbian coffee shops and bars to the Lesbian Feminist Center and Lavender Gang, whose memberships ran into the hundreds. Conferences, workshops, dance groups, consciousness-raising sessions, newsletters, and social parties were all part of the activities of these larger lesbian organizations. The movement in Japan was quick to form close alliances with other feminist groups and there has been a strong history of cooperation between gay and nongay women. Many lesbian women still express concern, however, that they feel marginalized within the feminist movement in Japan despite this history of frequent alliances around specific campaigns. Japanese lesbians also frequently speak of the difficulties in creating any shared agenda with the male homosexual community. Gay men's organizations are often criticized in this context as being bound to very traditional notions of the feminine and female sexuality. While there has been a continual, if gradual, increase in the number of women publicly identifying themselves as lesbians, on the whole it remains true that tolerance of male homosexuality is greater than of lesbians. Despite the incorporation of gay couples into a 1992 special presentation of a popular Japanese television dating game, the day when lesbian couples might also appear in prime-time programming seems far away. Similarly, special gay-culture issues of major critical theory journals over the last several years have focused on male homosexuality and made minimal if any reference to lesbianism.[46]

The focus of much of the discussion of sexuality during the heyday of the *ribu* movement was indeed closer to the call for sexual liberation in the 1960s in North America. However, even by the mid 1970s there was a marked shift beyond the politics of individual sexual freedom toward attempts to achieve substantive structural change within the institutions that had come to define a woman's sexual identity and her relationship to her body and to reorganize women's relations to those institutions. A key stimulus of this new focus was the 1970s conservative campaign to reform the Eugenic Protection Law. The attack on access to abortion demanded a thorough critique of the legal and medical institutions if the antireform movement was to mobilize sufficient support to defeat the proposed amendment, which would remove the so-called "economic reasons" clause. This clause had effectively offered a loophole for access to legal abortion in the postwar period. The first antiabortion campaign was defeated in 1973. Recognizing that this was not to be an isolated event, concerned women organized a group known as the Fighting Women, which was committed to the protection of abortion rights.

The conservatives mounted another major public campaign for reform in 1983, but with ten years of research and activism behind them the women of the antireform movement rallied a coalition that extended far beyond the women's movement. A decade earlier the focus had been direct action and lobbying, but in 1982 and throughout the 1980s the strategy focused on mapping the interconnectedness of what had previously been treated as separate women's issues. Special editions of journals such as *Agora* and *Onna Eros*, the many publications of the *minikomi*, dozens of feminist books and monographs, and thematic conferences and community workshops drew attention to the continuities between the abortion-law reform campaign, employment equity, the growing pressure for the privatization of welfare, and increased military spending. The pro–abortion rights coalition of 1982 included some seventy organizations representing the diversity of interests groups whose concerns converged around this one issue.[47]

Another reform campaign began in 1989 when the Right shifted its strategy away from the elimination of the "economic reasons" clause to focus on the legal period for abortion. The proposal to reduce the maximum limit for legal abortions from twenty-four to twenty-two weeks was finally approved by the Health and Welfare Ministry despite extensive lobbying and organized protest. Highly emotive images of foetuses at twenty-four weeks of development and documentation of improvements in life-support technologies for premature births within the second trimester convinced those who were not prepared to withdraw access to abortion that there was a basis for reducing the legal period. Feminists have conceded that they were unprepared for the shift in strategy.

The medical and legal professions came under still further scrutiny in the 1980s as a result of a series of investigations into malpractice in gynecological and obstetrics clinics. Women were shocked by disclosures of staggeringly high numbers of unnecessary surgical procedures in specialized clinics, botched hysterectomies, and excessive levels of intervention in births. The feminist response to these scandals took various forms, including local educational initiatives, midwife support networks, the publication of works dedicated to the demystifying of both the female body and the medical institution itself (e.g., the project to translate *Our Bodies, Ourselves*),[48] national conferences, and local action groups (e.g., the Tokyo Association for the Examination of Maternity Clinics and the Association for Rethinking Women's Bodies and Medicine).

The debate surrounding the Equal Opportunity Law in the 1980s also involved feminist critiques of the convergence in the Labor Standards Law of certain dimensions of the medical and legal framing of female sexuality. The protective clauses were interpreted as unnecessarily problematizing the working woman's reproductive functions—menstruation, pregnancy, breast-feeding, menopause—in ways that defined clear limits to women's capacity to participate in the work force. The ongoing privileging of the reproductive function encoded in the protective clauses was seen to be a direct throwback to earlier eugenic policies based on the German model at the time of World War II. Many women who did not support the removal of bans on night shifts and overtime did support moves to withdraw those protective clauses specific to women's reproductive functions. Concerns emerged that the problematization of women's reproductive functions in the context of work was directly related to a concurrent general trend toward the overmedicalization of the female body. Women's groups began to draw links between protective employment practices, the new high profile afforded menopause, the "discovery" of a plethora of housewive's diseases ranging from "fear of supermarkets" to "high-rise apartment phobia," the continued opposition to the legalization of the contraceptive pill by both conservative politicians and the medical profession, and the recurring conservative campaign for an end to legal abortion. The point of continuity was seen as the management of women's bodies.

In a country where there is already such extensive criticism of the level of institutional intervention in the area of reproduction, it is not surprising that feminists have been quick to respond to the new reproductive technologies and biogenetics industry. A key concern is the absence of an ethical or legal framework adequate to the rapidly emerging challenges posed by the potential of the new technologies. The existing Eugenic Protection Law actually lends itself well to a conservative agenda of increased monitoring of both the prenatal mother and fetus and the postnatal infant. As recently as 1986–1987 the government approved Ministry of Health and Welfare recommendations for the expansion of the already demanding system of compulsory health and immunization checks for preschool and school-age children. A nationwide system of "mothercare" clinics already closely tracks pregnancies for any sign of abnormality from the time of conception to birth in what many critics see as an unnecessarily high level of fetal monitoring. Gender-differentiated birth statistics for Asia are already showing a marked trend toward gender-selection procedures favoring male live births. In Japan both feminists and the disabled are closely examining the risks of abuse of fetal screening technologies given the current legislative controls. The potential for eugenic screening is still implicit in the Eugenic Protection Law, and there is sufficient evidence of profit-motivated corruption in the medical profession to justify the suspicion that women who can afford genetic and gender screening will increasingly seek access to these options.

Critics of the critics of the new technologies argue that it is inconsistent to fight for women's right to manage their bodies and then reject out of hand the personal choices of some individual women to take advantage of the availability of new procedures. This is not the first feminist critique of technology. Since the mid 1960s there has been an ongoing analysis of the impact of office and industrial technology on women's health. As technological initiatives continue to break new ground and disrupt familiar ethical frameworks there is considerable potential for increased dissent between antitechnology revisionists, proponents of careful monitoring of the application of new technologies, and those who see them as liberating.

The establishment of the Tokyo Rape Crisis Center and extensive regional support groups for victims of sexual harassment and sexual violence demonstrate a new awareness of, and willingness to address, the various forms of aggression that restrict the freedom of movement of women whether that movement is along a city street, a subway route, an office, one's own home, or even a corporate promotion's ladder.[49] Here again, violence and harassment are interpreted as mechanisms for the containment or management of women's bodies and their sexuality. Nineteen eighty-seven marked an important shift in judicial practice with two key findings in sexual violence cases. In the first case a woman was acquitted of murder charges in the death of a man who was struck by a train after falling onto the subway tracks when she struggled against his sexual advances. In the second case a man was found guilty of raping his wife in the first legal acknowledgment in Japan of the concept of marital rape. Women's groups exploited media interest in sensational court cases to gain maximum publicity for their fight. Since the late 1980s and 1990s there has been a proliferation of books and media coverage on the topics of sexual harassment and sexual violence. In 1990 alone some ten separate books on harassment appeared, including "guides" for male coworkers that ranged from sensitization and consciousness-raising strategies to more basic "how not to" and "how to and not get caught" guidebooks.[50] In 1990 a Japanese network took what was at the time considered a bold step when it aired a prime-time made-for-television movie on one woman's experience of sexual harassment in the workforce.[51] Over the last several years various support and lobby groups have formed around both sexual harassment and sexual violence, including the Women's Network against Sexual Assault and the Committee for Women's Rights and Sexuality. In 1989 the Tokyo Lawyers Association for Equal Rights submitted to the government a call for clear policies and legal reform to address the issue of sexual harassment. Surveys organized by both municipal and prefectural governments from 1989 to 1991 indicated that 70 percent of women had experienced some form of workplace harassment and that 60 percent of resignations or transfers were the result of harassment. Feminist groups have been quick to point out that any implementation of the Equal Employment Opportunity Act is seriously jeopardized by such high levels of sexual harassment. In both 1991 and 1992 the office of the prime minister gave assurances that the problem of *hara*, as it has come to be known (from the English "harrassment"), was under review, but no concrete policy has yet been developed.

Some feminists have expressed doubts as to the extent of the structural changes achieved over the 1970s in relation to questions of women's sexual identity. There is no doubt that the *ribu* movement did create a dramatic shift in public attitudes toward premarital sex, as is clearly documented in the Moore reports on Japanese sexual practices.[52] However, it is argued that the liberalization of attitudes toward sex and attempts to encourage women to value their own sexual pleasure have at best rendered superficial changes, and that most of the shift in both attitude and practice has been limited to nonmarried women. Nakanishi Toyoko, who sponsored the translation of *Our Bodies, Ourselves* into Japanese had the following comment on the continuing power of traditional taboos to limit and distort women's ability to articulate both their fears and desires, "We have to be able to express our experience of our bodies and of reality to a lawyer, a policeman, a doctor, without any sense of shame. . . . We also have to be able to talk to our daughters, our mothers and each other. A wife has to be able to express to her husband why she isn't sexually satisfied, what she wants him to do to give her pleasure. . . . Japanese women don't have a sense of freedom of expression, don't even have the words to express their experience, their desires, regardless of whether they are in a doctor's surgery, a lawyer's office or their marriage bed."[53]

## THE NEW WAVE: ACADEMIC FEMINISM

The impact of sexual liberation strategies did not extend to the reform of the institution that is at the heart of gender and sexual politics in Japan, the family. The abortion-reform campaign and the recent development of complex critiques of the medical and legal professions around such issues as sexual and domestic violence, sexual harassment in the workplace, biotechnologies, medical malpractice, contraception, and protective labor codes have led to the emergence of a more theoretically oriented feminism. This new feminism has focused on the disclosure and analysis of the discursive practices that have functioned as the ideological architecture that has housed the dominant construction of female identity and sexuality over much of the last century. A new generation of what some describe as "academic feminists" has begun the work of constructing a contemporary Japanese discourse of sexuality.[54]

A central focus of the emerging discourse of sexuality has been the analysis of the role of the media in the construction of gender and sexual identity. At the level of direct action, groups such as Media Watch, Rethinking Gender in Advertising, Women's Network against Sexual Violence, and Women's Action Group have mounted high-profile public campaigns against the production and circulation of pornography and images of gender stereotyping. Targets have included television commercials, billboards, public advertising of sex clubs, call-girl services, telephone sex and party lines, and sexual violence in television programming and film. There have also been a considerable number of books published since the early 1980s that have developed a complex theoretical field of analysis of questions of representation.[55] The most controversial dimension of this location of the media within a discourse of sexuality has been the pornography debate. This controversy has centered largely around the issue of censorship, with procensorship feminists arguing for a direct causative relationship between the consumption of pornographic images and sexual violence and gender stereotyping in society. Anticensorship feminists have argued that there is no evidence of a causative link and have drawn on the experience of the war and Occupation-period censorship regulations to underline the risks of government intervention in cultural production.[56] The fact that special-focus issues on gender and sexuality have become common among mainstream journals of culture, literature, and philosophy is indicative of the currency of the new discourse of sexuality within the contemporary Japanese intellectual and cultural landscape.

The Japanese government frequently cites the fact that more women complete postsecondary education than men as one proof of the improved status of women in the 1980s and 1990s. These figures are misleading to the extent that they do not reflect the gender differentiations that characterize the male and female experience of postsecondary education.[57] Even though things may not be as rosy as the Ministry of Education would like to suggest, it is true that more women are now achieving significantly higher levels of education. This shift in the level of education of middle-class Japanese women has been pointed to as one explanation for certain changes in the focus and strategies of Japanese feminism over the last decade. The International Women's Year Action Group is a good example of the new trends. When the International Decade for Women came to an official end in 1985, the association reconfigured itself as the Women's Action Group and continued to maintain a high profile. While it still utilizes more familiar methods of lobbying, demonstrations, and rallies, it has also developed an ongoing structure of reading groups, research teams, and public lectures and publications. Direct action is now combined with long-term education projects and well-researched programs for legal and policy reform.

In 1979 the Women's Studies Association of Japan was founded. The activities of this group over the 1980s were typical of a growing pattern across Japan of an increased interest in the introduction of a more formalized concept of women's studies and feminist research. This included demands from coalitions of women scholars, PTAs, teachers, and local and national women's groups for the removal of sexual discrimination and gender stereotyping from school textbooks; the development of sex-education programs for schools; the incorporation of women's issues, experience, and achievement into curriculum materials; and equal access to all courses. At the postsecondary level there was a move to introduce women's studies programs and to increase the numbers of women faculty and graduate students. Changes within the universities have been slower in coming but there is today a small but influential group of feminist scholars teaching and pursuing research at the university level.

Another important development has been the proliferation of adult education courses available to women through culture centers and community outreach programs. Local and provincial governments have invested considerable amounts of money into women's resource and community centers over the 1980s. There are those who have criticized these centers and the programs they offer as a means of diverting the attentions and political energy of a large population of educated middle-class women with an increasing number of leisure hours. There does seem to be some basis for arguing that the government's motivation in supporting these centers is fundamentally conservative, but one commentator has observed that while "it is tempting to dismiss [them] as merely cosmetic . . . there may be more radical potential in these centers than was realized by anyone at a governmental level." [58] A visit to the Women's Resource Center in Idebashi in 1991 confirmed this sense that the politics of these centers has been renegotiated. At one table a group of Japanese and Filipino prostitutes were meeting with two academic feminists to develop a position paper for the prostitutes to present to a government enquiry into the status of illegal women workers in Japan. At the same time a group of Ainu women were consulting with the center's librarian, who was helping them locate comparative materials in the center archives for use in their campaigns for the recognition of the particular problems faced by women of indigenous populations. Such alliances are frequent and belie any clear-cut distinction between an academic and nonacademic feminism in Japan.

Chizuko Ueno, perhaps Japan's most internationally well-known feminist and a contributor to this volume, has related how important it is to her in the Japanese context to be able to present her work effectively on any given topic to an audience of either academic feminists or community-based feminists. She points out that at many feminist conferences in Japan it is not possible to take for granted the language one is using and that foreign feminists who have criticized her for a popularization of feminism in Japan are failing to recognize the distinct challenges and strengths of a movement that requires accessible and open forms of communication. [59] Many of Japan's most influential and popular feminist critics and theorists are located outside the university system. These "independent" or "freelance" feminists are the source of some of the most challenging of the new academic feminist criticism. The shelves of the women's studies section in Japanese bookstores are lined with the works of these institutionally nonaffilliated feminists. While the continuing institutional barriers to women in the academy are one explanation for the emergence of this group, many of these women have made conscious choices to locate their work outside the academy, closer to specific sites of cultural and political activity. Their theoretical and critical writings weave in and out of the fabric of the daily life of women.

Over the 1980s the expanding field of feminist theory and research produced a new space within the public domain for the examination of the multiple discourses that intersect around the female body, ordering and organizing that body within a gendered and clearly differentiated role in relation to the goals and priorities of the body politic. A growing consensus among feminists is that major reforms cannot be achieved before a far-reaching redefinition of the family and the concept and practice of motherhood in Japanese society. This has essentially led the feminist movement back full cycle, yet again, to the "motherhood debate." One of the first major theoretical debates within the new academic feminism developed around Aoki Yayoi's use of the term "female principle" as a central concept of her theory of ecofeminism. She used the term to describe an alternative conceptualization of social values and practices. The term was criticized as an essentialist romanticization of the "female" that locked women into the traditional nurturing role at the same time as it called for a feminization of men. Ironically, some of Aoki's strongest critics went on themselves to call for the return of the father to the family and a more equal distribution of the nurturing role between men and women.[60] *Bosei* (motherhood) remains one of the most contentious issues within feminism. While some groups are firmly committed to the sanctity of motherhood and the domestic role, others would identify the current condition of *bosei* as what ails contemporary Japanese society. Still others are committed to an examination of the complex ways in which women internalize the dominant ideological construction of motherhood and its relation to both the family and the state. Some feminists call for a feminization of Japanese society while others decry this as a romanticization of conservative or traditional gender differentiations. The one point of agreement is that the family and motherhood are the primary sites of contestation and negotiation for Japanese feminism as Japan moves through the 1990s.[61]

Feminists I have interviewed in recent years, both in their discussions with me and in their writings, express a deep concern over what might be coined the "comfort zone" inhabited by so many Japanese women today. There is a general sense that the current level of material comfort achieved by Japanese middle-class women is creating a new complacency. The 1989 elections are often cited as proof of this. The media generally cited the so-called "woman problem" of Prime Minister Uno as the reason the women's movement was able to mobilize large numbers of middle-class women to vote against conservative candidates in the election of that year and elect the most women in a single election campaign since 1946. However, feminists point out that the affair between Prime Minister Uno and a geisha, and his subsequent payoffs to that woman for her silence, were far less significant to women voters than the ongoing revelation of financial scandals unfolding around the LDP and the recently introduced consumer tax. The level of attention paid to this tax in the various campaign speeches of women candidates in the 1989 election and in the *minikomi* publications in the period leading up to the election leads many feminists to identify the consumption tax as the primary cause of women's disenchantment with the government in 1989. The continued revelation of even more outrageous financial scandals has not provoked protests or action that come close to matching the outrage women expressed when confronted with a concrete increase in the cost of daily life in an already tightening domestic economy.

This reading of the 1989 election reinforces concerns that the potentially powerful political block of middle-class women is now focused primarily on quality-of-life issues—maintaining the "comfort zone." The media has dubbed this the "Hanako generation" after a women's magazine of that title that specializes in life-style articles and up-market advertising for upwardly mobile housewives. Ueno has described their situation in the following terms, "These women make very practical and realistic choices in the context of contemporary Japanese society. . . . They make careful choices between the necessary household income and their desired leisure time. . . . Lifestyle is a very real concept for these women but it is a commodity that is purchased rather than a freedom that is fought for. . . . They are only doing what is reasonable given the limited options available to them. It is the fact that their lifestyle is so comfortable that makes them so unlikely to leave it or do anything that would unsettle it."[62] Looking at the proliferation of luxury and special-focus consumer magazines, books, television programs, life-style oriented adult-education courses, mail-order catalogs, and so on over the last several years in Japan, it would indeed appear that one of the greatest challenges facing feminism in Japan in the 1990s will be the need to develop strategies to motivate this influential block of women to move beyond the "comfort zone." No transformation of the institution of the family will be possible as long as the Hanako generation remain entrenched in suburban consumer life. The titles of new feminist releases in the bookstores leave no doubt that feminists continue to see the family as the primary site for the renegotiation of female identity. Not surprisingly, this feminist attention to the family has generated a quick response from conservative scholars decrying the "crisis in the family." Commenting on this conservative defense of the family Toyoko Nakanishi laments, "There is no crisis in the Japanese family. If only it were true! The new class of leisured women is firmly committed to the institution. The challenge facing us as feminists in Japan today is to create just such a crisis."[63]

## NOTES

1. Chiyo Saito, "Nihonkei no feminisumu to Agora," *Agora* 34, 116.
2. This article focuses on postwar Japanese feminism. There is still much work to be done to address the history of prewar feminism in English scholarship. I refer readers seeking works on prewar feminism to Sharon Seivers, *Flowers in Salt: The Beginnings of a Feminist Consciousness in Modern Japan* (Stanford, Calif.: Stanford University Press, 1983); G. L. Rubenstein, *Recreating Japanese Women: 1600–1945* (Berkeley: University of California Press, 1991). In Japanese, see Hideko Maruoka, *Fujin shisoo keiseishi nooto* vol. 1 (Tokyo: Domesu, 1982); and Kikue Yamakawa, *Nihon fujin shisoo* (Tokyo: Daiwa shobo, 1981).
3. My article "Altered States: The Condition of Being Woman" in Andrew Gordon, *Postwar Japan as History* (Berkeley: University of California Press, 1993), also deals with the impact of state policy on women's lives over the postwar period.
4. *Ibid.*
5. See Sumiko Tanaka's discussion of this shift in the attitudes toward domestic unpaid work and the status of working women in *Josei kaiho no shiso to kodo* (Tokyo: Jitsushinsha, 1975), chapter 1, part 4 and chap. 2, parts 1 and 2. The recent volume *Koodo seicho no jidai*, edited by Onnatachi no ima o tou kai (Tokyo: Inpakuto Shuppankai, 1991), offers a useful collection of essays dealing with the major concerns faced by women over the early years of rapid economic growth.
6. Policy details and employment statistics for this section are drawn from Buckley, "Altered States."
7. Dorothy Robins-Mowry, *Women of Modern Japan* (Boulder, Colo.: Westview Press, 1973), 180.
8. Takashi Takimoto develops a brief but insightful introduction to the gendered nature of *naishoku* in Yamamoto Tetsuji, ed., *Keizai, sekkusu to jendaa*, in the *Unplugging Series*, Shinhyoron, Tokyo, 1983.
9. Saito's account of this period is offered in her interview in Buckley, *Broken Silence*, forthcoming (Berkeley: University of California Press, 1995).
10. Aoki interview in Buckley, *Broken Silence.*

11. Sachiko Ide's work on women and language in Japan examines the highly gendered nature of communication and its implications for feminist strategies in that country. See Ide, *Onna no kotoba, otoko no kotoba* (Tokyo: Nihon keizai tsushinsha, 1979); Ide, Hanaoka, and McGloin, eds., *Aspects of Japanese Women's Language* (Tokyo: Kurosoi Publishers, 1990). In English, see her more recent work discussed in Ide's interview in Buckley, *Broken Silence*.

12. Robins-Mowry is well positioned by virtue of her close contact with the leaders of these organizations, and her account of their development is helpful. See her *Women of Modern Japan*, 197–212 in particular.

13. *Ibid.*, 183.

14. *Ibid.*, 179. For more detailed discussion of the shifts in women's employment patterns over the 1970s, see Buckley, "Altered States"; Maruoka, *Fujin shisoo keiseishi nooto*, chap. 5; and Kayako Nakamura, *Paatotaimu Q&A* (Tokyo: Gakuyo shoin, 1983). Nakayama's work was one of the earliest comprehensive reviews of the new conditions of women's employment. See also Hisako Takahashi, ed., *Kawari yuku fujin rodo* (Tokyo: Yuhikaku, 1983) for another excellent collection of essays on the conditions of women's work in the 1970s.

15. For a representative selection of articles on employment equity and the relationship between women's working conditions and welfare policies in the 1970s and early 1980s, see *Danjo byodo, bosei hogo*, special issue of *Agora* 22 (1980).

16. For further analysis of policy developments over the 1970s and 1980s, see Buckley, "Altered States"; and Maruoka, *Fujin shisoo keiseishi nooto*, chaps. 5, 6, and 8.

17. For details of the early development of the *paato* workforce, see Nakamura, *Paatotaimu*.

18. *Agora* 23 (1980) was a special issue devoted entirely to the Copenhagen conference.

19. Salary range drawn from statistics listed in 1987–1990 timelines of the annual *Fujin hakusho*, ed., Nihon fujin dantai rengokai (Tokyo: Horupu Publications).

20. For discussion of the continuing growth of the part-time labor force, see "Naze onna wa paatotaimu os shitai no ka?" *Agora Monthly*, no. 133 (September 1988).

21. See the analysis of day-care policy implications for working women in Akiko Fuse, "Japanese Family in Transition," parts 1 and 2, *Japan Foundation Newsletter*, November and December 1984.

22. Timeline, *Fujin hakusho* (1983).

23. Timeline, *Fujin hakusho* (1991).

24. Timeline, *Fujin hakusho* (1987).

25. *Ibid.*

26. For details of the Agnes-chan debate, see *Agnes ronsoo o yomu*, ed. Agnes ronsoo o tanoshimukai (Tokyo: JICC shuppankyoku, 1988).

27. Timeline, *Fujin hakusho* (1990).

28. Timeline, *Fujin hakusho* (1991).

29. Timeline, *Fujin hakusho* (1986).

30. Timeline, *Fujin hakusho* (1991).

31. Gender-based wage differentials and other employment statistics are available annually in *Facts and Figures of Japan* (Tokyo: Foreign Press Center) and *Statistical Handbook of Japan* (Tokyo: Statistics Bureau).

32. Timeline, *Fujin hakusho* (1984, 1985).

33. See *Eijizumu*, special issue on aging of *New Feminism Review*, vol. 4 (Tokyo: Gakuyo shobo, 1992).

34. Yayori Matsui has written extensively on the relationship between Southeast Asian women's lives and Japanese economic development. Her *Josei kaiho to wa nani ka* (Tokyo: Miraisha, 1975) offers a good introduction to this more international dimension of the emergence of Japanese feminism in the 1970s and the role of the UN Decade of Women and Development in this process. See also her *Onnatachi no ajia*, (Tokyo: Iwanami shinsho, 1987); and *Sekai kara* 17, a special issue entitled, *Ajia josei roodoosha no genzai*, (Tokyo: Pacific Asia Resource Center, 1983).

35. Vera Mackie, "Feminist Politics in Japan," *New Left Review* 167 (1988): 67.

36. See Robins-Mowry, *Women of Modern Japan*, 85–113; and *Onna to senso*, special antiwar issue of *Agora* 24 (1981).

37. Toshiko Ando, *Kita fuji no onna tachi* (Tokyo: 1982). I am indebted to Vera Mackie for introducing me to the work of Ando.

38. Mackie, "Feminist Politics," 53–76.

39. For a more detailed discussion of the postwar history of Japan's defense policy, see Buckley, "Pacific Overtures," *Alphabet City*, no. 2 (1993): 52–62.

40. See *Japayuki-san no ima*, special issue of *Gendai no esupuri*, no. 249 (1989).

41. For an introduction to the issue of the "comfort women," see Hwangbo Kangja, "Shitte doosuru no ka?" in *Fuemiroogu*, no. 3 (Kyoto: Genbunsha, 1989): 3–26.

42. For Mitsu Tanaka's own account of this period, see her *Inochi no onnatachi* (Tokyo: Tabata shoten, 1972).

43. Yayoi Aoki interview in Buckley, *Broken Silence*.

44. The headline appears in a reproduction of newspapers from the period in *Impakushon* 73.

45. Yuko Kakefuda, "Onna Erosu," *Impakushon* 73, 137.

46. The special issue *Gei karuchaa* of *Yurika*, no. 5 (1993) exemplifies this pattern of absenting lesbianism from theoretical discourse.

47. For details of the abortion reform debate, see *Onna ni wa umenai toki mo aru*, ed. Senso e no michi o yurusanai onnatachi, (Tokyo: Gogatsusha, 1983); and *Onna no sei to chuuzetsu*, ed. and dist. Shakai hyooronsha (Tokyo, 1983).

48. This project was developed by Toyoko Nakanishi through her Kyoto-based bookstore Shokado. The title of the Japanese translation is *Karada watashitachi jishin* (Kyoto: Shokado, 1988).

49. See *Reepu kuraishisu*, ed. Reepu kuraishusu sentaa (Tokyo: Gakuyoshobo, 1990).

50. Kadono Seiko has written a report on sexual harassment in schools that offers

one of the more carefully developed analyses of the issue of harrassment in the Japanese case: *Sukuuru sekushuaaru harasumento* (Tokyo: Gakuyo shobo, 1989).

51. The feminist writer Keiko Ochiai developed the film script for the program, which was simply entitled "Sexual Harrassment."

52. *Moore Report: Women's Body and Sexuality* and *Moore Report Now* (Moore Report Editorial Collective, Tokyo, 1983 and 1992).

53. Nakanishi interview in Buckley, *Altered States*.

54. The recently published series *New Feminism Review*, 6 vols. (Tokyo: Gakuyo shobo, 1991–1993) offers a representative sample of both feminist theory and theoreticians. See also Yoshiko Miya, *Sekushuaritei: Otoko to onna no sei to sei* (Tokyo: Gendai shokan, 1989); and Akiko Yamashita *et al.*, eds., *Nihonteki sekushuaritei* (Tokyo: Sanshodo, 1991).

55. See, for example, Harueko Kato *et al.*, eds., *Josei to medeia, Sekaishisoosha* (Tokyo: 1992); and Medeia no naka no seisabetsu o kangaerukai, ed., *Medeia ni kakareru joseizoo* (Takaoka: 1991).

56. For a more detailed discussion of the pornography debate in Japan, see Buckley, "Techno-porn: Censored," in B. Massumi, *Politics of Everyday Fear* (Minneapolis: University of Minnesota Press, 1993).

57. Accurate statistics for high-school graduation, progression to tertiary education, and gender-differentiated attendance at both two- and four-year universities, are available annually in *Statistical Handbook of Japan* and *Tokyo Educational Statistics Yearbook*, ed. and dist. Tokyo Federation of School Teachers.

58. Mackie, "Feminist Politics," 66.

59. Ueno interview in Buckley, *Broken Silence*.

60. The exchange was primarily between Aoki and Chizuko Ueno, although other feminists were also involved on both sides of the debate. See Yayoi Aoki, "Feminizumu no uchu" in *Unplugging Series* (Tokyo: Shinhyoron, 1983); *Feminizumu to ekorojii* (Tokyo: Shinhyooron, 1986); and Chizuko Ueno, *Onna wa sekai o sukueru ka?* (Tokyo: Keiso shobo, 1986).

61. For representative arguments across the range of positions on the family and motherhood, see Kimiko Yagi, *Ideorogii to shite no bosei* (Josai daigaku, 1991); Chizuko Ueno, *Mazaakon: Shonen no matsuro* (Nagoya: Kawaai bunka kyooiku kenkyuujo, 1986); Rumiko Kora, *Bosei no kaihoo* (Tokyo: Tsuki shobo, 1985); Bosei kaidoku kooza guruupu, ed., *Bosei of kaidoku suru: Tsukurareta shinwa o koete* (Tokyo: Yuuhikaku, 1991); *Josei to kazoku no henyoo: Posuto fuamirii e mukete*, ed. Mizuta Noriko (Tokyo: Gakuyo shobo, 1990); Kaneko Yoshimi, ed., *Onna to ie* (Tokyo: Dooseisha, 1988); *Henbo suru kazoku shiriizu*, vols. 1–8 (Tokyo: Iwanami Shoten, 1991–1992).

62. Ueno interview in Buckley, *Broken Silence*.

63. Nakanishi interview in Buckley, *Broken Silence*.

# II ❖ KOREAN WOMEN

# 8

## Status of the Family and Motherhood for Korean Women

ELIZABETH CHOI

IN this chapter, the status of Korean women will be explored from the perspective of how different roles have been shaped over time. The burdens that were imposed on women in a traditional culture are discussed to provide a framework. In addition, the changing status and roles of women will be viewed in both historical and contemporary perspectives. Specifically, the central role for women that was sanctioned and maintained in a Confucian society was motherhood. Contemporary motherhood will be examined in relation to child-rearing attitudes and maintenance of the Korean cultural belief system regarding pregnancy and birth.

Korea is changing from a traditional into a modern culture. However, the social structure and cultural norms have not changed sufficiently to support the economic development transition. This creates a state of flux and uncertainty since new models are not always in place to replace old and familiar ones. For women, this poses a conflict rooted in disparities between motherhood and family roles and the opportunities of a modern society.

In 1988 and 1989 as a Fulbright Scholar I was sent to the Republic of Korea (ROK) to conduct a research project entitled "The Korean Mother-Infant Interaction in the First Six Months." During that time I met with academics, intellectuals, writers, and artists. Furthermore, I met periodically with forty women subjects (from the last trimester of pregnancy to the first six months of their infant's lives) who were interviewed extensively regarding the woman's changing role as a mother through home visits when their infants were one, three, and six months old. It was a historical moment when major social changes were occurring. As part of the new political climate, new art

189

forms called *Ma Dang Guk*, which involved audience participation, sprang up around the campuses. New awareness for women's oppression was often part of the dramas. The United States Information Agency sponsored a lecture series on "Women's Status" with scholars presenting the state of the art in their respective fields, such as the creative arts, media, and literature. What was evident throughout the symposia was how few professional women were represented in fields that were not traditionally women's occupations.

It was also the year that Ewha University Women's Studies department sponsored its first "sexuality" conference. Prior to that time it was not possible to discuss sexuality openly in a public forum. As George Hyde stated, "Although women are becoming emancipated, apparently sex is a taboo topic in many of Korea's homes and schools, where it is considered a subject unfit for the well-bred ears of properly raised young women until [the] wedding day." [1] Sung Moon Pie considers 1987–1988 as a period when the ROK crossed the threshold and achieved nearly complete democracy. [2]

South Korea, envied for the most rapid economic development among all the developing countries during the 1970s and 1980s, is moving at full gallop toward the realization of a long overdue political miracle, democracy. [3] This chapter presents a combination of firsthand observation, discussions, and subsequent review of the literature on women's changing roles and the changing nature of family relations in a democratizing Korea.

Women's status is not static but dynamic. It has been influenced by historical, cultural, social, political, and economic forces within the society. Since World War II, the ROK has undergone rapid industrialization and modernization. As part of societal change, women's status has changed, yet inequality has been maintained. Inequality in women's opportunities are maintained through an elaborate system of role relationships that are rooted in and rationalized by Confucian customs; they are socially mandated and often legally condoned. [4] The ROK is recognized as the nation with the strictest adherence to the Confucian ethical heritage. [5]

The status of women will be examined using Ogundipe-Leslie's framework in examining current women's conditions in Africa as the six mountains burdening women: first, oppression from outside (foreign intrusions); second, the heritage of tradition; third, her backwardness; fourth, man; fifth, her color and her race; and sixth, herself. [6] First I will examine the six mountains that burden Korean women, then how these burdens have affected women's experiences in the context of the family and motherhood.

## THE BURDEN OF OPPRESSION FROM OUTSIDE: FOREIGN INTRUSIONS

Korean women's lives have been influenced by China's cultural heritage, which dominated Korean society at different times in its history. The early influence of Buddhism allowed women relative freedom and status between the Silla (4th century A.D.–918) and the Koryo dynasties (918–1392). However, with the advent of neo-Confucian philosophy (derived from the Chinese classics), which stressed a rigid hierarchical order of human relationships based on age, sex, and inherited social status, women were often exploited and deprived of basic human dignity. During the Koryo period, single commoner girls had been drafted by the state and sent to the Mongolian court as yearly tribute. In order to avoid this, they married as early as thirteen or fourteen years of age.

This long-established exploitation of young women continued into the twentieth century, when as late as World War II tens of thousands of young women were sent to war zones as entertainers (de facto prostitutes) for Japanese soldiers.[7] A lawsuit filed by three Korean women threatens to upset the Japanese government's habit of evading its militarist past. The Japanese Bar Association's International Relations Committee says that about 170,000 to 200,000 Korean women were forced or enticed to become prostitutes.[8]

Even today, under the guise of economic development, prostitution is encouraged to attract tourists and foreign exchange. There are estimated 260,000 prostitutes in South Korea. Most of the women need their earnings to support families in rural areas. These women suffer widespread health problems.[9] Multinational corporations further exploit women's labor. For example, Pico Products closed its Korean plant without notice while owing workers, largely women, U.S.$1 million in wages and severance pay.[10]

## THE BURDEN OF THE HERITAGE OF TRADITION

The ideology that men are naturally superior to women in essence and in all aspects of life affects the modern organization of societal structures. This belief system has continued to prolong the attitudes of negative discrimination against women.[11]

In traditional Korea, the influence of women was largely confined to the house, for the outside world belonged to men. Men are still dominant in public life. Before the twentieth century ordinary Korean women bore no name and had no say in their choice of mate. Their lives were bound by the mores of seven arbitrary "evils": failure to give birth to a son; disobedience to parents-in-law; talkativeness; stealing; jealousy; adultery; and hereditary disease. Violation of any became a sufficient condition for the husband to divorce the wife, although this was not always practiced. An ideal woman was passive, quiet, and chaste; she was expected to be an obedient daughter-in-law, devoted wife, and dedicated mother, and this image of the ideal woman is still deeply entrenched in Korean values.[12] Women were largely defined by their roles as a daughter who is dependent on her father, as a mother dependent on her husband, and as a widow dependent on her son. Her life cycle was continuously dependent on the males in her family.

Despite this, women enjoyed a considerable degree of freedom and status during the periods preceding Yi Korea (1392–1910). In the Silla period, three women rulers occupied the throne and queen-mothers often acted as regents for young kings, exerting enormous political influence and power. During this era the female right to head the family was acknowledged. During the Koryo period, when Buddhism was predominant, women interacted with men outside the house relatively freely. Koryo poetry and songs written by women vividly portray their freer and flexible image. Marriage in the Koryo period meant the bridegroom's entry into the bride's home and living with her parents until children were born and raised. Remarriage by women was widely practiced and socially accepted; property inheritance was equal between sexes; and women of the Koryo court exerted a significant influence in politics as royal consorts, secondary wives, and regents of kings. Female shamans were active ritual leaders and at times exercised great influence over royal families. However, with the advent of Confucianism during the Yi dynasty period, society maintained a strict authoritarian system based on a rigid hierarchical order. Every human relationship was governed by that order, which was determined by social class, sex, generation, and age. The concept of equality, including that between the sexes, had no roots in Yi society.[13] Following the Yi dynasty, changes in traditional systems came about with the country's contact with Western ideas and its responses to foreign domination. Yu Eui Young named this an "eye-opening period." This was followed by "the Japanese period," when many pioneer women activists went underground or fled the country in order to join overseas independence efforts. Some improvement was made in women's experiences during this time. The spread of Christianity, Japanese-induced industrialization, expansion of the modern educational system, and independence movements all helped to improve the position of women.

In the post-1945 period there have been many important changes. The concept of equality between sexes was written into the 1948 constitution, but the most significant gains occurred in education. Also, the pattern of women's economic participation has changed drastically since 1945. The period from 1960 to 1985 marks a transformation of society under government policies designed to achieve maximum economic growth. The country transformed itself from a predominantly agricultural society to a rapidly industrializing nation. The industrialization of the country greatly expanded employment opportunities for both men and women. Rapid economic development and urbanization, however, have not been accompanied by commensurate improvements in the social, political, and legal status of women.

Despite some of the obvious gains they have achieved in terms of education and economic participation, the idea and practice of male superiority strongly persists within the family and society. Middle- and upper-class women with college degrees are idled at home after marriage, often against their wishes. Most working women take jobs out of economic necessity, and their work status does not necessarily change the male-dominated authority structure in the family. Sexism and paternalism remain very much alive. Women toil at home and work, but they are treated as second-class citizens in almost every realm of society. In terms of status and role, tradition remains strong.[14]

Since the family is the basic social unit, the woman has been given social status and honor by her family. A woman, however, as an "individual" or as a "member of society" often does not possess self-identity beyond a family existence.[15] From the traditional past also come notions of the physical control of a woman's body and its products. Under the Confucian code, the birth of a son was the chief means for advancing the wife's position, and the birth of additional sons further enhanced her status. A woman who brings her husband no children at all is especially discredited.[16]

Attitudinal forms, too many to enumerate, have been inherited from the traditions of the past. These attitudes derive from the socioeconomic formations in existence at the time and have lasted into the modern period in the fields of law, politics, religion, education, and a philosophy of life that is systematically biased against woman. Serious work has to be done to educate the Korean population to develop new attitudes.

## OTHER BURDENS

The other burdens ("mountains") facing Korean women are her backwardness, men, her color and her race, and herself. I will comment only briefly on these aspects of female culture in Korea.

Her backwardness is a product of five hundred years of neo-Confucian relationships that language, law, and education have regulated strictly along gender lines. Over time, women have internalized their secondary-citizen status. This status is perpetuated in family life through different socialization patterns for boys and girls that extends even to selective abortions based on gender. Because many Koreans believe that women born in the Year of the Horse make bad wives, some observers fear that an alarming rise in abortions of female fetuses occurred in 1990, a Year of the Horse. Earlier, concern about possible misuse of prenatal gender tests led the government to forbid doctors to reveal fetal gender, but some still do. To prevent an increase in abortions, the government is cracking down on doctors who perform gender tests.[17]

South Korea is cited as a country where the ratio of male-to-female births has been reversed as a consequence of women choosing to undergo ultrasound scans and then frequently aborting their female fetuses.[18] When family resources are in question males get more education and preferential treatment. In a related problem, because society desires boys more than girls, researchers found that small families consist mainly of boys whereas large families consist of girls. The last member of a family is more likely to be a boy regardless of family size. Sons by and large tend more than daughters to receive the benefits of growing up in small families, such as better education, nutrition, and medical care. Thus, in a society that is already male-dominated, females may be even more discriminated against. Current analyses seem to indicate that the attitude of son preference strongly affects Korean fertility.[19]

Women have to throw the fourth mountain off of their backs, men. Steeped in five hundred-year-old attitudes of patriarchy, which they do not wish to abandon because male domination is advantageous to them, even the most politically progressive men are not completely free from patriarchal attitudes and feelings of male superiority. Thus it is up to women to combat their social disabilities and to fight for their own fundamental and democratic rights. The liberation of women in society is not simply about sexual freedom for women, as most men tend to think and fear. It is about the larger problems of redistribution of privilege, power, and property between men and women.[20]

The women's movement in Korea emerged along with Korean people's acute realization of the needs of "modernization" and "enlightenment." The Confucian view of women, which had dominated Korean society for centuries, posed an enormous obstacle. Women, regardless of their social status, had been expected to be obedient and to practice the "virtue" of submission.[21] This women's movement may propel the changes needed in men's attitudes toward women that are required to reshape society for egalitarian relationships. Such changing attitudes foster growth and development of women in their choices as individuals.

A woman's race is important since the international economic order is divided along race and class lines. Race affects the economics and politics of North-South interaction. The ROK has been under the influence of cold-war superpower struggles since 1945. Human rights were suppressed as long as an identifiable enemy was lurking and women's rights were largely ignored.

The sixth mountain, woman herself, is the most significant burden for women. Women are shocked by their own negative self-image based on centuries of the internalization of the ideologies of patriarchy and gender hierarchy that was condoned under neo-Confucianism. As Kim Chong Ui stated, "because of the wrong socialization process in our society, which has continued for too long, not only men but also women themselves tend to recognize the inferiority of women, at least unconsciously. This is what remains as the major obstacle to achieving equality between men and women." [22] A majority of women still believe that they should be good housewives and mothers. [23] This idea was strongly expressed by the new mothers I interviewed. They felt they should defer their own goals until children are older. The few women who continued to work experienced greater stress from role-conflict and less support for their dual roles of working and motherhood. They felt that there are inadequate choices for child care and they are largely dependent on family or hired help. In addition, it was striking how important a role husband supportiveness played in women's own professional work. It was emphasized over and over again by all the women professors who were interviewed that their husbands were instrumental in their success as professors.

This is another reflection that a married woman cannot succeed independently without the acknowledged approval and support of her husband in her pursuit of a professional career. This is another reflection of how women's lives are circumscribed by their family situations rather than by their own individual strengths. All these conditions work against women making their own choices in their lives. Women's own reactions to objective problems therefore are often self-defeating and self-crippling. It is clear that programs are needed to educate women about their positions, the true causes of their plight, and possible modalities for effective change. [24]

## FAMILY LIFE AND ROLE CONFLICT

I will now examine family life in a modern Korea in order to link women's status as it relates to the different roles they fulfill at different stages of life and what problems continue to persist in a family context. The major problem facing Korean families today stems from an incongruence in the expectation of the perfect life and the realistic family life in a rapidly changing society.

Traditionally, Korean women have been devoted to performing roles of child-bearing, child rearing, and homemaking in the male-based family system. The rapid industrialization since 1960 has brought changes in the social structure in general and in family structure in particular. However, in reality, a strong link remains to the functions and values of the male-based family system. There has been a cultural lag in the sense that the structure has changed but the functions have not. In appearance, the family system is a nuclear one in which the functions are based on the emotional bond between husband and wife. However, the Korean family has retained functions based on the values of the patriarchal society. The relationship of the husband and wife is not equal and priority is given to the couple's parents and to their offspring.

With the increased opportunity for a higher education and the economic structural changes brought about by industrialization, there has been a demand for the inclusion of women in the work force. This has resulted in questioning women's roles. However, the gap between reality and expectation added more to the dilemma. Nuclearization of the family system requires greater roles for the mother in child rearing and homemaking than in the traditional system where grandparents were present to share child-care responsibilities. But structural changes, such as increased child care and housework relief have, not occurred. Therefore, career women end up performing dual roles. Women in full-time homemaking, on the other hand, experience more social alienation and anxiety in nuclear family life than in traditional extended family life. The decrease of the size of the family and the simplification of family life have lessened the roles of homemaking. The dissatisfaction from the loss of roles has adversely affected women.

The changes in the family have undoubtedly contributed to new family problems. The most serious problem for the urban family that was transformed to the nuclear family is "family instability." Divorces, separation, and desertion bring about the dissolution of families and have become important issues in Korea in recent years.

Middle-class women who received higher education tend to have a "marriage shock." Women have not received a consistent education about roles of women after childhood. Women have not developed a consistent concept of their roles. Without this, women enter marriage and roles that are different from what the schools taught. This produces the "shock," which women overcome by creating a new self and adjusting to married life.

Women have children and concentrate on raising them, while otherwise settling down. However, women face a different stage of life by their early or mid thirties, after their children go to school. They experience increasing loneliness and anxiety. Women may find personal worth in raising children and looking after their husbands. However, reaching forty years of age, they find themselves released from these roles. The gap between the expectation and reality of roles as housewives and roles of husbands in the modern society is so great that women find their roles inferior to those of their husbands. This deteriorates the self-esteem of women.

Lee Dong Won suggests that Korean women are not happy over time in their marriages but remain married for two reasons. First, maintenance of the family's stability is valued at the expense of an individual. This follows the traditional value of family centeredness. Placing a higher priority on parents and children than on their spouses, women preserve the traditions and try to regulate their own behavior. Second, the Korean family maintains stability. This may have something to do with how women alleviate their loneliness and dissatisfaction by substitution.

Korean women tend to overprotect their children or have unrealistic expectations for them. Women are placed in the position of playing excessive roles in the nuclear family in the child-rearing phase. However, the subsequent loss of roles after the departure or growth of children makes the woman feel isolated and lonely. Additionally, they face conflicts in roles resulting from the gap caused by the lag between changes of society and family. These conflicts have negative effects on the roles of housewives and child rearing.[25]

Korea has a relatively successful agricultural sector. However, with the availability of cash employment, many people have left farming. The urbanization and industrialization of Korea since 1965 seem to have created problems similar to those in Japan. Both sons and daughters of farm families often leave home early in their teens to take jobs for cash payment. This creates a shortage of farm labor long before any thought of marriage may produce this shortage and a difficult future for the farm economy.[26] According to Cho Hyoung, in the 1980s, 55 percent of all rural women aged fourteen years and over were economically active.[27]

A study determining how changes in the family status influence elderly women in Korea found that family status will not deteriorate very sharply or very fast in the next few decades. The demographic changes in the future will be that the proportion of widows will decrease gradually. This change will offset the increase in the proportion of women with no surviving son and will lead to a decrease in the proportion of widows with no effective source of family support. The shortage of support is likely to be generated not by the absence of children but by a smaller number of children available. For elderly women in this predicament, family expectations have to be changed to have more child involvement for both sons and daughters and even for more distant relatives in assisting elderly women without economic means for survival. If social welfare machinery cannot be created rapidly to deal with the Korean demographic transition, there will be a drastic deterioration of living standards for the whole population.[28]

A study to determine the power of decision making by the elderly found that among female elderly, age and residential area were salient in determining decision-making power, indicating that younger elderly women who live in rural areas are more likely to have decision-making power. The position of elderly females in the extended family mostly depends upon their spouse's status in the family, unless the women have their own economic resources.

Finally, filial piety was studied in a sample of 817 people, 67 percent of whom were females who had received a special prize from the government for their filial piety. Of the parents served by the filial persons, 65 percent were female. In a second phase, a random sample of 106 people was selected to validate the main ideas formed from the earlier study. They found the motives for filial piety as having three dimensions: value commitment, service commitment, and emotional commitment. They identified women as the major providers of filial care. Sons provided emotional and financial support and resources outside the family, but they were less likely to help with instrumental, hands-on services. Indeed, the declining future availability of women to serve as primary care-givers to old parents has emerged as a major social concern in Korea. Family members were involved in a set of complex interpersonal relationships with elderly parents and others in the family support network. Obviously, the extent of filial piety was contingent upon positive interpersonal relationships between family members. Caring for impaired parents will cause even greater difficulties. One should also consider the strain of care giving on filial women who also have marital obligations.[29] Filial piety may be another continuous burden to a majority of women who end up taking care of elderly parents and parents-in-law without a societal policy that addresses the needs of the total population and avoids placing an undue burden on a particular segment of the female population. This is yet another example of role expectations in a Confucian society without a corresponding recognition of the changing role of women in society.

## THE ROLE OF MOTHERHOOD

Motherhood is a major role given to women in society. However, there is a paucity of data actually describing the process of how one assumes that role. This needs to be explored more systematically from mothers' perspectives.

Park Young Sook, through naturalistic inquiry and journals kept by Korean mothers, studied twenty-one women in their transition to motherhood.

The sample consisted of homemakers (71.4 percent) and women working outside the home (28.6 percent); 76.2 percent came from nuclear families and 23.8 percent came from extended families. Women from nuclear families did not feel like a mother for the first three weeks, and realized that taking care of a newborn infant is a very difficult task. Between three and five weeks after the birth of their infant they felt they were mothers, and by the eighth week they became familiar with the mothering role and felt comfortable.

There were no significant changes in their relationship with their husbands in comparison to the period prior to delivery, but they felt they were neglecting their role as a wife as a result of discomfort that arose from taking care of their infants. Communication between the mother and the father focused on their infant. A woman's transition to motherhood can be viewed in four distinctive phases. The first phase of the transition to motherhood (the first ten days) is an Identifying Phase. During that time the mother discovers and identifies her baby by passive observation, focusing her attention on her baby with amusement.

The second phase of the transition to motherhood (eleven days to three weeks) is an Accepting Phase. The new mother accepts her infant by learning to relate to her or him and by actively observing her infant. The mother is still dependent on her care giver for infant care and experiences fatigue and sleep deprivation. Her difficulty in providing direct care to her infant is related to her anxiety and lack of confidence in her mothering role. She still does not accept herself as a mother but admits her maternal responsibility.

The third phase of the transition to motherhood (three to five weeks) is a Shaping Phase. The mother shapes an image by perceiving and internalizing her infant positively through interaction with her active and lively infant. The mother has recovered physically, has more self-confidence in infant care, assesses her maternal behavior and adapts herself to fit the needs of the infant by developing an appropriate maternal role.

The fourth phase of the transition to motherhood (five to eight weeks) is a Stabilizing Phase. The woman acquires a stable feeling of happiness and pleasure by interacting with her infant, who is able to exhibit cooing and smiling behaviors. She has incorporated her maternal role and is able to branch out and begin to show interest in social activities in addition to her infant care but also complains of pain in the extremities and the shoulders from daily activities. She has developed her unique style of the maternal role, fully recognizes herself as a mother, and has higher self-confidence in her infant care.[30] This study explicates the transition to motherhood in the first eight weeks after the delivery and explains the complexity in developing a motherhood role that recognizes the mother's physiological and psychological changes. The giving and enlarging of self by incorporating another human being in her inner psychic process and mental image of herself is explained by the study.

In Confucian societies motherhood, as the central role and status of women, depends largely on the ability to produce sons. This role continues to be a major burden for most women. The reminder of this chapter will focus on a study of Korean mothers I conducted in 1988 and 1989. This analysis will provide insights into what mothers' experiences are in contemporary Korea. For this data analysis, thirty-six completed data sets were utilized.

In the sample, maternal age ranged from twenty-four to thirty-five, and the mean age was 27.6. This figure reflects the increased age of marriage from 19 (in 1955–1960) to 25 (in 1985) and decreased fertility, from 6.2 live births to 2.5 live births.[31] Maternal education ranged from high school to graduate school but the majority (69.4 percent) had obtained a college degree. This is far higher than the total college enrollment of women, which is 26 percent.[32] The women in this sample were married from 2 to 10 years, with a mean of 2.8 years. Housewives comprised 66.7 percent of the sample population, and the remaining 33.3 percent of the women worked outside of the home. This reflects the fact that only one-third of college-educated women ever work.[33] Before marriage 44.4 percent never worked, and the rest worked from 2 to 10 years. Fathers' ages ranged from 23 to 39 (the mean age was 29.3 years). Fathers' education was from high school to graduate school, and again a majority (77.8 percent) were college graduates. Fathers' occupations were mostly in white-color or professional categories (83.3 percent). Among fathers, the only one who never worked was a medical student, and the rest worked from 1 to 12 years. Overall, this group had middle-class socioeconomic status.

Regarding the gender of the first born, 16 women desired sons first, 20 desired daughters first, and 52.8 percent stated that the gender of the infant did not matter. Only 2 people did not desire any son, but 15 (41.7 percent) desired one son only, 6 (16.7 percent) desired two sons, and 13 (36.1 percent) desired three sons. Nineteen (52.8 percent) desired one daughter, 10 (27.8 percent) desired two daughters, 3 (8.3 percent) desired three daughters and 4 (11.1 percent) desired four daughters. Overall, regardless of the gender, 12 (33.3 percent) desired one child only, 3 (8.3 percent) desired two children, and 21 (58.3 percent) desired three children. These results validate the traditional influence of desirability of children in a modern Korean society.

Reaction to pregnancy was very proud for 24 (66.7 percent); 11 (30.6 percent), proud; and only 1 (2.8 percent), neutral—no negative feelings were expressed. All the subjects had a conceptual dream (*Tae Mong*). This demonstrates strong cultural continuity of the Korean belief system in the value of heralding the onset of pregnancy and recognition of the need to practice fetus education (*Tae kyo*) during pregnancy. Fetal education is the belief that if women experience beauty in nature and calm and harmony in their lives, these attributes will be transmitted to the fetus. When asked if children were important, 12 (33.3 percent) thought they were very important; 18 (50 percent), important; and 3 (8.3 percent), not sure. One (2.8 percent) felt children were not important, and 2 (5.6 percent) felt strongly that they were not important. Abortion was considered by 18 (50 percent) at least once or occasionally, whereas 18 (50 percent) never considered it. For desiring pregnancy, 16 (44.4 percent) wanted pregnancy, 18 (50 percent) had no feelings about pregnancy one way or the other, and 2 (5 percent) did not want pregnancy at the time. Emotional feelings before delivery consisted of: 2 (5.6 percent), very proud; 6 (16.7 percent), proud; 9 (25 percent), in between; 3 (8.3 percent), anxious; and 16 (44.4 percent), very anxious. Regarding the ideal time for having children, 2 (5.6 percent) responded immediately; 13 (36.1 percent), after a year, 11 (30.6 percent), after two years; 3 (8.3 percent), after three years; and 7 (19.4 percent), any time. The traditional belief system regarding frequent rest during pregnancy was disavowed by the majority of respondents, with only one woman in agreement. Similarly, a majority (30, or 83.3 percent) practiced food taboos during pregnancy and 4 (11.1 percent) did not. The question of when a mother should resume activity after delivery elicited a range of responses: 9 (25 percent) said immediately; 7 (19.4 percent), after one week; 2 (5.6 percent), after two weeks; 9 (25 percent), after three weeks; and 7 (19.4 percent), after one month. Special postpartum food management was carried out by 24 (66.7 percent) women; 3 (7.5 percent) did not follow this practice and the remaining 6 (16.7 percent) respondents stated they ate nutritious food. Overall, the emotional experience of delivery was rated as very good by a strong majority 32 (88.9 percent) and good by 3 (8.3 percent); one person did not rate the experience. Physical discomfort during labor and delivery was rated as very painful by 19 (52.8 percent), painful by 15 (41.7 percent), and not painful by only 2 (5.6 percent). This may be related to the practice of not permitting a support person to be present during labor and delivery. In addition, prenatal education is not stressed at this point in Korea.

Preparation for an infant's arrival was rated as very enjoyable by 1 (2.8 percent) woman, enjoyable by 20 (55.6 percent), in between by 13 (36.1 percent) and not enjoyable by 2 (5.6 percent). Sleeping with the baby next to the mother was strongly supported by 32 (88.9 percent), supported by 1 (2.8 percent), and uncertainty was expressed by 3 (8.3 percent). Again, this follows the traditional practice of continuous contact between infant and mother. When asked at what age infants should go to public places, the responses were: several days old by 25 (69.4 percent), at 1 month by 7 (19.4 percent), and at 3 months by 4 (11.1 percent). Preference for breast-feeding was expressed by 6 (16.7 percent), formula feeding by 24 (66.7 percent), both by 5 (13.9 percent), and no preference by 1 (2.8 percent). The preferred methods for feeding were: always hold the infant while feeding by 16 (45.7 percent), usually hold the infant while feeding by 11 (31.4 percent), feed while lying or holding the infant by 6 (17.1 percent), and feed while the infant is lying down by 2 (5.7 percent). When asked who feeds the infant, the responses were: always the mother by 17 (48.6 percent), either mother or father by 15 (42.9 percent), family members by 2 (5.7 percent), close friend by 1 (2.8 percent). This is a changed practice from traditional culture, where breast-feeding was almost exclusively done for a long period of time. Also, hospitals separate mothers and infants from each other, and no rooming-in is allowed since many new mothers share rooms with others due to space limitations. This discourages breast-feeding during hospitalization.

Relationships with husbands during the pregnancy were rated as definitely good by 22 (62.9 percent), good by 12 (34.3 percent), and as usual by 1 (2.8 percent). The question was your husband satisfied with the gender of the infant? brought responses of very satisfied by 21 (60 percent), satisfied by 8 (22.9 percent), and uncertain by 5 (14.3 percent). Husband's attitudes to the newly born infant were: very proud by 20 (57.1 percent), proud by 12 (34.3 percent), and not certain by 3 (8.6 percent). Overall, this data suggests continuities in the Korean traditional belief system regarding childbearing and child rearing. The only exception to this seems to be decreased breast-feeding.

The changes occurring in the first month were multidimensional adjustments for both mothers and infants. New mothers were overwhelmed with integrating new roles and recovering physiologically. Fatigue and sleep deprivation were major complaints at this point. Infants were also going through biological adaptation. Many infants had problems in day and night reversal. Most mothers choose to stay in their own family home during this recovery period. There was a strain between husband and wife, since most wives felt they were neglecting their husbands.

The changes between the one- to three-month period when infants established routines and started smiling and cooing made mothers feel that they were recognized by their infant. Mothers continued to recover physically but still felt fatigued. Between three and six months almost all the subjects felt better physically, infant care became easier, and many of the mothers started to have some personal time. They were committed to their original goal of either staying home or working. The reasons given for staying home were (1) that mothers felt that at every stage of infant growth and development the infant needed them and (2) that substitute care was not an adequate solution. Career women remained committed to work but expressed difficulty managing home and work adequately. They received help from their own parents as well as from hired help, which they brought in to provide some infant care. One mother chose to have her infant stay at her mother's home and only had the infant on Sundays. Mothers all expressed how unprepared they were for the mother's role physically, but eventually grew to accept the responsibility and took pride in creating a new person.

In summary, motherhood is a major role transition for Korean women and from the very beginning sets the pattern for their future lives as either full-time homemakers or career persons. This decision may have an impact on their future choices.

## WHAT IS TO BE DONE?

How do Korean women overcome their six burdens? At the present time, Korean women are faced with several underlying problems that make it difficult to foster changes in sex-role relationships and equality. First and foremost, a Confucian code maintains strong gender bias for women.

Often, discrimination does not spring from legislation but from practices originating in the psychological and cultural environment. This can be seen in the Korean culture. Constitutional guarantees are helpful, but it takes social transformations of the power structure, public institutions, and family and work life to foster equality in political, economic, and family life. As Marian Lief Palley notes, in as much as the social mores deny women an equal role with men in the workplace, it has been difficult to change people's expectations regarding women working outside of the home.[34] Meaningful change in women's status will occur when the total population's consciousness is raised to understand human equality not based on gender.

On the bright side, there is a hope that with the 1992 election of President Kim Young Sam changes will take place. He has appointed three women to cabinet positions for the first time in the history of the Republic of Korea. This may signal a new openness and presence of women's leadership at a higher government level. The cabinet ministers of Health and Human Services and Environmental Protection and a cabinet ministry with the portfolio to coordinate women's policy are headed by women.[35] This may herald the beginning of a shift in government policy whereby women's issues are not relegated to different agencies but rather where there is coordinated policy that will address sexual inequality in a meaningful way. However, this is a small step to undo systematic gender bias that is rooted in centuries of inequality.

## NOTES

1. Georgie D. M. Hyde, *South Korea: Education, Culture, and Economy* (New York: St. Martin's Press, 1988), 242.

2. Sung Moon Pae, "Korea: Leading the Third World in Democratization," *Asian Affairs* 18, no. 4 (Winter 1992): 94.

3. *Ibid.*

4. Marian Lief Palley, "Women's Status in South Korea," *Asian Survey* 30 (December 1990): 1136–1153.

5. Howard A. Palley, "Social Policy and the Elderly in South Korea: Confucianism, Modernization, and Development," *Asian Survey* 32 (September 1992): 787.

6. Molara Ogundipe-Leslie, "African Women, Culture, and Another Development," *Presense African*, no. 141 (1987): 123–139.

7. Yu Eui Young, "Women in Traditional and Modern Korea," in *Korean Women in Transition: At Home and Abroad*, ed. Yu Eui Young and Earl H. Phillips (Los Angeles: California State University Press, 1987), 45–70.

8. Karl Greenfeld, "War and Amnesia," *Nation*, 16 December 1991, 764–65.

9. Jill Gay, "The 'Patriotic' Prostitute," *Progressive*, February 1985, 34–36.

10. Rachel Thompson, "Korean Women Pin Down U.S. Boss," *Progressive*, April 1991, 15.

11. Ogundipe-Leslie, "African Women," 133.

12. Yu Eui Young, "Women in Korea," chap. 1.

13. *Ibid.*, 15–27.

14. *Ibid.*

15. Yoon Hoo Jung, "The Nature and Directions of Korean Women's Issues," *Challenges for Women*, ed. Chung Sei Wha (Seoul: Ewha Woman's University Press, 1986), 67.

16. Elizabeth Choi, "Unique Aspects of Korean-American Mothers," *Journal of Obstetrics and Gynecological Nursing*, September–October 1986, 396.

17. "Bad Year For Girls?" *Newsweek*, 16 April 1990, 81.

18. "Discarding the Females," *World Press Review* 34 (March 1989): 5.

19. Park Chai Bin, "Preference For Sons, Family Size, and Sex Ratio: An Empirical Study In Korea," *Demography* 20 (August 1983): 333–52.

20. Ogundipe-Leslie, "African Women," 135.

21. Kim Yung Chung, "Women's Movement in Modern Korea," in *Challenges*

*for Women: Women's Studies in Korea*, ed. Chung Sei Wha (Seoul: Ewha Woman's University Press, 1986), 77.

22. Kim Chong-Ui, "On Male Chauvinistic Cultural Attitudes," *Korean Women Today* (Seoul: KWDI, Spring 1988): 4.

23. M. L. Palley, "Women's Status," 1153.

24. *Ibid.*, 1135–36.

25. Lee Dong Won, "The Changes in the Korean Family and Women," in *Challenges for Women: Women's Studies in Korea*, ed. Chung Sei Wha (Seoul: Ewha Woman's University Press, 1986), 230–54.

26. Clark Sorensen, "Farm Labor and Family Cycle in Traditional Korea and Japan," *Journal of Anthropological Research* 40 (Summer 1984): 306–23.

27. Cho Hyoung, "The Position of Women in the Korean Work Force," in *Korean Women*, ed. Yu Eui Young and Earl H. Phillips, 86–112.

28. Lee Yean-Ju and Alberto Palloni, "Changes in the Family Status of Elderly Women in Korea," *Demography* 29 (February 1992): 69–92.

29. Sung Kyu Tail, "A New Look at Filial Piety: Ideals and Practices of Family-Centered Parent Care in Korea (Filial Piety Prize System)," *Gerontologist* 30 (October 1990): 610–17.

30. Park Young Sook, "Transition to Motherhood of Primiparas in Postpartum Period" (Ph.D. diss., Seoul National University, 1991), 177–82.

31. Lee Yean Ju and Alberto Palloni, "Family Status of Elderly Women," 69–92.

32. Cho Haehong, "Korean Women in the Professions," in *Korean Women*, ed. Yu Eui Young and Earl H. Phillips, 46–70.

33. *Ibid.*, 48.

34. M. L. Palley, "Women's Studies."

35. "Wide-Open Women's Cabinet Ministers," *Cho Sun Daily News*, 2 March 1993.

# 9

## *Overcoming Confucian Barriers: Changing Educational Opportunities for Women in Korea*

CHO KYUNG WON

---

ISSUES of educational opportunities for women in Korea are complex. Although education has been very important in Korean society, where Confucianism has been influential, historically women did not profit. Their informal education was limited to traditional feminine tasks and virtues, not allowing intellectual study. Not until the end of the nineteenth century did formal education for women begin to develop.

As the idea of equality between the sexes began to gain acceptance in Korea in recent decades, women's educational attainments have gradually increased, partly due to the expansion of a nationwide compulsory educational system. Most Korean parents now tend to provide the same educational opportunities for their daughters as for their sons.

Until recently, the idea of equal opportunities between the sexes in Korea was approached mainly in terms of access to formal education. Women indeed came to have equal access to elementary and secondary levels of education. Female enrollment levels still are much lower than male's at the highest levels of education.

The increase in educational attainment among women has not brought improved status for women. The idea of equal opportunity in terms of access to education does not guarantee that students, regardless of sex, are given the actual opportunity to realize their full potential.

The traditional image of the virtuous Confucian woman is deep-rooted in the actual process of socialization and education. Not only do gender biases exist in curricular and school practices, but also the male perspectives continue to dominate the school society. The value structure of schools have been deeply connected to the patriarchal Confucian culture and material forces of Korean society. Gender inequalities underlying school practices are closely connected to discrimination in the labor market, the hierarchical power relations in school, and the labor division in the family. Those factors are mutually reinforced.

Under the circumstances, women tend to make contradictory decisions. Resisting the traditional sex roles and norms, they eventually come to accept those roles that are structured deeply and historically in their everyday lives in order to avoid tensions and conflicts they face. The traditional image of "wise mother and good wife" dies hard and has been an obstacle to the liberation of women through education.

Below I examine how educational opportunities for women have been expanded in Korea and clarify recent problems of educational opportunity for women. The first two sections will examine the Confucian views of women and their education, since those views have been major obstacles to women's liberation.

## CONFUCIAN VIEWS OF WOMEN

The Confucian image of women based on the theory of yin-yang has exerted tremendous influence on the Korean belief system in which men and women are seen as having totally different roles and functions. It limited female education to feminine virtues and domestic skills. This section examines the Confucian views of women, which resulted in the systematic control and subjugation of women during the Yi dynasty (1392–1910).

Confucius's central concerns were the virtuous or superior man and a well-ordered society. His teachings are represented by *jen*, a body of thought that specifies the moral virtues that make man a true man and which, taken together, mean humanity. The most important of these are filial piety, sincerity, righteousness, fraternal love, faithfulness, wisdom, courage, and propriety.[1] Confucius believed that a society would be well-ordered when it was governed by a virtuous man who had achieved *jen*. To become such a virtuous man is the ideal of the educated man. Everyone can achieve *jen* through education, which has been much emphasized in Confucian culture.

To examine Confucian views of women, it is necessary to look at the transition from ancient Confucianism to neo-Confucianism.[2] Philosophically, Confucianism became almost overwhelmed by the theory of yin-yang, which is the central theme of the *I Ching*. According to this theory, creation of the universe begins with the Great Ultimate, which engenders the negative material force yin and the positive force yang.[3] Under the tremendous influence of the theory, neo-Confucianism came to be and to emphasize the study of the nature of man and things (or nature). It assumed the correspondence and the unity of man and nature.

Neo-Confucians believed that the principle of nature could be realized if selfish human desires and feelings could be eliminated through moral efforts or cultivation. The first step toward this cultivation was the investigation of things. When things are investigated and one's knowledge extended, one's will is rendered sincere, one's feelings are correct, and one's personal life is cultivated. When this is done, one will fully develop one nature.[4] Although neo-Confucianism gave *jen* new meaning because of its metaphysical philosophy, it emphasized man's moral efforts or education for achieving *jen* in the same way as ancient Confucianism.

In this way, Confucians emphasized the intellectual and moral dimension of education for men's development. But they tended to limit education for women to domestic matters. Unlike men, intellectual or learned women were not highly esteemed. The limitation of women's education resulted from Confucian, especially neo-Confucian, ideas of women based on the doctrine of yin-yang.

It seems difficult to define exactly how Confucius himself regarded women. He does not seem to mention directly women's subordination to men.[5] Rather he seemed to assume the separation of functions between men and women for a harmonious family.[6] While ancient Confucians tended to emphasize the virtuous or moral example that man should set, neo-Confucians stressed woman's obedience to her husband.[7] And where ancient Confucians blamed men for sexual indulgence, neo-Confucians stressed that women should be faithful and chaste.

One would interpret the relationship between male and female or between husband and wife as a union of complementary equals.[8] However, commentaries on the *I Ching* that were, in general, composed in the Ch'in and Han dynasties already took for granted the hierarchical relationship between men (heaven) and women (earth).[9] The commentaries said that heaven and man are noble but the earth and women are mean. This kind of interpretation of the relationship between man and woman was orthodox in both Confucianism in the middle period and the neo-Confucian tradition.[10]

It is clear that neo-Confucians restricted women's activities more than ancient Confucians, assuming the separate functions between the sexes in the name of the law of nature. Such ideas go hand in hand with the development of a patriarchal social system. Woman's subordination to man was supposed to be a kind of moral law, much like the relationship between subject and ruler. These views led to the glorification of rulers in this period. Indeed, women are described as inferior to men in the Confucian patriarchal family system, in which the patriarch as husband and father was endowed with supreme authority.

## TRADITIONAL EDUCATION FOR WOMEN DURING THE YI DYNASTY

The Confucian image of women limited female education to feminine virtues and domestic skills in Korea. Women were excluded from the formal educational system because it was believed that an intellectual wife would harm her family (and society) by neglecting household affairs.

During the Koryo dynasty, which preceded the Yi dynasty, Buddhism was dominant although classic Confucian texts were taught in schools.[11] By the beginning of the Yi dynasty, Confucianism, especially neo-Confucianism, had spread widely in Korea. The Yi-dynasty rulers emphasized Confucianism against Buddhism as the state ideology in order to justify the new establishment of the revolutionary government. The Yi dynasty rulers set out to enlighten the people through neo-Confucian ethics in order to maintain a well-regulated state. The proper social relationship between subject and ruler was based on a rigidly hierarchical family model in which the female and younger members remain strictly obedient to the commands of the older males. The teachings of neo-Confucians inspired absolute loyalty for the monarch, filial piety for parents, and chastity for women. Throughout the Yi dynasty the Confucian norms of conduct came to permeate the whole society.[12]

Neo-Confucians during the Yi dynasty, who took for granted the separate but hierarchial role distinctions between men (yang) and women (yin) as a kind of law of nature, believed that social order and norms were deeply violated by Buddhists who abandoned the social world. Under the influence of neo-Confucianism, the formerly free Koryo women were repressed.[13] The Yi rulers began to emphasize the chastity of women and urged women to achieve Confucian female virtues by publishing the *Samganghaengsil-to*, a collection of stories about loyal subjects, filial devotion, and highly commendable chaste women (The principle of proper conduct), in 1432.

According to *Naeoebop*, a set of rigid rules concerning the distinctions of the roles of husband and wife, upper-class women spent most of their lives at home, shut off entirely from the outside world. Houses were divided into male and female sections, and it was considered improper for men to enter the women's section (or women to enter the men's section) unless the master of the house gave his permission. Women were not educated in intellectual matters, but instead were taught home management, self-discipline, courtesy or propriety to their husband's family, and how to rear and educate children. This kind of education was illustrated in *Naehun*, which was written by Sohei, the queen mother of King Songjong. *Naehun* was the first book of instruction for women. It is divided into seven chapters: manners of speech and conduct, filial piety, matrimony, marital relations, motherhood, family relations, and thrift.

*Naehun* advised women to speak calmly and sincerely, to be tender, beautiful, and faithful, and not to sit face-to-face with and talk with men or brothers-in-law. Married women were to obey their husband's parents. One section counseled, "Always follow what the parents-in-law ordered. Don't be idle. . . . If the parents-in-law call you, answer promptly and obediently." [14] The basic aim of such education for women was to indoctrinate and cultivate wifely virtues by presenting the exemplar of the virtuous Confucian women. Many fathers or grandfathers wrote additional texts for women within their family tree.

A virtuous woman was an honor to her family. [15] For example, *Yollyomun* (monument gates for chaste women) gave great honor to the whole family. Families with *Yollyomun* gates were granted various privileges: They were exempted from taxes, received a pension, and were given rice, for example. Yi women had little independence. They had to obey their fathers before their marriage, their husbands upon their marriage, and their sons in widowhood. Their status was closely related to the patrilineal kinship system.

There were numerous legal devices designed to maintain male dominance and the patriarchal social system. Widows were effectively prohibited from remarrying because their offspring would be barred from becoming public officials. Yi women were also subject to being expelled from their homes if they committed one of the seven evils, which originate in Confucian teachings: disobeying their parents-in-law, failing to bear a son, committing adultery, being jealous, carrying a hereditary disease, being garrulous, and stealing. The Yi women were required to be educated in the manner devised by the patriarchal neo-Confucian society.

The Yi society excluded women from the formal educational system because women's academic learning was supposed to be improper and contrary to the way women as mother and wife should behave. That is, an intellectual wife would harm her family and society by neglecting household affairs. The belief was based on law-like assumptions that the social roles between the sexes are dramatically different and that social order depends on the role differentiation.

The following sayings show such a social climate: "Teach sons, but do not teach daughters," "If women were learned or educated, their life would be very unhappy." Even scholars who argued for modernization and for demolishing the distinction of classes in the late Yi dynasty era warned that since reading books and learning were tasks for men only, women's reading and learning would be attended by many evils. A few women who were more interested in academic learning became *Kisaeng* (professional entertainers) or educated women, but they were denigrated by Yi society.

The Yi women, who were never given even a name let alone human rights, were indoctrinated with the Confucian beliefs about women. That is, women's education during the Yi dynasty can be called indoctrination in that it aimed to fix in their minds the belief that the Confucian ideal woman should be passive, obedient, chaste, and subordinate to men. Throughout the Yi dynasty women themselves internalized the Confucian ideal woman and took for granted their dependence on men and, thus, their inferior status. The nature of educational goals for Yi women were instrumental and far from being ideals of personal development.

In the domestic sphere, however, women ostensibly were as powerful as men. They managed the household finances. Children were supposed to obey both of their parents. However, men retained all the significant rights and privileges, and the institutional suppression of women actually extended to the family.

To attain virtue in Yi society, women had to lead lives of complete self-sacrifice. Eventually they became dissatisfied with such submission, and by the time Korea began to move into modern times, some Korean women were ready for more freedom and poised to overcome this Confucian view of women.[16]

## WOMEN'S EDUCATION IN THE MODERN ERA

The beginnings of education, especially formal schooling, for Korean women can be traced to the nineteenth century. Educational opportunities also changed for women during the Japanese occupation (1910–1946).

In the nineteenth century, Korea began to undergo many drastic changes. Harbors were opened to Japan and Western nations after the long isolation of the Yi dynasty. Korean people realized acutely the need for modernization and enlightenment. At the turn of the century, a few traditional leaders began to call for the education of women, who represented half of the population.

To most Koreans, however, schooling for women threatened both traditional Confucian views of women and the patriarchal order of Korean society.

Protestant missionaries, who had observed the earlier failure of Catholic missionaries to convert Koreans, adopted indirect methods of promulgating Christianity by establishing hospitals and schools as well as churches. Christian schools began to proliferate toward the end of the century.

Ewha Haktang, Korea's first school for women, was established in 1886 by Mrs. Scranton, a missionary. The aims of the school were to provide a thorough Christian education and to make better Korean women.[17] Ewha Haktang taught that all human beings were equal before God, aiming at liberating women. The school contributed to improving the position of Korean women through education. Many Christian schools for girls began to be established following the establishment of Ewha Haktang.

Korean parents did not want to send their daughters to foreign missionaries.[18] Thus, Mrs. Scranton experienced difficulties in getting students in the first year.

Meanwhile, the Kabo Reform of 1894 by the Korean government had abolished the traditional class system, permitted a widow's remarriage, and modernized the government examination for selecting officials. A new national educational system was developed by the Ministry of Education. However, no specific provision was made for women's education, and most Koreans continued to believe that women should be educated only in the domestic virtues.[19] Other religious groups, such as Tonghak, also called for equality between the sexes, although there remained many inequalities between the sexes in their religious practices.

One group, however, spoke out in favor of women. The Independence Club led by So Chai P'Il came out publicly in favor of women's education. They said that traditional views that women are inferior were wrong and that, since half of Korea's population was female, the need for women's education was urgent.[20] They argued that if women were not given education, their ignorance would jeopardize the education of future generations and the national well-being. Their activities contributed greatly to the awakening and enlightenment of the nation. The Independence Club emphasized equal opportunity for women and tried to create a new image of woman as a human being equal to man.

Encouraged by the Independence Club, founded in 1898, women began to demand independence and equality. Korea's first women's group, Chanyanghoe, was formed, and in it turn founded and funded Sunsong School for girls.[21] The school had to close in 1901 because of financial difficulties when it became impossible to make the girl's school a tax-supported public institution. Although the members of Chanyanghoe could be condemned for their friendship with the Japanese, they did contribute to spreading the idea of education for women.[22]

In 1910, Korea was annexed by Japan. Under Japanese colonial policy, Korean children were indoctrinated to become subjects of the Japanese emperor.[23] With the sovereignty of the nation and the nation's children at stake, Korean people believed that education was the way to modernize and perhaps ultimately free Korea.[24] Women, now that they had begun to enter the mainstream of education, were included in these efforts—more girl's schools were opened, and more girls were encouraged to attend them. It became clear that traditional forms of women's education were inadequate to meet modern needs, and the scope of women's education was altered to fit Western ideas. During this period, many efforts for women and education were made in the context of patriotic movements to free Korea, such as the National Debt Redemption Movement.

Japanese educational policy for women, by and large, was based on the ideology of "good wife and wise mother." Girls' schools established by the Japanese government differed from boy's schools not only in educational aims and curricula but also in years of schooling. The Confucian image of the woman as a good wife and wise mother continued to be a deep-rooted obstacle to modernizing education for women. However, the contribution of Japanese schools lies in the fact that the national formal educational system was extended to include women, who previously had been limited to a few private schools.[25] Once women were given educational opportunities, the traditional Confucian emphasis on a broad and scholarly education was extended to include them. Gradually, Koreans became as enthusiastic about educating girls as they were about boys, at least in terms of access to education.

## THE EXPANSION OF EDUCATIONAL OPPORTUNITIES FOR WOMEN

As the idea of educational equality between the sexes took hold in Korea, especially since the independence of Korea in 1945, women's schooling has gradually increased. Today, women are on average nearly as well educated as are men. Below I will discuss how rapidly women's education has increased, with first a quantitative overview of the change and then an examination of the limitations in educational opportunities for women.

Since the idea of equal educational opportunity between the sexes has

TABLE 9-1  *School Enrollment Rate by Sex*

| Level | 1965 (%) Female | Male | 1975 (%) F | M | 1985 (%) F | M | 1990 (%) F | M |
|---|---|---|---|---|---|---|---|---|
| Elementary | 95.1 | 98.1 | 103.4 | 103.0 | 101.4 | 100.7 | 103.2 | 101.8 |
| Junior High School | 33.0 | 50.9 | 67.0 | 80.8 | 100.4 | 101.6 | 97.0 | 96.9 |
| Senior High School | 19.6 | 35.0 | 35.0 | 51.1 | 75.2 | 82.5 | 85.0 | 90.0 |
| College or University | — | — | 4.5 | 10.8 | 21.1 | 47.1 | 23.8 | 50.4 |

NOTE: School Enrollment Rate: Students at each level of school divided by school age population.
SOURCE: Ministry of Education, *Statistical Yearbook of Education*.

been approached mainly in terms of access to formal education, the situation today is dramatically different from that of Korean society before independence. Boys and girls have equal access to elementary and secondary education. The gender gap in educational attainment has narrowed during the last 2 decades (see Table 9-1). Educational inequalities between the sexes become evident at entrance to senior high school and especially at the university level.

Recent educational enrollments in a variety of professional fields—from engineering to medical sciences—show significant increases in the numbers of women students, although such increases have produced little if any positive changes in women's employment status.[26] It is widely acknowledged that hurdles for women become higher as the level of education increases. Female *ratios* in enrollment at the highest levels of education are much lower than male *ratios*. The number of women relative to men decrease as one proceeds from bachelor's to master's to doctor's and professional degrees (see Table 9-2). Furthermore, female enrollment in higher education tends to be concentrated in such academic areas as art, education, humanities, and nursing (see Table 9-3).

Women's decision making regarding major academic areas and vocational roles derive from their socioeconomic context and the prevelance of sexual stereotyping. Although they want to get a job after graduation, college-educated women face sexual discrimination in the labor market.

Moreover, the Ministry of Education often limits educational opportunity for women rather than coming up with new insightful policies by remaining conservative and unresponsive. For example, the Seoul National University of Education, supervised by the ministry, instituted a rule limiting the number

TABLE 9-2  *Female versus Male College Degree Recipients*

| Degree | 1965 (%) | | 1975 (%) | | 1985 (%) | | 1991 (%) | |
|---|---|---|---|---|---|---|---|---|
| | Female | Male | F | M | F | M | F | M |
| Bachelor's degree | 16.9 | 83.1 | 28.9 | 71.1 | 36.1 | 63.9 | 36.9 | 63.1 |
| Master's degree | 10.4 | 89.6 | 18.3 | 81.7 | 18.5 | 81.3 | 23.8 | 76.2 |
| Doctor's degree | — | — | 2.3 | 97.7 | 10.2 | 89.8 | 13.3 | 86.7 |

SOURCE: Ministry of Education, *Statistical Yearbook of Education.*

TABLE 9-3  *Female Composition Rate in the Distribution of Majors in University*

| Major | 1965 (%) | 1975 (%) | 1985 (%) | 1991 (%) |
|---|---|---|---|---|
| General | — | 29.7 | — | — |
| Linguistics | 43.3 | 38.3 | 45.0 | 51.0 |
| Arts | 70.4 | 77.2 | 67.8 | 63.6 |
| Humanities | 36.4 | 21.3 | 34.1 | 37.9 |
| Social Science | 6.7 | 8.9 | 14.2 | 18.9 |
| Physical Education | 31.6 | 34.9 | 37.0 | 34.8 |
| Natural Science | 40.4 | 47.3 | 43.4 | 34.3 |
| Engineering | 0.9 | 1.3 | 2.7 | 6.5 |
| Medical Science | 33.8 | 36.5 | 32.8 | 35.5 |
| Agriculture | 6.8 | 11.2 | 13.2 | 25.8 |
| Fishery | 0.9 | 2.3 | 4.0 | 10.6 |
| Teachings/Education | 55.1 | 52.9 | 56.8 | 59.7 |

SOURCE: Ministry of Education, *Statistical Yearbook of Education.*

of women accepted for admission. Until 1989, the proportion of women in the university could not exceed 60 percent (now 75 percent) of the total students, even when female applicants have higher entrance examination scores than males. But the ministry has never instituted any kind of rule to limit the number of men when the proportion of men was dominant. Such conservative responses seem to be indifferent to the issue of educational opportunities for women.

There has been a gradual improvement of women's position through education. Also, there are some changing trends in parents' decision making for their children's education. In the past, parents have been more willing to send a son than a daughter to college. Indeed women from the lower classes have often financially supported their brothers' higher education, giving up even their own secondary education. A more recent report shows that Korean parents now want to send to college a high-achieving child, regardless of sex.[27]

Nonetheless, the idea of equal access to formal education does not guarantee that students, regardless of sex, are given the actual opportunity to realize their full potential. While women's participation in the educational process at all levels has increased, this participation remains within marked boundaries.

## GENDER INEQUALITIES IN THE PROCESS OF EDUCATION

As important as equality of access is the nature of the learning experience. Most high school girls express resistance to traditional sex roles and expectations. And young university women face contradictions between expectations and reality.

Research has suggested that there are gender biases in curriculum and textbooks and in the process of education.[28] Examples of this are differentiation in subject specialization, differentiated literature, and social relations in the classroom.[29] Men are the predominant policymakers in education. Male curriculum experts and educators usually formulate the detailed contents of the main textbooks that are used nationwide in elementary and secondary school. The curriculum is centrally designed and controlled by the Ministry of Education. As a result, the male experience tends to become the norm. Their insensitivity to and unconsciousness of gender problems or sexual inequalities lead them to male-dominant value systems and sex-role stereotyping in textbooks.[30]

Girls in elementary schools have higher test scores than boys, but they fall behind boys in achievement tests at the secondary level. While there has been no clear explanation of why this happens, women tend to internalize their roles as intellectual inferiors and feel considerable emotional strain in a competitive achievement. Teachers tend to act on their gender-linked expectations. A study of coeducation in secondary schools shows that teachers' attitudes and evaluations of students are gender biased.[31] They tend to respond to boys much more for "masculine" attributes (achievement, independence, aggressiveness) and to girls for "feminine" attributes (neatness, politeness, docility). This kind of differentiation between the sexes is apparent in the analysis of boys' and girls' school moral lessons.[32] Another study argues the gender structure of the hidden curriculum of Korean schools.[33] The problem of gender inequality in eduational aims lies in the actual ideology governing the process of education, not in the official aims of education. The hidden curriculum exerts influence despite official policies.

Although research to show unequal participation in the actual process has been insufficient, one cannot deny that the predominant Confucian image of women continuously plays a significant role in contemporary education by exerting a negative influence upon the educational aspirations and opportunities of girls. Young university women tend to reject the traditional Confucian image of a woman who gives up her own chance for self-realization. They do not want to become like their mothers, although they appreciate the sacrifices of their mothers for the family. Nonetheless, while valuing intellectual ability, they tend to think that it is incompatible with happiness in marriage.[34] Higher education for women has tended to be seen primarily as a means for their advantageous marriage and secondarily for their career. While they expect their sons to go to prestigious universities and to succeed in their careers, Korean parents do not express the same desires for their daughters.[35]

Most high school girls tend to disagree with the traditional sex-role norms. They value "ability" rather than "femininity." Since the university entrance examination is highly competitive, most high school girls study hard in order to achieve high grades, even though many of them in the long run fail the entrance examination. Emphasis on femininity tends to be reduced to some extent since parents and teachers as well as girls themselves care only for academic achievement. This is not surprising since Koreans as a people place a very high value on university education. Nonetheless, they accept those sex-role norms when they could avoid the conflicts and tensions they face by taking the traditional sex roles.[36] The definitions of femininity can act as both a prison and an escape route for girls. Because they are female, their academic failure is often legitimized.

Equal participation in the actual educational process should be emphasized as a crucial dimension of equal educational opportunities. The Confucian image of women continues to play a significant role in Korean education by exerting a negative influence upon the educational aspirations and opportunities of girls. The traditional values and beliefs rooted in the Confucian-oriented culture are not consonant with values that are considered important for a stable democracy.

Accordingly, there have been efforts to overcome the Confucian image of women. Some feminist scholars have argued for persuading girls to go into science and technology, revising the portrayal of the sexes in school textbooks, and changing stereotyped perceptions of girls and boys. But these efforts have not had much impact on everyday school life, especially on power relationships between men and women and decision making in education.

Gender inequalities underlying school practices are intimately connected to the discrimination of the labor market, the hierarchical power relations in school, and the division of labor in the family. These factors are mutually reinforced. The lived experience of girls or women in school is closely related with their lived reality out of schools. Women working outside the home usually experience negative attitudes toward and discrimination against themselves. Most Korean women are pressured toward the feminine role. The inverse correlation between educational levels and the labor-force participation of women shows that less-educated women are more likely to work than better-educated women.

The value structure of schools is closely connected to the culture and material forces of Korean society. While the most overt biases are being eliminated, an analysis of the more subtle biases that exist is needed. And Koreans, both men and women, must confront the deep-rooted, often unconscious Confucian attitudes toward women that they all hold before women will be able to free themselves from the views of traditional Confucianism.

## CONCLUSION

The Confucian view of women's education has had both negative and positive effects on women. During the Yi dynasty, women were taught filial piety, chastity, self-discipline, child rearing, and home management. Education was supposed to make women "wise mothers and good wives"—concepts that impeded the modernization of education for women in Korea. Nonetheless, the traditional Confucian emphasis on education has indirectly aided the expansion of women's education. Once they became part of the educational mainstream, women benefited from the importance that was given to education. Now, most Korean parents tend to do their best to provide the same educational opportunities for their daughters as for their sons. As a result, more women are able to realize their full human potential and have improved their position somewhat.

The traditional Confucian view of women continues to be an enormous obstacle to modernizing education for women. In order to provide education for women's self-realization, first of all, such efforts as consciousness-raising and gender-free policymaking in education, including curricular construction, have to be accomplished. For these efforts to be effective, future research should focus on more subtle ways in which gender operates within educational processes and on the manner in which schools and Korean society make girls conform to subordinate positions. This should illuminate the meanings of the contradictions and tensions Korean women confront and negotiate in their everyday lives. In illuminating them, it must be noted that for centuries women had neither the education nor the material conditions that fostered autonomy. Women's education should be an organic part of the struggle to transcend the privatized concerns and resistance against gender oppression. Every effort to overcome discrimination against women in education should be made to raise women's own consciousness as well as to foster institutional changes.

## NOTES

1. Kim Hak Joo, trans., *Lun-yu* (Seoul: Seoul National University Press, 1985): Filial piety is the most important among these virtues, and filial obligation is the most important of all social relationships. So, to achieve *jen*, one must start with obedience and love for one's parents.

2. The history of Confucianism can be divided into three parts: ancient period (until 221 B.C.), middle period (221 B.C.–A.D. 960), and modern period (960–A.D. 1912). Here I intend to use the term "ancient Confucianism" for the Confucian thought in the first period, and "neo-Confucianism" to refer to the third, especially the Confucianism during the Sung dynasty (960–A.D. 1279).

3. The *I Ching* is a Confucian classic. It is not clear by whom and when the book was written. It is said that a legendary figure, Fu Hsi, invented the linear signs of the *I Ching*. This seems to mean that the linear signs antedate historical memory. It is also said that King Wen made the present collection of sixty-four hexagrams with brief judgments and that his son, the duke of Chou, wrote the text pertaining to the individual lines. Part of it existed in Confucius's lifetime. He devoted himself to reflection upon it in his old age. A valuable and detailed commentary on the individual lines was compiled later by Confucius's pupils. It survives only in fragments. In the Han dynasty (206 B.C.–A.D. 220), where Confucian scholars reemerged, a literature grew up around interpretations of the *I Ching*, whose fragments are found in the so-called Ten Wings. In this period the yin-yang theory was incorporated into Confucianism by the Han scholars, especially Tung Chung Shu (176–104 B.C.). Commentaries differ greatly with respect to content and intrinsic value. While Han scholars tend to treat the *I Ching* as a book of divination, Confucians in the Sung dynasty (A.D. 960–1279) see it as a book of wisdom. It had become customary to separate the old commentaries contained in the Ten Wings and to place them with the individual hexagrams to which they refer. The *I Ching* became a textbook relating to statecraft and the philosophy of life.

4. In other words, neo-Confucians applied the idea of *jen* to all things. *Jen* was then understood to be the chief characteristic of heaven and earth, the production and reproduction of things. It is inherent in man's nature; man's duty is to develop it and put it into practice.

5. Kim Hak Joo, *Lun-yu*, 400: Confucius did blame man for sexual indulgence in *Lun-yu*. He also said, "Women and small fry are very hard to deal with."

6. Han Young Woo, *A Study of Social Thought in the Early Yi Dynasty* (Seoul: Jisiksanob-sa, 1983), 62–66: The following shows Confucian views of the five human relations in society: "Between father and son there should be affection, between ruler and minister there should be righteousness, between husband and wife there should be attention to their separate functions, between elder and younger brothers there should be order, and between friends there should be good faith." See Mencius, *Mencius*, trans. Cha Joo Whan (Seoul: Myungmoon-dang, 1970), Duke wen of T'eng, part 1.

7. According to ancient Confucians, no father should be so-called unless he acts like one, and no ruler deserves his position unless he fulfills his function. See Park Young Ock, "A Reexamination of the Confucian View of Women in Korea," *Journal of Korean Women's Studies* 1 (1985): 7–43.

8. The basic idea of the *I Ching* is that the world of being arises out of the change and interplay of yin and yang by continously transforming one force into the other. The relationship between yin and yang is not static, but dynamic and changing, forming a harmonious whole.

9. The attributes of ch'ien and k'un were tough/tender, willfulness/docility, integration/disintegration, and active/passive.

10. In contrast to the neo-Confucian interpretation, Taoism, to which Confucian literati were hostile, regarded women and earth not as mean but as more fundamental, depending on the same theory of yin-yang. See Lao-tzu, *Tao-te ching* (Seoul: Sangmoon, 1973). This view of women was analyzed in Chung Sei Wha, "A Critical Examination of the Educational Ideas for Korean Women from the standpoint of Ii-Ki Philosophy" (Ph.D. diss., Yonsei University, Seoul, 1991).

11. Confucianism itself probably entered the country along with Chinese characters around the time of Christ, though there are several theories on the subject. It did not gain influence immediately. Since the period of the Three Kingdoms (Kokuryo, Baekje, and Silla), which preceeded Koryo dynasty, schooling had been based on the Confucian classics. Confucian teachings became more important since officials were selected through competitive examination on the Confucian classics in both the later Koryo and the Yi dynasties.

12. At the beginning of the Yi dynasty, the Confucian norms were most prevalent among upper-class people. In the middle period, through *Karye* (home manners) and the community *Kye* (where villagers made certain promises to help one another), Confucian ethics started to be accepted by the lower class.

13. About 70 percent of the Koryo songs and poems were works of women expressing thoughts and emotions in their free and active life.

14. Queen Sohei, *Naehun*, trans. Lee Chung-Lim, chap. 2 (Imanuel, 1985).

15. Choi Tae Ho, "The Study of Genyo-yakon," *Journal of Asian Women* 17 (1978). This study examines a father's instruction for his own daughter, who became a young widow.

16. Ha Hyun Gang, "Changing Attitudes toward Women in the Late Dynasty," *Ewha Sahakyon'gu* 9 (1976): 7–10, argued that the traditional Confucian view of women had gradually undergone change since the seventeenth century. He asserted that the change of the Confucian view of women began from evils resulting from the prohibition of widow's remarriage, the issues of women's chastity ceased by the invasions of the sixteenth and seventeenth centuries, women's fresh perspectives gained through literary activities, and the gradual destruction of the hierarchial social status.

17. Song Gil Sop, "Christianity and Education in Modern Korean History," *Kyoyuk Gwa Sahoi (Education and Society)* 6 (1983): 210–13.

18. *Ibid.*

19. Kim Young Chung, *Women of Korea: A History from Ancient Times to 1945* (Seoul: Ewha Woman's University Press, 1979), 216.

20. Kim Young Chung, "The Women's Movement in Modern Korea," in Chung Sei Wha, *Challenges for Women* (Seoul: Ewha Woman's University Press, 1986), 80–82.

21. Chung Sei Wha, "Modern Women's Education in Korea," *The History of Korean Women II* (Seoul: Ewha Woman's University Press, 1972), 297–303.

22. Kim Young Chung, "Women's Movement," p. 84.

23. Sohn In Soo, *Hanguk Kundae Kyoyuk-sa (The History of Modern Education)* (Seoul: Yonsei University Press, 1971).

24. At the beginning of the Japanese colonial period Koreans preferred private education provided by Korean teachers to public education provided by the Japanese colonial government.

25. Chol Sook Kyung and Chung Sei Wha, "Formation of Korean Women's Modern Consciousness in the Enlightenment Period (1890–1910)," *Journal of the Korean Cultural Institute* 2B (1976): 325.

26. "Medical science" here includes all of medicine, pharmacy and nursing. Females are especially prominent in nursing.

27. This parental attitude has a significant influence upon education since college expenses are high.

28. Here I use the term "gender" instead of "sex" because the term implies more psychological and cultural (rather than biological) definitions of the "masculine" and "feminine" dimensions within social institutions and ideologies.

29. Separate home economics for girls and technology for boys courses were offered until 1991. In 1992 the two subjects were unified into one.

30. Han Myung Hoe, "Gender Role Concepts and Morality in Education," Fifth Seminar for the Revision of Morality Curriculum in Primary and Middle School, Korean Educational Development Institute, Seoul; and Kim Jung-Ja, "A Study on

Gender Roles in the Secondary School Curriculum," *Women's Studies Forum* 5, no. 1 (1986): 65–105.

31. Chung Sei Wha and Cho Kyung Won, "Equal Educational Opportunity and Women," in Korean Women's Institute, ed., *Women's Studies in Each Academic Area* (Seoul: Ewha Woman's University Press, 1989), 265–345.

32. Chung Sei Wha, "Socialization of Korean Women," in Korean Women's Institute, ed., *Women's Studies* (Seoul: Ewha Woman's University Press, 1979), 353–69.

33. Han Mynug Hee, "The Gender Structure in the Aims of Korean Education," *Journal of Korean Women's Studies* 3 (1987): 7–49.

34. Chung Sei Wha, "Socialization and Women," 179.

35. Chung Sei Wha, *Challenges*, 177.

36. Shim Mi Ock, "Variation of High School Girls' Sex Role Perceptions" (Ph.D. dissertation, Ewha Woman's University, 1990).

# 10

## Korean Women's Groups Organize
## for Change

LISA KIM DAVIS

FUELED by rising expectations of improved quality of life that accompany rapid industrialization, economic modernization, and gradual transfer of power from military dictatorship to an elected government, women's groups of various political ideologies in South Korea are taking on health issues that, when considered collectively, can be said to form an emerging feminist health agenda in the late twentieth century.[1] The resistance of Korean women to subordination under Confucianism dates back to the early 1800s, but gender-specific issues of female bodies and sexuality have always been overshadowed by nationalist and interclass struggles, with some justification. Women have participated as leaders and in organized contingents incorporating a women's rights agenda within peasant rebellions, church and education reforms, nationalist and independence movements, reconstruction efforts following the Korean War (1950–1953), industrialization and community development in the 1960s and 1970s, and, most recently, democracy, labor, and reunification movements in the south of the divided country.[2]

However, South Korean policies focusing on health in the postwar era were driven by the authoritarian central government's Malthusian assessment of what would be best for national economic development, without women as a group having a role in national level decision-making even when their own bodies were being regulated. Women's participation took place in the context of a Confucian patriarchal authority structure that continues to dictate role-relationships based on Confucian traditions. The increased organizing of South Korean women's groups around topics of health is less reminiscent of United States feminist efforts in the 1980s and 1990s addressing systems of health care and medicine than it is of the Western battered-women's movement's politicization of personal experience. Elizabeth Fee analyzes the women's movement approach to health care in terms of the traditions of social criticism of three branches of the women's movement—liberal feminism, radical feminism, and Marxist feminism.[3] Women's groups in Korea choose among these as well as socialist and Christian ideologies, all colored to varying degrees by anticolonialist, nationalist leanings, and they take on different health issues in accordance with their respective emphases. However, the emerging canvas of health-related policy demands reflects the shock of sudden economic, political, and resulting social transformations with a corresponding multiplicity of effects on various segments of the South Korean population. Demands concerning the health of the various women's groups tend to have common appeal rather than polarizing the feminist movement.

Current areas for mobilization are the officially sanctioned enslavement and systematic rape of Korean and other Asian women by Japanese troops during World War II (*Jungshindae*); the strengthening of legal provisions for women related to sexual violence, maternity leave, and employment termination after pregnancy; and campaigns addressing sex tourism, sexual and reproductive health, domestic violence, rape, occupational health hazards for women workers, and abuse of prenatal sex-determination testing due to son preference and resulting abortions of female fetuses. Health issues are also reflected in the formation of research sections at academic feminist research institutions on health and sexuality and by the proliferation of scholarly writings, dissertations, and study groups.

## THE HEALTH SITUATION AND BASIC HEALTH INDICATORS

The health of the population in South Korea has improved markedly since the inception of the first Five-Year Economic Plan in 1962, including improved health status for women. Enormous economic growth fueled by centrally planned, export-oriented industrialization brought about increased national and individual income. This enabled concrete improvements in standards of living and public health brought about by postwar rebuilding of housing, enhanced nutrition to alleviate starvation, water treatment, sanitation, improved roofing and weatherproofing, and primary health care.

Although the wealth has been distributed unevenly, enormous reductions in infant, maternal, and infectious-disease mortality have been achieved, along with a marked increase in life expectancy. It would be interesting to further analyze overall improvements in basic health indicators for social-class differentials. With industrialization, chronic diseases common to the West have emerged as leading killers, along with one of the highest traffic accident rates in the world, according to the Ministry of Transportation.[4] At present, public-health planners work on problems of environmental pollution, occupational hazards, an aging population, escalating health-care costs, smoking, alcoholism, and mental-health disorders resulting from displacement and social alienation. Koreans treat ill health with a variety of means, including the latest in high-technology biomedicine; herbal medicinal systems; the corner drugstore staffed by pharmacists who diagnose minor ailments and dispense drugs, many without prescription; and folk healers. For three thousand years, Koreans have utilized shamans, mostly women, performing the roles of healer, diviner, and communicator with the spirits.[5]

South Korea's basic health indicators are characteristic of a newly industrialized nation. Average life expectancy increased from 48.8 years in 1938 to 52 years in 1960, 63.2 years in 1970, and 70.8 years in 1990.[6] For women, life expectancy grew from 53.7 years in 1960 to 66.7 years in 1970 and 74.9 years in 1990.[7] Also, the infant mortality rate has fallen steadily, from 100.1 per thousand live births in 1953 to 53 in 1970 and 12.4 in 1990.[8] The major causes of death have shifted from infectious to chronic diseases for women and chronic diseases and accidents, mainly automobile, for men.[9] Although problems with intestinal parasites and drinking-water–related illnesses persist, changes in the social and physical environment have brought new major causes of morbidity and mortality for women as well as for men, including cardiovascular and circulatory disorders, stress, cancers, substance abuse, and tobacco-smoking–related ailments.

## THE UNIVERSITY'S ROLE IN DEFINING HEALTH ISSUES

Academic feminism and social activism in Korea have a tradition of integration, perhaps more so than in Western countries.[10] Women students active in "circles" in the 1970s and 1980s at Korean universities participated in the politics of the democratization movement, with undergraduates on the front lines of rallies and demonstrations replacing graduate students who were forced underground to escape police crackdowns. After finishing studies, socially and politically active women graduate students went on to form their own journals and research institutes. Given the end to military dictatorship in 1988, it is not surprising that groups active in the democracy movement have called for an end to police use of excessive tear gas, which has been held responsible for increased miscarriage rates near university gates where much of the fighting occurred.

Consideration of health as a women's issue is supported by formal and informal groups of scholars and writers, with informal organizations playing an important function in addressing new and controversial topics. For example, a women's health group has met at the Seoul National University School of Public Health since 1988 to study biomedical and psychosocial presentations of health topics such as mental illness, childbearing, and sexuality from a gender-specific perspective as covered in Western writings and to debate how to conceptualize "women's health" in the Korean context.[11] An informal study group on the world HIV/AIDS pandemic and prevention for Korean women began meeting in 1991, hosted by the Yonsei University School of Nursing and composed mainly of prominent women scholars, activists, and health-care professionals. This group sent a representative to the WHO Asian regional HIV conference in the fall of 1992. As of early 1994, eight private organizations are involved in AIDS work, and the women's study group continues to provide a forum for developing expertise on women's HIV-related needs.

Women working on the sex-industry issue have met regularly for years, including advocates, social workers, and, increasingly, students and journalists. Crisis management and empowerment issues that are raised often revolve around health matters, including tuberculosis, battering, alcohol and drug dependency, and AIDS. However, the health issues are not considered separated from the economic, political, and sexual context in which they occur.

The August 1992 *Journal of Korean Women's Studies* featured a special-edition focus on "Women and the Body," including articles on feminist health perspectives, cancer, menopause, and women in the health-care professions. Heavily debated within the text was the dominance of the biomedical approach to health and the limits of this framework for solving the health issues of Korean women.

### SEXUALITY AND THE POLITICS OF SEXUAL RELATIONS

Developing a feminist approach to health for Korean women revolves around addressing core issues of sexuality and the politics of sexual relations between persons, including female-male relations in the context of the Confucian patriarchal system. Characteristics of the hegemonic system include the separateness of male and female culture, cultural values emphasizing the family and social group over individual freedom, covert homosexual and bisexual subcultures, tacit acceptance of some degree of sexual freedom outside of marriage for men but not for women, and a large domestic and international sex industry. Almost all of the health issues on the agendas of women's organizations bear some relationship to sexuality, but only recently have Korean women's groups directly addressed sexuality and sexual relations. Several informal lesbian groups meet privately in Seoul; they lack the public gathering places of gay males. Academic women's research institutes are also adding projects on health, sexuality, and women's bodies in the 1990s.

Alternative Culture (Ttohanaui Munwha) is one group that is attempting a reconsideration of women's sexuality. The collective, composed of feminist scholars, students, and journalists, began in the late 1980s to discuss broad theoretical change in social consciousness about women and in male-female relationships through reconstructing culture, ideology, and methodology.[12] Their eighth annual journal, published in 1991, focuses on "rewriting sexuality" (*Seoro Suhnen Song Iyagi*) and contains more than 350 pages of new essays and poems on topics such as "Illusion and the Myth of Liberation," "Sexual Desire," "Sex, Love, and Marriage," "Campus Sexual Culture," "Sexual Assault in the Workplace," and "Public Hearing on Sex and Love for our Generation."[13]

REPRODUCTIVE HEALTH

Reproductive-health issues for Korean women in the 1990s include matters related to sexuality, physical ailments, relationships, the role of motherhood, breast-feeding, the particular concerns of working women, abortion, and son preference. These areas may overlap; for example, data on breast-feeding patterns of 5,430 women from a national fertility study show that female babies are significantly less likely to be breast-fed.[14] Feminist critiques of government health policies resist the defining of women's reproductive health only in the context of national population and economic policies and reflect an introspective struggle to widen the possibilities of women's experience while protecting the right of motherhood.

*Feminists and family planning*

Although South Korean women did not make the policies, they were included as important participants in harnessing population growth in postwar decades. At the beginning of the First Five-Year Economic Plan of the Republic of Korea in 1962, the Korean government implemented a national family-planning program that is now considered a model for many developing countries, even though it is contested whether the reduced population-growth rate resulted from the family-planning program directly or from changing social norms resulting from economic growth, the move away from an agriculture-based economy, and rapid urbanization and crowding. Probably all factors combined to contribute to an unusually rapid decline in population growth.

The authoritarian military government's economic development plan made family planning a priority as the country is one of the most densely populated in the world. The average number of children born per woman fell from 6.1 in 1961 to 1.7 in 1987, and the population-growth rate fell from 3 percent to 0.97 percent in the same time period.[15] The comprehensive program combined community-organizing techniques, state-of-the-art communications campaigns including utilization of mass media, and supporting government policies awarding tax exemptions and free child-delivery services for small families and monetary subsidies for low-income recipients of voluntary sterilization.

Initially, family planning was introduced in a massive program of the Ministry of Health and Social Affairs, which attempted to organize Maternal and Child Health Classes in all rural and urban areas in 1963. The effort failed within a year due to the expense of staffing 45,000 small organizations. In the 1960s discussion of contraceptives was taboo and family-planning field-workers were reportedly beaten frequently by village males, young and old. Use of birth-control methods was sometimes hidden from husbands and especially from in-laws. In 1967 the Planned Parenthood Federation of Korea, a semigovernmental body, organized 16,868 Mothers' Clubs, identifying female community leaders and asking them to join a small group of twelve to fifteen persons that would be run by volunteers. In addition to promoting contraceptive use and providing peer support to overcome the social taboo against contraception practice, the Mothers' Clubs each received the sum of $5.68 in U.S. dollars for meeting expenses and sometimes additional small loans that were used to invest in small enterprises such as rice-saving campaigns, village cooperative stores, collective labor at harvest or seeding time, cattle breeding, and other shared projects for community development.[16] The voluntary Mothers' Clubs uniquely contributed to family-planning acceptance until absorbed in 1977 by the national government's Saemaul Women's Clubs, which required compulsory membership for all women ages eighteen to sixty years of age, and which were unfortunately vulnerable to political manipulation efforts by the military regimes.[17]

Today, many feminist groups find that despite the push to encourage contraception use for the good of the national economy, the burden was unfairly placed on women, not men, and that women's health needs were left unmet. For example, research published by the Korean Women's Research Association (Hanguk Yosong Yong-gu-weh) calls for sex education for young women who leave rural hometowns to live alone in factory dormitories, who are ill-informed about pregnancy and sexuality and often subject to sexual assault by supervisors and coworkers.[18] The Planned Parenthood Federation of Korea operates seven counseling centers in industrial complexes to assist youth, and the services should be expanded to reach many more young male and female laborers, particularly in the export-free industrial zones.[19] In addition, the continued monetary awards to low-income women accepting voluntary sterilization has prompted the accusation that the government is coercing cooperation from lower socioeconomic class women, resulting in permanent infertility instead of use of temporary contraceptive measures. Another concern for feminists in South Korea, as in other countries, is the low rate of male involvement in contraceptive responsibility, with an estimated condom-use rate of 8.7 percent and a vasectomy rate of 14.3 percent compared to a female sterilization rate of 48.2 percent.[20] This rate of condom use is not enough to protect Korean women from sexually transmitted diseases like hepatitis B, estimated to be carried by 20 percent of the population, or from HIV. Improperly monitored IUD use also results in infections, especially among women who lack quality health services or time off from work to go see a doctor. Several studies report of women complaining of chronic pain from complications of IUD's, sterilization, and abortions, with difficulty in receiving responsive medical care for those conditions.[21]

## Abortion

Contraceptive prevalence rates among married persons in the Republic of Korea was reported at 77 percent as of 1990, but at the same time, according to government figures, 52 percent of Korean women of childbearing age had had at least one abortion.[22] It could be expected that this figure lies on the low side of actual experience. By age group, this ranges from 27 percent of women aged fifteen to twenty-four to more than 63 percent of women aged thirty-five to thirty-nine.[23] In another survey, 53 percent of married women polled had undergone abortions. Of women who had experienced at least one abortion, the average number of abortions was 2.1 each.[24] By law, abortion is restricted to cases when the health of the mother is threatened, including cases of rape, incest, and detection of genetic defects in the fetus, but in practice abortions are readily available for as little as $125, even without an appointment.[25]

Comparing abortion rates among countries is difficult due to inconsistencies in the data collected. According to a leading international think-tank on reproductive health, in the United States there were approximately 28 abortions per thousand women aged fifteen to forty-four in 1985, 50 percent to 200 percent greater than figures for other Western nations also showing data believed to be complete. In Japan, incomplete data from 1987 reports 18.6 abortions per thousand women aged fifteen to forty-four, which is considered to be an underestimate, and a different survey from 1975, which is considered to be more complete, counts 84 abortions per thousand women aged fifteen to forty-four—an overestimate for 1990. Abortions are permitted for "social or socio-medical reasons" in Japan, which is less of a legal restriction than in Korea, and are freely available but underreported. A 1984 survey showed South Korea with 53 abortions per thousand women aged fifteen to forty-four, and this figure is estimated to be at least 20 percent too low due to underreporting. Korea has one of the highest abortion rates in East Asia, and ranks among the top ten countries in the world in terms of this measure of abortion rate, similar to Cuba, Turkey, and the former Eastern Bloc countries.[26]

The discrepancy between contraceptive practice of married Korean couples and the high abortion rate suggests that sex is occurring prior to marriage and that there is either a low rate of use of contraception outside of marital relationships or possibly a high contraceptive failure rate. The issue of abortions is not a priority for women's movement organizations as long as inexpensive and safe abortions remain available, but if regulations are tightened, given the high rate of use of the method to handle unwanted pregnancy, the illegality of abortions and payoffs to doctors would become more pressing.

### Son preference

Most of the explanation for the high abortion rate can be found in the continuing preference for male children. According to Byun, abortions of girl fetuses is high in the case of the third or fourth offspring. The male-to-female ratio among first children is 100 boys to 102 girls; for the fourth child it is 199 boys to 100 girls.[27] This can be interpreted to mean that a couple that already has several children stops using contraception in hopes of bearing a male child and is more likely to abort later female fetuses. Stories of families with eight or nine girls and one boy, the youngest, are not uncommon. A minority of

Korean women still go along with the husband taking a second wife in order to bear a male child.

Sex determination tests are banned, but it is common for the doctor to tell the parents what sex the child is during a prenatal office visit, if requested to do so. In that case, it is customary to pay the doctor extra money, although no specific fee is quoted. In 1992 a Korean judge convicted a doctor for giving this information, and the doctor's license was revoked. The reason for stricter enforcement of the ban on prenatal sex determination, as the male child population has grown disproportionate to the female child population, is to protect the "rights" of males to be able to get married and have offspring necessary for continuing the family line. Finding women to marry is expected to be a problem when the current preschool generation reaches marrying age. This trend reached a peak in infants in their first year of life in 1990, when there were 114.7 boys to every 100 girls.[28] A Planned Parenthood slogan in recent years attempts to gain increased acceptability of the one child, female child family, but smaller family size has not extinguished the desire for sons.[29] Women's organizations speak of son preference but have yet to use the language of female "fetus-cide" in pressing for less coercive state family-planning policy, better reproductive-health services, and enforcement of bans on sex determination tests.

## THE OCCUPATIONAL HEALTH OF WORKING WOMEN IN MANUFACTURING AND CLERICAL SECTORS

Women's groups addressing conditions for workers choose to speak and write about the effect of occupational hazards on reproductive health. They are concerned more about unintended abortion through miscarriage than about induced abortions. Other maternal health issues related to workers are the various effects of video display terminals and infertility or deformities resulting from hazardous substances like solder and mercury. Exposure to paint, dry-cleaning fluid, and chemicals used in the pharmaceutical industry are documented as increasing miscarriage rates, and there is evidence that heavy labor during pregnancy makes future conception more difficult.[30]

The Labor Division at the Korean Women's Research Association advocates better enforcement and quality monitoring of existing industrial safety laws, which include provisions for regular employee health exams and plant safety inspections. These laws have been found not to be uniformly applied.[31]

The consortium of Korean Women's Associations United (KWAU), representing over two hundred women's groups, included child care for families with working parents on its agenda for 1991. Child care has been considered a health issue since four cases of accidental infant death occurred in 1991 when the parents had to leave the children home unattended in order to go to work. Government or company subsidized child care is especially pressing for low-income workers, considering that the minimum wage in January 1991 was $1.15 per hour. Also in 1991, KWAU organized a public forum on ending the system of forced retirement of women after marriage or pregnancy, due to male-dominated customs.[32] Many traditional employers feel uncomfortable having employees who are married or who have children, a throwback to the days when the place for the good woman was inside the house (hence the old-fashioned Korean word for wife, *ahneh*, meaning "inside"), and some husbands still consider it an insult to their ability to provide for the family if the wife works away from home. Besides child-care facilities, laws requiring maternal leave and adequate sick days with pay for workers are supported by women's groups across the political spectrum.

## THE OCCUPATIONAL HEALTH OF WOMEN IN THE SEX INDUSTRY

The proliferation of the commercial sex industry, which has accompanied industrial growth and military buildup, involving Korean and foreign consumers, is a constant reminder to Korean feminists of the degraded status of women. One study by the YMCA found that, of fifteen- to twenty-nine-year-old females in South Korea, 20 percent will have employment experience in a sex-related industry.[33] In South Korea, the range of businesses that may be involved in the selling of sex is very broad, including food and beverage establishments, baths, barbershops, and almost any kind of entertainment business. This does not mean that all female staff sell sexual services, but the possibility of labeling workers as such is left open. Every imaginable variety of economic arrangement exists between management, worker, and client. The sex industry needs to be understood in the context of a global political economy where commercial sex is bought, sold, marketed, and traded, in which Korea participates with tacit official tolerance. Sex for money as it is practiced in South Korea can be seen as an expression of the economic situation of women; it also often is an expression of unbelievably brutal violence against women, which is socially condoned.

Examples of actions taken against the exploitation of women in the sex industry are a collaborative campaign led by Church Women United against the international sex tourism in major Seoul hotels, which succeeded in raising public awareness but failed to do more about ending the commerce than force the relocation of some of the business from Seoul to Cheju Island, a tourist development zone. They also led a campaign protesting the U.S. magazine *Hustler*'s 1988 special issue "Hustler's Olympic Goer's Guide to Korean Sex," which portrayed Korean women as sexual objects available for purchase.[34] "We began to take the problem of American influence on our culture through that kind of magazine seriously," writes one women's association, which proceeded to organize rallies for the withdrawal of United States army bases from Korea.[35] Neither of these campaigns appears to have had a major impact on working conditions in this industry, and regulation often has a punitive effect on the working woman rather than influencing conduct of purchasers.

One example of the public-health bureaucracy's lack of interest in women's health for the woman's own sake can be seen in the public-health inspection system in a U.S. military base area. In the Korean city of Tongducheon, home of the U.S. Army Second Infantry, near the zone dividing North and South Korea, women observed working in the sex industry experienced both reproductive and nonreproductive health problems such as complications from multiple abortions, sexually transmitted diseases, infected IUDs, overconsumption of alcohol, and respiratory infections. Although prostitution is illegal in Korea, women providing sexual services to U.S. military personnel are considered legal "entertainment" workers licensed by the government's Korean Special Tourist Authority, and they are required to undergo weekly testing for venereal disease and biannual HIV testing at the public-health clinic. Women report that routine venereal disease testing is performed in a perfunctory manner, and that the clinic personnel lack interest in checking for or treating any ailments of the woman beyond the obligatory tests and registering results on the identification card that workers are required to carry. The women interviewed said that they did not feel the health services were provided for the benefit of their overall health, as their other sicknesses were generally ignored, but just to keep their customers' employer happy.[36] Furthermore, condom use was reported anecdotally to be sporadic, for a variety of complex reasons.

VIOLENCE AGAINST WOMEN

As part of the worldwide feminist movement to include violence against women as a human-rights issue, various factions of Korean women's groups in the 1990s have worked together on the topic of violence against women, which, like in the United States, is one of the major causes of injury for women of reproductive age. Although drawing conclusions about the meaning behind comparative violence rates is difficult, according to 1992 figures from the International Criminology Institute, Korea recorded the third highest number of sexual offenses in the world, behind the United States and Sweden. An estimated 250,000 women were reported to have experienced rape or acts of indecency in 1990, a threefold increase over 1988. According to the World Bank, 17 percent of women surveyed reported experiencing attempted or actual rape.[37]

The increase reflects improved awareness and reporting of incidents, facilitated through new and rejuvenated groups such as the Women's Sexual Violence Counseling Center, founded by a graduate of Ewha Woman's University's Women's Studies Department, which is the first graduate program in gender studies in South Korea, as well as possibly increasing frustration in social relationships resulting from the change to a technology-based society and challenges of traditional gender roles. The new Counseling Center has made the issue more visible through reports covered by the media and publicity for its phone hot-line staffed in part by volunteer women college graduates, and an atmosphere of increased social acceptability of seeking assistance is emerging. In a survey on sexual violence in the workplace by the Korean National Council of Women (Yo-hyup), the government-sanctioned national association of women's groups, in October 1991, 84 percent of reported cases involved verbal assault, 24 percent involved physical assault, and 15 percent involved sexual assault.[38]

The film Because You are a Woman (Danchi Koodaega Yojaranun Eeyoumanero), directed by Kim Yu-jin, reenacted the true story of a woman who was sentenced to prison in 1989 for biting off part of the tongue of a college student who had raped her. Through a painful appeals process, in which the woman eventually is pronounced not guilty, the complex interplay of class and gender biases in the legal system is highlighted. The popular acclaim for this movie drew public attention to the frequency with which rape is tolerated, and the demand for strengthening laws against rape were in the national spotlight in 1993.

The Korean Legal Aid Center for Family Relations, founded by the first woman attorney in Korea, Dr. Lee Tai Young, has given legal aid to women experiencing family problems, including domestic violence, since 1956. Besides crisis intervention and education programs, the work of Dr. Lee has focused around advocating for change in the Family Law to entitle women to initiate divorce, to have a chance for child custody, and to receive inheritances.[39] Women's Hot Line was formed in 1983 to provide counseling and a safe house for abused women. According to a Women's Hot Line study in June 1984, 42.2 percent of surveyed women had experienced physical abuse by their husbands, 14 percent had been physically abused during the past year, and 1 percent reported being beaten more than once per month.[40]

Magdalena House, funded by the Catholic Church, provides a safe home for sex-industry working women experiencing battering, substance addiction, illnesses, and pregnancy in a blue-collar Seoul neighborhood, and two other outreach projects staffed by women counselors also assist sex-industry working women in Mia-Ri and Itaewon districts of Seoul.[41] My Sister's Place women's centers in two U.S. military base towns, funded by the Korean Presbyterian Women's Association, counsel and advocate for Korean women in relationships with U.S. servicemen, either wives, girlfriends, or sex-industry workers. Activities include counseling on domestic violence, cross-cultural relationships, career, and education, as well as a nursery school for working mothers, many of whom are single, and a bakery business for job retraining.

Police violence against females has received much press attention since 1986, when Kwon In-suk, then a college student activist, revealed that she had been raped by interrogators prior to serving a three-year term for labor organizing. In 1991, unprosecuted police rape of a woman who was stopped by the police but not charged with any crime caught the attention of the international Human Rights Watch and international women's groups, who conducted a letter-writing campaign.[42] Mainstream Korean women's groups often mobilize around particularly high publicity cases of brutality, often when foreign military are involved, because nationalist sentiments are of greater weight to many Koreans than feminist matters. Examples of this are the international *Jungshindae* movement and demonstrations of college students in the fall of 1992 after Yun E. Kum, a bar worker, was beaten to death by an American soldier.

## JUNGSHINDAE

Health implications of rape of women committed by foreign armies are just now being explored by international feminists, fueled by revelations of violence in recent military occupations. The most shocking tale of violence against Korean women has emerged since 1991, when decades of work of Professor Yun Chung Ok and colleagues and women's organizations in Korea and Japan unearthed documentation of the systematic rape of between 100,000 and 200,000 women, mostly Koreans, by the Imperial Japanese Army during World War II. In August 1993 the Japanese government acknowledged the practice but refused to admit that orders were given from top of the military hierarchy, as women's groups claim. Survivors continue to come forth to confirm official documents and written accounts and have received small amounts of financial compensation raised by the Council for the Reconciliation of Korean Women Drafted into Sexual Slavery.

Women's groups in Korea and overseas are unified in efforts to publicize the war crimes internationally, demanding retribution from Japan for living survivors as well as additions to history textbooks. *Jungshindae* is believed to be one of the most extreme expressions of territorial, ethnic, and gender domination resulting from the masculine abuse of power, domination, and aggression documented in the twentieth century.[43] For *Jungshindae* survivors, grave physical and mental health issues are numerous and are only beginning to be recognized and understood. Women who have identified themselves often display permanent scars from beatings and even vaginal deformities from abuse. Some women report lives of infertility due to injury to their reproductive organs. Long-term side effects of sexually transmitted diseases are also common, including fertility problems in adult offspring of survivors. Psychological disorders, which the women still suffer from, include insomnia, posttraumatic shock disorder, obsession with cleanliness, and inability to trust.

## CONCLUSION

The issues germane to Korean women's organizations in the south today are both familiar and foreign to Western feminists. Because of the recent replacement of a succession of military dictatorships with democratic elections, and because the country is still divided into north and south along the lines of the post–World War II Cold War, the feminist agenda in South Korea is still expressed primarily in terms of social, political, and economic issues having to do with national survival first and foremost, subordinating issues of patriarchy, sexuality, and male-female relations.

As Korean society struggles to synthesize the forces of economic modernization pitting Western influence against an equally ancient and proud culture, Korean feminists in various groups are invariably caught up in the dilemma of identifying to varying degrees with Third World women's movements and those of industrialized countries. Enormous industrial growth has not guaranteed change in a patrimonial social structure, posing difficult challenges for feminists who seek a new social order that will retain positive aspects of the Korean tradition.[44] Throughout the 1980s, a time of political disorder resulting in democratization, South Korean society was marked by fragmentation of values and cultural tastes, increased social stratification resulting from capitalist expansion, and gains in the freedom of expression and association, although the National Security Law remained in effect. The result is a mass of contradictions, with women's organizations ranging across the spectrum of political ideologies.

The health issues selected by the range of women's organizations are all important for the improvement of women's health status and life experience. The diversity of the topics taken up and the lack of overlap between health agendas of some of the groups is not an impediment to achievement, although in other areas the political stances of the groups conflict. While increased participation in a civilian government may in future years decrease extreme polarization among groups and possibly result in more disagreement over what stance to take on a particular women's health issue, today South Korean feminists have taken on a broad agenda of difficult issues covering the interests of different classes; many of the issues are of urgent interest to all Korean women. Looking forward to reunification between the north and the south, women leaders have sought to meet their counterparts, who may even be blood relatives. Reunification will bring new texture to the Korean feminist agenda as the north's Communist tradition of guaranteed child care and socialized health services merges with the south's greater economic strength.

## NOTES

1. For a general discussion of the effects of rapid economic and political change on women in Korea, see Marian Lief Palley, "Women's Status in South Korea: Tradition and Change," *Asian Survey* 12 (1990): 1136.

2. Kumari Jayawardena, "Women and Resistance in Korea," in *Feminism and Nationalism in the Third World* (London: Zed Books, 1986), 221.

3. Elizabeth Fee, *Women and Health* (New York: Baywood, 1982), 18. See also Robert W. Connell, *Gender and Power* (Palo Alto, Calif.: Stanford University Press, 1987).

4. For example, see "Seoul's Traffic Prompts Emergency Measures," *New York Times*, 3 November 1991, 11.

5. For example, see Jayawardena, "Women and Resistance," 213; and Laurel Kendall, *Shamans, Housewives, and Other Restless Spirits* (Honolulu: University of Hawaii Press, 1985).

6. Ministry of Health and Social Affairs, *Yearbook of Health and Social Statistics*, vol. 36 (Seoul, 1990), 308.

7. Yonhap News Agency, *Korea Annual 1990*, 27th ed. (Seoul, 1990), 239.

8. For example, "Ministry of Health and Social Affairs Report," *Korea Herald*, 12 April 1991, 3.

9. Korean Women's Development Institute, *White Book* (Seoul, 1990), 56.

10. Chung Sei Wha, *Challenges for Women: Women's Studies in Korea*, trans. Chang-hyun Shin *et al.* (Seoul: Ewha Woman's University Press, 1986), 38.

11. Lee Seung Ja, interview by author at Seoul National University, School of Public Health, Department of Public Health Nursing, Seoul, October 1990.

12. Choi Chungmoo, "Korean Women in a Culture of Inequality," in Donald N. Clark, ed., *Korean Briefing 1992* (Boulder, Colo.: Westview), 97.

13. Tto Hana-ui Munwha (Another Culture), *Rewriting Sexuality* (Seoul: Tto Hana-ui Munwha Press, 1991).

14. R. Nemeth, "Son Preference and Effects on Korean Lactation Practices," *Journal of Bioscience* 17, no. 4 (1985): 451.

15. Planned Parenthood Federation of Korea, *Report on Programs and Activities* (Seoul: PPFK, April 1988), 5.

16. Chung Kyung Kyoon, *Studies of Family Planning Mothers' Clubs* (Seoul: Planned Parenthood Federation of Korea, 1987), 12, 18, 30–31.

17. For example, see Kathryn S. March and Rachelle Taqqu, *Women's Informal Associations and Their Organizational Capacity for Development* (Boulder, Colo.: Westview, 1986).

18. Lee Gunjeong, "Women Laborers in Manufacturing and Maternal Health," in *Women and Society*, vol. 2, *Changjak Kwa Bipyong* (Creativity and Criticism) (Seoul: 1991), 76.

19. Planned Parenthood Federation of Korea, *Final Report of the Establishment of Sex Education Centers for Youth*, prepared for the United Nations Family Planning Agency and the Ministry of Health and Social Affairs, Seoul, December 1988, 1–36.

20. Lee Gunjeong, "Women Laborers," 21.

21. Kim Eun Shil, "The Construction of Normality, Health, and Women's Gender Identity in Korea" (paper delivered at the Asian Studies Association Annual Conference, Washington, D.C., 1992), 8. See also Lee Gunjeong, "The Health and Maternity Protection of Women Factory Workers" (Seoul: Association for the Study of Korean Women, 1992), 14.

22. Planned Parenthood Federation of Korea, *Report on Programs*, 5.

23. Korean Women's Development Institute, *White Book*, 64.

24. Hong Sung Bong, "Changes in Induced Abortions," *Korean Gynecological Bulletin* 31, no. 11 (1988): 1509.

25. Stanley K. Henshaw, "Induced Abortion: A World Review 1990," *Family Planning Perspectives* 22, no. 2 (The Alan Guttmacher Institute): 77.

26. *Ibid.*, 78.

27. Byun Wha Soon, "Women and Population Policy," *Women's Studies Quarterly* 9, no. 3 (1991): 114.

28. Korean Institute of Population and Health, *Demographics* (Seoul, 1990), 85.

29. Laurel Kendall, "Women in Korea—Media Briefing" (New York: The Asia Society, August 1988), 26.

30. Lee Gunjeong, "Women Factory Workers," 11. See also Han Hee Jeong, "Working Conditions and the Health of Women Workers" (Master's thesis, Seoul National University, School of Public Health, 1989).

31. Lee Shi Baek and Han Hee Jeong, "Research on the Health of Women Workers in Various Working Environments" (paper presented at the Korean Council on Health Education Annual Meeting, Seoul, 1988).

32. Yosong-ui Yonhap (Korean Women's Associations United), "Report on the Activities of KWAU, Second Half of the Year 1992" (Seoul, January 1993), 1.

33. Cho Hyung and Chang Pil Wha, "Perspectives on Prostitution in the Korean Legislature," *Women's Studies Review* 17 (1990): 84.

34. *Hustler*, October 1988.

35. Yosong-ui Yonhap, "Interim Activity Report, July to December 1988" (Seoul: self-published, 1988), 5.

36. Du-rae Bang (My sister's place), author's interviews with women at women's center, Tonducheon, February 1991.

37. World Bank, *World Development Report 1993: Investing in Health* (New York: Oxford University Press, 1993), 50.

38. Korean Women's Development Institute, *White Book*, 64.

39. Sunny Strawn, interview with author at Korean Legal Aid Center for Family Relations, Seoul, September 1990.

40. Choi Kum Suk, "Rise in the Legal Rights of Korean Women," *Koreana Quarterly* 4, no. 2 (1990): 14.

41. J. Maloney and O. J. Lee, interviews with author at Magdalena House, Seoul, December 1990.

42. Park Jiwon, "Report to Asia Watch" (Washington, D.C.: Human Rights Watch, October 1991), 1.

43. Kim Hyun Sook, *Jungshindae: Korean "Comfort Women"* (New York: KOA Women, forthcoming, 1994).

44. For example, see Norman Jacobs, *The Korean Road to Modernization and Development* (Chicago: University of Illinois Press, 1985); and Lee Man Gap, *Sociology and Social Change in Korea* (Seoul: Seoul National University Press, 1986).

# 11

## Women Workers in a Changing Korean Society

ROH MIHYE

WORKING women have been playing a significant role in Korea's rapid economic growth since the nation launched its first five-year economic development program in 1962. The economic success that Korea has achieved since then owes much to working women in the manufacturing industries. It is undeniable, however, that women workers, whether in high-level professional positions or in low-level manual labor, have been discriminated against compared to their male counterparts in the working world.

Korea has experienced a sharp increase in the number of women in the work force whose status and responsibilities have been upgraded. During the early stage of economic development, young female laborers worked primarily in unskilled jobs in labor-intensive manufacturing industries. In the 1970s, when there was an exodus of males and young females from rural areas to cities and industrial areas, the aged and middle-aged women had to fill in for the labor shortages caused by these migrations from the agricultural sector. In the 1980s, the majority of married women from the urban poor strata were absorbed in low-level jobs in the manufacturing and service sectors. And, as industries progressed into advanced stages, the demand for women workers increased and spread to highly technical, administrative, and managerial sectors as well. Yet, in the overall employment structure, women in managerial and professional positions still form a small minority, while the majority of women workers are engaged in low-paid, unskilled manual labor and service-sector jobs.

Problems in women's economic activities are not limited to the occupational segregation that is characterized by women's heavy concentration in traditional "women's work," such as low-level manual labor, sales, and service jobs. Stigmatized by blatant sexual discrimination, women workers have been forced to leave their jobs upon marriage or childbearing and to retire earlier than their male counterparts.

Being aware of the problem, the government, female academics, and women's organization activists are pooling efforts to eliminate various discriminatory employment practices in the labor market. But women are still facing sexual discrimination in the labor market, such as restrictive recruitment practices, wage differentials between the sexes, limited opportunities for promotion, and the "crowding-out effects" of vulnerable "women's work" (low wages, long working hours, and unstable employment status). And social-support systems for working mothers, such as public or private child-care facilities, do not meet their needs in quality or quantity.

## CHARACTERISTICS OF WOMEN IN THE LABOR FORCE

### Women's economic activity

The economically active female population fifteen years old and above has shown a 264 percent increase from 2,835,000 in 1960 to 7,474,000 in 1990 (see Table 11-1). The female labor-force participation rates have also increased, from 37.0 percent in 1963 to 47.0 percent in 1990, and female shares among the economically active population have steadily increased from 34.4 percent in 1963 to 40.4 percent in 1990.

### Economic activity and residential area

Looking at labor-force participation rates in 1963, 1970, 1980, and 1990 for urban and rural women respectively, it is evident that there was a sharp increase in the participation rate for rural women from 1963 to 1970 and then a smaller rate of increase followed by a sharp increase during the 1970s (see Table 11-2). The sharp increase in the participation of rural women through the 1960s until 1970 seems to stem from the high participation of middle-aged women filling in for the shortage of labor caused by the migration of many males and young females for the cities (see Table 11-3).

### Economic activity and marital status

The labor-force participation rate of married women (i.e., women who were ever married), including the widowed, divorced, and separated, was 36.9 percent in 1963, 7.4 percent less than that of single women. Married women's

TABLE 11-1  *Labor Force Participation Rates*

| Year | Participation Rate (%) | | Economically Active Population | | |
| | Females | Males | Total (× 1,000) | Females | Proportion of Females |
|---|---|---|---|---|---|
| 1963 | 37.0 | 78.4 | 8,230 | 2,835 | 34.4 |
| 1970 | 39.3 | 77.9 | 10,062 | 3,615 | 35.9 |
| 1975 | 40.4 | 77.4 | 12,193 | 4,371 | 35.8 |
| 1980 | 42.8 | 76.4 | 14,431 | 5,412 | 37.5 |
| 1985 | 41.8 | 72.3 | 15,592 | 5,995 | 38.3 |
| 1990 | 47.0 | 73.9 | 18,487 | 7,474 | 40.4 |

SOURCES: Economic Planning Board, *Annual Report on the Economically Active Population Survey* (1963–1985); National Statistical Office, *Annual Report on the Economically Active Population Survey* (1990).

NOTE: Since the 1987 survey, the lower age limit of the economically active population was raised from fourteen to fifteen years of age, and earlier labor statistics were adjusted accordingly by the EPB.

TABLE 11-2  *Female Labor-Force Participation Rates of Farm and Nonfarm Households*

| Year | Entire Country (%) | Farm Household (%) | Nonfarm Household (%) |
|---|---|---|---|
| 1963 (A) | 37.0 | 41.6 | 30.8 |
| 1970 (B) | 39.3 | 49.3 | 30.4 |
| 1980 (C) | 42.8 | 55.3 | 36.9 |
| 1990 (D) | 47.0 | 61.6 | 44.2 |
| (B)−(A) | 2.3 | 7.7 | −0.4 |
| (C)−(B) | 3.5 | 6.0 | 6.5 |
| (D)−(C) | 4.2 | 6.3 | 7.3 |
| (D)−(A) | 10.0 | 20.0 | 13.4 |

SOURCES: Economic Planning Board, *Annual Report on the Economically Active Population Survey* (1987); National Statistical Office, *Annual Report on the Economically Active Population Survey* (1990).

participation rate surpassed that of single women by 0.8 percent points in 1990. A number of factors are assumed to be responsible for the increase in the rate of married women's labor-force participation. First, women are receiving more education than before.[1] They are, therefore, delaying the onset of work,

TABLE 11-3   *Sex Ratio of Rural to Urban*
*Migrants by Age Group*

| Age | 1976–1980 | 1981–1985 |
|------|-----------|-----------|
| 15–29 | 77 | 76 |
| 30–55 | 116 | 112 |

SOURCE: Korean Women's Development Institute, *White Paper on Women* (1991), 46.
NOTES: "Sex ratio" is the number of males per 100 females. The urban population ratio increased sharply from 28 percent in 1960 to 74.4 percent in 1990. See *1960 Population and Housing Census Report* (Seoul: Economic Planning Board, 1962), and *1990 Population and Housing Census Report* (Seoul: National Statistical Office, 1992).

and the gap is being filled by middle-aged women. Second, increased living standards and educational expenses for children prompt housewives to earn money to supplement their husband's incomes. Third, many contemporary women have a stronger desire to take part in economic activities and be able to adapt themselves to careers more readily than women in earlier generations.

*Economic activity, age, and residential area*

When looking at the labor-force participation rate by age groups, there are two rates to be especially noted (see Table 11-4). First, the decline of participation for the age group between fifteen and nineteen since the 1970s is caused by the rise in the school enrollment ratio.[2] Second, the decline of participation for the childbearing age group (twenty-five to twenty-nine) seems to derive from the dip for rural women that began to emerge in the mid 1970s, but did not exist in the 1960s and the early 1970s.

Besides these two young age groups, participation has increased for all other groups. Comparing the participation patterns of urban and rural women, the age-specific participation patterns of rural women in 1970 does not show an M-shaped curve, while an M-shaped curve of labor-force participation was more obvious for urban women both in 1980 and 1989. Hence, not only was the degree of decline in labor-force participation during childbearing ages relatively small for rural women in 1980, showing a 56 percent participation rate, but also the rates for ages thirty and over was higher than for the younger group both in 1980 and 1989. On the contrary, for urban women the decline during the childbearing ages was quite large and the younger group had a higher

TABLE 11-4   *Female Labor-Force Participation Rate by Age Group (in percent)*

| Age | 1963 | 1970 | 1980 | 1990 |
|-----|------|------|------|------|
| Total | 37.0 | 39.3 | 42.8 | 47.0 |
| 15–19 | 37.2 | 44.1 | 34.4 | 18.6 |
| 20–24 | 43.4 | 47.1 | 53.5 | 64.5 |
| 25–29 | 36.2 | 34.6 | 32.0 | 42.8 |
| 30–34 | 39.2 | 38.3 | 40.8 | 49.6 |
| 35–39 | 41.6 | 42.7 | 53.0 | 58.0 |
| 40–44 | 48.4 | 47.0 | 56.7 | 60.5 |
| 45–49 | 44.9 | 46.5 | 57.3 | 63.9 |
| 50–54 | 38.5 | 41.2 | 54.0 | 60.0 |
| 55–59 | 32.5 | 37.1 | 46.2 | 54.4 |
| 60+ | 10.7 | 14.7 | 16.9 | 26.5 |

SOURCES: Economic Planning Board, *Annual Report on the Economically Active Population Survey* (1987); National Statistical Office, *Annual Report on the Economically Active Population Survey* (1990).

participation rate than the middle-aged cohort. The exceptionally high rate of 70 percent economic participation for the middle-aged group (thirty-five to fifty-five) in rural areas can be seen as making up for migration of male and female youth to cities.[3]

### Working women and education

A look at the number of workers by educational attainment reveals that 40.7 percent of male workers have the educational achievement levels of middle-school graduation or below, while the comparable figure for female workers is 60.6 percent. In other words, approximately two-thirds of female workers have a low level of education. On the other hand, 17.4 percent of male workers and 8.3 percent of female workers are at least college graduates. However, female college graduates tend to have difficult times finding jobs because employers usually prefer to hire males. Female college graduates have difficulty finding positions appropriate to their educational level and often have to be satisfied with underemployment in secretarial or clerical positions.

### Women and unemployment

In 1990, the unemployment rate for all women was 1.8 percent, while that of female college graduates was 5.3 percent. Even though the unemployment rate of women decreased during the 1980s, a positive relationship between the educational level of women and the unemployment rate was retained. The number of women who were not seeking employment but who desired employment was 1,319,000 in 1989. These women were the "discouraged unemployed" who had given up job seeking because either they believed that there were no job opportunities or they could not find any job. College graduates amounted to 10.7 percent of this number.[4] These discouraged unemployed were not linked very well with job openings because of the lack of employment opportunities and information.

EMPLOYMENT STRUCTURE OF FEMALE WORKERS

*Industrial distribution*

The proportion of female workers in the primary sector has rapidly decreased while the proportions of female workers in manufacturing and the tertiary sectors have steadily increased during the 1963–1990 period (see Table 11-5). In 1990, out of the total 7,341,000 women employed, 51.6 percent were in social overhead capital and other service industries, followed by 28.0 percent in mining and manufacturing industries and the remaining 20.4 percent in agriculture and fishery industries. Compared to 1963, these figures show that the number of women in the primary sector decreased by 48.3 percent while those in the secondary and tertiary sectors moved up by 21.1 percent and 27.2 percent, respectively.

In the secondary-industry sector, female workers have been concentrated especially in the labor-intensive industries in manufacturing fields such as textiles, clothing, rubber products, food processing, paper and printing, electronics (fabricated metal), and computers (see Table 11-6). Since the early 1970s, especially during the 1975–1985 period, wholesale and retail trades, restaurants and hotels, insurance, and social and personal-service sectors showed a sharp increase in female employment in accordance with the rapid growth of these tertiary industries.[5]

*Occupational distribution of female workers*

The largest number of female workers, accounting for 1,875,000 or 25.6 percent, were engaged in production work in 1990, followed by those engaged in the agricultural, fishery, and forestry work (20.4 percent), sales work (16.9 percent), service work (16.7 percent), clerical work (12.8 percent), and professional, technical, and managerial jobs (7.7 percent). Between 1970 and 1990

TABLE 11-5 *Distribution of Employed Women by Industry and Proportion of Females among the Employed by Industry (in 1,000 persons and percent)*

| Year | Total[1] Females[2] | Agriculture, Forestry, and Fishery | | Mining and Manufacturing | | Social Overhead Capital and Other Services | |
|---|---|---|---|---|---|---|---|
| | | Females | Proportion of Females | Females | Proportion of Females | Females | Proportion of Females |
| 1963 | 2,633 (100.0) | 1,808 (68.7) | 38.0 | 182 (6.9) | 27.7 | 643 (24.4) | 30.0 |
| 1970 | 3,513 (100.0) | 2,012 (57.3) | 41.5 | 428 (12.2) | 31.1 | 1,074 (30.5) | 31.6 |
| 1975 | 4,261 (100.0) | 2,210 (51.9) | 41.4 | 740 (17.3) | 33.1 | 1,311 (31.8) | 31.8 |
| 1980 | 5,222 (100.0) | 2,034 (39.0) | 43.7 | 1,166 (22.3) | 37.9 | 2,022 (38.7) | 34.0 |
| 1985 | 5,833 (100.0) | 1,619 (27.8) | 43.4 | 1,356 (23.2) | 37.1 | 2,858 (49.0) | 37.7 |
| 1990 | 7,341 (100.0) | 1,499 (20.4) | 45.5 | 2,058 (28.0) | 41.8 | 3,785 (51.6) | 38.6 |

SOURCES: Economic Planning Board, *Report on the Economically Active Population Survey* (1987); National Statistical Office, *Report on the Economically Active Population Survey* (1990).

[1]In 1,000 persons.

[2]In percent.

TABLE 11-6 *Distribution of Female Workers in Manufacturing and Proportion of Female Workers in Each Manufacturing Industry (in percent)*

| Industry | 1966 | 1970 | 1980 | 1989 |
|---|---|---|---|---|
| Total Distribution of Female Workers | | | | |
| Food and Beverage | 11.1 | 7.7 | 8.3 | 10.4 |
| Textile, Clothing, and Leather | 73.4 | 64.0 | 55.4 | 42.5 |
| Wood Product | 1.6 | 1.9 | 2.0 | 2.2 |
| Paper and Printing | 1.8 | 2.8 | 3.4 | 4.0 |
| Chemical | 5.5 | 5.6 | 7.6 | 6.1 |
| Nonmetallic Mineral | 1.5 | 1.7 | 2.3 | 2.3 |
| Basic Metal | 0.2 | 0.3 | 0.8 | 0.5 |
| Fabricated Metal | 2.4 | 4.2 | 15.3 | 22.8 |
| Other | 2.5 | 11.9 | 4.9 | 9.0 |
| Total | 100.0 | 100.0 | 100.0 | 100.0 |
| Proportion of Female Workers in Each Manufacturing Industry | | | | |
| Food and Beverage | 22.8 | 22.7 | 34.0 | 41.2 |
| Textile, Clothing, and Leather | 64.8 | 62.8 | 59.0 | 51.3 |
| Wood Product | 8.2 | 10.5 | 13.8 | 19.0 |
| Paper and Printing | 13.2 | 16.5 | 21.9 | 25.6 |
| Chemical | 19.5 | 22.5 | 29.3 | 26.6 |
| Nonmetallic Mineral | 8.9 | 11.3 | 19.3 | 20.5 |
| Basic Metal | 5.0 | 4.9 | 7.3 | 6.2 |
| Fabricated Metal | 5.3 | 10.1 | 22.7 | 22.5 |
| Other | 29.9 | 55.1 | 41.3 | 45.8 |
| Whole Manufacturing | 33.6 | 28.9 | 36.2 | 33.4 |

SOURCES: Economic Planning Board, *Population and Housing Census* (1966, 1970, 1980); National Statistical Office, *Annual Report on the Economically Active Population Survey* (1989).

women production workers and clerical workers showed rates of increase of 10.9 and 10.0 percent while the proportion of female workers in sales and service works went up by 6.3 and 5.9 percent, respectively. The proportion of professional and technical workers grew by 5.4 percent, but that of agricultural workers dropped by 39.4 percent.

When looking at the age distribution of female workers by occupation by 1990, 69.8 percent of clerical workers were in the fifteen to twenty-four age group, while 60.2 percent of professional workers were twenty to twenty-nine years of age. This implies the existence of the voluntary or involuntary retirement-with-marriage practice in these occupations. Among women service and sales workers, one-third were aged thirty to thirty-nine, while 80 percent of agricultural workers were over forty years of age. It is notable that the proportion of production workers in the fifteen to twenty-four age group remained above 60 percent until 1985 but declined to 20.6 percent in 1990.[6]

*Occupational concentration and segregation*

When looking at the occupational distribution of workers by sex in detail it is clear that men and women are concentrated in different occupations. As of 1988, 64.7 percent of female workers were concentrated in just twenty occupations, while 9.6 percent of male workers were engaged in those same jobs. Moreover, within occupational categories women and men are often found disproportionately at different levels, with men concentrated in the more skilled, responsible, and better-paid positions. Put in somewhat different terms, there exists both horizontal and vertical segregation between men and women in the workplace. As to the number of workers by employment-status classification and sex, 10.9 percent of the male workers were section chiefs (*kye-jang*) or above, but only 0.6 percent of female workers held this rank. Of the male workers, 86.6 percent were at the low level of ranking compared with 97.9 percent of the female workers. Consequently, female workers, who tend to be concentrated at the low level of employment, have limited chances for promotion (see Table 11-7).

In the executive branch of the government, 23.7 percent of the civil servants in 1990 were women; 90 percent of them were concentrated in the low levels of seventh class or below, and 22.6 percent of all the female civil servants were in the lowest, or ninth, class. Among the higher levels (fifth class and above), women were only 1.0 percent of the employees. Women are usually concentrated in the special posts, such as counseling and health care, which provide limited opportunities for promotion.[7]

*Employment status of workers*

Looking at the status of employment, unpaid family workers accounted for 56.0 percent of female workers in 1963 and decreased to 24.6 percent in 1990. The self-employed among women were 22.2 percent in 1963 and decreased to 16.1 percent in 1990. Paid female employees increased from 21.8 percent in

TABLE 11-7  *Workers by Sex and Hierarchical Positions (in Persons and Percent)*

|  | All Workers | | Male | | Female | |
|---|---|---|---|---|---|---|
| Directors | 45,380 | (1.0) | 43,409 | (1.4) | 1,971 | (0.2) |
| Department Managers | 65,843 | (1.5) | 64,066 | (2.1) | 1,777 | (0.1) |
| Bureau Chiefs | 153,232 | (3.4) | 149,950 | (5.0) | 3,282 | (0.2) |
| Section Chiefs | 76,512 | (1.7) | 73,348 | (2.4) | 3,164 | (0.2) |
| Foremen | 1,909 | (0.0) | 1,651 | (0.1) | 258 | (0.0) |
| Under Foremen | 37,319 | (0.8) | 27,001 | (0.9) | 10,318 | (0.7) |
| Team Heads | 73,574 | (1.6) | 62,663 | (2.1) | 10,911 | (0.7) |
| Wage Workers | 4,048,389 | (89.9) | 2,582,224 | (86.0) | 1,466,165 | (97.9) |
| Total | 4,502,158 | (100.0) | 3,004,312 | (100.0) | 1,497,846 | (100.0) |

NOTE: Includes establishments with ten workers or more.
SOURCE: Ministry of Labor, *Report on the Occupational Wage Survey* (1989).

1963 to 56.6 percent in 1990. Although the rate of paid workers is on the increase, the rate of nonwage workers such as the self-employed and the unpaid family workers is still high. In the case of the self-employed, many of them are street-shop owners or peddlers; even among paid female workers, about 23 percent of them are daily employees. This means that many women are employed in the informal sectors or have a quite unstable employment status.[8]

## WORKING CONDITIONS AND SOCIAL-SUPPORT SYSTEMS

### Women's monthly wages

The average monthly wage of female workers as of 1990 was 323,691 won, which is only 55.0 percent of that of male workers. However, wage differentials between men and women have undergone considerable improvement since 1971 (see Table 11-8). When comparing the monthly wage by age and sex, for men it increases continuously until fifty years of age, then turns down, then increases again after sixty years of age. For females, it increases only up to age thirty-four; after that, it decreases.

The wage differential according to the level of education is wider for female workers than it is for male workers. As of 1990, if the wage of middle-school graduate female workers is set at 100.0, a high-school graduate was paid

TABLE 11-8  *Monthly Wage by Sex and Wage Differentials*

|  | Monthly Wage in Won | | Female Percentage of Male Wage |
|---|---|---|---|
|  | Females | Males |  |
| 1971 | 11,937 | 27,365 | 43.6 |
| 1976 | 36,396 | 82,871 | 43.9 |
| 1980 | 85,674 | 192,589 | 44.5 |
| 1985 | 158,486 | 328,177 | 48.3 |
| 1987 | 198,734 | 390,139 | 50.9 |
| 1989 | 277,610 | 512,931 | 54.1 |
| 1990 | 323,691 | 588,320 | 55.0 |

SOURCE: Ministry of Labor, *Report on Occupational Wage Survey* (1971, 1976, 1980, 1985, 1987, 1989, 1990).

114.4; junior-college graduate, 144.2; and college graduate, 208.2. If the baseline is also set at 100.0 for male middle-school graduates, the comparable figures for male workers were 108.1, 117.2, and 167.3, respectively. The lower the educational level of the employee, the greater was the wage differential between the sexes. That is, in the case of junior-college graduates it was 72.0 percent, 59.8 percent for high-school graduates, and 57.0 percent for middle-school graduates or under.[9] Women university graduates had a wage differential of 68.4 percent. This is largely a function of underemployment and resistance of employers to hire better-educated and trained women.

The male and female wage differential in the transportation, storage, and communication sectors was the lowest, with a wage ratio of 76.5 percent. The female-to-male wage ratio in the public and personnel-service sector was 58.7 percent; the wholesale, retail, food, and hotel sectors stood at 56.2 percent; and the finance, insurance, and real estate industries reached 52.5 percent. In contrast to the above sectors, the electricity, gas, water, and construction sectors had more serious wage differentials of between 46.6 percent and 47.7 percent. In manufacturing industries that employ mostly females, the female-to-male wage ratio was only 50.5 percent.

When we examine the male and female wage differentials by occupation, we find that administrative and managerial occupations had the lowest, with a wage ratio of 83.0 percent, followed by the service occupations (72.0 percent), and professional and technical jobs (67.1 percent). Among the occupations, clerical jobs showed the most serious wage differential, with a rate of 55.6 percent. Results of a study on wage differentials between the sexes in 1988 showed that only 37.8 percent of the male and female wage difference was nondiscriminatory, stemming from differences in worker's characteristics, and the remaining 62.3 percent was due to discrimination against women.[10]

## Working hours

Average monthly working hours for female workers are 216.5, which is longer than that of males by 0.6 hours. Difference in average monthly working hours between the sexes has, however, been lessened recently.

Female average monthly working hours are the longest for production workers (228.7 hours) and the shortest for professional, technical, managerial, and clerical workers. In the professional, clerical, and service occupations, working hours of female workers are shorter than those of males, while in the rest of the occupational groups women are working longer hours than men.

## Child-care facilities

Industrialization has resulted in changes in the employment structure, improvement in women's education, a tendency toward nuclear families, and changes in family life-cycle. As a consequence, the rate of women's participation in economic activities had increased to 47.0 percent in 1990. The rate was 47.2 percent even for married women, which is a little higher than that of single women (46.4 percent). Thus, child care for married women workers with young children has become a serious social problem. Child care has been considered to be primarily the responsibility of the mother. However, child care should be considered as a social problem related to labor-force participation.

Excluding those children who can be taken care of by other family members, there are 820,000 children who need childcare. However, the current day-care facilities are not sufficient to meet these needs. In 1990 there were only 2,323 day-care centers, accommodating 73,300 children, which was only 8.7 percent of those who needed child care.

The government established 300 additional day-care centers in low-income, densely populated areas by 1992, and there are plans to transform 94 of the existing New Town Nurseries into day-care centers. As a result, 86,800 children in urban low-income areas now benefit from the government services.[11] The problems with existing day-care facilities are: insufficient number, short or inflexible hours, high expenses for poor families, poor quality of child care, and insufficient governmental support.

TABLE 11-9   *Number of Union Members and Membership Rate by Sex*

|      | Union Members (in 1,000 persons) | | Union Membership Rate (%) | |
|------|--------|--------|--------|--------|
|      | Female | Male   | Female | Male   |
| 1985 | 312    | 692    | 15.2   | 15.9   |
| 1986 | 311    | 725    | 14.2   | 16.2   |
| 1987 | 367    | 900    | 15.0   | 18.5   |
| 1988 | 475    | 1,232  | 18.1   | 23.9   |
| 1989 | 530    | 1,402  | 18.5   | 26.0   |

SOURCE: Ministry of Labor, *Women and Employment* (1990).

### Female workers and trade unions

South Korea has a company-union system. As of 1989, the Federation of Korean Trade Unions had 17 industrial trade-union associations, 4 national units, and 7,861 union branches. It had 1,932,415 members, which accounted for 19.8 percent of all eligible workers (see Table 11-9). Female labor-union members accounted for 27.4 percent of the total union members.[12] Union membership among eligible female workers was 18.5 percent in 1989. It has increased in the 1990s, but was still 7.5 percent lower than that of male memberships in 1993.

The labor union movement has been active since 1987. However, there are very few women at the top levels of decision making. Recently, female union leaders of company unions have appeared in sectors where female workers are concentrated, such as textiles, chemicals, and electronics.[13] In 1989, 2.5 percent of the local chapters and branches were led by female leaders (198 out of 7,861 branches).[14] Women's participation in the trade-union movement, both in joining unions and assuming decision-making roles, is very sluggish. Women's activities in trade unions have not led to much improvement in women's low positions in the workplace and poor working conditions.

### The Equal Employment Act

The Equal Employment Act was enacted in December 1987 and went into effect on 1 April 1988. The act consisted of twenty-four articles and was partially revised on 1 April 1989 as a result of demands made by women's organizations and groups. The act contains the principle of equal pay for equal work, maternity protection, and the concept of the right to continue employment after marriage and childbirth. In the cases of the breach of the equal wage provision and of discriminatory practices of termination of employment on the basis of marriage, pregnancy, or childbirth, the employer is subject to a jail term up to two years or a fine up to 5 million won, and 2.5 million won for discriminatory practices in recruitment, placement, on-the-job training, promotion, and violation of the maternity protection provisions on child-care leave and breast-feeding facilities at the workplace. In case of labor disputes on sexual discrimination or maternity protection, the Employment Dispute Mediation Committee, which consists of fifteen representatives of women workers, employees, and women experts, mediates a settlement.

Although the Equal Employment Act provides the basis to protect women's rights in employment, it has not been effectively implemented. In order to implement the act effectively, it is important first to publicize it to a wide public. Second, it is necessary to strengthen the activities of the Committee of Working Women under the Ministry of Labor, which was formed on 6 December 1990 as a result of the act. Third, a concrete and clear standard should be suggested for what constitutes equal work. Fourth, the Employment Dispute Mediation Committee should be reorganized and reformed to function as a quasi-judicial organization with binding decisions. Fifth, heavier penalties should be imposed in case the provisions on the rights of workers are broken. Sixth, women themselves need to report on breeches of the law, and women's organizations should carry out organized movements to boycott the products of employers violating the act. Finally, continuous efforts should be made especially by the government to change the prevailing conservative attitudes toward women.

## PROSPECTS

The rate of population increase dropped sharply in South Korea from 2.9 percent in 1960 to 0.97 percent in 1990. The total fertility rate decreased from 6.0 persons in 1960 to 1.7 persons in 1990. Women's average age at their first marriage increased from 21.6 in 1960 to 25.5 in 1990. The average expected life span at birth for women increased from 53.7 years in 1960 to 75.0 years in 1990.[15] The reduction in the number of children and the extension of life expectancy have brought about changes in women's family life-cycle. The delivery of the last baby occurs before thirty years of age and his or her entrance to primary school before thirty-five years of age. Women tend to be emerging from the busiest time of child rearing at a relatively young age. Thus, life planning for them for some additional forty years is necessary. Also, women have more leisure time than before as they spend less time in household duties and child care.

Years of schooling for women is expected to increase continuously in the future. Attitudes toward women's roles at home and in society have been changing, with the increased level of education and the spread of the idea of equality between men and women taking root in Korean society. At the same time, women's desires for self-realization through social participation have been increasing. All these factors combined will bring about a steady increase in the number of women engaging in various social and economic activities.

On the other hand, Korea's economic structure will change its physical infrastructure in order to adapt to the trends of the world economy. First, the trend toward the internationalization of industry will reduce the need for labor-finishing, export-oriented industrialization and promote the balance between industrial development in rural and urban areas, large and small enterprises, and export and domestic-demand industries. Second, it is possible that the new industrialization may advance the employment structure through the "Third Industrial Revolution," with the innovation and information technologies, promotion of heavy chemical industrialization, office automation, and promotion of the rationalization of employment organization and employment order.[16] Third, it is possible that the trend toward democratization will lead to policy decisions respecting human rights by encouraging participation and autonomous bargaining, especially regarding the industrial autonomy of labor and management.

Along with the increase in the number of economically active women participants, changes in the education and training of female workers will progress. Therefore, women's labor will change from unskilled to semiskilled, and the voluntary and involuntary departure from the paid work-force upon marriage or childbearing will decline. With the increasing shortage of skilled labor, part-time employment of middle-aged and older housewives will increase.

As we have seen, there are a host of obstacles to the improvement of the status of women in the labor market today: higher unemployment among female college graduates, employers' unfair labor practices, occupational segregation based on sex, low wages, insufficient support systems for working women, poor working conditions, and a growing preference to hire women as part-time workers.[17] These are the problems we may expect to solve successfully only through the concerted and continuing effort of the government, especially of the Second Ministry of Political Affairs, the organ of the South Korean government in charge of women's affairs, women's organizations, labor unions, concerned scholars, and public research institutions such as the Korean Women's Development Institute. Our joint efforts should be directed first at such issues as strengthening agencies and committees in charge of the Equal Employment Act, revising the act to improve its effectiveness, strengthening the vocational guidance system for women, expanding vocational training opportunities, developing more promising occupations for women, adopting unemployment insurance, enlarging the function of the women's employment information center, expanding day-care services, and adopting administrative and legal means to effectively implement these measures.

## NOTES

1. Average years of schooling for females were 8.2 years in 1990, up from 4.72 years in 1970. Average years of schooling for females twenty to twenty-nine years of age were 10.38 years in 1990, up from 8.32 years in 1970. See *Social Indicators in Korea* (Seoul: National Statistical Office, 1991), 167.

2. Of girls fifteen to seventeen years of age, 88.7 percent were enrolled in high school in 1990, while the rate was 19.6 percent in 1963. See *Statistical Year Book of the Ministry of Education* (Seoul: Ministry of Education, 1963, 1990).

3. Korean Women's Development Institute, *White Paper on Women* (Seoul: 1991), 46.

4. Economic Planning Board, *Report on the Employment Structure Survey* (1990), 383–85.

5. Tak Hi Jun, "Women and Manpower Utilization in Korea," in Korean Women's Development Institute, *Women's Studies Forum* 3 (1987): 69–116.

6. Economic Planning Board, *Annual Report on the Economically Active Population Survey* (Seoul: 1991).

7. Korean Women's Development Institute, *White Paper on Women*, 220.

8. The urban informal sector includes the wholesale and retail trades including street sales, peddlers, and small shops and also restaurants and hotels, social and individual service works including home-based work, small-scale manufacturing, and daily housekeeping jobs. Since the urban informal sector consists of various strata with diverse characteristics, it is very difficult to make women's labor statistically visible.

According to the definition of the informal sector based on the size of the establishment (four workers or less), the number of workers in the urban informal sector was estimated at 4,911,000 in 1989. Female workers accounted for 2,122,000, which was 52.5 percent of all female workers in the urban area (versus 36.5 percent of male workers). If we exclude professional, technical, administrative, and managerial workers, the number of women workers in the urban informal sector decreased to 1,941,000. About half of women workers in the urban area were concentrated in the informal sector. See Economic Planning Board, *Report on the Employment Structure Survey*.

9. Ministry of Labor, *Women and Employment* (Seoul: 1990), 97.

10. Roh Mihye, "A Study on Male-Female Wage Differentials," in Korean Women's Development Institute, *Women's Studies Forum* 7 (1991): 34.

11. Economic Planning Board, *The Seventh Five-Year Social and Economic Development Plan* (Seoul: 1991).

12. Ministry of Labor, *Women and Employment* (1990).

13. Tak Hi Jun, "Women and Manpower Utilization in Korea," in Korean Women's Development Institute, *Women's Studies Forum* (1987): 108.

14. Ministry of Labor, *Women and Employment*, 110–11.

15. National Statistical Office, *Social Indicators in Korea* (Seoul: 1991).

16. Tak Hi Jun, "Women and Manpower Utilization," 108–9.

17. Employers preferred to hire women as part-time workers to reduce labor costs in manual or repetitive work. See "A survey on Part-Time Employment" (Seoul: The Council of Korean Employers' Organizations, 1993). There are no official statistics on part-time workers in Korea. As of 1991, the proportion of women working thirty-six hours or less was 10.2 percent. See National Statistical Office, *Annual Report on the Economically Active Population Survey* (Seoul: 1992).

# 12

## Agenda for Social Reform: Women's Political Participation in South Korea

SOHN BONG SCUK

DEMOCRACY can be defined as politics in which various groups of people enjoy fair shares of power and decision making. The goal of democracy is to rid society of discrimination and inequality and realize these universal values for members of society. A democratic polity should allow different groups of people to articulate their interests and express them through political organizations and parties. Electoral freedom and competition need to be respected so that spokespeople of various groups can find their places in government through popular voting. Accepting such definitions for democracy, one ought to ask how successful are different groups in society in sending their representatives to the National Assembly, and how actively can they advance their (or their clients') opinions in the political arena? Does democracy allow more groups, especially those who were formerly denied power, to share responsibility and participate equally in politics?

Korean society has always had strong traces of bureaucratic authoritarianism. But in the course of rapid industrialization, urbanization, and improvement in education, various new social forces have emerged demanding substantial changes. Despite the presence of political parties and elections, it has been true that workers, farmers, the poor, progressive intellectuals, and women have been deprived of an equal opportunity to participate in the political system. As the democratization process has progressed in recent years, it is natural that these groups have demanded more equal shares of power and responsibility, even to the extent that the institutions of government cannot absorb these demands.

This chapter examines the issue of fair political representation in South

Korea from a feminist political perspective. As of 1989 more than 7 million women were economically active. The number accounted for 46.5 percent of the total female population in Korea. Of the total population employed, women accounted for 40.4 percent, 2.1 percent higher than in 1985, which illustrates that women's participation in the economy is increasing. Compared to this, women's participation in politics has been minimal, and the role of women in politics has been almost negligible. It seems that, while women are encouraged to contribute economically, their participation in politics is frowned upon. In fact, it can be said that Korean society depends heavily upon the female labor force but rejects female participation in politics.

Statistics show that the average number of women representatives in past legislatures in Korea has been, at most, 2 percent. The number dwindled to 1 percent in the Fourteenth Congress (1992–1996). In local legislatures, women represent 0.9 percent of the total. In 1993 there were only three women at the ministerial level. Among those above the fifth level (the "upper level" in civil service classifications), women hold only 1.5 percent of all high government positions. Among the members of political parties, women make up 40 percent of the total membership, yet most of the leadership positions are held by men.

These simple statistics, which will be examined in greater detail below, give evidence to the fact that women's place in politics is extremely limited. This also leads one to wonder to what extent women's concerns will be heard in Congress, in the government, and in political parties. Women simply lack representatives of their own sex. Despite the multiple-party system and regular elections, women's chances to advance in the political system appear to be very slim. I will first examine how Korean politics in the past has been systematically biased against women in holding public offices and sharing power. This will be examined by analyzing to what extent women in Korea today are involved in political activities in different spheres: the legislative branch, the executive branch, the judiciary, the local assemblies, the political parties, and in local and national elections. Then I will explore the main reasons for women's low rates of political participation by pointing out the problems of the sociopolitical structure and system and the sociocultural characteristics that are unique to Korea. Lastly, I will argue that improving women's political participation is an important task of national development and democratic reform. With this point of view, I will consider what kinds of positive effects we can expect from an increased level of political representation and participation of women, and what can be done to achieve them.

*The legislative branch*

In a representative democracy, the national legislature is the foremost authoritative body that is supposed to represent opinions and interests of different social groups of people. With this presumption, one can raise the question, "How many women, compared to men, have been elected to the National Assembly in Korea?"

From the first general election in 1948 to the thirteenth in 1988, the total number of women elected to the National Assembly was sixty-one. However, if one takes into consideration the fact that some of those assembly women were reelected, the actual number of women who have been elected to the National Assembly is merely forty-two. This figure accounts for only 2 percent of the total of 2,934 members of the National Assembly. Among them, the number of women elected to the National Assembly through direct election (by popular choice) is sixteen, of which the actual number of women, excluding those who were reelected, is seven. Only seven women have been sent to the National Assembly through the people's direct election. This figure clearly illustrates the extent to which women in Korea have been excluded from the political arena.

A national constituency system was adopted at the Sixth National Assembly, by which about one-third of the legislature is appointed from functional areas. The number of women legislators who have been elected to the National Assembly from this national constituency is forty-five, of which the actual number of women excluding those who were reelected is thirty-five. This shows clearly that more female members of the National Assembly are recruited by the system of national constituency than are elected from the district constituencies. This pattern was repeated during the Thirteenth National Assembly in 1988. Of the seventy-five national constituency seats, the ruling Democratic Justice party apportioned five to women, and the main opposition party, the Party for Peace and Democracy, "spared one." However, of 224 district constituency seats, not a single woman was able to secure a seat. Consequently, only six of the 299 assembly seats were held by women in the thirteenth term of the National Assembly, occupying only 2 percent of the total seats.

Looking at the Fourteenth National Assembly, which was installed in June 1992, one notices that women's participation was even lower than before.

During the fourteenth general election, which took place on 24 March 1992, a total of nineteen women candidates competed for seats in district constituencies, but none of them was successful. If we look at them by parties, the ruling Democratic Liberal party (DLP) and the main opposition party, the Democratic party (DP), nominated only two female candidates each.[1] The Unification National party nominated three female candidates, as did the New Justice party. Nine remaining female candidates ran as independents. As in the thirteenth general election, not a single woman was elected from the district constituencies. Only three women, two nominated by the DLP and one by the DP, became members of the national assembly. Thus, in the Fourteenth National Assembly, women occupied barely 1 percent of the total seats, a figure that is even lower than in previous terms.

International comparisons also suggest that South Korea is appallingly low in the rate of women's legislative representation. On average, among 131 countries in the world as of 1991, women occupied 11 percent of the legislative seats. The formerly socialist countries of Eastern Europe and the former Soviet Union had relatively high rates of women's participation, although the number has been declining due to rapid political changes. In the Scandinavian countries of Finland, Denmark, and Sweden, women's representation in the national legislatures in 1991 accounted for around 30 percent, the highest in the world. In North Korea the corresponding figure was about 20 percent. In general, women's advancement into the national legislatures in the world is an increasing trend.[2] Korea still remains a country in which women are seriously underrepresented in national politics.

*The executive branch*

As of 31 December 1991, the total number of public servants within the government bureaucracy was 823,831, of which women accounted for 202,307 (24.6 percent). To be more specific, women account for 29 percent of the total employees in the national bureaucracy and 16 percent in the local bureaucracies. Since the new Equal Employment Law was enacted in 1987, legal discrimination against women for government posts has disappeared in all branches. Also, due to the revision of Article 2 of the Official Appointment Regulation, women officers in the executive branch have been increasing. The figures indicate that women's representation in the executive branch is higher than in other branches. However, few women are in higher positions. For example, female officers comprise only 1.7 percent (388) of 22,357 administrative posts that are in charge of decisionmaking, that is, those who are level five or above in grade. The figure is 1.6 percent of central government officers at level five or above, while among local government officers it is 1.9 percent.[3]

Although there has been an increase in the rate at which women are being recruited for jobs in the government bureaucracy, women are usually concentrated in low-ranked positions, temporary employment, or specially appointed functional jobs. There are two channels through which officers are recruited in Korea: the state examination and special employment without the examination. A majority of women at the level of fifth grade or above in government have been recruited through special appointment. They are usually appointed as functionaries and, in many cases, on a temporary basis, and after a certain period of time they are transferred to regular positions, simply bypassing the on-the-job screening test. Hence, it is rare that women enter regular government services of high rank through the state civil service examination.

In the executive branch the highest government position ever occupied by a woman has been a ministerial position. In 1994, three women were serving as ministers. In total, nine women have held ministerial positions in the past. As of 1991, there were eleven women holding positions of general director, equivalent to the level of third grade or above. The number amounts to a tiny 1.9 percent of all general-director positions. In an international comparison, ninety-three countries do not have any women in ministerial positions, 3.5 percent of all countries have one or more women in ministerial or equivalent positions, and women occupy more than 20 percent of the ministerial positions in three countries. In six countries out of 159 UN member nations, the heads of government were women (3.8 percent) as of the end of 1990.[4]

### The judiciary

A total of 4,890 lawyers and judges have passed the state law examination since 1949. Fifty-seven of them are women, comprising a tiny 0.01 percent of the total. The first woman passed the state law examination in 1951. There were barely ten female jurists in Korea up until the early 1980s. However, starting in 1981 when the government allowed the number of examinees to be passed each year to increase to three hundred, the number of female jurists has gone up. Consequently, as of March 1991 there were a total of fifty-five female jurists in Korea, including thirty-five judges, two public prosecutors, and eighteen lawyers. If one counts the judicial apprentices who were in the Judicial Research and Training Institute after having passed the state law examination, the total number was fifty-seven.

In comparison with the male jurists in Korea, the number of female jurists is still quite minimal. Looking at the present trend, one can be more optimistic about future prospects of more women entering the judiciary. However, the judiciary is still regarded as the most conservative and male-dominated sphere of public life in South Korea.

### Local assemblies

The year 1991 was a turning point in the history of local politics in Korea. Local assemblies were reinstated for the first time since General Park Chung-Hee dissolved them immediately after the coup in May 1961. In order to elect representatives for the new local assemblies, the election of assemblies at the basic-level local government was held on 26 March 1991. The assembly members of the higher level—provincial and metropolitan—governments took place on 20 June 1991. In the basic communities a total of 10,120 candidates competed, 122 of them were women. Out of 4,303 total seats, 40 were won by women. In the high-level assembly, 63 (out of the total of 2,877) female candidates ran for offices, winning 8 out of the total 866 seats. Women secured a tiny 0.9 percent of all seats in the local assemblies.[5]

The function of local assemblies is to help improve the welfare of the local communities. It is generally known that women are more needed and better qualified to run the local assemblies. The preelection mood in the country was also that many women would run and win their seats. The results of the elections, however, clearly showed that women were still at a great disadvantage in this domain of Korean politics as well. Looking at the more optimistic side, one can presume that those 185 female candidates who ran in the local elections gained valuable campaigning experiences, and that these experiences in turn would serve as an important stepping stone for future political participation of women in Korea.

### Political parties

The only women's political party that has ever existed in Korean history was the Korean Women's National party, founded on 18 August 1945. But it is questionable whether this was a party of coherent organization and political significance. In 1963 a woman legislator, Mrs. Park Soon Chun, was elected the chairperson of the Democratic party by a unanimous decision of 779 representatives. She served in the office for four years. Since then, the participation of women in political parties, measured by their membership, has increased to a great extent. For example, as of June 1989, the Democratic Justice party drew 40 percent of its membership from women. The proportion was 60 percent for the Democratic party, 20 percent for the Peace and Democratic party, and 40 percent for the Republican party. However, very few women have been able to hold high-ranking positions in those parties.

The ruling Democratic Liberal party (DLP) was founded in 1990 with the merger of three parties. It reserved one seat for women on the supreme council, but had yet to appoint one by early 1994. Of the three deputy secretary generals in the DLP, one is a woman, and of the eight members of the party advisory council, one is a woman. There is no woman in the fifty-member party executive council. Only 4.4 percent of the members of the standing committee of the DLP are women, and only 2 out of a total of 224 district party chairmen were women as of the end of 1991. As far as officers of the party headquarters are concerned, 2 out of 57 directors, 2 out of 56 vice-directors, and 3 out of 79 departmental heads were women.

In the Democratic party, one of the eight supreme council members is a woman. Only one woman was elected to the national assembly from the national constituency list, and another was appointed as the deputy party chairwoman. Three of the seventy party executive members are women, comprising 4.3 percent of its membership. Of the 180 district party chairmen, 2 (or 1.1%) are women. Among the 160 party bureaucrats, one out of every 10 directors and 30 vice-directors is a woman, and 5 out of 60 department heads are women. In summary, there are only 7 women (out of 160) who had any significant influence in the party policymaking process in the Democratic party headquarters.

The United People's party emerged as the second major opposition party after the general election in March 1992, securing a caucus group within the National Assembly. But the role of women in this party is questionable; although it has pledged to emphasize women's issues, there has not been enough time to observe the party's actions. Furthermore, the Progressive People's party, which consciously promotes women's entry into the National Assembly, failed to gain any seat. Since it could not acquire more than 2 percent of the total votes, the party had to be dissolved. Thus, statistics attest to the fact that, as far as women's representation in high-rank party positions is concerned, parties in Korea are not much different from one another. This is a clear indication of the male dominance in South Korea's party politics.

In summary, the number of women in the political parties has grown. However, a small number of women hold any significant party positions. In addition, most of the women in those positions are assigned to works related to women's affairs. Serious constraints are imposed on women preventing them from power sharing within the parties, keeping them usually as service women rather than as activists.

### Voting participation

As a citizen in a democratic society every woman in Korea has the right to vote for a candidate of her preference in elections. However, women in general have been less inclined than men to use their legal voting power. To illustrate this point, in 1992, right before the fourteenth general election, the number of eligible female voters was 14,707,355 (50.7 percent of total eligible voters), compared to 14, 296,473 of eligible male voters. Thus women outnumbered men by 410,882. However, women's turnout rate fell marginally short of men's. In the past, the marginal difference between males and females varied between 1.3 percent at the minimum and 4.8 percent at the maximum.[6]

Not only has women's turnout been lower than that of men, but women have usually been strongly influenced in their voting behavior by the political views of their husbands or fathers. However, recent surveys show that the trend of conformist voting among women is declining, and young, educated, and urban women are more likely to vote independently. If women voters could organize their votes and use their voting power more effectively to press for change, the chances for women to enhance their political standing could be improved. In fact, the idea is being promoted among women's organizations.

## WHY ARE WOMEN UNDERREPRESENTED IN POLITICS?

Reasons for women's low rates of political participation can be explained in several ways. I will examine them in the context of South Korea's social structure, cultural characteristics, and factors attributable to women themselves.

Korea's political structure is strongly male-oriented. Its political process has long been authoritarian in style. The system of elite recruitment and promotion have been relatively closed, informal, and patriarchal. Thus, political power has been concentrated in the hands of a few authoritarian figures who have strong personal ties with their subordinates. Besides these informal ties among politicians, important policy decisions are often made behind closed doors, often bypassing open, official, and democratic channels. The more important the issue, the more likely it will be discussed and settled in informal settings by the exclusive few. Given the close, personal relationships among politicians and the unofficial political process that are rather important in Korean politics, women are greatly handicapped in their efforts to establish personal ties with political leaders. They are quite often left out of the informal, yet important, decision-making process.[7]

Authoritarianism, centralization, and an oligarchical power structure are even more apparent in the party system and political organizations. Korean political parties are organized around a few central political leaders. Therefore, the party organizations are run mostly by men who are close associates of those party leaders. A typical patriarchal bond is formed between these men. This kind of paternalistic structure puts women at great disadvantage in participating in important party activities. Parties are often run by factional ties, in which factional leaders usually help "their men" to secure nominations and political money.

This also helps to explain why women are less successful in getting nomination and acquiring election funds. Women usually occupy low-ranking positions in the party organizations, and when they want to run in a national election, they often lack the party's organizational and financial supports. The present small-constituency system further makes women candidates' success difficult. Because many candidates vie for only one seat in the district, the campaign often becomes overheated. The electoral competition is fierce and the expense to maintain the district offices is far too high for women candidates, who are usually less endowed financially than men. Running a campaign costs between 20 and 50 million won per month ($25,000 to $62,000). These funds don't come from the central office. The district party manager has to raise them. They are usually supplied by businessmen who want to advance their interests through politics. They are reluctant to "invest" in women politicians since they figure that the chance of a woman being elected is fairly slim. Corrupt election practices, limitations imposed on female politicians by the election law, and other systematic constraints are additional factors that limit women's power-sharing in Korean politics.

Social and cultural elements have also limited women's political participation. Despite the equal rights for men and women promised in the constitution, Korean political culture is predominantly male-oriented and authoritarian. It has strongly discriminated against women in the political arena. Throughout the history of Korea, gender difference has assigned men to the public arena and women to the private, domestic sphere. The rigid definition of role differentiation is not as valid today as it was in the 1980's, but its legacy has strongly remained in the society. This makes Korean women's participation in politics even more difficult.

According to a survey reported prior to the local elections in 1991 by the Center for Korean Women and Politics, 46.3 percent of the public still perceived that the most important reason why there were so few women candidates in local elections was that "people have negative views on women going into politics."[8] A great many people still believe that women belong in the home. The prevailing view is that it is not womanly to have an interest in and to participate actively in the political process. Cultural factors discourage women from running for office and also keep people from voting for female candidates. The negative image of political women also affects the election process. For example, 40 percent of the candidates who ran in the local self-government election in 1991 pointed out that the greatest disadvantage for female candidates was "voters' preference for men over women."[9]

Another problem rests with Korean women themselves. How do they perceive political women? The culture of gender discrimination is deeply rooted in the social structure. Through education and socialization, women themselves come to accept these gender biases as a matter of fact. They tend to stay politically uninvolved, accepting the fact that woman is politically inferior to man. Traditional women consider that women should stay away from politics and that political women are unfeminine. They are brought up, in other words, to accept the tradition of passive women and to depend on men in politics. These stereotypical and traditional images are also reinforced by the media. Such massive social indoctrination to "feminize" women has led women to believe that they don't deserve to rule their own destiny, and even causes them to hesitate to vote for and support women candidates.

## TOWARD THE TWENTY-FIRST CENTURY:
## PREDICTIONS

Women have been largely alienated from politics in South Korea. Will the trend be corrected in the future? What is the prospect for gender politics in the twenty-first century? What are some of the ways in which women can participate in politics more effectively?

Many of the problems in Korean politics today stem from the inability of the established political institutions to accommodate the changes that have taken place in various realms of the society. Hence, political reforms are required in the political-administrative system, which has fallen far behind the rapid changes in social structures. For a more democratic and productive operation of these institutions, it is also necessary that current political representation and recruitment practices be drastically changed.

In democracy, different and competing groups of people should be accounted for by enabling them to choose and send their representatives into the decision-making process. A political system that permanently isolates a significant portion of its people from sharing power cannot maintain its long-term stability and legitimacy. Therefore, political reforms need to be introduced so that an excessive gender bias can be corrected. A new and more democratic system of political representation is not only a necessity but a natural course for social change in the twenty-first century.

Futurologists offer predictions on possible directions of change in our political, economic, social, and cultural life in the next century. Important changes, according to them, will also take place in gender politics. It is said that in coming years women's leadership will become more visible, important, and effective in problem solving than now. And political participation of women will be remarkably enhanced. Evidence to support such statements is not difficult to find.

First, it is expected that many social issues of our daily life will become more political. As society becomes more pluralistic and the functions of the government more complex, politicians will be expected to have professional expertise in their lawmaking and other political activities. As much as contemporary politics is fed up with debates on ideology and institutions, the focus of future politics will be built around specific problems of people's daily life. Hence, politicians will be tested by their skill and ability to solve these problems and improve the actual living conditions of the people. In fact, President Kim noted the changing public mood and shrewdly pledged an era in which politics will serve the people.

The growth-oriented development strategy in Korea has brought the people material prosperity. However, serious environmental degradation accompanied the economic development. The major issues confronting South Korea's politicians are such environmental problems as clean air, clean water, and recycling, and the associated problems of community health and social welfare. Women are better informed on these community issues and usually more interested in solving these problems than men. As these community-based issues become more politicized, women may be able to participate in politics on a more equal footing with men. An increasing number of women will also find themselves fit to take leadership positions. The restoration of local self-government has opened new opportunities for political women. Hence, women's position in the realm of politics is expected to improve in Korea.

Second, the future will not tolerate the present gender bias in political representation. Women's level of education and political consciousness are growing rapidly in Korea. Inequality and discrimination is being questioned by more and more women. The past political practices, which have been monopolized by men, cannot remain unchanged forever. Korean society is becoming more and more modern, complex, and pluralistic. Different social groups, such as workers, farmers, the young, and the poor, who have been alienated from power and economic benefits for so long, have begun to assert their legitimate place in society and now vie for positions in local and national politics. The women's movement is an important part of this wind of change, for women are also inadequately represented in politics. Therefore, it is natural to expect that women, whose causes lie in realizing a more just and harmonious social order, will intensify their efforts and struggles to expand the scope of their leadership and representation.

Third, as democratization in Korea continues, women's representation in the political arena should also be improved. Democratization will bring changes in governmental practices and its decision-making process, so that the political system will become more open and democratic. When the political process does become more open and democratic, irregular practices, unofficial channels, and private connections may no longer play as important a role in elite recruitment. Male-dominated, authoritarian, under-the-table politics have so far kept women away from politics, and this in turn, seems to have encouraged corruption. When elections and policy deliberations are conducted in open and democratic forums, the type of politics that relies heavily on the informal, private favor-exchanging and exclusive networking will disappear, eventually widening the scope of women's political participation, and women will no longer have to face the disadvantage of "being women" in politics.

The above analysis suggests an optimistic view of change in gender politics, although the progress may be slow. Korean women still face a great challenge, and there are a number of things that women and their organizations must do to improve their status in politics.

## AGENDA FOR FUTURE

The patterns and practices of contemporary society tend to keep women from equal access to politics. Some of them are embedded in the culture and others in policy failures. Therefore, reforms are required not only in the area of policies but also on the level of social and cultural consciousness. Traditions and thought patterns do not change overnight. As well as demanding reforms in discriminatory laws and policies, women must relentlessly pursue changes in the culture and in the way political women are viewed and depicted in the society.

Below, I will explore three issues. First, I will examine how policies and laws can be reformed to reduce and eventually eliminate the disadvantage that women face in entering the political arena. Second, I will suggest a number of things that can be done to improve women's skills and abilities as politicians. Finally, I will deal with possible ways of changing the negative image that the society and its people have of political women.

*Reforms in policies*

What are the mechanisms that can be utilized to bring more women into leadership positions? First, the laws and policies should be reformed so that more women can be recruited into public offices. Elections are one of the best and perhaps most natural ways to bring women into politics. The laws and practices, both visible and invisible, discouraging women to run for and succeed in races for the national and local legislatures need to be changed. The election laws should be amended in the following ways: expansion of the size of the constituency, public management of the elections, and introduction of clean campaigns and equal opportunity to raise political funds.

Political parties should provide women with higher positions and more responsibilities. They also need to nurture and aid women politicians more effectively. Until women gain enough strength to compete with men, the parties should reserve a certain percentage of their candidacies for women. Also, more women should be appointed to important government positions. Some positions should be clearly delineated as ones for which it is more advantageous to have women assigned. These positions should be reserved for women. Job descriptions for these positions need to be carefully analyzed and widely publicized.

Women need to urge the government and private enterprises to fill a certain percentage of their jobs with women. Some might argue that this is unfair and discriminating against men, and hence undemocratic. Yet, women have not had the same kind of opportunity as men for such a long time. The temporary privilege is perhaps the only way to help women overcome the disadvantages they have suffered in the past.

In order to realize the above propositions, women and their groups can form legitimate pressure groups and demonstrate a show of organized power. A significant reform can be made if women, who account for more than 51 percent of the votes, would exercise their voting rights to press for change and use them more effectively. Women's organizations can serve as effective means of organizing women voters. Until now, many of the women's groups have been focusing on promoting and encouraging women's active participation in social activities. They have emphasized equal rights in legal positions, attaining equal educational and employment opportunities, and so on. Remarkable progress has been made in this respect. Now is the time for women to find effective ways to utilize these newly earned rights and opportunities in order to upgrade the level of their political representation. To achieve this, it is imperative that more women leaders emerge and take part in politics. Women leaders should be included in important decision-making processes, such as those affecting the most basic and authoritative allocation of values. Government policies for women have often been criticized as relying on insincere tokenism and the assigning of a few symbolic positions to women politicians. These kinds of political practices should be carefully reexamined. As long as women remain passive and satisfied with the minimum offered by the present system, effective reforms cannot take place. At the same time, it is women's (and their leaders') responsibility to prove to the public that women in power can make the world different, new, more creative and democratic. Women's organizations can also help to promote clean, moral, and people-oriented images of politics, as opposed to the images made by power-oriented male politics.

*Educating and training women politicians*

Preparing women for successful participation in politics requires appropriate training and education. One important educational focus should be on the training of political candidates. This training should not only include the candidates themselves, but also the campaign managers and the entire supporting staff. These people need special training in various areas; preparations for candidacy, selection of the district, procurement and management of the campaign funds, analysis of the voters and campaign strategy, public address skills and image management, and publicity management. Once elected, women officials need leadership development training. They need education that can help them adjust to and work effectively within the existing political structure.

A politician also has to maintain an ongoing relationship with the constituency that elected her. She should continue to meet and talk with the people of her district, show them what the priority projects of the district are and what she is going to do about them. She should remember to consolidate her support base and continue to expand it. Constant communications with women's groups and other social organizations will help guarantee their continuous support.

Women politicians should learn how to utilize the media to their benefit. We live in the media age. It is not much of an exaggeration to say that the success of today's politicians largely depends on how much media coverage they get. Knowing how to portray favorable images through the media and how to get the voters' attention can lead the woman politician to a successful career. Women also need to study and monitor carefully how the media treat women politicians. Also, women in senior—or even retired—positions should be encouraged to meet and exchange their knowledge and experiences with prospective leaders. Those who lose in reelections need to be trained to manage their districts more effectively the next time.

Women's groups and other civic organizations have great potential for leadership training. Their education programs should include consciousness-raising seminars for both the prospective and the incumbent leaders. Most social organizations, however, lack funds and cannot afford to organize training programs on their own. Therefore, the government should support them by providing facilities and money. Women's organizations should take an active role in receiving support from the government and private industries. Training women leaders is necessary not just for the female population, but also for the betterment of the entire society. It is an important means of human resource development as well.

*On social consciousness*

The socialization process is the main culprit in leading many women to feel inferior and helpless in politics. This has to be corrected through social-education programs. Changing the values and attitudes of the people requires well-conceived theories and comprehensive planning. It also takes a long time to help women to be more active and concerned about social and political issues. Women need to change their traditional views of politics. The curricula for the general education of women have to be renewed so that the consciousness level of women on political issues can be upgraded. Traditional values and attitudes can be changed also by having more women involved in various social activities and civic movements. There are many projects in which women can become involved. Civic movements that focus on consumer protection, environmental awareness, community activities, fair-election campaigns, and voluntary work will help women develop social consciousness and improve their leadership skills.

One should also think of ways to help women support and choose women candidates. If women elect women candidates, they can help women occupy half of the seats in representative assemblies. Voting is one of the most important political acts. Women should create a voting bloc for themselves. Women's organizations should encourage more women to run and win in elections. They can raise funds for women candidates, campaign for them, and educate voters to participate in elections and vote for women candidates.

## CONCLUSION

Women's issues are no longer only for women. They affect the happiness and well-being of the entire society and constitute the core element of democracy and national development. They should not be treated as separate from other major sociopolitical issues. A transformation is needed in the way people view the problems of women. The problem of gender discrimination is rooted in both history and culture as well as in political practices. People's negative perceptions about women in politics will not go away overnight. They must be addressed through the combined efforts of the media, education, and institutional changes.

In addition, women and their organizations should work together and cooperate with other sectors of society in order to bring democratic changes and facilitate structural and institutional reforms. Democracy for women cannot come unless there is democracy for the whole society. Women's activities and political participation need to focus on helping political parties to better aggregate demands for reform. Women's organizations can also watch the elections or see to it that elected officers do their best in serving the people.

There are many challenges for feminist groups in Korea. They can do a better job articulating women's needs and in organizing their votes for appropriate causes. They can educate the public on the gender problem and possible solutions. Feminist groups ought to persuade both men and women that women have a place in everyday politics and can perform leadership roles as well as men. They should also promote education and training programs for female politicians to become more effective in competing with men in elections.

Politics in the twenty-first century will require new cohorts of individuals and groups to play important roles. No society that traps a major portion of its population in a political alienation trap can achieve democracy and stable economic development. Democracy has to allow competing social forces to represent their interests in a way that makes them work productively with others. Gender discrimination is an enemy of peace and democracy. Reform in South Korea, therefore, requires a reform in its gender politics.

NOTES

1. The Democratic Justice party, which was the ruling party in the Thirteenth National Assembly, merged with two opposition parties and was renamed the Democratic Liberal party (DLP), becoming a large ruling party. The Party for Peace and Democracy first merged with another opposition (minority) group, renaming itself New Democratic party. Then, it again merged with another opposition party, the Democratic party, and was renamed the Democratic party (DP), becoming by far the largest opposition party.

2. United Nations, *The World's Women 1970–1990: Trends and Statistics* (New York: United Nations, 1991), 32.

3. Ministry of Government Administration, *Government Officials Annual* (Seoul, 1992).

4. United Nations, *World's Women*, 31.

5. Sohn Bong Scuk *et al.*, *The Study of Female Candidates for Local Assembly Elections* (Seoul: Center for Korean Women and Politics, 1991).

6. Central Election Management Committee, *Yearbook of National Assembly Elections* (Seoul, 1988).

7. Sohn Bong Scuk, *The Study on Women Legislators* (Seoul: Center for Korean Women and Politics, 1991), 35.

8. Center for Korean Women and Politics, *Public Opinion Poll on Local Self-Governments* (Seoul, 1991), 13.

9. Sohn Bong Scuk *et al.*, *Female Candidates*, 41.

# 13

## Feminism in a Confucian Society: The Women's Movement in Korea

### MARIAN LIEF PALLEY

THE Republic of Korea (South Korea) has experienced very rapid industrial growth and economic modernization since the end of the Korean War.[1] Although the society's material change has been substantial, behavioral adjustments to the economic developments have occurred slowly and have sometimes been justified by tradition. Thus, inequities in women's opportunities are maintained through an elaborate system of role relationships that are rooted in and rationalized by Confucian customs; they are socially mandated and often legally condoned. However, despite the cultural limits on behavioral change, a women's-rights movement has developed in Korea over the past several years, and it is addressing issues of equity, worker exploitation, and sexual violence—universal concerns of modernized societies. The interaction of tradition with the calls for change issued by this women's-rights movement is the focus of this study.

This examination of the groups in the women's movement and their issue orientations is based in large measure on interviews conducted in 1988 and analysis completed in 1990. Additional interviews were conducted in 1993, and the movement circa 1993 appears to have made some adaptations to new issues and new political realities.

### INDUSTRIAL DEVELOPMENT AND THE CHANGE IN WOMEN'S EXPECTATIONS

Many nations have industrialized and modernized their economies in the post–World War II era. Much attention has been focused on this development in Asia, since countries such as Japan and the "Four Tigers" (South Korea,

Taiwan, Hong Kong, and Singapore), to name just a few, have been very successful in their efforts to compete in world markets with the more established industrial giants of Western Europe and North America.

However, even though a nation's productive capacity may become modernized, it does not necessarily follow that its social and political values, which have evolved through the centuries, will be completely supplanted. The Republic of Korea has industrialized and economically modernized a substantial portion of its productive capacity in the past two decades. Yet despite its rapid transition toward becoming a modern industrial society, there are cultural and social values that are sometimes used to justify social institutions and expectations that arose in earlier eras. Put in somewhat different terms, culture can be described in terms of its material and behavioral components. While the material culture in South Korea has modernized and been affected by Western influences, its behavioral culture maintains and embraces some Confucian traditions, and it is slow to change.[2] Part of this behavioral culture is reflected in the inequities in women's roles.[3]

Modernization and industrialization have led to improved educational opportunities for many Korean women.[4] Employment options have changed, and if women do not share the same job alternatives as men, they do have more workplace opportunities than they had ten years ago. Professionally trained and other upper-class women seek adjustments in the status of women through political action—mostly using the parliamentary process but not shunning altogether protest tactics. Women's political activity increasingly attempts to place issues on the national public-policy agenda that had previously been deemed private and thus inappropriate for public scrutiny. Questions relating to family and work roles for women are now raised in public debate, and policymakers are pressed to make decisions on these issues. There has been "a process of . . . deprivatization of female roles (which) coincides with a growing number of women perceiving themselves to have a greater stake in altering existing arrangements of public roles."[5] As this has occurred, numerous women's organizations have developed in order to foster political participation by and on behalf of women.

During the 1980s, political turmoil was nearly a daily occurrence in South Korea. Demands for democratization, reunification with North Korea, and human-rights reforms were the three pillars of discontent that articulated and fueled the country's ongoing strikes, protests, and demonstrations. Much of the underlying cause of political opposition, however, seems to have been rooted in discomfort with some of the consequences of South Korea's rapid industrialization and modernization.

Women participate in the social movements, which issue these calls for change, but they do not hold leadership positions. Neo-Marxist rhetoric sometimes colors the discourse, and when the women in these campaigns for social and political change discuss women's issues, this rhetoric tends to carry over. However, often women-specific issues are buried within the broader concerns of these social movements. Other politically active women not involved with the social movements are more specifically connected with women's volunteer organizations, which perform community services, provide leisure-time activities, or offer professional associations that reinforce occupational status. During the 1980s many of these groups also began to address issues of sexual inequality. The vast majority of Korean women, however—as with most men and women in all nations—have no involvement with any organization that is concerned with changing society in any way.

The history and role of women in Korean society have been studied, but women's organizations and their role in effecting changes in female expectations and attitudes by and toward women have not yet been considered seriously by most observers of Korean politics.[6] This study will look at traditional women's roles in South Korea, consider the groups involved in the contemporary women's movement, and see how they try to redress seemingly entrenched and tradition-bound, sex-role relationships. Many socially conscious Korean women perceive that they have not yet achieved equal status with Korean men. They believe that if there is to be any change in this relationship then a leadership must be in place to help facilitate an expanded awareness among women regarding their situation, to alter male attitudes about women and their appropriate roles in the family and in society, and to help shape the nation's policy agenda. Such a leadership group has developed in Korea, and an awareness of the need for these changes is beginning to occur. A cadre of women that is engaged in fostering some attitude changes can be found in the numerous women's organizations that exist in South Korea. Ultimately, these women will have to mobilize a large enough following of active members and other supporters who are willing to contribute time, energy, money, and other resources to their efforts to produce greater gender equality in Korean society.

To discern the role of women's organizations as they attempt to alter women's status in Korean society, it was necessary to examine the position of women in Korea and understand the cultural constraints under which women and their organizations operate. Also, women activists were interviewed for their views on the changing conditions that influence the status of women in their society.

These interviews took place from June through August 1988, and follow-up interviews were held in June and July 1993. The interviews were with women who held leadership positions in eighteen women's groups (there are over forty women's organizations that have some relationship—sometimes tangential—with the women's movement in South Korea). In order to sketch out the scope of sex-role relationships and the relative position of women in Korean society, twelve women professors of sociology, political science, and women's studies were also interviewed. In addition, several women who now serve in the House of Delegates, three women who served in the House of Delegates prior to 1988, and several people in leadership positions at the Korean Women's Development Institute were interviewed.

At the outset of this research, a reputational approach was utilized to draw the sample. Several faculty members from the Women's Research Institute at Ewha Woman's University suggested the names of leaders in women's-rights groups. Interviews were scheduled with these people. At each of these meetings the interviewee was asked for the names of other women who were thought to be appropriate for this study. In other words, people provided the names of women who were perceived to be influential in the women's movement. Appointments were then made with any women whose names were mentioned at least twice in this context. The respondents were asked questions that addressed attitudes, organizational development, and changing sex roles in the "New Korea" as well as political strategy and tactics. In 1993 some women were reinterviewed and some additional people were selected for inclusion in the sample due to their public positions or their visibility in the women's movement.

## WOMEN IN KOREA: A CULTURAL PERSPECTIVE

An understanding of Korean culture and society is not possible without comprehending the nature and role of Confucian thought—it would be like tying to grasp the nature of American development without sensing the significance of liberalism, the Protestant ethic, or the frontier. While Americans are concerned foremost with freedom and individualism, Koreans, steeped as they are in a Confucian moral code, are more deeply concerned with relationships. Therefore, to understand the role of women's rights organizations and their leaders as they try to alter women's status in Korean society, it is useful to bear in mind some of the basic assumptions of Confucianism that are often used to justify women's unequal roles.

"In traditional Korean society, women have long been in a disadvantaged position."[7] Korean social structure consisted of a royal monarch, strong class consciousness, and a patriarchal, extended family system that emphasized the maintenance of family lines. This structure tended to maintain separate and unequal roles for women from those of men.[8] In large measure, this separation is rooted in Confucianism. One of the tenets of Confucianism requires three obediences of women: to the father when young, to the husband when married, and to the son in old age.

Confucian thought is sometimes applied and appreciated unevenly, that is, some portions of the code are upheld while others are observed in the breach. Thus, it should not be too surprising that sometimes the code is used to justify a separate and unequal role for women. Despite centuries of inequality between the sexes and the inferior position of women in traditional Korean society, industrialization and modernization have wrought some changes in female lives. But a gap exists between industrial development and cultural response, between material and behavioral culture. Kim Chong Ui wrote in *Korean Women Today*, a publication of the Korean Women's Development Institute (a government agency), that "because of the wrong socialization process in our society which has continued for too long, not only men but also women themselves tend to recognize the inferiority of women, at least unconsciously. This is what remains as the major obstacle to achieving equality between men and women."[9] Women do work outside of the home today. Yet they have no expectation that men will assist them in their home and child-care responsibilities. As in many other countries, there are almost no public programs to assist the working mother, and very few private employers provide supports that could facilitate the dual roles of women as mother/wife and worker.

Women are employed in light industry, agriculture, and some of the professions, especially teaching. Opportunities for professional mobility are very limited, and on average women earn approximately 45 percent what men earn. It has been estimated that over 70 percent of the workers in the poorly paid garment and textile, toy, and electronics factories that manufacture goods for export are women.

Women's suffrage was included in the 1948 constitution. Article 8 of the Constitution of the Republic of Korea states that all citizens are equal before the law and that there shall not be discrimination in political, economic, social, or culture life on account of sex, religion, or social status. Often the reality is at variance with the America-influenced constitution. In 1993 there were three women cabinet ministers and only five women serving in the National Assembly, which has 299 members. And despite the language of equality that was incorporated into the constitution, Korea has only recently (effective 1 January 1991) modified its family law, which had included legal provisions that placed women in a disadvantaged position vis-à-vis men with respect to inheritance and other family status roles.

The influence of the United States in drafting the Korean Constitution is clear, particularly in the article that addresses equality. This language reflects a diffusion of rhetoric from the American to the Korean experience, although there was no initial comparable diffusion of cultural beliefs and attitudes. Thus, Korea has had a constitution and a family law that were at variance with one another with the latter reflecting the reality of life in Korea more than the former. However, the constitution provides an ideological baseline that some people, such as members of reformist women's groups, strive to reach.

## THE CONTEMPORARY WOMEN'S MOVEMENT

The vocabulary of the Korean women's movement needs to be understood. There are presently two types of women's organizations that seek improved conditions for women in Korea. They are usually identified by women activists as either "radical" or "reformist" in orientation. These terms must be understood in the context of the women's movement in Korea and should not be confused with American usage of these constructs.

Radical women's groups in Korea have been identified with broader human-rights issues, such as the torturing of prisoners, democratization of the political system, and reunification with North Korea. These concerns have sometimes preceded radical women's groups' identification with women-specific issues. It can be argued that opposing torture and indefinite detention and advocating for the democratization of the political system are hardly "radical" in a society that has a history of repression. Also, the use of unconventional tactics such as strikes and demonstrations do not qualify as "radical" methods to many. Moreover, it is possible that the violence associated with the strikes and demonstrations has been the conscious tactical choice of the demonstrators. Shin Nakyun, president of the Korean League of Women Voters, told me, however, that the fall of the Communist-bloc countries along with the 1992 election of President Kim Young Sam, a very popular democratic leader, may have influenced some "deradicalization" of the radical women's groups.

When the term "radical" is used to describe women's groups it does not mean to imply support for radical changes in women's role and status. The term is sometimes used interchangeably with support for human-rights reforms. At times the rhetoric used by members of these groups is very harsh within the context of Korean society, and the language is often neo-Marxist and out of touch with the political mainstream of society. Today, neo-Marxism and nationalism go together, many radical women proclaim. Although there is widespread opposition to the oppression of recent Korean regimes, it is important to remember that most Koreans are not prone to support neo-Marxist movements. These groups at times employ traditional lobbying methods but they also join in demonstrations and strikes that sometimes become violent. They supported the Party for Peace and Democracy in the 1988 election and consequently were identified as antigovernment. In 1992 they split their support. Thus many radical women supported the Democratic Liberal party and its candidate, President Kim, while other self-identified radical women supported the opposition Democratic party.

Put in somewhat different terms, the radical women's groups do not necessarily support radical shifts in women's roles, although they do tend to support political change in society, which their leaders believe will eliminate the restrictions on individual freedom that they see in Korea. The tactics that they are willing to use are nonconventional (strikes, marches, demonstrations) as well as traditional, conventional modes of participation.

The reformist groups—which women activists refer to as "traditional" or "mainstream" organizations—appear, in contrast to the radical groups, to be moderate to conservative in bent, although many would be viewed as liberal in the American political context. That is, they work for change in women's role within the constraints of the existing society. They seem to be using concepts employed by groups that operate in the American women's movement—to be effective you must be perceived as legitimate; to be perceived as legitimate you must focus on incremental issues; it is important to be involved in the definition of the problem; and, at the very early stages of the policy process, it is helpful to try to manipulate symbols favorable to your cause.[10] Some of these groups have been very effective in bringing significant demands for changes in the position of women in society to the attention of public policymakers, and at times these organizations have been credited with fostering real changes in the role of women in Korean society. Finally, unlike the radical groups, women in the mainstream organizations utilize only traditional lobbying techniques. They are involved in education, influencing decision makers, drafting legislation, and so forth. These groups tend to support the ruling party and are therefore identified as progovernment.

The problems and concerns of South Korean women cannot be grouped into one neat aggregation. Rather, a fivefold classification of women and their backgrounds provides a more accurate picture.[11] Farm women, working-class women, professional women, middle-class housewives, and poor women all have different problems and concerns. Policy priorities for these five groups of women are often quite different, though sexual violence seems to be a coalescing issue. Of course this situation is true anywhere, and it is certainly the case in any complex or developing society. It should be noted that even though different cohorts of women have different needs and interests, most of the women's groups have middle-class leaders and tend to reflect the interests of middle-class women.

Farm women are not concerned with the right to work—they work to survive. In agricultural societies all able-bodied people participate in productive endeavors. Korea is no exception, for it has a very labor-intensive agricultural sector, and as a result women are by necessity involved in most aspects of agricultural production. However, when heavy machinery is brought onto a farm, men operate the machinery. Working-class women often work out of the home too, and their major concerns are work related, especially pay equity and improved working conditions. Some analysts have observed that South Korea's "economic miracle" was achieved in large measure as a result of female labor since women have been very heavily involved in some of the labor-intensive industries, such as the garment trades.

With Korea's modernization there has been an improvement in education and professional training for women. However, professional women often cannot find employment positions at all, or, if they do find jobs, they often are not commensurate with their skills and training. These women want better job opportunities and fringe benefits. In Korea today it is easier for women high-school graduates to find employment than it is for women with university degrees. Less than one-half of women university graduates can hope to find employment out of the home. Yet a survey conducted at the Ewha Women's University in 1987 showed that over 90 percent of the students wanted to work after completion of their education.

Professionally trained and educated women are concerned also with the provisions of the Family Law. Despite its modifications, the law still maintains a system of patrilineal family headship, defines relationship in a different manner for a woman's family than for a man's, and restricts marriage between people with the same name and place of origin—even if they are very distant relatives.

Middle-class housewives often need outlets for their physical and intellectual energies. These women are the mainstay of the voluntary sector in South Korea. Many leaders of the women's groups are educated middle-class homemakers. They are concerned with changing the provisions of the Family Law and with issues as far ranging as consumer protection, education for children, job training for poor women, sexual violence, and career opportunities for women who wish to work outside their homes.

Finally, poor women require education, job training, social programs, and employment. Most often these women and their problems are defined as welfare concerns and are not included under the rubric of women's issues. The groups in the women's movement seldom address these concerns, although there are some traditional groups that maintain job-training programs for poor women.

### The groups in the women's movement

Numerous organizations representing women's interests have emerged in Korea in the past decade. There are in addition some groups that predate the current concerns with women's rights and can trace their origins to the pre–World War II era and the immediate post-1945 period. However, prior to the mid 1980s, these groups were not particularly concerned with issues relating to women's rights and equality. Any efforts to divide neatly the forty-plus women's organizations into two discrete clusters will have its limitations, but it is nonetheless useful to consider Korean women's groups in the terms used by women activists themselves. Thus, one talks of two separate sets of groups—the more established mainstream groups that tend to be reformist in perspective and the radical groups. Some of the reformist organizations are affiliated with the Council of Korean Women's Organizations (CKWO), an umbrella organization that acts to foster coalition behavior among these other-wise separate groups. The radical groups tend to be more recent entrants into the political process, being less than ten years old. These groups tend to af-filiate with Korean Women's Associations United (KWAU), another umbrella organization that works to foster group interaction and coalition building. As noted previously, among the women involved in the women's movement in Korea, the more established mainstream reformist groups are often referred to as "traditional" organizations. In English this usage is a misnomer since the women in these groups are working to change some traditions, in particular those that keep women in a subordinate position in relation to men.

The membership of the mainstream groups tends to be middle class. Its leadership is well educated and attended elite universities. The more radical groups tend to have very small memberships and the leaders of its groups are also middle class, well educated, and graduates of the same elite universities as the leaders of the reformist groups. Of the women who were interviewed for this study, all but three were graduates of the Ewha Woman's University. Of the three exceptions, two were graduates of Seoul National University and one was a high-school graduate who headed the Korean Women's Workers Association.

What often distinguishes the leaders of the different types of groups is age. The leaders of the radical groups tend to be younger. Also, while the women in the reformist groups are usually willing to speak English, the radical-group women would only speak Korean. Since the women in both groups are similar in their social and educational backgrounds, language choice seemed to be a symbolic statement. The reformist women are willing to accommodate to the linguistic limitations of the interviewer whereas the radical women seem to be making a nationalist and anti-American statement with their unwillingness to use English and preference to rely on an interpreter.

It would be impossible to discuss all the groups associated with the women's movement in Korea separately in these pages. However, it is useful to consider a representative sample of organizations in the movement to gain an appreciation of the range of issue concerns and strategies employed by the different associations.

THE MAINSTREAM ORGANIZATIONS. The mainstream groups tend to be mass membership groups. For example, the Young Women's Christian Association (YWCA), established in Korea in 1922, has thirty thousand paid members, and in the course of any year over two million women participate in its programs. It has thirty-one chapters, all of which conduct programs for their regions. Local chapters are involved in various service projects that assist poor women, and the YWCA has taken a strong position and developed a program emphasis relating to creative education, peace and unification, economic self-reliance, and environmental conservation. They regularly provide political support for women's issues, although the YWCA is traditionally a service organization. It is, however, often difficult to develop a unified position for the YWCA since there are numerous local groups, and the memberships of these locals sometimes find it difficult to agree on single perspectives.

Members of the YWCA have been active politically. In recent years, the majority of women who have served in the National Assembly have been YWCA members. Also, members of the YWCA are active in other organizations. They talk with many people, meet with other groups, and speak with government officials.

The Korean Center for Family Law, established in 1954 by Lee Tai Young, is seen by most women involved in the women's movement as one of the key organizations. The Center for Family Law has coordinated efforts to change the Family Law since 1954. Its organizational leadership takes the position that central to women's role is the family and that there is a need to alter the Family Law. Originally the organization focused on women's affairs exclusively, but now it provides legal aid to all poor people. It is affiliated with the Korean National Council of Women (KNCW) and works with the KNCW when there is a need for coalition effort. But Kwak Bae Hae, the supervisor of counseling at the center, told me that coalition efforts were not particularly successful when working to alter the Family Law. Although the Center for Family Law is not affiliated with the KWAU, the center is involved with human rights activities, and the KWAU is also intimately involved with such activities.

Among the more established mainstream groups are the Business and Professional Women (BPW) and the Korean Association of University Women (KAUW). The BPW is a small organization that attracts members who are married, professional women. As an organization it has supported reform of the Family Law, which Kim Hyun Ja, a former president of BPW (and vice president of the YWCA and former member of the National Assembly), told me was akin to Korea's Equal Rights Amendment, as well as the Equal Opportunity Act. The BPW usually can be counted on to support programmatic changes that will improve the status of women.

The KAUW was founded in 1950 to foster understanding and friendship among women, and to enhance educational opportunities for university women. More recently it has expanded its concerns to include opportunity building for women. The KAUW has one thousand members who are organized into five chapters. The major issues with which the organization is concerned relate to equal job opportunities for women, especially women college graduates who are often forced to stay at home because they cannot find suitable employment. The group tends to support most of the positions taken by the other traditional women's groups, including reform of the Family Law and implementation of the Equal Employment Act. However, members of the KAUW identify their organization's main purpose as education. They are particularly concerned with educating the public and changing the education system itself. One of its primary concerns is reform of the college-entrance system, which is based on an examination system. (In 1988, 200,000 out of 1 million high-school graduates entered college.)

In addition, there are professional organizations for nurses, hairdressers, and others affiliated with the Council of Korean Women's Organizations that are concerned with the employment status of their members. They too are involved with supporting changes that will improve the status of all Korean women. Finally, there are the two largest women's groups in Korea, the Korean National Mother's Association (KNMA) and the Korean Federation of Housewives' Clubs (KFHC). The mothers' organization, founded in 1958, has between 40,000 and 50,000 members, and the housewives' group, established in 1963, has a membership of 180,000 organized into 198 clubs. These latter two groups are seen as being at the most conservative and tradition-bound end of the women's groups' spectrum.

It is interesting that it was the KNMA that helped to spearhead the planned-parenthood drive in the later 1950s, and along with the housewives' group, they support changes in the Family Law and the Equal Employment Opportunity Act and the need to equalize women's status in society with that of men. The stated main purposes of the KNMA is to educate mothers about family planning and help women adapt to the changing society. The primary concerns of the KFHC relate to support of the consumer movement and the fair evaluation of domestic labor. This latter programmatic perspective effects their position on divorce and the Family Law more generally. At present, women receive in divorce settlements only what men want to provide to them. It is the contention of the KFHC leadership that divorce settlements would be more equitable if domestic labor was defined as productive labor.

The mainstream groups, with the exception of the YWCA, are affiliated with the Council of Women's Organizations, which was founded in 1959. It attempts to coordinate the coalition activities of the women's groups. However, by most accounts, coalition building has not been too successful.

As noted above, the mainstream groups are concerned with changing the provisions of the Family Law, equal employment opportunity and jobs, and consumer protection. By 1993 most women's groups also supported legislation that would define sexual violence as a criminal act. In recent years reformist groups have lobbied for the passage of the Equal Employment Opportunity Act, which went into effect in April 1988. This legislation provides for equality for women in job placement, on-the-job training, promotions, retirement, and compensation for maternity and maternity leaves of up to one year for each child. The more radical groups have criticized the law and the mainstream reformist groups, which supported it, on the grounds that it has no mechanism for implementation. The mainstream groups' leaders respond that one must begin some place and that the symbol of the law and what it means is very important. They contend that now that they have a law, albeit a minimalist one, they can work for tools to implement it.

Efforts to alter the Family Law have been far more difficult. The 1987 agreement by each of the political parties to consider changes in the Family Law was supported by all of the women's organizations, mainstream and radical. The amendment proposed by all of the women's organizations would have eliminated the family headship system, abolished the prohibition of marriage between members of the same clan, altered child-custody arrangements so that a child would not automatically go to the father in cases of divorce, altered the inheritance system so that all surviving members of the family of a deceased man would receive equal shares rather than the present system in which the eldest son receives a larger portion of the resources, and changed the rules for property division in divorce so that women could receive proper alimony and not be at the mercy of the exhusband. When this proposal came before the National Assembly, sixty-one members signed a petition in support of the changes. But the Confucian elders launched a countercampaign against the changes and got twelve of the delegates to remove their names from the supporting petition. Also, they were able to exert sufficient influence—based on a fear that they would mobilize voters to vote against any delegate who supported the amendment—so that the proposal to amend the Family Law was never brought to the floor of the National Assembly for debate and a vote.

In 1989, the National Assembly did enact legislation that changed some of the provisions for the Family Law that the women's organizations found most offensive. On 1 January 1992 child-custody arrangements changed. Children no longer automatically go to the father in cases of divorce. The inheritance system was revamped so that all surviving children—regardless of gender, marital status, or birth order—will share equally. Also, although the family headship system is retained, some of the duties and responsibilities of the family head can be shared, by law, with other members of the family.

THE RADICAL ORGANIZATIONS. The radical groups, with limited memberships, do not have as much money as the mainstream groups and thus find it difficult to be as active as the older, more moderate organizations. There are twenty-four groups that belong to Korean Women's Associations United, a coalition of the more radical women's organizations. The largest of these groups is the Women's Society for Democracy, which is a multi-issue women's rights group under the leadership of Professor Lee Hyo Jae, a member of the Sociology Department at the Ewha Women's University. Along with Lee Oo Jeong, appointed to the National Assembly in 1993 by the Democratic party and formerly the president of KWAU, she is seen by most of the radical women as a symbolic leader of the contemporary women's movement in Korea. Other radical groups include the Women's Hot Line, the *Women's Newspaper* (now the *Women's News*), Korean Women Workers Association, Korean Catholic Farmers, Women's Committee, and numerous church-related organizations (in fact, Lee Oo Jeong was also president of Korean Church Women United). In 1991 the Sexual Violence Relief Center (SVRC) was formed. The SVRC, along with the Women's Hot Line, has been in the forefront of a campaign against sexual violence that seems to have brought all of the women's groups—mainstream and radical—together in a common cause (see below).

The Korean Women's Society for Democracy (KWSD) was founded in 1987 after the Women's Society for Justice and Equality, which had been organized in 1983 to deal with women's labor issues and the patriarchal system, died from internal splits between members who advocated labor reforms, which would benefit women, and those who were more concerned with democratic reforms of the political system. In 1988 the KWSD had 150 active members and directed its attention to a wide range of issues that affect women, including women's labor rights, prostitution, and sex torture. They are also involved in efforts to alter the Family Law. However, the leaders of the organization believe that it is premature to confront men on issues of sexual equality until more general concerns regarding human rights, reunification, and democratization are addressed and resolved.

The Women's Hot Line, in contrast, is a single-issue group that was founded in Seoul (and continues to operate only in Seoul) in 1983 to address problems associated with spouse battering, rape, and prostitution. Its organizational leaders express concern about AIDS, especially as it affects prostitutes who work around American military installations. The Women's Hot Line runs Shelter House, a facility for battered wives, and also receives hundreds of phone calls each month asking for information and advice. In addition, this organization tries to bring the issue of sexism in the workplace to the attention of the public through the publication of printed materials and public demonstrations. Members of the Women's Hot Line tend to be younger than members of the more traditional, mainstream groups. Hee Lo Youn, a representative of this organization, told me that attitudes of women and men about women were changing as a result of heightened social consciousness. She did, however, argue that women and labor are the most oppressed groups in Korea, and that the liberation of women is hampered by contradictions of class, sex, and nationality. This rhetoric fits well into the discourse of the more overarching social movement that addresses human rights reform, democratization, and reunification of North and South Korea.

The SVRC focuses more broadly on sexual violence. The group was formed in 1991 by Ewha Woman's University graduates who had been women's-studies students. In addition to it's lobbying efforts for the passage of a sexual-violence special law, the SVRC provides counseling and maintains a shelter for victims of sexual violence.

Kim Sue Ja, manager of the *Women's Newspaper* (*Women's News*), agreed with Hee Lo Youn's assessment of women's situation in Korea. She noted that although there has been some change achieved since 1980—especially regarding women's attitudes about themselves—substantive changes will require changes in social institutions. Social institutions have not been altered, and as a result substantial changes in the unequal status of women have not been addressed. However, she told me that women have modified their Confucian ideological perspective and have developed greater social awareness, but added that it is possible to balance improved status for women with a modified Confucian belief system emphasizing relationships. The *Women's Newspaper* (*Women's News*) is a newcomer to the women's-rights scene, having been founded in 1986 as a research group for women's organizations. Initially illegal, in April 1988 the newsletter became legal. Its first issue was published in October 1988, and it is now a weekly women's newspaper that targets a middle-class readership and seeks to raise the consciousness of women and educate young children to be androgynous.

While most of the organizations discussed thus far focus their energies and attention on issues that are of central concern to middle-class women, the Korean Women Workers Association (KWWA), created in 1987, has a different orientation. Lee Young Soon, president of the organization, told me that the group is concerned specifically about the status of women workers. In particular, the differential pay and promotion opportunities afforded women workers is seen as inequitable, and other labor organizations do not address problems that are women-specific. Married women workers often leave their jobs when they have children. But, increasingly, families need the women wage-earner's income in order to make ends meet. Thus, in 1987, 40.7 percent of women who were working in production prior to marriage continued to work after marriage. Women who continue to work after they have families have not necessarily improved their situation since they then must perform the dual roles of housewife and work-force participant. The KWWA is working to educate women to try to overcome what they identify as this disadvantaged position. They support the development of day nurseries for children (and run one day nursery themselves). Although the KWWA supports changes in the Family Law, the law is not considered to be of particular concern to poor and working-class women because its immediate affects upon them are not seen as being great.

A somewhat different perspective on women and their role in Korean society is provided by the Korean Christian Farmer's Association (KCFA), which works for the improvement of farmers. In an interview with me in 1988, Kim Min Hee, executive secretary of this organization, said that they want "to change the structure that exploits the rural areas." In rural areas, she said, women are producers along with men, and the problems men and women confront are similar. In 1984 the KCFA established a Women's Department in order to involve women with the men in "participating in the struggles" to improve conditions. The issues that are of particular concern to KWAU and its Women's Department at this time involve problems associated with the import of agricultural products. As far as support programs for women workers are concerned, Kim Min Hee believes that the KCFA cannot provide such supports. The problems are rooted in the "feudal consciousness" of rural areas, which leave women's role unchanged, she noted. Moreover, to raise the consciousness of men and women, support would have to come from national public policy changes, as personal or regional efforts would not be sufficient. The KWAU Women's Department spokeswomen, like those of the KWWA, do not see that the economic problems of farmers will be solved by reforms in the Family Law.

Changes in Korean society have led to the rise of radical groups. Whereas many of the mainstream groups were established originally as social and voluntary organizations for and by middle-class women, the radical groups are a product of the latter half of the 1980s. In the 1970s, mainstream women's organizations were influenced by the women's movements of the West, and especially the United States, where numerous Korean women were educated. Also, media presentations affected the direction that Korean women's organizations took in the 1970s. In fact, the ideology of these Korean women's organizations followed very closely that of the American women's rights groups.

The 1980s began to see the rise of a countermovement to Western influences. In particular, the "Third World" influences regarding equality were added to the women's movement's ideological baggage. This concern for equality in the Korean context was translated into "human rights." The women in the radical women's organizations believe that women can only achieve their goal of equal status with men if there is a change in the political mechanism. As noted earlier, there tends to be a willingness among these women to place women's issues in abeyance until the broader political goals of democratization, human rights, and reunification are met. Concerns about sexual violence seem to provide an exception to this perspective.

The groups affiliated with the KWAU have worked with the more mainstream women's organizations to try to bring about changes in the Family Law. However, as noted above, some of the women who I interviewed and who represented farm women and factory workers observed that the Family Law was of secondary importance to them because the issues of inheritance, divorce, custody, and the like are not too important to the people whom they represent. The issues that concern workers are work conditions and pay equity, and the issues that most affect farmers relate to economic inequities that the political system maintains.

The Equal Employment Law was not endorsed by any of the radical groups. In part this was a conscious strategy by the groups' leaders, who believed that support for this legislation would be a "sell out" since it has no implementing mechanism. In fact, these organizations opposed the law, and their unwillingness to lobby for the law's passage was seen as a reflection of their distaste for the bill. When they are involved in trying to effect some policy change, either for women or in the context of the broader radical politics of the nation, these groups are as likely to utilize protest tactics—street marches, strikes, and rallies—as they are traditional lobbying techniques—education campaigns, media presentations, and one-on-one lobbying of members of deliberative assemblies.

Two other important groups are the Korean League of Women Voters (KLWV) and the Women's Research Institute at the Ewha Woman's University. The KLWV is a small group, established in 1969, and modeled closely after the League of Women Voters in the United States. As an organization, it is concerned with voter participation and education. Particular interest in recent years has been the issue of local autonomy. The KLWV is interested in home rule and is involved in educating voters about the potential of local autonomy in what has been a highly centralized polity. The KLWV, seen as radical by mainstream organizations and as moderate by radical groups, remains unaffiliated with either of the major coalition groups. In the past two years it has increased its activities and visibility. In part this can be seen as a result of recent political liberalization. The Women's Research Institute at Ewha Woman's University is an important organization for the Korean women's movement. It provides a focal point for meetings, research, and publications. Also, it continues to educate new generations of women students to be conscious of their roles, status, and opportunities.

## SEXUAL VIOLENCE AS A CROSSCUTTING ISSUE

The 1992 national election brought to power Kim Young Sam and the Democratic Liberal party. The election of Kim, a very popular leader, was seen by women, many of whom supported the LDP, as a victory for democracy and human rights. Also, they saw in Kim a supporter of women's rights. In fact, during the election campaign all of the presidential candidates voiced support for women and women's concerns. In return for their support, leaders of the women's-movement organizations wanted women appointed to public office and support for their policy agenda. High on the list of concerns were issues of child care, implementation of the Equal Employment Act, and sexual violence.

Sexual violence is an issue that seems to have exploded on Korea's sociopolitical scene in 1991–1992 when the Sexual Violence Relief Center (SVRC) began to make media presentations that addressed sexual violence as an issue. Many people responded by pronouncing that it was a mistake to generate a problem where none existed. However, the SVRC persisted in it's campaign. In part, the campaign took root because Interpol issued data that showed Korea had the third highest rate of reported sex crimes against women in the world. Also, there were two highly publicized sexual violence cases that generated public outcries against sexual violence.

Concerns about sexual violence brought together all of the women's groups into a coalition to support legislation that would make sexual violence a criminal violation. The Sexual Violence Relief Center and the Women's Hot Line have been seen as the leadership groups in the coalition.

Sexual violence has been defined as rape, sexual assault, sex talk, exposure, sexual harassment, gang rape, and marital rape. The women's movement groups are all in agreement in their support for legislation that would criminalize sexual violence. They have had some disagreements among themselves as to whether or not marital violence, and especially marital rape, should, at the present time, be included in a law. However, Kim Young Jung, a former member of the National Assembly and director of the Ewha Women's University Women's Research Center, who is currently a vice president of the Korean Red Cross, told me that she believes that some women go along with men and separate domestic violence from sexual violence, but that most women believe that domestic violence (including marital rape) should be included in a law that defines sexual violence as a crime.

The concern for chastity is very strong in Korea and many women will not report sexual violence, especially rape, because of the negative stigma associated with the violation of one's chastity. In fact, some support for a law is based on deep concern and commitment to female chastity. Other women see violence against women as a human-rights violation. Thus Lee Kei Kyling, president of the *Women's News*, suggested to me that some women see sexual violence as a human-rights issue. And, Jung Young Ae, the manager of counseling at the Women's Hot Line told me that women's issues are human-rights issues. Moreover, she noted, democratization is becoming a reality in Korea with the election of President Kim and reunification will take a long time to achieve. It is, she said, necessary to address women's issues now and not wait for the completion of a national agenda that would bring reunification. This point was underscored by Choi Yong Ai, director of the SVRC. "A quick transformation of radical women has occurred," she told me. "As recently as the late 1980s women's issues were secondary to democratization, human rights violations, and reunification with the North."

## CONDITIONS TODAY

Korean women face several underlying problems that make it difficult to foster change in sex-role relationships and equality. To begin with, an underlying Confucian moral code that assumes a primary role for women in maintaining family relationships is very strong. It is maintained by custom and is further reinforced by the Family Law. Inasmuch as the social mores deny women an equal role with men in the workplace, it has been difficult to change peoples' expectations regarding women working outside of the home. This condition is particularly vexing since many women are, in fact, workplace participants in Korea. They work until they marry or have families. They tend to hold poorly paid, dead-end positions. Professionally trained women often do not have the opportunities for employment, and Korean society, which has been transformed economically, is losing much of its trained people power to the influence of traditional norms and expectations.

Some changes have occurred in recent years. Women's attitudes about their own roles have been changing. Men's attitudes have been changing too, although more slowly. A vice-president of the Korean League of Women Voters told me that the "major problem is women's consciousness. Women still believe that they should be good housewives and mothers. There is some change but it is very, very slow." What is most significant seems to be the very fact that the question of women's rights is discussed at all. Some of the concerns that women's groups articulate have moved onto the nation's policy agenda. Thus an Equal Employment Opportunity Law was enacted, and there have been changes in the Family Law. Also, concerns about sexual violence are openly discussed and there is every expectation that the National Assembly will enact legislation that defines sexual violence as a crime.

The women's-rights movement is relatively new in Korea. Although there have always been women's societies, the concern with issues of sexual equality and equal opportunity is of very recent vintage. There has been some cultural diffusion from the West as a result of American influences as well as the UN Decade of Women. Also, media presentations, Western education, and the rise of women's studies programs have all affected the emergence of the movement.

It is important to keep in mind that there is not just one adaption to industrial modernization—there are as many adaptations as there are societies. Thus, in Korea the material culture has changed substantially while the behavioral culture has adapted within the constraints justified by tradition. When considering the role of women and the influence of the women's-rights movement in affecting the relative position of women in society, it seems naive to assume that the movement and its groups will look like a reflection of a Western campaign for change or that the changes that will take place in Korea will make it look like a Western society. Moreover, it is unlikely that the women who lead the struggle for change even want reform through the imposition of individualistic, Western-style behavioral norms and values, since family and relationships remain central to most Koreans. However, concerns with gender equity, an end to labor exploitation, and protection against sexual violence do seem to reflect universalized and generalized concerns of a "modernized" society.

## NOTES

1. Support for this research was provided the author by the Fulbright Foundation (1988) and the Korea Research Foundation (1993). An earlier version of this chapter, "Women's Status in South Korea—Tradition and Change," appeared in *Asian Survey* 30 (December 1990): 1136–1153.

2. Koh Yong Bok, "Traditionalism and De-Traditionalism," in *Korean Society*, ed. Chun Shin Yong (Seoul: The Si-sa-yong-o-sa Publishers, 1982), 137; Chung Chai Sik, "Confucian Tradition and Values: Implications for Conflict in Modern Korea," in *Religions in Korea*, ed. Earl H. Phillips and Yu Eiu Young (Los Angeles: California State University, Center for Korean-American and Korean Studies, 1982), 99–116; Norman Jacobs, *The Korean Road to Modernization and Development* (Urbana: University of Illinois Press, 1985), chap. 1.

3. Confucianism also establishes role relationships for men. Moreover, behavioral roles are in place for many types of relationships and situations. Women are not alone in being confined in their behavior by established rules. However, limits that are placed on women are often justified by invoking traditional practices of Confucianism, and it is these role relationships and behavioral expectations as well as the contemporary response that are being examined in this research.

4. "Modernization" is being defined "as the introduction of novel means in order to improve society's performance, but with the aim that those changes not chal-

lenge, and in fact reinforce, certain cherished goals and organizational procedures." The stimulus for change may come from either internal or external sources, and in the case of most Asian nations it has been derived directly or indirectly from the United States or Western Europe, and is usually referred as a "Westernization." Jacobs, *The Korean Road*, 6.

5. Joni Lovenduske and Jill Hills, "Introduction," in *The Politics of the Second Electorate* (London: Routledge and Kegan Paul, 1981), 3.

6. Recent literature in English includes Kim Ynug Chung, *Women of Korea* (Seoul: Ewha Woman's University Press, 1976); Hyoung Cho, "Household Economy and Gender Division of Labor in Korea" (photocopy, Seoul, 1988); Pilwha Chang-Mitchell, "Women and Work: A Case Study of a Small Town in the Republic of Korea" (University of Sussex, Ph.D. dissertation, 1988). See also collections of articles in *Challenges for Women*, ed. Chung Sei Wha (Seoul: Ewha Woman's University Press, 1986); and *Women Studies Forum*, vol. 1–9 (1985–1993) (Seoul: Korean Women's Development Institute).

7. Korean Women's Development Institute, *Status of Women in the Republic of Korea* (Seoul: KWDI, 1985), 7.

8. *Ibid.*

9. Kim Chong Ui, "On Male Chauvinistic Cultural Attitudes," *Korean Women Today*, Spring 1988, 4.

10. Joyce Gelb and Marian Lief Palley, *Women and Public Policies*, rev. ed. (Princeton: Princeton University Press, 1987), chap. 1.

11. This classification was suggested to me by Lee Yong Suk, cultural affairs officer, United States Information Agency, Seoul, 6 July 1988.

# ABOUT THE CONTRIBUTORS ❖ INDEX

# About the Contributors

SANDRA BUCKLEY, formerly professor of East Asian studies at McGill University, is presently teaching at Griffith University in Australia.

ELIZABETH CHOI is associate professor of nursing at George Mason University. In 1988 she was a Fulbright Lecturer at the College of Nursing at Seoul National University, where she studied mothering patterns.

LISA KIM DAVIS is a doctoral student at the School of Public Health at the Johns Hopkins University. In 1990 she was a Fulbright Scholar at Seoul National University, where she focused her research on women's health problems.

KUMIKO FUJIMURA-FANSELOW is associate professor of comparative education and women's studies at Tokyo Ewha Woman's University.

JOYCE GELB is professor of political science and director of the Women's Studies Certificate Program and the Center for the Study of Women and Society at the Graduate School and University Center of the City University of New York.

ATSUKO KAMEDA is associate professor of education at Jyumonji Junior College in Tokyo.

KIMIKO KUBO is secretary general and chief of research and publishing in the Section on Women's Issues at the Fusae Ichikawa Memorial Association in Tokyo.

ROH MIHYE is the director of research at the Korean Women's Development Institute (KWDI) in Seoul.

MIHO OGINO is associate professor of women's studies and Japanese language at Nara Women's University in Nara.

MARIAN LIEF PALLEY is professor of political science and international relations at the University of Delaware.

SOHN BONG SCUK is the director of the Center for Korean Women and Politics in Seoul.

EIKO SHINOTSUKA is professor of economics in the School of Human Life and Environmental Science at Ochanomizu University in Tokyo.

CHIZUKO UENO is associate professor of sociology in the Faculty of Letters of the University of Tokyo.

CHO KYUNG WON is an assistant professor of education at the Ewha Woman's University in Seoul.

# Index

Abegglen, James, 101

Abortion in Japan: economic grounds for, 72, 87–88, 174, 175; feminist work to protect legal, 174–75; guilt about, 82–83; legalized, by Eugenic Protection Law, 15, 72–73, 87–90, 174; among married women, 76–78, 79; movement against, 87–90, 174; in pre–World War II period, 68–71; rate of, 74, 75(table), 79(table), 230; screening for gender and, 176

Abortion in Korea, 229–30; gender preference and, 194, 230–31

Abuse. See Violence against women

Academic feminism: in Japan, 178–82; in Korea, 225–26

Academic programs in Japan, gender and selection of, 46, 48(table), 50, 54–55, 62

Academic programs in Korea, 214, 215(table)

Adult education in Japan, 180

Advisory Committee on Policy for Women Workers, 114

Age discrimination in Japan, 37

Agnes-chan incident, Japan, 165

*Agora* (periodical), 15, 150

Agora Resource Center, 157

Agricultural workers, Korean, 8, 281

AIDS prevention, 84, 233, 287

Akamatsu, Ryoko, 142

Alliance of Feminist Representatives, 138

Almond, Gabriel, 1

Alternative Culture (T'tohanaui Munwha), 227

Asia, Japanese feminism in, 167–72

Asian Women's Association, 169, 170

Asian Women's Forum, 170

Aspirations for male vs. female children in Japan, 51–52, 57

Association for the Promotion of the Study of Homemaking by Both Sexes, Japan, 54

Association for Working Women, Japan, 129

Association of Women in Agriculture, Japan, 151

Atsuko, Konishi, 82

Attitudes in Japan: on women in politics, 121, 144–45; on women returning to work, 30–31, 153–55; women's, toward female body and contraception, 78–82; on women's education, 50–53

Attitudes in Korea: on appropriate female behavior, 191–92; on role of women, 292–93; on women in politics, 266, 271–72; women's negative self-image, 195

Ayatoshi, Kure, 70

Bank of Creativity, Japan, 157

Basal body temperature (BBT), fertility control and, 76, 77(table)

Baseball clubs, Japanese, 56–57

*Basic Survey of the Employment Structure*, Japan, 28, 36

*Because You Are a Woman* (film), 234

Beechey, Veronica, 26

Biogenetics, 176

Birth rates, declining: in Japan, 17, 87, 89, 114, 153; in Korean, 17, 228, 253–54

Buddhism: gender roles and, 5, 6; requiem services for aborted fetuses provided by, 82–83. See also Komei party, Japan

and developments in, 60–64; sexism and gender stereotyping in, 53–58; social norms and attitudes on gender roles and, 50–53; teaching profession and, 58–60

Education of Korean women, 206–22; conclusions on, 218–19; Christian missionaries and, 4, 212; Confucian views of women and, 207–9, 217; current status of, 213–16; in family planning, 228; gender inequalities in modern, 216–18; in modern era, 211–13; in politics, 270–71; traditional, during Yi dynasty, 209–11

Ei, Wada, 103

Elder care, 9, 134–35, 166, 198

Employment, Japanese system of lifetime, 101, 104, 109

Employment patterns, of Japanese women, 9–10, 23–25, 27–29, 34–37, 96–98. *See also* Women workers, Japanese

Employment patterns, of Korean women, 7–9, 241–49

Employment Policy Research Committee, Japan, 115

Enterprise unions in Japan, 101

Entrance exams, Japanese educational, 49, 57–58

Environmental movement: Japanese, 14, 135, 136, 140–41; Korean, 267

Equal Access Child-Care League, 165

Equal Employment Opportunity Act, Korea, 10, 12, 13, 252–53, 260, 284, 285, 290

Equal Employment Opportunity Law, Japan, 10, 34–37, 62, 106–7, 109, 134, 163–64, 175–76; limitations and problems of, 111–12; sexual harassment and, 177–78; women managers under, 112–13

Eugenic Protection Law of 1948, Japan, 176; abortion legalized under, 15, 72–73, 87–90; conservative attempts to reform, 88, 174

Ewha Haktang school, 212

Executive branch of government: women in Japanese, 141–43; women in Korean, 248, 260–61

Expectations for male vs. female children: in Japan, 51–52, 57; in Korea, 216–17

Family background as asset for Japanese women, 29–30

Family Law, Korea, 13, 281, 284, 285–86, 288

Family life, Japanese, 104–5; women workers and, 38–40

Family life, Korean, 193, 195–98, 285–86

Family planning services: in Japan, 73–74; in Korea, 227–29, 285

Federation of Korean Trade Unions, 252

Feminine behavior: Japanese standards of, 52, 121; Korean standards of, 191–92

Feminist movement, international, 2, 152, 289

Feminist movement, Japanese, 14, 15, 18, 122, 150–86; academic feminism and, 178–82; cultural discourse on female sexuality and, 172–78; on employment and labor, 35, 152–55; on oral contraceptives, 85–87; post–World War II government policies on women and, 151–61; pre–World War II, 71; *ribu*, 172, 174, 177; United Nations Decade for Women and, 161–66

Feminist movement, Korean, 13, 274–94; cultural perspective on Korean woman's role and status and, 277–79; current conditions, attitudes, and, 292–93; health issues as defined by, 225–26; industrial development, changes in women's expectations, and, 274–77; mainstream reformist, 280, 282, 283–86; occupational health of women and, 231–33; political participation of women and, 268, 269–70; radical, 279–80, 286–90; reproductive health and, 227–31; sexual violence and, 233–35, 290–92; survey of contemporary, 279–90

Fertility control in Japan: antiabortion movement and rights of, 87–90; features of, 76–78; oral contraceptives, 83–87; post–World War II, 71–74; pre–World War II, 68–71; recent trends in, 74–76; women's attitudes toward, 78–82. *See also* Abortion in Japan

Fertility control in Korea, 227–29

Foreign intrusions, effects of, on Korean women, 191, 235–36

27, 96–101; proposed participation of, in Peace-Keeping Operations, 169

Japanese League of Women Voters, 151, 157, 168

Japanese-style management, impact of, on women workers, 96–97, 101–5, 115

Japanese women: economic participation of, 9–10 (see also Women workers, Japanese); education of (see Education of Japanese women); feminist movement and (see Feminist movement, Japanese); life patterns in work and family life, 24–25, 27–30, 31–32, 38–40; marriage age of, 36; political participation of, 13–16 (see also Political participation of Japanese women); reproductive rights of (see Reproductive rights in Japan)

Japan Family Control Association, 77

Japan Family Planning Association, 73, 87

Japan Family Planning Federation, 73

Japan Women's Council, 167

Japan Women's Union, 152

*Journal of Korean Women's Studies*, 226

Judiciary: women appointed to Japanese, 120, 143; women appointed to Korean, 261–62

*Jungshindae* women in Korea, 135–36, 171–72, 191, 235–36

Jung Young Ae, 291

Kabo Reform of 1894, Korea, 212

Kamakura period, Japan, 5

Kawahashi, Sachiko, 127

Kazuo, Koike, 109

Ken'ichi, Tominaga, 101

Kim Chong Ui, 4, 195, 278

Kim Hyun Ja, 284

Kim Min Hee, 288–89

Kim Sue Ja, 287–88

Kim Young Jung, 291

Kim Young Sam, 203, 279, 280, 290

Kim Yu-jin, 234

Komei party, Japan, 123, 124(table), 127, 128, 134

Korea: Confucianism in, 3–5, 192, 193, 217,

277–78, 293 n. 3; declining birthrates in, 17, 228, 253–54; democracy movement in, 225–26, 275; economic development in, 6–7, 197, 224, 227–28, 274–77; health situation in, 224–25; Japanese occupation of, 211, 213

Korean Association of University Women (KAUW), 284

Korean Catholic Farmers, 286

Korean Center for Family Law, 283–84

Korean Christian Farmer's Association (KCFA), 288, 289

Korean Church Women United, 286

Korean Federation of Housewives' Clubs (KFHC), 284–85

Korean League of Women Voters (KLWV), 290

Korean Legal Aid Center for Family Relations, 234

Korean National Council of Women, 234, 284

Korean National Mother's Association (KNMA), 284–85

Korean Special Tourist Authority, 233

Korean women, 189–205; economic participation of, 7–9; education of (see Education of Korean women); effect of foreign intrusions on, 191; elderly, 197–98; exploited during World War II (see "Comfort women" [*Jungshindae*] of Korea); family life and gender role conflicts, 195–98; fostering change for, 203–4; health of (see Health of Korean women); motherhood role of, 198–202; political participation of, 11–13 (see also Political participation of Korean women); race, class, and self-image of, 195; secondary-citizen status of, 193–94; shortage of, 231; traditional gender roles of, 191–93; working (see Women workers, Korean)

Korean Women's Associations United (KWAU), 231–32, 282, 286, 289

Korean Women's Development Institute (KWDI), 12, 278

Korean Women's National party, 262